Paint Shop Pro™ 7 For Dummies®

Tools of the Tool Palette

Button	Tool Name	What It Does
	Arrow tool	Select image windows or drag images within windows.
	Zoom tool	Left-click to zoom in; right-click to zoom out.
	Deformation tool	Click selected areas to change dimensions or rotation.
	Crop tool	Drag a rectangle then double-click to crop an image.
	Mover tool	Drag selections or vector objects.
	Selection tool	Drag a rectangle or other shape to select an area.
	Freehand tool	Select an area by tracing around it.
	Magic Wand tool	Select an area of similarly colored pixels.
	Dropper tool	Click to pick up color from the image.
	Paint Brush tool	Drag to paint.
	Clone Brush tool	Brush a copy. Right-click on the source area, move, left-drag.

Button	Tool Name	What It Does
	Color Replacer tool	Paints foreground color as you drag over background color.
	Retouch tool	Lightens, smudges, and other effects.
	Scratch Remover tool	Drag to remove photo scratches.
	Eraser tool	Erases (or paints background color on main layer).
	Picture Tube tool	Pastes multiple images as you drag.
	Airbrush tool	Applies color while you mouse down.
	Flood Fill tool	Fills an area with solid color, patterns, or gradients.
	Text tool	Creates text, outlined and/or filled.
	Draw tool	Draw lines or shapes freehand, outlined and/or filled.
	Preset Shapes tool	Draw roundish and squarish shapes, outlined and/or filled.
	Vector Object Selection tool	Selects vector objects (text, shapes).

Doing Stuff with Layers

To Do This	Do This
Create layer	Click New Layer button, top left
Select a layer	Click its name
Go to background layer	Ctrl+1
See content thumbnail	Pause cursor over name
Delete layer	Drag to trash can icon
Hide/view layer	Click eyeglass icon

IDG BOOKS WORLDWIDE

Copyright © 2001 IDG Books Worldwide, Inc. All rights reserved.

Cheat Sheet $2.95 value. Item 0693-5.

For more information about IDG Books, call 1-800-762-2974.

For Dummies®: Bestselling Book Series for Beginners

Paint Shop Pro™ 7 For Dummies®

Cheat Sheet

Brush size and other tool attributes

Use the Tool Options window, shown below. To open the Tools Options window:

Click this button

Or press this key
O (the letter)

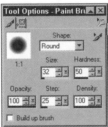

Colors, styles, and textures

To choose color, style, and texture of paint, use the Color Palette, shown below with basic instructions.

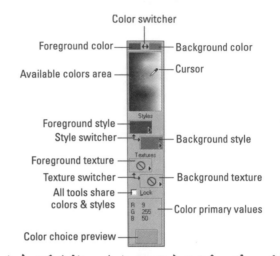

- Color switcher
- Foreground color
- Background color
- Available colors area
- Cursor
- Foreground style
- Style switcher
- Background style
- Foreground texture
- Texture switcher
- Background texture
- All tools share colors & styles
- Color primary values
- Color choice preview

Layers

To use layers, open the layer palette, shown below. Your actions apply only to the currently selected layer. To open the layer palette:

Click this button

Or press this key
L (the letter)

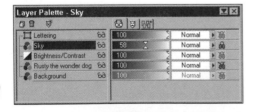

Helpful shortcut keys

Action	Shortcut
Open browser	Ctrl+B
Undo	Ctrl+Z
Redo	Ctrl+Alt+Z
Toggle tool options window	O
Toggle layer palette	L
Toggle open palettes	Tab
Select All	Ctrl+A
Select None	Ctrl+D
Paste as new image	Ctrl+V
Paste as selection	Ctrl+E
Paste as new layer	Ctrl+L
Paste vector object	Ctrl+G
Make image full color	Ctrl+Shift+0

For Dummies®: Bestselling Book Series for Beginners

™

References for the Rest of Us!®

BESTSELLING BOOK SERIES

Are you intimidated and confused by computers? Do you find that traditional manuals are overloaded with technical details you'll never use? Do your friends and family always call you to fix simple problems on their PCs? Then the *...For Dummies*® computer book series from IDG Books Worldwide is for you.

...For Dummies books are written for those frustrated computer users who know they aren't really dumb but find that PC hardware, software, and indeed the unique vocabulary of computing make them feel helpless. *...For Dummies* books use a lighthearted approach, a down-to-earth style, and even cartoons and humorous icons to dispel computer novices' fears and build their confidence. Lighthearted but not lightweight, these books are a perfect survival guide for anyone forced to use a computer.

> *"I like my copy so much I told friends; now they bought copies."*
>
> — Irene C., Orwell, Ohio

> *"Quick, concise, nontechnical, and humorous."*
>
> — Jay A., Elburn, Illinois

> *"Thanks, I needed this book. Now I can sleep at night."*
>
> — Robin F., British Columbia, Canada

Already, millions of satisfied readers agree. They have made *...For Dummies* books the #1 introductory level computer book series and have written asking for more. So, if you're looking for the most fun and easy way to learn about computers, look to *...For Dummies* books to give you a helping hand.

1/99

Paint Shop Pro™ 7

FOR

DUMMIES®

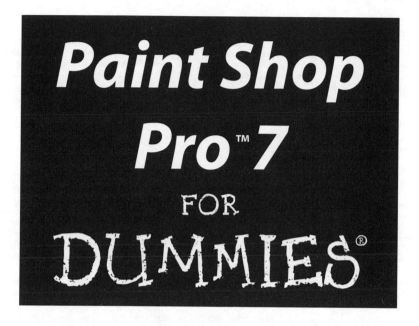

Paint Shop Pro™ 7 FOR DUMMIES®

by David Kay

IDG BOOKS WORLDWIDE

IDG Books Worldwide, Inc.
An International Data Group Company

Foster City, CA ◆ Chicago, IL ◆ Indianapolis, IN ◆ New York, NY

Paint Shop Pro™ 7 For Dummies®

Published by
IDG Books Worldwide, Inc.
An International Data Group Company
919 E. Hillsdale Blvd.
Suite 400
Foster City, CA 94404
www.idgbooks.com (IDG Books Worldwide Web Site)
www.dummies.com (Dummies Press Web Site)

Library of Congress Control Number: 00-103649

ISBN: 0-7645-0693-5

Printed in the United States of America

10 9 8 7 6 5 4 3 2 1

1B/SU/RQ/QQ/IN

Distributed in the United States by IDG Books Worldwide, Inc.

Distributed by CDG Books Canada Inc. for Canada; by Transworld Publishers Limited in the United Kingdom; by IDG Norge Books for Norway; by IDG Sweden Books for Sweden; by IDG Books Australia Publishing Corporation Pty. Ltd. for Australia and New Zealand; by TransQuest Publishers Pte Ltd. for Singapore, Malaysia, Thailand, Indonesia, and Hong Kong; by Gotop Information Inc. for Taiwan; by ICG Muse, Inc. for Japan; by Intersoft for South Africa; by Eyrolles for France; by International Thomson Publishing for Germany, Austria and Switzerland; by Distribuidora Cuspide for Argentina; by LR International for Brazil; by Galileo Libros for Chile; by Ediciones ZETA S.C.R. Ltda. for Peru; by WS Computer Publishing Corporation, Inc., for the Philippines; by Contemporanea de Ediciones for Venezuela; by Express Computer Distributors for the Caribbean and West Indies; by Micronesia Media Distributor, Inc. for Micronesia; by Chips Computadoras S.A. de C.V. for Mexico; by Editorial Norma de Panama S.A. for Panama; by American Bookshops for Finland.

For general information on IDG Books Worldwide's books in the U.S., please call our Consumer Customer Service department at 800-762-2974. For reseller information, including discounts and premium sales, please call our Reseller Customer Service department at 800-434-3422.

For information on where to purchase IDG Books Worldwide's books outside the U.S., please contact our International Sales department at 317-572-3993 or fax 317-572-4002.

For consumer information on foreign language translations, please contact our Customer Service department at 1-800-434-3422, fax 317-572-4002, or e-mail rights@idgbooks.com.

For information on licensing foreign or domestic rights, please phone +1-650-653-7098.

For sales inquiries and special prices for bulk quantities, please contact our Order Services department at 800-434-3422 or write to the address above.

For information on using IDG Books Worldwide's books in the classroom or for ordering examination copies, please contact our Educational Sales department at 800-434-2086 or fax 317-572-4005.

For press review copies, author interviews, or other publicity information, please contact our Public Relations department at 650-653-7000 or fax 650-653-7500.

For authorization to photocopy items for corporate, personal, or educational use, please contact Copyright Clearance Center, 222 Rosewood Drive, Danvers, MA 01923, or fax 978-750-4470.

About the Author

Dave Kay is a writer, engineer, and aspiring naturalist and artist, combining professions with the same effectiveness as his favorite business establishment, Acton Muffler, Brake, and Ice Cream (now defunct). Dave has written more than a dozen computer books, by himself or with friends. His titles include various editions of *Microsoft Works For Windows For Dummies, WordPerfect For Windows For Dummies, Graphics File Formats*, and *The Internet Complete Reference*.

In his other life, as the Poo-bah of Brightleaf Communications, Dave writes and teaches on a variety of subjects. He and his wife, Katy, and Golden Retriever, Alex, live in the wilds of Massachusetts. In his spare time, Dave studies animal and human tracking and munches edible wild plants. He also has been known to make strange blobs from molten glass, sing Gilbert and Sullivan choruses in public, and hike in whatever mountains he can get to. He longs to return to New Zealand and track kiwis and hedgehogs in Wanaka. He finds writing about himself in the third person like this quite peculiar and will stop now.

ABOUT IDG BOOKS WORLDWIDE

Welcome to the world of IDG Books Worldwide.

IDG Books Worldwide, Inc., is a subsidiary of International Data Group, the world's largest publisher of computer-related information and the leading global provider of information services on information technology. IDG was founded more than 30 years ago by Patrick J. McGovern and now employs more than 9,000 people worldwide. IDG publishes more than 290 computer publications in over 75 countries. More than 90 million people read one or more IDG publications each month.

Launched in 1990, IDG Books Worldwide is today the #1 publisher of best-selling computer books in the United States. We are proud to have received eight awards from the Computer Press Association in recognition of editorial excellence and three from Computer Currents' First Annual Readers' Choice Awards. Our best-selling ...*For Dummies*® series has more than 50 million copies in print with translations in 31 languages. IDG Books Worldwide, through a joint venture with IDG's Hi-Tech Beijing, became the first U.S. publisher to publish a computer book in the People's Republic of China. In record time, IDG Books Worldwide has become the first choice for millions of readers around the world who want to learn how to better manage their businesses.

Our mission is simple: Every one of our books is designed to bring extra value and skill-building instructions to the reader. Our books are written by experts who understand and care about our readers. The knowledge base of our editorial staff comes from years of experience in publishing, education, and journalism — experience we use to produce books to carry us into the new millennium. In short, we care about books, so we attract the best people. We devote special attention to details such as audience, interior design, use of icons, and illustrations. And because we use an efficient process of authoring, editing, and desktop publishing our books electronically, we can spend more time ensuring superior content and less time on the technicalities of making books.

You can count on our commitment to deliver high-quality books at competitive prices on topics you want to read about. At IDG Books Worldwide, we continue in the IDG tradition of delivering quality for more than 30 years. You'll find no better book on a subject than one from IDG Books Worldwide.

John J. Kilcullen
John Kilcullen
Chairman and CEO
IDG Books Worldwide, Inc.

**Eighth Annual
Computer Press
Awards ➤1992**

**Ninth Annual
Computer Press
Awards ➤1993**

**Tenth Annual
Computer Press
Awards ➤1994**

**Eleventh Annual
Computer Press
Awards ➤1995**

IDG is the world's leading IT media, research and exposition company. Founded in 1964, IDG had 1997 revenues of $2.05 billion and has more than 9,000 employees worldwide. IDG offers the widest range of media options that reach IT buyers in 75 countries representing 95% of worldwide IT spending. IDG's diverse product and services portfolio spans six key areas including print publishing, online publishing, expositions and conferences, market research, education and training, and global marketing services. More than 90 million people read one or more of IDG's 290 magazines and newspapers, including IDG's leading global brands — Computerworld, PC World, Network World, Macworld and the Channel World family of publications. IDG Books Worldwide is one of the fastest-growing computer book publishers in the world, with more than 700 titles in 36 languages. The "...For Dummies®" series alone has more than 50 million copies in print. IDG offers online users the largest network of technology-specific Web sites around the world through IDG.net (http://www.idg.net), which comprises more than 225 targeted Web sites in 55 countries worldwide. International Data Corporation (IDC) is the world's largest provider of information technology data, analysis and consulting, with research centers in over 41 countries and more than 400 research analysts worldwide. IDG World Expo is a leading producer of more than 168 globally branded conferences and expositions in 35 countries including E3 (Electronic Entertainment Expo), Macworld Expo, ComNet, Windows World Expo, ICE (Internet Commerce Expo), Agenda, DEMO, and Spotlight. IDG's training subsidiary, ExecuTrain, is the world's largest computer training company, with more than 230 locations worldwide and 785 training courses. IDG Marketing Services helps industry-leading IT companies build international brand recognition by developing global integrated marketing programs via IDG's print, online and exposition products worldwide. Further information about the company can be found at www.idg.com. 1/26/00

Dedication

This book is dedicated to my sister, Pam, and her sons Ben and Bob, all ornaments on the family tree hanging happily amongst the coconuts.

Author's Acknowledgments

I would like to acknowledge the support and tolerance of my wife Katy and of my friends and family, from whose company I am sadly removed while writing these books.

I would like to also acknowledge Bob Selling, an invaluable member of First Parish Church, Unitarian Universalist, of Stow and Acton, and supporter of this work.

Thanks also to Matt Wagner and the rest of the folks at Waterside, and to the congenial editors at IDG Books Worldwide, including:

- Acquisitions editors Laura Moss and Tom Heine for their finely honed acquisitiveness and pseudo-omnipotence.
- Editorial manager and project editor draftee Kyle Looper for long-suffering.
- Copy editor Nicole Laux for her light hand at the controls.
- My technical editor, Lee Musick.

Publisher's Acknowledgments

We're proud of this book; please register your comments through our IDG Books Worldwide Online Registration Form located at `http://my2cents.dummies.com`.

Some of the people who helped bring this book to market include the following:

Acquisitions, Editorial, and Media Development

Project Editors: Kyle Looper, Jade Williams

Acquisitions Editors: Tom Heine, Laura Moss

Copy Editor: Nicole Laux

Proof Editor: Teresa Artman

Technical Editor: Lee Musick

Media Development Manager: Laura Carpenter

Media Development Supervisor: Richard Graves

Editorial Assistant: Sarah Shupert

Production

Project Coordinator: Emily Wichlinski

Layout and Graphics: Brian Drumm, LeAndra Johnson, Barry Offringa, Jill Piscitelli, Kendra Span, Julie Trippetti

Proofreaders: Laura Albert, Corey Bowen, Susan Moritz, Charles Spencer, York Production Services, Inc.

Indexer: York Production Services, Inc.

General and Administrative

IDG Books Worldwide, Inc.: John Kilcullen, CEO; Bill Barry, President and COO; John Ball, Executive VP, Operations & Administration; John Harris, CFO

IDG Books Technology Publishing Group: Richard Swadley, Senior Vice President and Publisher; Mary Bednarek, Vice President and Publisher; Walter R. Bruce III, Vice President and Publisher; Joseph Wikert, Vice President and Publisher; Mary C. Corder, Editorial Director; Andy Cummings, Publishing Director, General User Group; Barry Pruett, Publishing Director

IDG Books Manufacturing: Ivor Parker, Vice President, Manufacturing

IDG Books Marketing: John Helmus, Assistant Vice President, Director of Marketing

IDG Books Online Management: Brenda McLaughlin, Executive Vice President, Chief Internet Officer; Gary Millrood, Executive Vice President of Business Development, Sales and Marketing

IDG Books Packaging: Marc J. Mikulich, Vice President, Brand Strategy and Research

IDG Books Production for Branded Press: Debbie Stailey, Production Director

IDG Books Sales: Roland Elgey, Senior Vice President, Sales and Marketing; Michael Violano, Vice President, International Sales and Sub Rights

◆

The publisher would like to give special thanks to Patrick J. McGovern, without whom this book would not have been possible.

◆

Contents at a Glance

Cartoons at a Glance

By Rich Tennant

page 7

page 71

page 203

page 125

page 353

page 311

Fax: 978-546-7747
E-mail: richtennant@the5thwave.com
World Wide Web: www.the5thwave.com

Table of Contents

Introduction

Congratulations! Brilliant person that you are, you use Paint Shop Pro! Thousands of other brilliant people also use Paint Shop Pro, and for one very intelligent reason: It does darned near anything you could want it to do, from fixing photographs to animating Web graphics, and — unlike certain more famous programs — it doesn't set you back a day's salary.

Guided by that same intelligence, you're probably asking yourself, "Is there a book that gives me what I want, quickly, without dragging me through a tutorial? One with an attractive yellow-and-black cover, so it doesn't get lost in the clutter on my desk? Preferably cheap?"

Welcome to *Paint Shop Pro 7 For Dummies,* the attractive, inexpensive, yellow-and-black book that lets you get great graphics out of Paint Shop Pro without making you feel like you're going back to school in an attractive, yellow-and-black school bus.

What Can You Do with this Book?

Books are useful, elevating things. Many people use them to elevate their PC monitors, for instance. With that fate in mind, *this* book has been created to serve an even higher purpose: enabling you to do the kind of graphics stuff that you really want to do. Here's a smattering of what you can do with the help of this book:

- Download photos from a digital camera.
- Fix up fuzzy, poorly exposed or icky-colored photos.
- Print album pages or other collections of photos.
- Paint, draw, or letter in all kinds of colors, patterns, and textures.
- Draw using lines and shapes that you can go back and change later.
- Apply cool special effects to photos and drawings.
- Change colors of objects.
- Combine photos with other images.

- ✔ Alter the content of photos and other images.
- ✔ Remove unwanted relatives from family photos.
- ✔ Add wanted relatives to Wanted posters.
- ✔ Retouch unsightly relatives on Wanted posters.
- ✔ Create transparent and other Web page graphics.
- ✔ Create animations rivaling *South Park* and *Chicken Run*.
- ✔ (Well, OK, that last item may be a bit ambitious, but you *can* make neat animated Web banners and other short action flicks.)

Is This the Book for You?

Is this the Paint Shop Pro book for you? Depends. If, like me, you tend to leave chocolate fingerprints from your bookstore *biscotti* on the books you're browsing, it's definitely yours now.

In addition, this book is for you if:

- ✔ You find most computer books boring or useless
- ✔ You need solutions rather than lessons
- ✔ You find parts of Paint Shop Pro 7 confusing
- ✔ You haven't done much with graphics programs before
- ✔ You have used other Windows programs before
- ✔ You need Paint Shop Pro for business or home use
- ✔ You really like bulleted lists

How Is this Book Organized?

Computer software "manuals" document features because that's the easiest way to write one: "The File menu presents the following choices. . . ." If features on the File menu exactly matched what you had in mind, that would be great — but how are you to know to use the Clone Brush tool when what you're really looking for is the "Fix Uncle Dave's hair transplant scars" tool?

Some computer books are organized into lessons, teaching you how features work. They give you examples of basic tasks, and then more complicated ones. Along the way, hopefully, before too long, you find an example resembling what you had in mind.

This book is organized by different kinds of tasks, like working with photos, or painting pictures, or adding text. Where possible, it tells you exactly what to do in numbered steps. Where that's not possible, it gives you explanations of how things work in non-technical language.

You don't have to read it in any order. Just skip to the section or chapter you need. Go right to the index, if you like — or the Rich Tennant cartoons! In detail, this book is organized as follows.

Part I: Getting the Picture

This part puts you in the picture and your picture in Paint Shop Pro. Chapter 1 puts you in the picture, explaining how to get control over all the various doo-dahs floating around the Paint Shop Pro screen. It also gives quick synopses of what the various tools do, which is particularly useful for anyone who just needs a few hints to get going. Chapter 2 tells you how to open up an image file, start a new image, or save an image as various file types. It tells you how to use Paint Shop Pro's neat image browser that lets you see your various files before you open them. Chapter 3 tells you how to get existing images into Paint Shop Pro, whether from a scanner, a digital camera, or your PC screen.

Part II: Painting the Picture

Part II is for anyone who plans to paint, draw, or otherwise doodle in Paint Shop Pro. Chapter 4 addresses Paint Shop Pro's new Color palette, showing you how to get not only the color you want, but also paint in the wild gradients, patterns, and textures that Paint Shop Pro version 7 offers. Chapter 5 tells you how to use the basic painting tools of Paint Shop Pro, and also how to control the way Paint Shop Pro paint tools work: brush size, spraying patterns, brush shapes, paint density, and more. Chapter 6 shows you how to do something you've seen only in cartoons: make images flow right off a paintbrush. I explain two features that are useful for retouching there: Paint Shop Pro's cool new Picture Tubes tool (a kind of spreadable clip-art), and the Clone Brush tool.

Part III: Improving Appearances

When you have an image that needs some sprucing up, Part III is the place to turn. Chapter 7 shows you how to use Paint Shop Pro's hand tools to brush away wrinkles from portraits, fix scratches, and remove red-eye. Chapter 8 gives you nearly instant ways to correct overall photo problems, such as bad exposure, poor color, blurry or speckly images, or just brighten up the colors of a photo taken on a dim day. Chapter 9 takes you to fun and exotic lands of special effects, where you can twist, bend, make three-dimensional buttons, do cutouts, create patterns, or make your image look like it was done in neon or burnished copper! Chapter 10 helps you cope with the inescapable reality that, yes, you really are using a computer, and if you want the most from Paint Shop Pro, you need to understand just a little about how it deals with color. Chapter 11 shows you how to fine tune the quality of your image for contrast, brightness, and color, and tackle the more subtle problems of certain photos.

Part IV: Changing and Adding Content

Part IV opens the door to a brave (and fun) new world: changing the content of an image. Chapter 12 shows you how to change the size, proportions, orientation, and, if you were leaning a bit to the left at cousin Suzie's wedding, the rotation of your image. It also shows you how to crop your image to get the composition you want, or flip it into a mirror image. Chapter 13 gives you one of the key tricks for changing content: selecting parts of your image. Because Paint Shop Pro has no idea where cousin Suzie begins and her husband ends, it's up to you to tell Paint Shop Pro, "Suzie's the one in white," or to outline her by hand, when you want to abstract her into a solo portrait. Chapter 14 shows you ways to move, copy, or re-shape the parts you select. Need a flock of jumping sheep when you have only a few? Chapter 14 is just your style. Chapter 15 shows you how to divide images into layers, or use layers to combine images. Layers are a powerful tool that make later editing much easier, and produce stunning image overlays. Chapter 16 lets you add layers of easily edited text and shapes to your image, using Paint Shop Pro 7's expanded vector graphics tools. Chapter 17 gives you a time-tested tool for combining images, called *masking,* that lets you paint out unwanted parts and paint in the stuff you need.

Part V: Taking It to the Street

All this fooling around in Paint Shop Pro is great, but, in the end, you probably want your image to appear somewhere else: on a piece of paper, on the Web, or as part of an animation. Chapter 18 shows you how to best fit your image onto paper. It also tells you how to print multi-image pages for photo albums, collages, or portfolios. Chapter 19 tells you how to get exactly the image file you want for the Web, and gives you tips for getting the fastest-downloading images with the least sacrifice in quality. Chapter 20 shows you the fastest way to create animations, either letting Animation Shop generate cool text or image effects, or integrating your own frames from Paint Shop Pro.

Part VI: The Part of Tens

Problems often come in threes, so this book tackles them by the tens, just to be sure. Part VI has fixes for the ten most wanted issues that people run into when they're trying to use Paint Shop Pro. Chapter 21 untangles the ten most common confusions and perplexing problems of Paint Shop Pro while Chapter 22 gives you ten quick fixes for photography problems.

Shortcuts and Conventions in this Book

This book doesn't have too many conventions. We in the U.S. had quite enough of those in the recent elections, thank you. This book does, however, employ one basic shortcut that is a convention in all *For Dummies* books:

Rather than saying, "Click the word File in the menu bar and then click the word Open in the menu that drops down," this book says "Click File⇨Open." Saves time, saves trees, and keeps you from falling asleep. (The underlined letters are the same ones you find in all Windows programs. They indicate that if your mouse breaks, you can press the Alt key on your keyboard along with the underlined letter's key to get the same result as if you clicked on the word with your mouse.)

The other convention this book uses is IDG Books Worldwide's famous icons, taking your eye quickly to valuable tips, telling you about something you need to keep in mind, or alerting you to technical stuff you can skip. They're self-explanatory (as any good icon is), so I don't bother showing them here. Instead, I leave them as yet another temptation for you to. . . .

Read on!

(Oh, yes, and please buy the book now. Thanks.)

(Oh, and by the way, IDG Books and I would love to hear from you. Register your copy of this book along with your comments at http://my2cents. dummies.com and IDG Books Worldwide will forward your comments or questions to me. Or, drop me some e-mail at psp7@brightleaf.com. I'm just one guy, with no special connections to Jasc and no helpers, so I may not be able to answer your questions, but I'll try.)

Icons Used in This Book

This icon points out important issues or tidbits of information that you want to be sure to remember. Just remember to look for Remember.

An all-purpose workhorse, this icon offers advice or shortcuts that can make your life a whole lot easier.

Skip over this one if you'd like. This icon marks geekfest stuff you don't really need to know, but might find interesting.

Tread lightly when you see this icon because something unpleasant could happen if you proceed without following this cautionary note.

Part I
Getting the Picture

In this part . . .

Need to get *in the picture* quickly? Do you need to get a picture quickly into or out of Paint Shop Pro? Start here.

The Paint Shop Pro screen has more controls, tools, and objects floating around in it than the space shuttle has. In Chapter 1, I briefly summarize what all this stuff does, help you bring the various floating windows under your control, and show you how to use fundamental features like the command history and undo/redo features. If you already have some experience with graphics programs, read Chapter 1 for a fast way to discover Paint Shop Pro's unique quirks and features.

Throughout the rest of Part I, I show you how to get pictures into and out of Paint Shop Pro. Do you already have an image file on your PC? I give you different ways to open up or start existing image files in Chapter 2. For instance, Paint Shop Pro provides a great image browser that lets you see tiny, thumbnail images of your various files before you open them. And also in Chapter 2, I tell you how to make the various choices involved in starting a new image, such as size, resolution, or number of colors. Plus, I point out the pros and cons of saving images as different types of file.

If you're downloading an image from your digital camera, scanning an image from paper, or capturing it from your PC screen, turn to Chapter 3 for help. Discover the best ways to scan printed images, the two different ways to get images from cameras, or the various ways Paint Shop Pro lets you grab the exact object you want from a computer screen.

Chapter 1

Introducing Paint Shop Pro

. . . .

In This Chapter

▶ Recognizing stuff in the Paint Shop Pro window

▶ Displaying and unrolling palettes, windows, and toolbars

▶ Understanding the color palette

▶ Locating tool options

▶ Choosing layers

▶ Turning on rulers, gridlines, and guidelines

▶ Keeping an overview of where you are

▶ Undoing and redoing commands

. . . .

Sometimes all you need is a good introduction. At a party, your conversation may be going nowhere until someone says, ". . . and Pat, here, breeds bandicoots!" As it happens, you've been fascinated by bandicoots for years, (well, who wouldn't be?) and that introduction is all you need.

And so it goes with software: Sometimes all it takes is an introduction. Someone points out, "By the way, this is the thing that controls how your paintbrush works," a light bulb turns on above your head, and you're making progress in no time.

In that spirit, this chapter is a quick introduction to the parts of Paint Shop Pro that you may currently be trying to understand, plus a few fundamentals about how Paint Shop Pro works. You may discover some features as exciting as bandicoots, but mainly you'll see how to work with Paint Shop Pro.

Firing Up Paint Shop Pro and Finding What You Need

To fire up Paint Shop Pro, choose Start⇨Programs⇨Paint Shop Pro 7. Soon you are treated to a window like the one in Figure 1-1 (but without the picture of the cute dog).

You don't see all the tools and menu selections of Figure 1-1, however, until you have an image of some kind to work on. See Chapter 2 for help with opening images or creating new ones. Any image will do for now, if you just want to experiment with the various parts of Paint Shop Pro. To get a blank image for that purpose, choose File⇨New and then click OK in the New Image dialog box that appears.

(As many programs do, Paint Shop Pro displays a Tip of the Day dialog box when you launch it. Like daily vitamins, these tips are beneficial, but sometimes bothersome. Deselect the Show Tips on Startup check box if you want to prevent these tips from appearing again. Click the Close button to make the tip go away. You can always view tips by choosing Help⇨Tip of the Day.)

Menu bar   Toolbar   Image window   Tool options window, unrolled

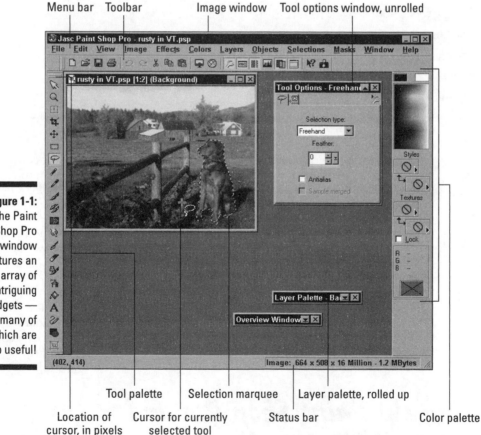

Figure 1-1:
The Paint Shop Pro window features an array of intriguing gadgets — many of which are also useful!

Tool palette   Selection marquee   Layer palette, rolled up

Location of   Cursor for currently   Status bar   Color palette
cursor, in pixels   selected tool

So what's all the stuff in the window? Well, *tools* (buttons that, when clicked, turn your cursor into a paintbrush or something else that you guide by hand) are stacked on the left side of the interface in the *Tool palette*. The colors that you paint with are situated on the right, in the *Color palette*.

Other features (the ones that you don't guide by hand) lurk up in the menus. These include commands for brightness, contrast, color controls, and various effects for anything from cleaning up a bad photo to giving Uncle Dave a swirly haircut.

Some parts of Paint Shop Pro are undoubtedly familiar to you from other programs, like many of the buttons on the Toolbar. Other important parts of Paint Shop Pro are more subtle, maybe even invisible at the moment. Some parts seem to spring into action as you pass your cursor over them. Read on.

Operating Toolbars, Palettes, and Windows

Paint Shop Pro uses panels of controls, calling them *toolbars, palettes, windows,* and such. All these terms, however, mean pretty much the same thing: a collection of stuff. You can move these panels around, open or close them, and turn them off or on.

In Paint Shop Pro, the toolbar just under the menu bar has the distinction of being called the *Toolbar* (also known as the Standard Toolbar) as Figure 1-1 shows. Don't confuse the Toolbar with the Tool palette, which runs down the left side.

Unrolling and moving toolbars, palettes, and windows

Certain panels are already visible when you first open up Paint Shop Pro. But, they initially appear only as title bars floating on your screen, labeled, for instance, Overview Window or Layer Palette (refer to Figure 1-1).

These panels open up and display their contents rather startlingly when you pass your mouse cursor over them. They then scroll back up into their own title bars when your cursor clicks elsewhere. They are considered *roll-up* panels, despite the lack of alfalfa sprouts, avocado, and other extras any self-respecting roll-up should have. Table 1-1 tells you how to control rolling and unrolling.

Table 1-1	Working with Roll-Up Panels
To Do This	*Do This*
Enable (display) or disable (hide) a panel	Click panel's button on Toolbar, press shortcut key, or select in Toolbars dialog box — see the following section.
Move a panel	Drag it by its title bar, kicking and screaming. You can even move it outside the limits of the Paint Shop Pro window.
Open (unroll) a panel	Move your mouse cursor to the panel's title bar. The panel "unrolls" from the title bar, a feature called *Automatic Roll-Up.*
Close (roll up) a panel	Click an area outside of the roll-up: on the image, on the title bar of Paint Shop Pro itself, or on the title bar of some other panel.
Disable rolling and unrolling	Choose View➪Toolbars and deselect the Enable Automatic Roll-Ups check box (in the Toolbars dialog box shown in Figure 1-2). Now, any panel you've enabled appears fully open.
Lock a panel open	Click the down-arrow in the upper-right corner of the panel. The arrow now points up. Whenever you enable (display) this panel, it appears unrolled.
Unlock a locked-open panel	Click the up-arrow in the upper-right corner of the panel. The arrow now points down.

I find that locking panels open works best for me. The constant unrolling and rolling is too distracting.

The toolbars, palettes, and windows that litter your screen at random locations *float,* which means that you can drag them around instead of leaving them sitting like censorship strips across the exciting parts of your image.

Certain panels (the Tool palette, Toolbar, and Color palette, for example) don't normally float, but are instead left *docked.* A docked toolbar object is attached to the left, top, and right edges of the Paint Shop Pro window. You can make docked panels float by dragging them away, or you can dock them to a different edge, if you like.

Move a docked object by dragging it by the very top (if it runs vertically) or far left end (if it runs horizontally) of the bar. Only an outline of the bar goes with you as you drag, until you release the mouse button. To redock a bar, drag it to a Paint Shop Pro window edge and release the mouse button. You probably have to try a few times to find the right position to make the bar dock.

Enabling and disabling toolbars, palettes, and windows

Besides being able to roll or unroll the various panels in Paint Shop Pro, you can selectively choose which ones to disable (hide) or enable (display). Or, more simply put, you can turn them on or off. Table 1-2 shows two ways to hide or display palettes, toolbars, and the like: clicking buttons on the Toolbar, or pressing shortcut keys on the keyboard.

Table 1-2	Showing and Hiding Palettes and Such		
To Show or Hide This	*What It Is*	*Click This Button*	*Or Press This Key*
Color palette	Supplies color, patterns, and textures		*c* for *color*
Histogram window	Shows distribution of color values		*h* for *histogram*
Layer palette	Shows & controls image layers		*l* for *layers*
Overview windows	Shows entire image at all times		*v* for *views*
Toolbar	Contains editing, viewing, and other buttons	No button	*t* for *tools*
Tool Options window	Controls tool (brush) behavior		*o* for *options*
Tool palette	Contains brushes and other hand tools		*p* for *palette*

Where's Waldo? Finding and hiding panels

Palettes and windows have a tendency to hide in all the clutter — and, sometimes, to disappear altogether. To find one that's hiding (or perhaps was never enabled), click its button on the Toolbar a few times. (See Table 1-2 for buttons.) The missing object should pop on and off.

On the other hand, if your currently enabled, floating palettes or windows are cluttering up

your view, press the Tab key to hide them. Press the Tab key again if you want to reveal them.

Likewise, to temporarily clear the screen of your enabled toolbars, press the T key on your keyboard. Press T again to restore them. Press it again to hide them. Isn't this fun? Beats working! Press it again. . . .

Yet another way to control which toolbars, windows, and palettes are displayed is to use the Toolbars dialog box. Choose View➪Toolbars, and the Toolbars dialog box jogs into action. As Figure 1-2 tells you, select the check boxes next to the toolbars (okay, toolbars, palettes, or windows) that you want to display and click the Close button.

Figure 1-2: Toolbar central: Click in the check boxes to display or hide toolbars.

If you do a lot of photography, Web illustration, or use a lot of Paint Shop Pro's effects, try enabling the Photo, Web, or Effect toolbar, respectively. Their buttons provide handy shortcuts to important functions for those jobs.

The Toolbars dialog box also lets you change how the buttons and text look using the Display Large Text check box, the Icons on Palettes check box, and the Display Flat Style Toolbars check box. To see what these check boxes do, just fiddle with them (click the check box on and off and click OK). A more important check box is the Enable Automatic Roll-Ups, which I cover in the next section.

Knowing and customizing toolbars

The role of Paint Shop Pro Toolbars, like toolbars everywhere, is to give you buttons to click for tasks that you can also accomplish by using the menu bar, but not as conveniently. The left end of the Standard Toolbar (or just the Toolbar to its pals) contains the familiar cast of characters that most Windows programs offer. From left to right, the buttons you've undoubtedly seen before are New (start a new image), Open, Save, Print, Undo, Redo, Cut, Copy, and Paste.

To the right of the usual buttons are the ones unique to Paint Shop Pro. See Figure 1-3 for these guys. From left to right, you have a button for full-screen previewing, one for normal zoom (*normal* meaning full-scale or 1:1 viewing), and then the buttons to toggle various palettes and windows on or off.

Figure 1-3:
The
Standard
Toolbar, with
buttons
unique to
Paint Shop
Pro called
out.

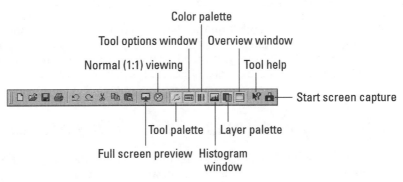

You can add buttons to the toolbar, too. For that matter, you can add or remove buttons to any toolbar. For instance, if you do a lot of digital camera work, you could add an Access Camera button. (Otherwise, you'd have to choose File➪Import➪Digital Camera➪Access.) To add buttons, follow these steps:

Near the far right end of the toolbar, the **?** icon gives you help on any tool: Click the **?** icon, click the tool that you need, and the Help window charges to the fore. (Click the X in the upper-right corner of the Help window to banish it.)

1. **Right-click on the toolbar you want to change.**

   You can click anywhere on the Toolbar, but you can't click farther right than the last button.

   A pop-up menu appears.

2. **Choose Customize.**

   The Customize dialog box displays its wares. The left side of the dialog box lists all the available buttons. The right side lists (from top to bottom) all the buttons that currently appear from left to right on your Toolbar.

3. **On the right side of the dialog box, click the location within the buttons where you want your new button to appear.**

   Your new button will go above the button you click on, which means that, on-screen, it appears to the left of that button (or above that button, if the toolbar runs vertically).

4. **On the left side, click the new button you want, and then click the Add button in the center of the dialog box.**

   If you then need to move the position of your new button, click Move Up or Move Down.

To remove a button, click it on the right side of the dialog box and then click the Remove button. Click the Reset button if you want to restore the original button set. Click the Close button when you've finally got all your buttons. Click Close on the Toolbars dialog box, too.

Meeting the tools of the Tool palette

Tool palette seems like a peculiar name to me, invoking images of mechanics in berets, carrying their tools about on wooden platters. . . . Maybe it's just me. The Tool palette is simply the place where the graphics tools live — tools being features like paintbrushes that enable you to paint or otherwise modify the image by dragging or clicking your mouse on the image.

You can find the full details of these tools throughout this book, but in general, using a tool from the Tool palette involves three steps:

1. **Click the tool in the Tool palette.**

2. **Adjust the tool's settings in the Tool Options window and Color palette.**

   If you don't see the Tool Options window anywhere, click the Tool Options button in the Toolbar to display that window, or press the *O* key on your keyboard.

3. **Click or drag on the image.**

If the tool applies colors, you may also want to choose colors by clicking on the Color palette. You can choose colors at any time: before choosing a tool or just before you click or drag the image. Table 1-3 briefly describes each tool. For details about selecting colors, see Chapter 4. For more information about painting, beam yourself to Chapter 5.

Table 1-3		Tools of the Tool Palette
Button	*Tool Name*	*What You Can Do*
	Arrow tool	Select an image window by clicking on its title bar. Or, for images that are larger than the window, drag the image to view areas outside the window.
	Zoom tool	Click on an area of the image to zoom in on that spot; right-click to zoom out.
	Deformation tool	Click on selections or just on layers to change size of a selected portion of an image, or to rotate it using the frame that appears.
	Crop tool	Trim the edges of a picture. Click where you want one corner, drag to opposite corner, then double-click anywhere on the image.
	Mover tool	Drag selections or entire layers around.
	Selection tool	To select an area of the image, define the area by dragging across it. (A moving dashed line called a *marquee* surrounds selected areas. Refer to Figure 1-1.)
	Freehand tool	Select an area by tracing around it; the Tool Options window provides several variations that make tracing easier.
	Magic Wand tool	Select an area of similarly colored pixels by clicking on any point in that area. The Tool Options window provides important variations on this theme.
	Dropper tool	Pick up a color to paint with from your image (make it the foreground color) by clicking on any colored area. Right-click to set background color.
	Paint Brush tool	Paints your foreground color (chosen from the Color palette) onto the image as you drag. The Tool Options window controls brush size and other important factors.
	Clone Brush tool	Lets you repeat an image (like a pantograph, for you fans of old art tools). Right-click on the source image, move to where you want to paint a copy, and then drag with the left mouse button to paint.

(continued)

Table 1-3 *(continued)*

Button	Tool Name	What You Can Do
	Color Replacer tool	Paints the foreground color as you drag over areas having the background color. In the Tool Options window, you set color finickiness (better known as tolerance).
	Retouch tool	Does wonderful but mysterious smudgy things to areas you drag over. Exactly what it does is set by (you guessed it) the Tool Options window.
	Scratch Remover tool	Drag over a scratch to remove scratches from photographs.
	Eraser tool	Erases, sort of. When you use it on the background layer (the *only* layer, if you have only one layer), it actually paints in background color.
	Picture Tube tool	Bizzarro, kewl special effect of appliquéing (pasting) images as you drag.
	Airbrush tool	This spray painter applies foreground color as you hold the mouse button down. Paint gets denser if you repeat strokes or stay in one place.
	Flood Fill tool	Fills an area of similarly colored pixels with solid foreground color, or with patterns or fades *(gradients)* of two colors. The Tool Options window and Color palette play key roles here.
A	Text tool	Add text with this. Click where you want the text to appear and then type the text in the dialog box that appears. Text goes on a special vector layer. You can redimension or rotate the text with the frame that appears.
	Draw tool	Draw any shape, filled or not, using lines and curves, foreground and background color, patterns, gradients, and textures. Can get pretty complex; the Tool Options window and the Color palette have a lot to do with the results.

Button	Tool Name	What You Can Do
	Preset Shapes tool	Nice, simple roundish and squarish shapes, or custom shapes, outlined and/or filled, as the Tool Options window and Color palette dictates.
	Object Selector tool	To choose one of several objects (text blocks, lines, or shapes) on a vector layer, click the object with this tool. Or, drag around objects and use controls in the Tool Options window to group or position objects.
Missing	Panic button	Personally, I think a Panic button ought to be available somewhere in all programs, but Paint Shop Pro doesn't have one. (Your best alternative is to press Ctrl+Z, or click the Undo button on the Toolbar, to undo your last action.)

Paint Shop Pro enables you to create an image using multiple layers of super-imposed images. If you use layers, the tools and most menu commands work *only on the currently active layer.* What's more, you can select an area to limit your actions to that portion of the image. If any area of the image is selected (as is Rusty the Wonder Dog, back in Figure 1-1), the tool works *only in the selected area!* If a tool doesn't appear to be working, you may be trying to use it outside the selected area or on the wrong layer. See the chapters in Part III for more about selections and layers.

Here are a few tips for using the tools of the Tool palette:

✔ Tools at the bottom of the toolbar — Text, Draw, Preset Shapes, and Object Selector — are sometimes called *vector* tools. Normally, they work a bit differently from the other so-called *raster* tools and require a special layer to work on. See Part IV for more information.

✔ If a large number of tools in the middle of the toolbar are grayed-out, then you're currently working on a *vector layer* (a layer that can contain only text, lines, or shapes). Press Ctrl+1 to return to the background layer.

✔ Many of the tools on the Tool palette apply the background color rather than the foreground color if you press the right mouse button instead of the left one as you click or drag with that tool. See Chapter 4 for more about foreground and background colors.

Hobnobbing with the status bar

The status bar (along the bottom of the Paint Shop Pro window) is a feature of most Windows programs. Its role in life is to tell you information that it thinks you may find useful. Some of the useful stuff it displays includes:

- **How to use a tool:** When you hover your cursor over a tool, the status bar gives you a very brief "what" and "how-to" description and lists options available if you press the Ctrl, Alt, or Shift key.

- **Current cursor position (where your tool is):** The status bar lists the position of the cursor in *pixels* (image dots) and displays the position within parentheses, such as (376, 340) — refer to Figure 1-1 for an example. The first number tells you how many pixels over from the left edge your cursor is (the so-called *X position*), and the second is how many pixels from the top edge your cursor is (the so-called *Y position*). When you're cropping, selecting, or drawing, this display also provides information about the dimensions of the area you're affecting.

- **How big your image is:** The far right end of the status bar gives image size, with three numbers in the form width x height x color depth. The width and height of your image is given in pixels. The color depth tells you how many colors your image can have.

Confronting the Color palette

The Color palette normally lives on the right side of the Paint Shop Pro window (although you can drag it elsewhere). The Color palette is where you choose the colors used by various painting and drawing tools and commands. You can also choose textures and patterns for the tool to apply. For full details about choosing colors and textures, see Chapter 4. Figure 1-4 shows you the basic parts of the palette.

Your cursor looks like an eyedropper while it hovers over the Available Colors area, as shown in Figure 1-4. This eyedropper icon tells you that your cursor is ready, willing, and able to pick up a color. As you pass your cursor over the available colors, the color choice preview area at the bottom shows a preview of the exact color you're poised over.

Click (left-click, that is) on any color in the Available Colors area to choose that color to paint or draw with. It becomes the so-called *foreground* (or *stroke*) *color,* the principal color you use. The foreground color sample (top, left in Figure 1-4) then shows you the color's appearance more clearly.

Right-click on a color in the Available Colors area to choose the *background* (or *fill*) *color,* an alternative or second color for painting or drawing. That color appears in the background color sample at the top, right of Figure 1-4.

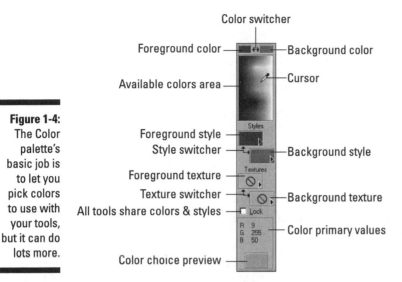

Color switcher

Foreground color — — Background color

— Cursor

Available colors area —

Figure 1-4:
The Color
palette's
basic job is
to let you
pick colors
to use with
your tools,
but it can do
lots more.

Foreground style —
Style switcher — — Background style

Foreground texture —
Texture switcher — — Background texture
All tools share colors & styles —

— Color primary values

Color choice preview —

In Paint Shop Pro, you don't just paint with colors, you paint with *style!* The Foreground Style and Background Style areas determine what kind of style you apply. Your foreground or background style can simply be your foreground and background color, as Figure 1-4 shows, or can be as complex as a rainbow-hued or woven pattern! Read more on styles in Chapter 4. To switch the background and foreground styles, click the *switcher.*

Textures are optional, and are turned off in Figure 1-4. They can give the appearance of rubbing color on various surfaces, like canvas, asphalt, or rocks.

Saluting the Tool Options window

 The Tool Options window is the Napoleon Bonaparte of Paint Shop Pro: small, but powerful. If you don't see it on your screen, click the Tool Options button (shown at left of this paragraph) on the Toolbar, or press the *O* key on your keyboard.

The Tool Options window controls a lot of the way your tools (from the Tool palette) work. If a tool isn't working the way you would like it (say, the brush size is wrong, or the paint is too thin), the Tool palette is one of the first places you need to go.

Every Tool Options window has two or three tabs you can click on to access important controls. Except for the last tab, the tabs change with every tool you use, so giving you detailed descriptions or a picture here wouldn't be much help. (I give you the details as I describe each tool in later chapters.) In general, however, the tabs are as follows, from left to right:

- Tab 1, with same tool icon as on Tool palette: the tool's principal controls, such as brush width. In Chapter 5, I give details of the controls that you most commonly find on tools.

- Tab 2, with meshed-gears icon, absent in most tools: options, such as *tolerance* (a sort of sensitivity) or *mode* (different ways of operating).

- Tab 3 (or Tab 2 if only two tabs are present), with icon that is oddly suggestive of dental hygiene: the Cursor and Tablet Options tab.

Getting a precise cursor or brush outline

The Cursor and Tablet Options tab has two check boxes that affect your cursor, as follows:

- **Use Precise Cursors:** Enable this check box to give you a crosshairs cursor that lets you see more precisely where you're placing the tool than the normal cursor does.

- **Show Brush Outlines:** Enable this check box to make the mouse cursor display the shape, size, and density you've chosen for your tool's brush on Tab 1. I think brush outlines are a pretty useful feature, but if you don't like it, clear the check mark.

Using a pressure-sensitive tablet

The Tablet options of the Cursor and Tablet Options tab only apply if you're using a pressure-sensitive drawing tablet. By checking off the various check boxes, the pressure you apply to the tablet can vary up to three things:

- The Vary Opacity check box allows pressure to change the opacity (transparency) of the paint you apply.

- The Vary Color check box lets you switch between foreground and background color by changing pressure.

- The Vary Width check box lets you change, by pressure, the width of the applied paint over a range from 1 pixel up to the brush width you specify on Tab 1.

Bowing to the Layer palette

You can make Paint Shop Pro images in layers, as if you were drawing on transparent sheets on top of the original (or *background*) layer. Layers are great for making changes that can be modified, removed, or switched on or off, but layers also take some getting used to.

When you use layers in an image, the painting or other changes you make happen only on one specific layer at a time. The *Layer palette* lets you choose which layer you are currently working on, specify which layer or layers are currently visible, group layers together, adjust their transparency, and many other features.

 To display or hide the Layer palette, press *L* on the keyboard or click the Toggle Layers button on the Toolbar (shown at left). Figure 1-5 shows the sort of thing you see.

Raster layer

Vector layer   Layers

Active layer

Figure 1-5:
Layers —
not for the
chicken-
hearted.

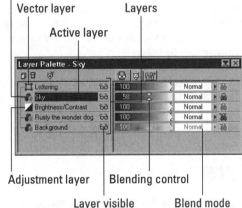

Adjustment layer   Blending control

Layer visible   Blend mode

The palette lists layers by name down the left side. The original image is usually on the Background layer. Text and drawn objects usually appear on separate layers. See Chapter 15 for details about layers and the Layer palette, but here are the main controls you can use:

✔ Hover your cursor over a layer (on the left side) and a tiny, or *thumbnail,* image of the layer appears.

✔ Click on a layer on the left side of the palette to make it *active* — the layer you're currently working on. That layer's name appears on the title bars of the image window (in parentheses) and Layer palette.

✔ Click the eyeglass icon for a layer to make the layer invisible; click again to make it visible.

Nodding to the Histogram window

 The histogram window is a sophisticated and rather abstract chart. If it were human, it would be an engineer. It is useful mainly to computer graphics experts, but a nodding acquaintance with it can occasionally be useful to normal mortals, too. Click the Histogram button (shown in the margin) on the Toolbar or press *h* on your keyboard to toggle the window on or off.

The height of the graph at any point is a count of how many pixels have that value. If your image has an area painted with a solid color, for instance, all pixels have the same value for each primary color. Spikes on the graphs represent that area because the image has many pixels with the same value.

A graph that is high at the left end in the red, green, blue, grayscale, or lightness curves means that the image has lots of pixels with low value (that is, shadows); if they are higher at the right end, it means the image has lots of high-value pixels (or highlights). If you increase, say, brightness, these pixels all move up in value, and the peaks and valleys on the line move to the right; decrease brightness, and they move to the left.

Sometime when you are fiddling with an adjustment in, perhaps, the Colors menu, observe how the histogram changes as you make changes. Nod wisely, and then forget about it.

Electing Your Rulers

If a cat may look at a king, you may certainly view Paint Shop Pro's rulers. Choose View➪Rulers, and rulers appear along the left and top edges of your image window. Perform that command again, and they go away.

As you move your cursor around, two tick marks appear on the rulers, showing you the position of your cursor. (The Status bar also gives you that position very accurately, in numbers of pixels — the dots that make up the image.)

Paint Shop Pro's rulers, as Paint Shop Pro is initially set up, give you distances measured in pixels. Distances are always measured from the top-left corner of the image.

You can change rulers from pixels to inches or centimeters this way:

1. **Choose <u>F</u>ile➪<u>P</u>re<u>f</u>erences➪<u>G</u>eneral Program Preferences.**

   The Paint Shop Pro Preferences dialog box appears.

2. **Click the Rulers and Units tab.**

3. **Click the Display Units list box, and choose Pixels, Inches, or Centimeters from the drop-down list that appears.**

   Click OK after you finish.

Getting on the Grid

Some work is easier to do "on graph paper" — that is, with a grid of lines over your image. For instance, when doing a floor plan of your dining room, a grid of lines at specific intervals helps you make sure that, from your seat at the table, you can reach the pork loin on the sideboard. Paint Shop Pro offers you a way to (ahem) "grid your loins" for such work.

Choose View➪Grid (or press Ctrl+Alt+G) to turn the grid on (or off). The grid isn't part of your image; it only appears in the Paint Shop Pro window, and you cannot print it. The grid now appears on all images displayed in Paint Shop Pro.

You can set the grid spacing and line color to any values you want, this way:

1. **Choose File➪Preferences➪General Program Preferences**

   The Paint Shop Pro Preferences dialog box appears.

2. **Click the Rulers and Units tab to display that tab.**

3. **In the Grid area of that tab (on the right), in the Units selection box, choose Pixels, Inches, or Centimeters.**

4. **Set the values in the Horizontal Spacing and Vertical Spacing text boxes to make the grid spacing wider or narrower.**

   Those values are in whatever units you chose in Step 3. For instance, if your units are pixels, a value of 10 means the grid is spaced at 10 pixel intervals.

To set line color, click the Line Color color swatch (initially gray), and then choose any color from the Color dialog box. For help with the Color dialog box, see Chapter 4. Click OK after you finish.

Aligning Objects to Guides

Getting things to line up is no problem if you follow Paint Shop Pro's guides. *Guides* are simply straightedges — horizontal or vertical — that you can set anywhere in your image. You can set as many as you like.

To create guide lines, you must display Paint Shop Pro's rulers (choose View⇨Rulers), and also display guide lines: Choose View⇨Guides. Choose View⇨Guides again to hide the guide lines.

To create a guide line, click on any point on a ruler, drag toward your image, and release your mouse button when the line is where you want it. To create a horizontal line, for instance, click on the horizontal ruler along the top of your image, and drag down.

To move or get rid of a guide line, first place your cursor on the ruler, on the tiny raised area where the guide line hits the ruler. (Your cursor, which is a set of crosshairs when it's over a ruler, gets a bit fatter when it's on the correct spot.) Then, to move the guide line, drag along the ruler. To eliminate the line, drag away from your image, off the edge of the image window.

You can make lines and other objects *snap* to guides or gridlines by choosing View⇨Snap to Guides. See Chapter 14 for more about moving and snapping objects.

Viewing and Zooming Your Image

Working with images on a PC involves a lot of *zooming* — changing the magnification of your view. Sometimes you need to work close-up, taking that nasty gleam out of Uncle Charley's eye, for instance (something Aunt Mabel has been trying to do for years). Other times, you really need to see the whole picture, but currently Uncle Charley's gleaming eye rather scarily fills the whole window.

Zooming does not change the actual size of your image (in pixels or in inches). It only changes how big Paint Shop Pro displays the image on-screen.

Zooming the image in the window

The easiest way to zoom in (view close-up) or zoom out (see the big picture) is to use the *Zoom tool,* the magnifying glass icon shown here in the margin. The tool is second from the top in the Tool palette.

Click on the Zoom tool. Your cursor changes to a magnifying glass icon. Then click with it on your image in this way:

- ✔ **Click (left-click) to zoom in.**
- ✔ **Right-click to zoom out.**

Using better screen settings

Your PC comes set to display a certain *resolution* and *color depth* on-screen. It may be able to do better, which would allow you to work on images in Paint Shop Pro more easily and accurately. (*Resolution* is how many dots or pixels your screen shows across and down; *color depth* determines how many different colors can be on-screen at once.)

To change your screen settings, right-click on your Windows desktop area. A menu appears. Click Properties from that menu, and then click

the Settings tab on the Properties dialog box that appears. At the bottom of the Settings tab, click the Colors selection box and choose a True Color (24 bit or 32 bit) setting (if that setting isn't already chosen or unavailable). Also, see if you can drag the Screen Size slider to the right by one or more stops. Click OK when you're done. An information dialog box appears; click OK there, too. After 15 seconds, either your screen changes or Windows quits trying and returns you to your original settings.

When you zoom in, click on the place that you're interested in seeing more closely. Paint Shop Pro centers the image on that area, which ensures that the portion you're interested in remains within the window when the image gets bigger.

Paint Shop Pro zooms in steps. It doesn't zoom continuously, as a camera might do, for instance. Sometimes finding the best zoom for you takes trial and error (alternately left- and right-clicking with the Zoom tool). Paint Shop Pro expresses each step as a *magnification ratio* (such as 1:2), also called the *zoom factor* and displays it on the title bar of the image window.

Zoom factor gives the ratio of the image's on-screen size to its actual size, in pixels. So, for example, a ratio of 1:2 means you're seeing the image at half scale (half as many pixels wide and tall). A ratio of 2:1 means you're seeing the image twice as large as it really is.

You can zoom in more convenient steps, too. To zoom your image to its true size (in pixels, not inches), click the Normal Viewing button on the Toolbar, shown here. For fast zooming, see the various Zoom choices on the View menu. Choosing View➪Zoom In By 5, for instance, takes you from a ratio of, say, 1:15 to 1:10 in one step.

Using an Overview Window to stay oriented

When you zoom in really close on an image, you can easily lose track of just which portion of the image you're looking at. The solution is Paint Shop Pro's

Overview Window. It always shows you the whole image, and a rectangle marks the area you've zoomed in on.

 Click the Overview Window button, shown in the margin, to turn the window on or off. An Overview window like the one in Figure 1-6 appears somewhere on-screen. You can drag it by its title bar to anyplace you like.

To move your view around within the image, drag the tiny rectangle around within the Overview Window. Your cursor changes into a hand icon when it's over the rectangle to indicate that you can drag. The main image window shows whatever is in the rectangle.

Figure 1-6: Zooming in on Rusty. The Overview Window shows the whole farm and the zoom factor (3:1).

Filling your screen with your image

Sometimes you wish you could just fill the screen with your image — and not see the Windows taskbar, the Paint Shop Pro window frame, and all the other stuff on-screen that is, for the moment, non-essential. Well, your wish is one of Paint Shop Pro's commands. Do the following:

1. **Zoom to the image size you want (right- or left-click with the Zoom tool).**

   Paint Shop Pro keeps the image size that you choose here, so set the zoom so that the image fills, or slightly more than fills, the Paint Shop Pro window.

 2. **To view the image, click the Full Screen Preview button on the Toolbar, shown in the margin.**

(Alternatively, you may press Ctrl+Shift+A, or choose View⇨Full Screen Preview.)

Your PC screen now displays only the image (and the blank area around it). But . . . but . . . without any buttons to click on-screen, how do you get back to Paint Shop Pro? Easy:

3. Click anywhere on the screen or press any key on your keyboard.

Your normal Windows desktop, with the Paint Shop Pro window, returns.

If you want to *edit* your image using the full screen, not just view it, choose View⇨Full Screen Edit or press Shift+A (not Ctrl+Shift+A). Your image, plus any toolbars or palettes that are currently active, are all that appear on-screen. Edit away! You can use keyboard shortcuts, like pressing T for the Toolbar, to turn toolbars, windows, and palettes on or off. To return to normal viewing, press Shift+A again.

Working on several images at once

You can open several images at once in Paint Shop Pro. Each one gets its own window. Having several images open is useful for tasks such as cutting and pasting between images. To help manage those windows, use the commands in Paint Shop Pro's Window menu. That menu contains the usual suspects of nearly all Windows programs: Cascade, Tile (Horizontally or Vertically), or Close All to close all image files.

Remember that Paint Shop Pro tools and commands only apply to whichever image window is currently *active* (the one with the colored title bar). Click an image window's title bar to make that window active and bring it to the front.

Undoing and Redoing

Make a mistake? Choose Edit⇨Undo. Or, press Ctrl+Z or click the Undo button (shown in the margin). Each time, you back up a step, undoing the preceding action. If you accidentally undo too far, you can redo the step with Edit⇨Redo. (Or, you can press Ctrl+Alt+Z, or click the Redo button on the Toolbar.)

A command history helps you see more precisely what commands you are undoing and redoing. Choose Edit⇨Command History (or press Ctrl+Shift+Z) and the Command History dialog box appears, providing enough command of history to finally understand the Peloponnesian War.

Okay, so nobody really understands (or correctly spells) the Peloponnesian War, but you *can* undo and redo your Paint Shop Pro commands with more insight now. All previous commands are marked *undo* to indicate that you may undo them.

To prepare to undo, click on any previous (lower-numbered) step, and Paint Shop Pro highlights all actions back to, and including, that step. Click the Undo button, and your highlighted steps are undone. Undone steps are now marked *redo* (to indicate that you may redo them).

To redo steps, click on any step marked Redo. All steps up to and including that one are highlighted. Then click the Redo button to redo those steps.

Notice that you can't undo or redo isolated steps within the history. That is to say, command history doesn't let you do anything you couldn't do by using Ctrl+Z and Ctrl+Alt+Z (or the Undo and Redo buttons on the Toolbar), but it does let you see what steps you're undoing.

Chapter 2

Starting, Opening, and Saving Image Files

● ●

In This Chapter

▶ Starting a new, blank image

▶ Saving time with clever file commands

▶ Opening image files

▶ Controlling zooming and windows

▶ Saving image files

▶ Working with different image types

▶ Reading image information

▶ Browsing visually through image files

▶ Downloading images from the Web

● ●

"**T**he truth," TV's *X Files* claims, "is out there." I beg to differ. The truth is *in* there — in the files — mysterious though those files may be. This chapter is where you discover the truth about files.

Are you seeking to spawn new files of your own? Here are the secrets of battling your way past the tough questions Paint Shop Pro asks about size, pixels, rasters, vectors, resolution, and color depth.

Or are you trying to make sense of files that have landed on your doorstep? Have aliens sent you cryptic files? Or perhaps you want to beam them down yourself from the Web, or adapt your images for the other, alien environments in which your colleagues live. Here's how to obtain, read, and write a variety of alien file types.

If you work with images very long, you're ultimately surrounded by a swarm of files on your disk drive. Paint Shop Pro's image browser can help you sort through the swarm and visually choose exactly the image you need to attack.

For you, the seeker of fact, the prober of files — the truth is not out there. It's in here! Read on.

Starting an Image from Scratch

 If you're going to create an image from scratch, you need a clean canvas. To start a new, blank image, either click the New button (shown in the margin) at the far left end of the Toolbar, or choose File⇨New.

The New Image dialog box makes the scene (its mug shot is shown in Figure 2-1) and raises a few questions about this new image you're proposing to make: size, resolution, color, and color depth. In the next few sections, I give you the answers to those questions.

 Don't bother creating a new, blank image if you're going to be working on an image file that already exists, downloading an image from a camera, or scanning an image.

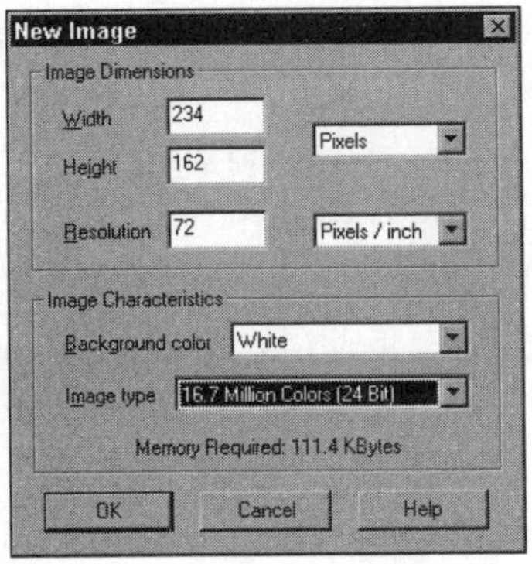

Figure 2-1:
How big,
what color,
and how
many colors
are among
the
questions
Paint Shop
Pro poses
for a new
image.

New Image
Image Dimensions
Width 234   Pixels
Height 162
Resolution 72   Pixels / inch
Image Characteristics
Background color White
Image type 16.7 Million Colors (24 Bit)
Memory Required: 111.4 KBytes
OK   Cancel   Help

Choosing the right image size

How big should your image be and should you give its size to Paint Shop Pro in pixels or in inches (centimeters)? You can do it either way, really, but most people find that following these general rules make life easier:

✔ If you expect the image mainly to be viewed on a computer screen (where pixels are the preferred unit of measure), enter values for width and height in pixels.

✔ If you intend the image mainly to be printed, give size in inches or centimeters. Click the selection box that reads `Pixels` in Figure 2-1 and select either the Inches or Centimeters option. Then type numbers for height and width (in inches or centimeters) into the Height and Width boxes.

Computer screens are measured in pixels (how many dots of color they can display). How many pixels should you use? The maximum size (width in pixels by height in pixels) that PC screens today display are:

✔ 640 x 480 (decreasingly common)

✔ 800 x 600 (still somewhat common)

✔ 1024 x 768 (common)

✔ 1280 x 1024 (increasingly common)

✔ Occasionally lots bigger

Your image should probably not be as large as the entire screen. If you know how many pixels high or wide you want your new image to be, enter those values into the Height and Width boxes in the New Image dialog box.

If you have no idea about size, try 400 pixels wide by 300 pixels high.

Choosing adequate image resolution

The New Image dialog box also has a setting for *resolution* — how many pixels your image has per inch or centimeter. Your choice of resolution tells Paint Shop Pro two things, depending on how you entered Width and Height (which I describe in the preceding section):

✔ Did you specify your image's width and height in inches? Then the value you give for resolution determines how many pixels wide and high your image is. If you specify an image 1 inch by 1 inch, for instance, and a resolution of 72 pixels/inch, Paint Shop Pro creates an image sized to 72 x 72 pixels.

✔ Did you specify your image's width and height in pixels? Then the value you give for resolution determines how big your image is on paper. If, say, you have an image 144 pixels wide, and specify a resolution of 72 pixels per inch, the image prints 2 inches wide (144/72). (On the other hand, because Paint Shop Pro allows you to print at scales other than 100 percent, resolution isn't a firm limit on how big your printed image can be.)

So, how much resolution is enough? Do you need to worry about it at all?

If you're just doing casual office or personal image work, you probably can just leave the Resolution setting in the New Image dialog box alone. The default of 72 pixels per inch works fine for most such work. You really only need to increase it if you are striving to create the highest-quality printed image your printer can do, at one of the printer's higher-quality settings.

Otherwise, here are a couple of general rules for choosing resolution:

- ✔ **If you're creating an image for viewing on PC screens:** Set your image size in pixels and don't worry about resolution.

- ✔ **If you're creating an image to be printed in a particular size (in inches or centimeters):** The lower the resolution you choose, the grainier, blockier, or more jagged the picture looks when you print it at the size you want. (You'll be able to see the tiny rectangles of color that make up the image, as shown in Figure 2-2.) The higher the resolution, the less grainy the picture looks, but it's also a much larger file on your computer, and Paint Shop Pro may run more slowly.

Choosing the color of your new image's background

After you create a new image in Paint Shop Pro, it begins life filled with some color. Click the down arrow in the Background Color drop-down list box (in the New Image dialog box) and you can choose that color from Paint Shop Pro's primary colors listed there by name — Red, Blue, or Green — and also White and Black.

Other options in the Background Color drop-down list box include options that read Transparent, Background Color, and Foreground Color. The Background Color and Foreground Color options allow you to use any color. They fill the image with either the background or foreground color, respectively, that you have chosen in the Color palette.

Selecting the best image type (color depth)

The last thing you have to decide when creating a new image (using the New Image dialog box) is the *image type* of the new image. Click the Image Type list box and various choices emerge: 2 colors, 16 colors, Greyscale, 256 colors, and 16.7 million colors. Seeing these options may give you the idea that type has something to do with the number of colors — if so, you're right.

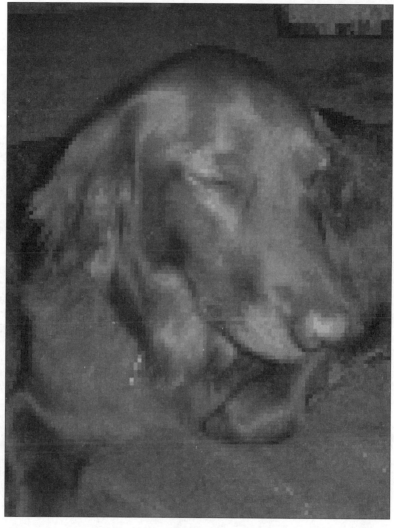

Figure 2-2:
Very low resolution images come out blocky. This image was originally printed 2 inches wide at 50 dpi (dots per inch).

The type setting for a new image is also called *color depth*. The number of colors is the third fundamental aspect of an image (besides width and height). Computer engineers, being the way they are, said, "Aha! A third 'dimension.' So what if it has nothing at all to do with the third dimension in a 3-D picture? Let's call it *depth* anyway to confuse people!" Also, rather than refer to images by the number of colors, engineers refer to them as being 1-bit, 4-bit, 8-bit, or 24-bit — terms you can find in parentheses in the Image Type list box of the New Image dialog box.

Selecting an unlisted background color

If you have already opened the New Image dialog box and want to choose a color for the image background that *isn't* already the foreground or background color in the Color palette, follow these steps:

1. **Click Cancel in the New Image dialog box.**

2. **Select the foreground color or background color you desire in the Color palette.**

3. **Reopen the New Image dialog box by choosing File⇨New.**

4. **Select the Background Color option or Foreground Color from the Background Color drop-down list box.**

Why should you care? Color depth refers to the maximum number of different colors *possible* in the image. This number matters to computers because they are forced to reserve more memory for the image if you intend to use more colors. It matters to you, too: More colors are great for a better-looking image, but adding colors can mean that Paint Shop Pro runs more slowly, that the file is slower to transmit by e-mail or over the Web, or that it doesn't fit on a diskette, if that's what you had in mind. If you're going to be printing your image professionally, you may also *want* to limit the number of colors to the printer ink colors available so you don't use a color that you can't reproduce.

On the other hand, many of the advanced Paint Shop Pro features work only on 16.7-million color (24-bit) images. So you have to choose the high color depth to take advantage of some features.

If in doubt, choose 16.7 Million Colors (24-bit). You're not stuck with your choice. You can change image type in Paint Shop Pro at any time, going either up or down in number of colors. See Chapter 10 for the details.

Here are choices you can make for various kinds of work:

- ✓ **2 Colors (1-Bit):** This displays images in black and white, which is generally okay for shapes and letters, line drawings, or drawings intended only to be faxed. If you paste a image that has shades of gray or color into a two-color image, the result is abstract black and white blotches.

- ✓ **16 Colors (4-Bit):** Images that use only 16 colors aren't generally useful for doing photos or similarly realistic painted images. If you're doing floor plans or mechanical drawings where the only color requirement is that colors be *different,* then this color depth is fine. It's also often good for drawing logos and other symbols. You start out with 16 fairly icky colors to work with, but you can change them by *editing the palette,* which I cover in more detail in Chapter 10.

✔ **Greyscale (8-Bit):** Greyscale images are like black-and-white photographs. The dots or shapes that make up an image can be in up to 256 different shades of gray.

✔ **256 Colors (8-Bit):** 256-color images begin to make realistic (photograph-like) color images possible. Many of the images used on the Web (drawn images, some photographs, and nearly all animations) use only 256 colors. You start out with a palette of 256 specific, Paint Shop Pro-assigned colors, but (as with 16-color images) you can change them.

✔ **16.7 Million Colors (24-Bit):** You want this depth for realistic or photographic color images, but it works fine for anything at all.

Discovering Time-Saving Commands for Image Files

The File menu is a logical place to turn for all things file-ish. The Paint Shop Pro File menu contains the usual suspects, choices that lurk in nearly all Windows programs (file open, save, save as, close, print, and program exit). It also has some convenient tricks among its offerings that can save you time and effort, as follows:

✔ **Browse:** Open files by looking at *thumbnail* (tiny) images of them. Cool way to go. See "Browsing and Organizing Files Using Tiny Pictures" later in this chapter.

✔ **Revert:** When you've totally wrecked an image in Paint Shop Pro, but haven't yet saved it, this command reloads the file as it was, pre-wreckage.

✔ **Save Copy As:** Use this command to make copies of your image (as files on disk) in different formats, or with various changes. It's like the Save As command that nearly all Windows programs have, only it doesn't change the name of the file you're currently working on.

✔ **Workspace:** This submenu contains commands that let you save your current Paint Shop Pro screen setup (including positions of toolbars, the active tool, and the currently open image), and restore it later.

✔ **Delete:** This command deletes the image you're currently viewing (the image whose title bar is in color, if you're viewing multiple images) from your disk drive. (This command saves you the trouble of switching to Windows to delete a file.)

✔ **Send:** This command sends your image as an attachment to a new message in your e-mail program. (It may not work if your e-mail isn't set up as Microsoft would like it to be.)

✔ **Import:** This submenu lets you acquire an image from your scanner, download an image from your electronic camera, or capture an image from your screen. See Chapter 3.

✔ **Export:** This submenu lets you make *picture tubes* (brush-on images), helps you produce images for Web pages, creates custom shapes for the Preset Shapes tool, and outputs to Jasc's online display site, `StudioAvenue.com`.

✔ **Page Setup, Print, Print Preview, and Print Multiple Images:** The usual suspects you find in any Windows program, all related to printing, plus a special print command for multiple images on a single page. See Chapter 18 for more about printing.

✔ **Jasc Software Products**: This command launches any of Jasc's other programs, if they're installed on your PC, including Animation Shop, which comes with Paint Shop Pro.

✔ **Batch Conversion:** If someone gives you a bunch of images in one format (say, Photoshop), and you need to convert them all to another format (say, GIF), this is the fast way to do it.

✔ **Preferences:** This command links you to various settings that control how Paint Shop Pro does things. See the Index of this book to find where I describe some of the various preferences.

As in most Windows programs, the bottom of the file menu also lists the files you've most recently worked on. Click one to reopen it, if it hasn't been moved, renamed, or deleted.

Opening Image Files

Paint Shop Pro can crack open most of the popular types of image files. You have three possible ways to do this (plus the image browser which I discuss later in this chapter):

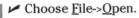

✔ Choose File->Open.

✔ Click the Open button on the Toolbar.

✔ Press Ctrl+O.

The Open dialog box appears (as shown in Figure 2-3). The Files of Type selection box is initially set to All Files, meaning that it displays *all* the various kinds of files in whatever folder you open (whether or not Paint Shop Pro is capable of opening them).

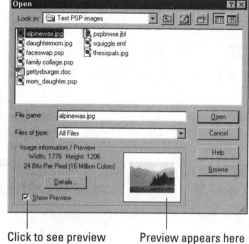

Figure 2-3:
The Preview
option
makes
opening the
right file
easier, if
slower.

Click to see preview   Preview appears here

If you double-click on your image file in the Open dialog box, Paint Shop Pro tries to load it. Often, however, you find that you're pouring over a big pile of files with similar names. Here are a few tricks to help you find the one you want:

✔ File names aren't alway descriptive enough, so to see a tiny preview of the image itself, select the Show Preview check box. Click on any file, and a preview appears in the Preview window. Refer to Figure 2-3.

✔ To show just one file type (say, you're looking for a GIF file), click the Files of Type drop-down list box and select the file type you're looking for from the many file types Paint Shop Pro can read.

✔ If the file you want isn't listed, make sure you didn't choose a different file type in the Files of Type drop-down list box! Choices in this box are *sticky* — the next time you open a file, the Open dialog box displays only that same file type. Choose All Files in Files of Type to see all files again.

✔ Image width, height, and color depth appear in the Image Information area as you click on each file.

✔ For more information about an image you've clicked on, such as date or file size, click the Details button.

Paint Shop Pro attempts to translate your image file into a form that it can use. For some files, especially *vector* image files such as DXF and WPG, Paint Shop Pro needs additional information from you, specifically, how many pixels wide and high you want the image to be. (See the section, "Using vector file types (drawing files)," later in this chapter for more information.)

How the FPX can I see the TIF, JPG, DXF, and other extensions!?

Image files are often referred to by the three-letter ending *(extension)* at the end of their file names. The file `polecat.tif`, for instance, is called a *TIF* (or TIFF) file. On many computers, Windows is set up to *hide* these extensions, which actually makes your life harder when using Paint Shop Pro. If, when you go to open a file in Paint Shop Pro, the files don't appear to end with a period and three-letter extension (such as `.psp`, `.bmp`, or `.pcx`), Windows is hiding valuable information from you.

To reveal the extensions, do this: Double-click the My Computer icon. In the window that appears, choose <u>V</u>iew⇨Folder <u>O</u>ptions to get the Folder Options dialog box. Click the View tab there, and under Files and Folders, Hidden Files, deselect the check box labeled `Hide File Extensions For Known File Types`. (Then click OK.)

Saving Your Image

You can save an image as many different types of file. Some types are good for one purpose, others for another. The choice depends on what you (or the people you give the file to) intend to do with the image. Another person, for instance, may not have Paint Shop Pro and may therefore want a Photoshop file instead.

The best idea, however, is to first save your image as a Paint Shop Pro (PSP) type of file, even if it started life out as a different type. Paint Shop Pro files are a good choice because, among other things, they save the layers and selections you may have created during the editing process. Most other file types don't save that stuff.

Then, if you (or the people to whom you're giving the file) also need a different type of file, save a *copy* as that other type of file. If you make changes to your image, always make the changes to the Paint Shop Pro file and then make copies of that file in the various file types you may need.

To save any image as a Paint Shop Pro file, first look at the file name in the title bar, at the top left of the Paint Shop Pro window. (The file name appears after the words *Jasc Paint Shop Pro.*) The file name should end in a period and three letters; if not, see the sidebar "How the FPX can I see the TIF, JPG, DXF, and other extensions!?"

If the file name has the extension .psp, choose File⇨Save or click the Save button on the Toolbar. You're done! (Your image was a Paint Shop Pro file already; you just updated that file with your latest changes.)

If the file name ends in anything *but* .psp, do the following:

1. **Choose File⇨Save As.**

   The Save As dialog box appears.

2. **Click the Save as Type box and select the Paint Shop Pro Image option.**

3. **Select a folder and type a name for the file.**

   Do this exactly as you would to save a file in any other Windows program.

4. **Click the Save button.**

After saving the image as a Paint Shop Pro file, if you also need the image in a different file type, do the following (or, to save Web files, see Chapter 19):

1. **Choose File⇨Save Copy As.**

   The Save Copy As dialog box appears.

2. **Select the file type you want from the Save as Type box.**

   If you want to save the file as a Paint Shop Pro file, but in a form that earlier versions of Paint Shop Pro can read, click the Options button. The Save Options dialog box appears; choose the version you want, and then click OK.

3. **Click the Save button.**

When you save a copy in a different file type, your currently open file isn't affected at all. It remains whatever file type it was.

If you've used layers (or floating selections) and save a copy as something other than a PSP file, Paint Shop Pro may have to merge (combine) those layers into a single image. Paint Shop Pro displays a dialog box to warn you, if so. That merge *doesn't* happen to the Paint Shop Pro image you're currently working on, only to the file copy you're creating. Click Yes to proceed.

Using Native and Foreign File Types

Sooner or later, someone will give you a file that is not a Paint Shop Pro file or ask you to supply one. Fortunately, Paint Shop Pro can read most of those and write many of them. The next sections describe a few of the most popular file types. Each file type is identified by the three-letter ending (extension) it uses. For instance, Paint Shop Pro files end with the extension .psp.

Here are some of the more common types of image file that you may need to open or create, and peculiarities to each type of file that you may need to know about. Most of the time, you don't have to do anything special to open a particular file type or to save your work as that type of file — but, then again, sometimes you do. Paint Shop Pro will, in most cases, simply ask you a few questions to resolve any problems when opening or saving a foreign file type.

Paint Shop Pro files (PSP)

PSP is the native Paint Shop Pro file type and is probably the best choice for storing your own images. When you save your work as a Paint Shop Pro file, you can save everything just as it is, including any areas you have selected with Paint Shop Pro's selection tools, plus your various kinds of layers, your palettes, your tool settings (like current brush width), transparency, and other advanced features. You can pick up almost exactly where you left off. Paint Shop Pro files can have any color depth you choose.

Programs other than Paint Shop Pro or Animation Shop don't often read Paint Shop Pro files (PSP), however. You may need to save a copy of your image in a different file type for someone who uses other software. Also, earlier versions of Paint Shop Pro can't read Paint Shop Pro 7 files. To output Paint Shop Pro 5.0 or 6.0 files, see the instructions for saving a copy of your image in the section, "Saving Your Image," earlier in this chapter.

BMP

BMP files are *Windows Bitmap* files; that is, they were designed by Microsoft for storing images, and many programs under Windows can read and write them. BMP files can have color depths of 1, 4, 8, or 24 bits. (Set your color depth by using Colors⇨Decrease Color Depth or Colors⇨Increase Color Depth; see Chapter 10 for details.)

BMP files that are 24-bit can be quite large. When you save a file as BMP, you can click the Options button in the Save As, or Save Copy As, dialog box to choose higher *compression* (make smaller files). Under Encoding (in the Options dialog box that appears), select RLE and then click OK. (RLE stands for *Run-Length Encoding,* a way of making image files smaller.) Now, when you save the file, Paint Shop Pro asks your permission to switch to a 256-color (8-bit) version of the BMP file. The resulting file is much trimmer than the original, although the color quality may diminish slightly.

TIFF

TIFF (or TIF) stands for Tag Image File Format (which, of course, tells you nothing useful). Many graphics programs on the PC and Macintosh can read and write TIFF files, so it's a good choice of file type when you don't know what kinds of files the other person can read.

TIFF files also offer advanced image features. One feature is something called an *alpha channel* that you can use to store a selection area (see Chapter 13) or a mask (see Chapter 17) that you've created in Paint Shop Pro. Besides Paint Shop Pro's own PSP file type, only the TIFF, TGA (Targa), PSD (Photoshop), and PNG file types, among Paint Shop Pro's repertoire of file types, can store this sort of advanced information.

TIFF files can be quite large unless you compress them. To compress a TIFF file, click the Options button when using the Save As or Save Copy As dialog box. Then choose LZW Compression option in the Compression area of the Options dialog box that appears. LZW gives you the best compression and compatibility with most other programs. (No image quality is lost by using LZW compression in TIFF files.)

For advanced users, TIFF is a good choice because it's capable of storing information not only in RGB primaries, but also CMYK (used for some high-quality printed images). It can also store advanced data for color accuracy such as gamma. See Chapter 10 for definitions of RGB and CMYK.

GIF

The Web uses GIF images all over the place. GIF is the most popular of three common file types used on the Internet. (JPG and PNG are the other two.) CompuServe developed GIF for Internet use, so it was optimized from birth for an online role.

Many programs read GIF files. (Older programs may read only the older GIF standard, GIF87, instead of the newer GIF89a; Paint Shop Pro lets you choose which standard to use when saving a GIF file if you click the Options button in the Save As or Save Copy As dialog box.)

GIF images have a maximum color depth of 256 colors, which allows fairly realistic images. 256 colors, however, are not enough to enable Paint Shop Pro to do all operations, so you may need to increase the number of colors. (See Chapter 10.)

GIF enables you to use some special features such as a *transparent color* (which lets the background of Web pages show through), and *interlaced display* (in which the entire image gradually forms as it is downloaded from the Web). GIF can use fewer colors than 256 if you want to save file size and, therefore, save people who view your file on the Web downloading time.

A special Paint Shop Pro tool called the *GIF Optimizer* can help you set transparency and otherwise optimize your image for Web use. See Chapter 19 for details of creating images for the Web using this tool.

Some GIF files actually contain a whole series of images to be displayed as an animation. You can view these images using Animation Shop; Paint Shop Pro only shows you the first image of the series.

JPEG

JPEG (or JPG) stands for Joint Photographic Experts Group, which sounds pretty impressive. JPEG images are very common on the Web for color photographs and other very realistic color images because their files are very small (relative to other file types) and download very quickly.

The disadvantage of JPEG is that it uses something called *lossy compression,* which means that the image quality is reduced a bit, especially around sharp edges like text. You can choose just how much compression or quality you want, but because some image quality is always lost, it's best to keep your work in some other format (preferably PSP). Use File➪Export or File➪Save Copy As to create JPEG files.

If you're reading JPEG files, Paint Shop Pro offers an effect that removes some of the problems, called artifacts. See Chapter 8.

As with GIF, Paint Shop Pro offers a special tool, the *JPEG Optimizer,* for adjusting JPEG images for the Web. See Chapter 19 for details of fine-tuning JPEG images with this tool.

PNG

PNG (Progressive Network Graphics) was designed to take over for GIF on the Web, although it is only catching on slowly. It does have some advantages over GIF, and accomplishes the same functions as GIF, so it may yet take over. As its main use is Web graphics, I discuss it a bit more in Chapter 19.

Using vector file types (drawing files)

Graphics images come in two main flavors: *raster* (also called *bitmap*) and *vector*. Here are the differences between them:

- **Raster (bitmap) images are made up of dots (pixels).** Most computer images are of this kind, and Paint Shop Pro is principally designed for this kind of image. It both reads and writes a wide variety of raster images.

- **Vector images are made up of lines, shapes, filled areas, and text.** Although Paint Shop Pro is principally designed for raster images, it allows you to create special vector layers that contain lines, text, and preset shapes. You can change text, lines, and shapes more easily if they're stored as vectors than if they're stored as bitmaps. Paint Shop Pro can read certain vector image files but converts them to rasters.

Vector files are typically created by popular *drawing* software (as opposed to *painting* software). AutoCAD, for instance, a popular drafting application, writes DXF (Drawing eXchange Format) files. Corel Draw writes CDR files, and Corel WordPerfect uses WPG files. Many other vector file types are in use, as well.

Like Paint Shop Pro files, some other file types can also contain a mix of vector and bitmap graphics. These include Windows Enhanced Metafiles (EMF, a Microsoft Windows standard), Computer Graphics Metafiles (CGM, a standard by the American National Standards Institute), PICT (a Macintosh standard), and embedded PostScript (EPS, by Adobe). Some files (like embedded PostScript) may in some cases contain both a bitmap and a vector version of the same image.

Opening vector files

Paint Shop Pro can open many kinds of vector (or mixed vector and bitmap) files. You can also copy drawings, using the Windows clipboard, from most vector programs that run under Windows, and paste the images into Paint Shop Pro.

Whether you're opening or pasting vector images, however, Paint Shop Pro converts them into bitmap images. To do the conversion, it pops up a Meta Picture Import dialog box that wants you to input a width and height for this resulting bitmap image, in pixels. (Any dimension information in the original file doesn't survive the translation, so Paint Shop Pro needs some help from you.)

TIP

If something other than Paint Shop Pro opens your files

If some program other than Paint Shop Pro automatically opens your graphics files when you click or double-click on them and you prefer Paint Shop Pro, here's what to do:

In Paint Shop Pro, choose File⇨Preferences⇨ File Format Associations. The File Format Associations dialog box appears.

To make Paint Shop Pro open all the various types of graphics files that it's capable of opening, click the Select All button.

To select exactly which type of graphics file Paint Shop Pro will open, click to enable the check box for each type you want in the list of file types shown. Click OK when you're done.

Select the Maintain Original Aspect Ratio check box if you want to keep the same proportions as the original image. Because Paint Shop Pro is translating between two very different kinds of image data, it may make a few mistakes that you have to clean up afterward.

Saving vector files — not

You can't save pure vector-type image files in Paint Shop Pro. You can, however, save your work as one of the file types that allows a mix of vectors and bitmaps such as EPS or CGM.

In those instances, PSP simply stores a bitmap image and leaves the vector part blank. Because no vector data is stored, a program that handles only vector graphics may not be able to read the file.

Fixing Files Where Some Paint Shop Pro Features Don't Work

When you work on some images, especially foreign file types (non-PSP), you may discover that some tool or command you need has gone gray (like this author).

Maybe you opened a GIF file and wanted to use some of Paint Shop Pro's filter commands. Paint Shop Pro appears to be saying, "Forget it! I just won't let you do it." The filter commands are grayed out. Or, you want to add a raster layer to that GIF file, and the New Raster Layer command has gone gray.

Your basic problem is a lack of depth. Well, not *your* depth: the color depth of your image. A number of Paint Shop Pro commands and tools don't work on images with less than 24-bit (16 million color) color depth. You need to change color depth.

I go into more detail about changing color depth in Chapter 10. The basic trick, however, is to choose Colors⇨Increase Color Depth⇨16 Million Colors (24 Bit). After increasing color depth, do your work, and then decrease the color depth again if you must in order to save it as the file type you want.

Reading or Storing Notes about a File

Sometimes you end up working with lots of different files that have similar names and contents, but different sizes or color depths. You can tell them apart when you choose File⇨Open to open a file. Just check out the Image Information / Preview section of the Open dialog box that appears. This section lists the image's width, height, and color depth. For even more information, click the Details button in that section, which can tell you if a file is the right or wrong one before you even open it.

After an image is open, you can get the same information and more by choosing Image⇨Image Information. The Current Image Information dialog box appears and displays information about the creator of the image: click the Creator Information tab. You can enter your own information there, too; just type it into the text boxes provided and click OK when done.

Browsing and Organizing Files Using Tiny Pictures

Pretty soon, your PC's disk drive is loaded with images and telling them apart or organizing them is like managing the Imelda Marcos' shoe collection, but less interesting. You haven't got much to tell the files apart, except, in this instance, for a file name. How do you find and open the file you want?

The solution is tiny thumbnail pictures. No, don't call in a manicurist. Use Paint Shop Pro's Image Browser and choose your file from a page of *thumbnails:* tiny pictures of all the image files in any chosen folder.

Choose File⇨Browse or click the Browse button in the Open dialog box. (Or press Ctrl+B if you're a keyboard kind of person.) Figure 2-4 shows the

Browse window, with the sort of images you see next. (Paint Shop Pro may take a few seconds to display all the images.) To close the window when you're done, choose File⇨Close or press Ctrl+F4.

Figure 2-4:
Paint Shop
Pro's
Browse
window
proves that
a picture is
better than
a thousand-
word file
name.

The left side of the Browse window looks and works like Windows Explorer. Click a folder to see its contents (thumbnail images of the graphics files in that folder). If the folder contains more folders, a + sign appears to its left. To open that folder, click the + sign; to close it, click the – sign that now appears where the + sign did.

On the right side of the window are the thumbnail images with their file names. Here are some important ways to chew on your thumbnails:

✔ To check image type, size, and date before opening the file, pause your cursor over any thumbnail. Paint Shop Pro displays the information near your cursor. For more detail, right-click the thumbnail and choose Information from the pop-up menu.

✔ To open an image file, right-click it and choose Open from the menu that appears.

✔ To rearrange your thumbnails in the right-hand pane of the browse window, drag them where you want them.

✔ To move an image to a different folder, drag the thumbnail from the right pane to your destination folder in the left pane.

✔ To copy a file to a different folder, drag the thumbnail to another folder while holding the Ctrl key down.

✔ To delete a file, right-click its thumbnail and choose Delete from the pop-up menu that appears.

 ✔ To rename a file, right-click its thumbnail, choose Rename from the pop-up menu and type a new name in the Rename File dialog box that appears.

 ✔ To select several files for opening, moving, copying, or deleting, hold down the Ctrl key and click their thumbnail images. To select a series, left-click the first (or last) image; then hold down the Shift key and click the last (or first) image. Follow the preceding bullets for opening, moving, copying, or deleting files.

To sort your thumbnails in different ways, follow these steps:

1. **Right-click on the blank area to the right of the pictures.**

   The Thumbnail Sort dialog box appears.

2. **Choose Ascending or Descending sort order from the Primary Sort tab.**

3. **Choose what to sort by in the Sort By area: file attributes such as date, or image attributes such as dimensions (size).**

4. **To sort within a sort (such as by file name within each file date), click the Secondary Sort tab and again choose a sort order and what to sort by.**

5. **Click OK to sort.**

Obtaining Images from the Web

The Web is a grab bag of goodies for graphics gurus. Here's how to get your hands on these fabulous fruits.

One of the best ways to get graphics is to find a Web site offering them free and clear. Most such sites provide instructions for downloading those image files. To save an image that you're viewing in your Web browser, use the following methods:

 ✔ Right-click the image and, in the pop-up menu that appears, look for Save Picture As or a similar choice. You're prompted for the location on your hard disk where you want the image saved.

 ✔ Right-click the image and, in the pop-up menu that appears, choose Copy. This choice copies the image to the Windows clipboard; open Paint Shop Pro and press Ctrl+V to paste the image as a new image. (See the Edit⇨Paste command for ways to paste the image into another open image.) Save the image by choosing File⇨Save.

A fair number of graphics images on the Web have transparent portions, especially their backgrounds. The transparent parts of such images actually have a hidden color (typically white), and that color may become visible in Paint Shop Pro. See Chapter 19 for more about transparency in Web images.

Most Web images are one of only a few different file types: GIF, JPEG; or PNG. GIF, and some PNG images, are *palette images,* with a limited number of colors (typically 256 colors); as a result, a few tools such as Paint Shop Pro effects may not work until you increase the colors to 16 million (24-bit). See Chapter 10.

Many, if not most, animations on the Web are GIF files. You should open animated GIF files in Animation Shop, not Paint Shop Pro (which only displays the first frame of the animation).

Chapter 3

Capturing Pictures from Paper, Camera, or Screen

· ·

In This Chapter

▶ Scanning images from paper

▶ Getting better scans

▶ Scanning printed images

▶ Downloading pictures from digital cameras

▶ Using TWAIN software

▶ Capturing images from the screen

· ·

*W*here do your pictures come from? From your new digital camera? From a piece of paper? Or, from your PC screen?

Ironically, most people don't actually *paint* pictures in Paint Shop Pro. They get an image from somewhere and then mess around with it. This chapter tells you how to get that image into Paint Shop Pro.

Scanning into Paint Shop Pro

With scanners almost as cheap as a carton of paper, scanning is one of the most popular ways to get an image into a PC. Many people are surprised that scanning is a more involved process than they expect. Getting an image *from* paper is not quite as simple as putting an image *on* paper — unless quality isn't all that important.

If your PC is equipped with more than one image-acquiring device (scanners, TWAIN-compliant cameras), you need to tell Paint Shop Pro which one you're using before going through the following steps. Choose File⇨Import⇨ Twain⇨Select Source. The Select Source dialog box appears. Select your scanner (source) and then click Select.

In most instances, the following steps scan an image from a properly installed scanner (although your scanning software may differ):

1. **Launch the scanning software that came with your scanner.**

   To do that, choose File⇨Import⇨Twain⇨Acquire in Paint Shop Pro.

   Or press the scan button on your scanner, if it has one.

   Some special software designed to run your scanner should appear. (If it doesn't appear, read the literature that came with your scanner and check to make sure your scanner is properly installed.) Because that software depends on the scanner manufacturer, I can't tell you a lot of details about it. I give you some tips, however, in the next section, "Using your scanning software."

   Figure 3-1 shows the two windows that appear if, for instance, you're using Microtek Scanwizard software.

Figure 3-1:
One example of scanning software. One window contains controls, another shows a preview. Your software may be different.

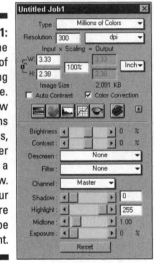

2. **Find and click the Preview button.**

   In Figure 3-1, for instance, the Preview button is in the Preview window. If you don't find a button labeled `Preview`, look for a similar word. The scanner starts to scan and shortly gives you a small preview image, as shown in the Preview window of Figure 3-1. This preview image shows the entire scanning area of the scanner (the glass area in a flat-bed scanner).

3. **Define the area you want to scan.**

   In most scanner software, you create a rectangle (the dashed line shown in Figure 3-1) in the Preview area to define the area that you want to scan. (Drag from one corner of the part you want to the opposite corner.) Usually, you can then drag this rectangle to adjust its position or drag its sides or corners to adjust its size. If you don't define the scan area in this way, you'll probably end up with an enormous image (your scanner's entire field of view) that you'll have to crop (trim) to the area you want.

Most scanner software allows you to enlarge (zoom in on) the preview image. Look for a magnifying glass icon, click it, and then click on the image.

4. **Adjust settings that control the resolution or number of colors, or that improve the appearance of the preview picture.**

   Scanner software often offers important features and controls, including whether you want color or black-and-white scanning. In the ScanWizard software of Figure 3-1, the controls are in the left window. I describe these and other useful controls in "Getting the most from your scanning software," just a bit later in this chapter.

5. **Find and click the Scan button.**

   If you can't find a Scan button, look for a Start or Begin button. Figure 3-1 shows a Scan button next to the Preview button. The scanner begins to scan again. (It may take longer or shorter than it did in Step 2.)

After the scanner is done, an image appears in Paint Shop Pro. You can now close the scanner software window or continue to scan more images (starting with Step 2). Each image gets its own window in Paint Shop Pro.

Remarking on TWAIN

Mark Twain loved high-tech gadgets (such as typesetting machines, the computers of his day). Although he'll never meet his namesake, the TWAIN interface, I think he would have loved the happy accident of having his pen name associated with today's high-tech scanners. (Incidentally, TWAIN, despite its capitalization, is not an acronym, although some wags have suggested that it stands for Technology Without An Interesting Name.)

TWAIN is a go-between that links scanners, cameras, and other image sources to PC image-processing software like Paint Shop Pro. Scanners are made by different manufacturers and,

therefore, speak different native languages. To make translation easier for your PC, most manufacturers have chosen to make their scanners comply with a standard called TWAIN. As a result, in graphics programs like Paint Shop Pro, scanning usually involves a menu choice called TWAIN.

But a scanner is a sophisticated instrument that needs software to control it. So when you scan, your PC launches a specialized TWAIN-speaking scanner-controlling program. Scanner manufacturers install this program on your PC during the scanner setup.

Scan-ty information

What exactly goes on in a scanner? Here's a quick tour. The scanner illuminates your image while it moves a light sensor in a series of straight lines across the page. As the sensor goes along, it periodically *samples* (takes a reading of) how much light is coming from one tiny spot on the image. Usually, the scanner uses three sensors combined, one for each primary color.

These readings are converted into digital numbers, one for each primary color. During the conversion process, the scanner makes an adjustment to account for the fact that electronic sensors don't see light the way the human eye does. (This adjustment is called *gamma,* and,

apart from scanning, it also has to be made by software when your PC displays colors to you on-screen.) The scanner may also make other adjustments as directed by the scanning software.

Scanners that offer more *bits* (as in 24-bit, 30-bit, or 48-bit) can pick up more subtle differences in color or brightness. Paint Shop Pro can only handle 24-bit data, so if your scanner does better than that, its capability is, to some degree, wasted. Those extra bits help the scanner make fine adjustments to the conversion in some scanners, however, and so actually do improve the quality of a "mere" 24-bit image.

Getting the most from your scanning software

Whatever software your PC uses to control your scanner, it undoubtedly offers you certain settings to play with. For casual scanning of images that don't have problems (such as underexposure), you can often ignore a lot of those settings and do all your fiddling in Paint Shop Pro. Sometimes, however, the controls in your scanner software make a difference that can't be easily duplicated using Paint Shop Pro alone.

You can usually adjust these settings *after* you do the Preview. Except for resolution and color settings, the Preview image reflects the changes without running your scanner again.

Most scanning software keeps its settings from one scanning session to the next. This is great if all your printed images are similar but not if they're very different. If your scanning software has a Reset button, click it to restore original settings before you adjust the settings for a new image. Usually a dialog box appears allowing you to select which settings to reset and which to leave the same.

Choosing the number of colors

To achieve the best quality possible with color photographs (and other images that either have many colors or very gradual, subtle shadings), you want the maximum number of colors the scanner can produce. Usually, this maximum is expressed as 24-bit or 32-bit color. If your PC has disk space for the large files this produces, scanning at this number of colors is best even if your final application requires fewer colors. For the sake of control, it's better to have more colors than you need to start with and use Paint Shop Pro, rather than the scanner, to reduce the colors (for which, see Chapter 10).

If you know that your final application for the image doesn't require such high quality and you're in a rush or your disk drive is short on space, you can save yourself a bit of time in Paint Shop Pro by choosing fewer colors during scanning.

Here are some scanner settings you may find, labeled type or color depth in the scanner software, that usually work well for the following uses:

- **Business or highest-quality personal use:** Choose 16 million colors (24- or 32-bit). (These images can then be color-reduced in Paint Shop Pro for faster downloading in Web or e-mail applications.)

- **Casual family or business Web page illustrations or snapshots to be sent by e-mail:** Choose 256-color if it's available, but it's not always offered as a scanner option. Use 16 million colors if the 256-color option is not available.

- **Black and white photos, pencil drawings and sketches, or line drawings with lines of varying weight:** Choose 256 shades of gray. Scanners typically scan such images by looking for one particular color. If your drawing is all in one color of pencil, such as green, it may not appear! Check your scanner manual for notes on scanning "grayscale" images or line drawings, or avoid red, blue, or green pencils.

- **Clear, original printed text with good contrast, or line drawings in dark ink or with thick lines:** Choose Two colors (1-bit), or *Line Art,* if available; otherwise, choose 256 shades of gray. If you have a line drawing with uneven line darkness, you can sometimes turn it into good line art by adjusting either the Line Art Threshold or the Highlight/Midtone/ Shadow settings. See "Contrast and other adjustments," later in this chapter, for more about the latter setting.

Choosing resolution

Resolution is the number of dots (or *samples*) per inch that your scanner reads from the paper image. Your scanning software has a control for resolution.

Higher resolution means you get more detail — more pixels — which is generally A Good Thing. For instance, if you scan a 4-inch x 6-inch snapshot at 300 dots per inch (dpi), you get an image of 4 x 300 (1200) pixels high and 6 x 300 pixels (1800) wide. (That's even more pixels than most PC screens can show at the same time.) You can always make a picture lower in resolution (reduce its size in pixels) in Paint Shop Pro if necessary but you can't add detail that isn't there in the first place.

Higher resolution also poses some problems. First of all, high resolution means bigger files! If you're just scanning a photo to e-mail to someone or to put on the Web, the people viewing your photo aren't going to appreciate the long wait for a large photo to download — especially if it's bigger than their screen! You can reduce a photo in Paint Shop Pro, of course, but why bother if you don't need to? Besides, sometimes the shrinking process (also called *resampling*) doesn't give quite as good a result as if you had chosen the lower resolution in the first place.

To judge what resolution to use, answer these questions:

- **How big an image do you need?** For most Web and e-mail work, an image 300 to 400 pixels on a side is plenty. Multiply the width or height of the region you are scanning (say, 6 inches wide) by the scanner resolution you're thinking of using (say, 300 dpi) to figure out the resulting width or height in pixels (1800 pixels wide, in this example). Select a lower resolution to get a smaller image in pixels.

- **How big a file do you want?** Scanning a 4-inch x 6-inch color snapshot at 300 dpi (and 24-bit color) can give you a file as large as 6 megabytes. Cutting resolution in half can reduce the file size by as much as a factor of four.

- **How finely detailed does the image need to be?** At 300 dpi, you can begin to see an individual human hair placed in your scanner.

You probably won't see any changes you make in resolution in your Preview image. To see the effect of resolution settings, you have to scan an image into Paint Shop Pro (click the Scan button in your scanner software).

Setting contrast and other adjustments

Some of the other adjustments available in your scanner software can make an enormous difference in the quality of your image. Fiddle with these after you have clicked the Preview button in your scanner software so that you have a Preview image to look at as you make your adjustments. You may have to poke around to find a button or command that reveals these adjustments.

Many of the adjustments that scanning software offers are pretty technical. I don't have room to fully do them justice here, but you probably won't need them anyway. I describe here a few of the important ones you may find:

- **Brightness:** Brightness makes all areas darker or lighter to the same degree.

- **Contrast**: This adjustment makes dark areas darker and light areas lighter.

- **Exposure:** Increasing Exposure makes dark pixels disproportionately darker and so brings out detail in the light areas.

✔ **Shadow/Midtone/Highlight:** The Shadow and Highlight values are also called the black and white points, respectively. Sometimes they're unnamed, appearing as sliding arrows under a histogram chart. These three settings are something like Contrast and Exposure, but more precise, which make an image's dark areas darker and its light areas lighter. They also bring out detail in the middle ranges of darkness and adjust a too-dark or too-light image to a more pleasing appearance. Each setting ranges from 0 to 255 (the numeric values correspond to brightness: 0 is black and 255 is white). The choices are:

- **Shadow:** To make the darker areas as dark as possible, adjust the Shadow value upward. All pixels *below* that value become as dark as you can make them without radically changing any colors.

- **Highlight:** To make light areas as light as possible, adjust the Highlight value downward. All pixels *above* that value become as light as possible without radically changing their colors.

- **Midtone:** If the rest of the image is, overall, kind of dark, adjust the Midtone value downward; if the image is light, set the value higher.

✔ **Descreen:** Software like Microtek Scanwizard and Umax Vistascan have special *descreen* abilities, which means they can minimize the moiré patterns that arise when you scan printed images. Generally, they offer several settings that depend upon whether you're scanning from a newspaper, magazine, or higher-quality printed source like a book. (You probably have to scan to see the result of descreening — it's unlikely that you can see it in the Preview.)

✔ **Unsharp Masking:** Try this feature (often lurking in an area called *filter* or something similar) if your photo doesn't look quite as sharp as it should. Without actually making the image sharper, this feature gives the illusion of sharpness. It raises the contrast around edges (where the pixel values change). Unsharp masking has three settings, as follows:

(The numbers used in these settings don't have any intuitive meaning, so don't look for one. Just adjust them up or down.) The settings are:

- **Amount:** This setting adjusts the degree of contrast enhancement (sharpness).

- **Radius:** This setting determines how far from an edge the effect extends.

- **Threshold:** This setting sets a limit, below which an edge won't be enhanced. A low threshold value means even small changes in pixel value get contrast-enhanced. A setting too low may make the image speckly.

If you forget to use Unsharp Masking *while* scanning, you can use Paint Shop Pro's Unsharp Mask effect *after* scanning. Choose Effects⇨Sharpen⇨Unsharp Mask and the Unsharp Mask dialog box appears. Make the same adjustments listed in the preceding bullet. Figure 3-2 shows the unsharp mask effect.

Figure 3-2:
Unsharp
Masking
refers to the
effect
illustrated
by this
before-and-
after pair of
images.

Many scanner programs offer check boxes to turn on automatic features (typically auto contrast and auto color correction). These features attempt to adjust various settings for you, based on the Preview scan. Sometimes they work well and sometimes they don't. Try enabling and disabling their check boxes to see the result in the Preview area.

You can find an excellent, detailed guide to using the features of scanning software — in fact, to using your scanner in general — on the Web at `www.scantips.com`.

Forever plaid: Scanning printed images

When you scan a printed image from a newspaper, magazine, or book, your image often acquires a blurry checkered plaid or barred pattern. This pattern, called a *moiré* (mwah-*ray*) pattern, is caused by conflict between the dots used to print your image and the dots that happen during scanning.

The next time you put your windows screens up or down, you can see this same effect if you look through two screens at the same time. Or, if you have a screen porch, stand outside and look through the two screens where they meet at a corner.

The moiré pattern may exist only on your PC screen in Paint Shop Pro and not in your image file, as Figure 3-3 illustrates. Try viewing the image at full scale (press Ctrl+Alt+N), or larger. If the pattern then disappears, the pattern is just the effect of using a zoom of less than 1:1. Don't worry about it. When the image is printed at a high printer resolution or used on the Web at full size, then that pattern probably won't appear. If the pattern is still visible at a 1:1 zoom, then it's permanent and you need to do something about it.

Dots not nice

Why do scans of printed images get moiré patterns? Unlike photographic prints and painted or drawn artwork, printed images are made up of ink dots of varying sizes at a certain spacing. This would not be a problem except that your scanner also uses dots, but of a different size and spacing.

Your scanner reads the image by sampling the image (looking at tiny spots on the image) at some spacing (your chosen resolution in dots per inch). The samples don't align exactly on the printed dots, except, say, every 10 or 20 pixels; the rest of the time they align partly on the dots, partly on the white background. The usual result is a checkered or barred patterning on the image. Something similar can happen when Paint Shop Pro displays the image on your PC screen, which also uses dots.

Figure 3-3:
A moiré pattern appears on this roof, but is not an image flaw. In this instance, the zoom of 1:3 (noted on the title bar) is responsible.

Permanent moiré pattern problems? Try these solutions:

- ✔ **Higher resolution:** The pattern may fade if you set the resolution of your scanner's software (the dots per inch value) higher.

- ✔ **Descreening:** If descreening is provided by your scanner software, use this option. See "Contrast and other adjustments," earlier in this chapter, for more information.

- ✔ **Special filter:** Choose Effects⇨Enhance Photo⇨Moire Pattern Removal. See Chapter 8.

Printed images pose more problems than just moiré patterns. Although they appear to have a wide variety of tones, printed images actually comprise alternating dots of primary colors (black and white photos have only two colors, for instance). When these images are scanned (particularly at high resolution), they retain that spotty, dotty character. Zoom in to see them.

As a result, Paint Shop Pro features that use color selection and replacement don't work as your eye would lead you to expect. An area that looks uniformly green, for instance, may be made up of blue and yellow dots. You can't select that green area of your scanned-in logo, for instance, because it's not really green! This problem gets worse at higher resolutions.

To partially solve this problem, you can apply Paint Shop Pro's blur filter (see Chapter 8) to make the dots blur together. If you have problems selecting a colored area with the Magic Wand tool (see Chapter 13), try increasing Tolerance in the Tool Options dialog box.

Getting Images from a Digital Camera

Paint Shop Pro can be a great tool for digital photography. First, however, you have to get your camera and your PC talking to each other. They have to connect (*interface* in geek-speak) physically and in software:

- **Physical interface:** Digital cameras physically connect to PCs in all kinds of ways. Your physical connection may be a serial port (a connector on the back of most PCs, if a modem or something else isn't already using it), a parallel (printer) port, a USB port, a FireWire port, a memory card that plugs into your computer, a diskette, an infrared beam, X-rays, semaphore flags, or magical auras — who knows what the camera people will come up with next? See your camera manual for details. You also probably have to set a switch on your camera to prepare it for sending images to the PC.

- **Software interface:** You also need a software interface, unless your camera stores photos on some disk or other device your PC can read. (In that circumstance, pop the diskette, memory stick, or whatever in the proper place in your PC, copy the files to a folder on your hard disk, and open the files in Paint Shop Pro.) This software interface may take one of two forms:

    - Paint Shop Pro may already have built-in interface software to talk to your camera. See the next section, "Configuring Paint Shop Pro for your camera."

- Most cameras come with their own interface software. If you want to use that software instead of Paint Shop Pro's, or if you discover in the next section that Paint Shop Pro doesn't have built-in software for your camera, skip "Configuring Paint Shop Pro for your camera" and see "Talking TWAIN to your camera" instead.

The camera's CD may also install software for you that competes with Paint Shop Pro. You don't need to install that, if the CD's installation software gives you the choice. If that software *is* installed, it may, in certain circumstances, open your graphics files instead of Paint Shop Pro opening your files. To give Paint Shop Pro control over your files, see the sidebar, "If something other than Paint Shop Pro opens your files," near the end of Chapter 2.

Configuring Paint Shop Pro for your camera

To read photos from your camera, you need to *configure* (set up) Paint Shop Pro. (You only configure it once, unless you switch between multiple cameras. In the latter case, you configure Paint Shop Pro each time you switch.)

If you do a lot of work with photographs in Paint Shop Pro, check out the Photo toolbar. It contains buttons that are shortcuts to many of the commands that I discuss here, as well as to the photo-enhancing effects that I discuss in Chapter 8. Choose View⇨Toolbars and enable the Photo Toolbar check box in the Toolbars dialog box that appears.

First, use the camera vendor's instructions to connect your camera to your PC by means of the cable that comes with it. Then, follow these steps:

1. **Choose File⇨Import⇨Digital Camera⇨Configure.**

   The Digital Camera Configuration dialog box appears.

2. **Click the Camera Type selection box.**

3. **Choose your camera model from the drop-down list.**

   If your camera isn't in that list, click Cancel and skip the rest of these steps. You need to read "Talking TWAIN to your camera," later in this chapter.

4. **Select the Download Thumbnails Immediately After Opening Camera check box.**

This choice tells Paint Shop Pro that you want to view thumbnail (tiny) images automatically when you connect to the camera. (Otherwise, you download thumbnails by using a command after you're connected.) I find thumbnails useful, as do most primates.

5. **Leave the port and speed settings in this dialog box alone.**

   Paint Shop Pro searches high and low for your camera and figures out how fast a data link the camera can use. Unless you know better than it does, using Paint Shop Pro's choices is usually faster and better than making your own choices.

6. **Click OK.**

Downloading and opening photos

To begin the downloading process, choose File⇨Import⇨Digital Camera⇨ Access. The Digital Camera dialog box, shown in Figure 3-4, arrives on the scene.

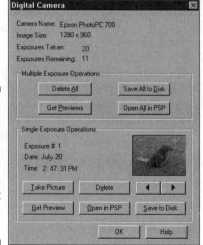

Figure 3-4: Transferring one or more photos to your PC with Paint Shop Pro's direct camera interface.

Controls in the Multiple Exposure Operations area near the top of that dialog box let you deal with all your photos at once. Controls in the Single Exposure Operations area near the bottom let you work with individual photos. Information about the dimensions of your currently chosen image and the number of exposures on the camera appears at the very top.

To download your photos, you can use any of the following ways (unless the option is grayed-out for your camera):

✔ **Download all photos — the whole enchilada:** Click the Save All to Disk button. *Downloading* means that your photos go directly to your PC's disk drive, as files. You don't see them in Paint Shop Pro. You then can open them in Paint Shop Pro with File⇨Open as you can any other image file (see Chapter 2).

✔ **Download selected images — the ones where your child is not sticking out his tongue:** Browse through the miniature images (also called *thumbnails* or *previews*) by clicking the left- and right-arrows under the thumbnail image. The exposure number, date, and time appear next to the image (for most cameras). When you come to a tongue-free or otherwise desireable photo you want to download to your PC, click the Save to Disk button. You then can open them in Paint Shop Pro with File⇨Open.

If you don't see a thumbnail image from your camera in the lower portion of the dialog box and you want to see the pictures that are on your camera before you download them to your PC, click the Get Previews button — in the *top* section of the dialog box. (The Get Preview button, in the *bottom* section, downloads a thumbnail of the individual image you have chosen with the right- and left- arrow buttons.)

If you do come upon a thumbnail of an image in which, say, your child or client is not being shown to his or her best advantage, click the Delete button (not the Delete All button) to remove it from your camera.

✔ **Open a particular image in Paint Shop Pro:** Browse through the thumbnails (as the preceding bullet describes) to that image. Click the Open In PSP button. You can also open *all* the images in Paint Shop Pro by clicking the Open All in PSP button, but that choice may use so much memory that Paint Shop Pro becomes sluggish. To save an open image to disk, see the instructions for saving a file in Chapter 2.

You can shoot pictures while your camera is connected to your PC — if, unlike me, you have something worth taking a picture of in your office. Click the Take Picture button and then click the Get Preview button. If you like the result, open it in Paint Shop Pro or download it as you would any other image.

After you download all the images you want to your PC and have checked them in Paint Shop Pro to make sure they are readable, you can return to the Digital Camera dialog box (choose File⇨Import⇨Digital Camera⇨Access). Click the Delete All button to clear your camera's memory or storage device. Click OK.

Talking TWAIN to your camera

Most camera makers — unaware that you have very cleverly chosen Paint Shop Pro and that you therefore have built-in interface software for many cameras — provide their own interface software. They probably direct you to install that software on your PC.

The camera vendor's interface software usually speaks *TWAIN,* a PC standard for connecting image acquisition devices like cameras and scanners. For further remarks on this standard, see the sidebar, "Remarking on TWAIN," earlier in this chapter.

Should you use the camera vendor's software? Use the camera vendor's TWAIN software if Paint Shop Pro doesn't list your camera among the ones it knows how to talk to (see the earlier section, "Configuring Paint Shop Pro for your camera"). Or, you can use the TWAIN software if it has features you particularly like.

Because you can have more than one TWAIN device (say, a scanner and a camera that both use TWAIN), you have to tell Paint Shop Pro which TWAIN device you want to use before you use it. Choose File⇨Import⇨TWAIN⇨ Select Source to access the Select Source dialog box. Various TWAIN interface names are listed. Determine which name is related to your camera and choose it.

To launch your camera's TWAIN software, which enables you to download photos to Paint Shop Pro, choose File⇨Import⇨TWAIN⇨Acquire. The camera's TWAIN software launches. Refer to the camera vendor's instructions to download your photos.

Capturing Images from Your PC Screen

There it is, on-screen: the exact image you need. But it's in some other program, not Paint Shop Pro. You figure that there must be some way to get it into Paint Shop Pro — after all, it's already in your computer.

Well, you're right. Paint Shop Pro has several different ways to capture that image. In fact, even if Paint Shop Pro didn't give you any help, Windows has a secret way of *capturing* (copying) images from the screen.

Quick captures with the Print Screen button

Windows has a well-kept secret that you may find useful: You can copy what you see on-screen onto the Windows clipboard. (The clipboard is that invisible area where text and graphics that you cut and copy are stored in Windows programs.) Use this technique for screen capture if you don't happen to have Paint Shop Pro handy — perhaps you're using someone else's PC or in too much of a hurry to launch Paint Shop Pro. Windows gives you these two ways to copy screen contents onto the Windows clipboard:

✔ **To capture the entire screen:** Press the Print Screen button on your keyboard (labeled PrtScn, Print Scrn, or some other badly spelled contraction).

✔ **To capture just a window:** Press Alt+Print Screen.

Nothing appears to happen when you press the keys, but now the image is on your clipboard. You can open any program you like (say, Paint Shop Pro) and use the Edit⇨Paste command (or Ctrl+V in most programs) to paste the image.

If the image is in a document in certain other applications, you may instead click the picture and then choose Edit⇨Copy to copy the image onto the clipboard. Sometimes, however, the colors come out better if you use one of the two Print Screen button methods.

If you're using a PC that doesn't have Paint Shop Pro and want to take the image with you, you can save the image that you've just copied with Print Screen as a clipboard file. On the Windows taskbar, choose Start⇨Programs⇨ Accessories⇨System Tools⇨Clipboard Viewer. (It may be located elsewhere on some systems. Poke around the Accessories menus to find it.) Hey! There's your picture! Choose File⇨Save As to save it as a clipboard (.CLP) file. E-mail or carry the file on a diskette to your own Paint Shop Pro-equipped system. Paint Shop Pro can open .CLP files.

Selective captures with Paint Shop Pro's capture features

The Windows Print Screen feature is okay for snaring your entire screen or a single window, but other species of Windows wildlife aren't so easily captured. For instance, you may want to capture only a particular part of an image, a toolbar from a program window, or where a mouse cursor is pointing in a program window. For these trickier captures, use Paint Shop Pro's capture features that you can find in the Capture menu.

Preparing to capture

To set your snare, take the following steps:

1. **Choose File⇨Import⇨Screen Capture⇨Setup from the menu bar.**

   The Capture Setup dialog box of Figure 3-5 comes to your aid.

   From left to right in Figure 3-5, you can see that you have three kinds of choices: what you want to capture, how you want to *trigger* (activate) the snare, and a couple of options (Include Cursor or Multiple Captures).

Figure 3-5:
Setting your
snare for
elusive
Windows
wildlife.

2. **Choose what to capture.**

   Paint Shop Pro can capture five different species of Windows wildebeest. In the Capture Setup dialog box, choose one of the possibilities listed in column 1 of Table 3-1.

Table 3-1	Using Different Types of Capture
Type of Capture	*What it Does*
Area	Captures a rectangular area that you define anywhere on-screen
Full screen	Captures the whole nine yards, the entire enchilada, the full Monty — everything on-screen
Client area	Captures everything in a window except the title bar
Window	Captures the application window that you specify (don't use for a document window; use Object for that)
Object	Captures an application window, a document window, or any individual feature in a window, like a toolbar — a very useful catch-all category that works for toolbars, menu bars, scroll bars, palettes, and sometimes portions of those objects.

3. **Choose your trigger.**

   You must choose a trigger, to use after setup is done, that tells Paint Shop Pro to start capturing stuff. Without a trigger, capture would start immediately. All you would ever capture is Paint Shop Pro itself! In the Capture Setup dialog box, shown in Figure 3-5, you can see that you have three choices for triggering the capture. Select one of the following options:

- **Right mouse click:** A right mouse click begins the capture.

- **Hot key:** From the Hot Key selection box, choose a key to serve as a trigger. You can choose any of the function keys, F1 through F12, alone or in combination with Shift, Alt, or Ctrl. F11 is initially chosen for you.

- **Delay timer:** Select this option and then enter a delay time (in seconds) in the Delay Timer box.

4. **Choose options.**

   Paint Shop Pro gives you two options:

   - **Capture multiple images:** If you plan to capture a series of on-screen images, select the Multiple Captures check box in the Capture Setup dialog box (Figure 3-5). You're then able to simply snap a series of images without returning to Paint Shop Pro each time. If you're creating a tutorial for using some software, for instance, you can set up Paint Shop Pro and then easily capture a screen for each step.

   - **Include mouse cursor in capture:** You may want to show the mouse cursor in your screen captures to point out some feature. If so, select the Include Cursor check box in the Capture Setup dialog box (Figure 3-5).

Using the Include Cursor option may not work if you're only capturing an object. You need to use your cursor to select the object, placing the cursor somewhere other than where you want it in the picture.

Making the capture

After you're set up to capture from the PC screen in Paint Shop Pro, you're ready to make the capture. To capture an image, take the following steps:

1. **Click the Capture Now button in the Capture Setup dialog box.**

   The Capture Now command starts the capture process. If the Capture Setup dialog box is no longer on-screen, click the Start Capture button on Paint Shop Pro's Toolbar (a camera icon at or near the right end of the Toolbar) or press Shift+C.

   Paint Shop Pro discreetly shrinks to a button on the taskbar to get out of your way.

2. **Make any last-minute changes to the thing you want to capture.**

   You have a final opportunity to adjust the appearance of the screen area that contains the image — before you trigger the capture. If you have chosen the option of capturing the mouse cursor, position the cursor now.

3. **Trigger the capture (or wait for the timer to trigger it).**

Depending upon the kind of trigger you chose (see Step 3 in "Preparing to capture"), either right-click with your mouse, press your hot key (say, F11), or wait for the time interval to elapse.

If you're capturing a full screen, Paint Shop Pro restores itself to full window size now. You're done and can skip the next steps. Otherwise, Paint Shop Pro waits for you to choose your capture area.

4. **Choose the capture area (unless you're capturing the full screen).**

How you choose the capture area depends on what kind of capture you have chosen, as shown in Table 3-2.

After you choose the capture area, the capture occurs instantly. Paint Shop Pro immediately restores itself to its original window size (unless you have chosen the multiple capture option) and displays the capture as a new image.

5. **Repeat Steps 3 and 4 if you have chosen the multiple capture option.**

Paint Shop Pro acquires each capture as a separate image. You don't see them because Paint Shop Pro remains minimized as a button on the taskbar. To restore Paint Shop Pro, click its button on the Windows taskbar.

Table 3-2	Pointing Out Your Quarry to Paint Shop Pro
Type of Capture	*What to Do after Triggering the Capture*
Area	Left-click once where you want one corner of the area. Then, with your mouse button released (don't drag), move your cursor diagonally to where you want the opposite corner and click again.
Full screen	Do nothing; after you trigger, Paint Shop Pro immediately restores itself to full window size.
Client area	Left-click on the window you want.
Window	Left-click on the window you want.
Object	A black rectangle encloses whatever object is directly under your mouse cursor. You don't have to keep that object. Move your cursor around and, when the black rectangle encloses the object you want, left-click.

For better and easier captures, read and heed the following tips:

✔ Set up your screen the way you want it to look before you enable the trigger (before you press the Capture Now button or press Shift+C). If you try to make adjustments after you set the trigger, you may accidentally trigger the capture.

✔ The color depth of the new image matches your screen settings; therefore, it's either a *palette* image (typically 256 colors or fewer) or a so-called *true color* (16.7 million color) image. You may want to upgrade a palette image to a true color image in order to use Paint Shop Pro's more advanced tools. See Chapter 10 for information on increasing the number of colors.

✔ If the computer on which you captured an image is set to 256 colors, the image's colors may come out awful. The capturing computer's palette (the set of 256 colors used to create the image) and Paint Shop Pro's palette probably aren't the same copy.

  If the PC on which you're capturing your image offers True Color, make sure the screen is set to that option: Right-click on the Windows desktop, choose Properties, click the Settings tab, select Colors, and choose True Color (24-bit or 32-bit).

✔ To enhance colors — for those captured colors that come out fairly accurate, but faded, murky, or otherwise less than satisfactory — see Chapters 8 or 11.

✔ If you're capturing an image from your Web browser, use save as or copy rather than Paint Shop Pro's screen capture. To save an image as a file in Internet Explorer, for instance, right-click the image and choose Save Picture As.

Part II
Painting the Picture

The 5th Wave · By Rich Tennant

"I THINK YOU'VE MADE A MISTAKE. WE DO PHOTO RETOUCHING, NOT FAMILY PORTRAI...OOOH, WAIT A MINUTE-I THINK I GET IT!"

In this part . . .

*1*f you need to paint, spray, fill, erase, or otherwise get creative with brushes and paint, start here. Begin with paint in Chapter 4. Paint Shop Pro's wild, new color palette goes beyond basic paint and lets you flow gradients (shadings), patterns, and textures right off your brush. Choose paint that simulates the texture of scribbling on surfaces like asphalt, brick, or wood, or apply a real woodgrain pattern. Simulate three-dimensional shading with gradient fills, or paint in patterns of neon colors.

In Chapter 5, I show you the magic of Paint Shop Pro's basic brushes and other hand tools. Discover how to get exactly the stroke and effect you want. Paint Shop Pro lets you easily control brush attributes such as shape, softness, paint transparency or thickness, spray patterns, and evenness of flow. Even erasing can be an art in Paint Shop Pro!

For real magic, I show you how to make images flow right off a paint brush in Chapter 6. Paint Shop Pro's cool new Picture Tubes tool applies a sort of spreadable clip art. Need a cloud of butterflies? Wave your Picture Tube tool. Here I also show you the magic of the Clone Brush tool, which is great for seamlessly retouching photographs by brushing a duplicate of patterns, backgrounds, or other areas that already exist in your photo.

Chapter 4

Choosing Colors, Styles, and Textures

· ·

In This Chapter

▶ Choosing colors

▶ Understanding foreground and background color

▶ Adjusting color

▶ Creating custom colors

▶ Using styles and textures

· ·

*B*efore you go flinging your paintbrush around with wild abandon, choosing a color to fling is a good idea. (Unless, of course, you're one of those devil-may-care creative types.) Here's where to get the inside story on the fastest and best ways to choose a color under various circumstances.

In Paint Shop Pro, however, you don't just paint with color. How boring and pedestrian! No, you paint with style! Style, in this case, refers either to plain old, boring color, or creative, multicolor designs of various types called *gradients* and *patterns* — all of which can flow off your brush at your command.

But wait, there's more! Not only does your paint have style, but it can also have texture. Your work can look like you're rubbing chalk on concrete, or spray-painting an elephant's ear, or doing something else far more interesting than just smearing paint or multicolor patterns smoothly on paper.

All of this excitement springs from the Color palette, which in Paint Shop Pro 7 hides more secrets than a black dog hides ticks. Figure 4-1 shows the palette and some of its more important features.

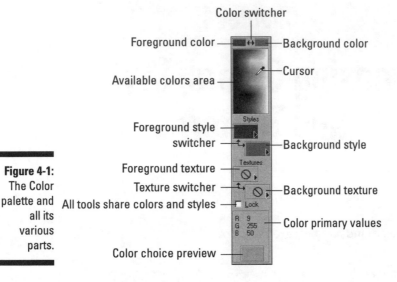

Color switcher

Foreground color ——— ——— Background color

——— Cursor

Available colors area ———

Foreground style —
switcher ———
——— Background style

Foreground texture ———
Texture switcher ——— ——— Background texture
All tools share colors and styles ———

R 9
G 255 ——— Color primary values
B 50

Color choice preview ———

Figure 4-1:
The Color
palette and
all its
various
parts.

Here's a brief summary of what the various parts shown in Figure 4-1 do:

- **Available Colors:** Click either of the mouse buttons on this area to pick up a color conveniently. Left-click and the color becomes the foreground (principal) color. Right-click and it becomes your background (secondary) color. If you see fewer colors than Figure 4-1 shows, your image has 256 colors or fewer. See "Working With 256 Colors or Fewer," later in this chapter.

- **Foreground Color:** I call this rectangle the foreground color *sample*. Unless you have chosen a fancier *Style* than plain paint, this sample shows you what you'll paint when you apply a tool to the canvas with the left mouse button pressed. (Paint Shop Pro also refers to this color as the *stroke* color.)

- **Background Color:** I call this setting a sample, just as I do with the foreground color. Background color is simply a second painting color used either for two-color operations, or as a convenient second color that gets applied by tools when you use the right mouse button. (Paint Shop Pro also refers to this color as the *fill* color.)

- **Foreground Style:** (I call this the Foreground Style thingy a *swatch* just to help you keep it separate from the Foreground Color sample.) This setting is the best single indicator of what you're going to paint. It has three alternative settings: plain paint (foreground color); a multihued pattern called a *gradient;* and a pattern called, well, a *pattern* (a geometric or photograph-like image). Paint Shop Pro also refers to foreground style as the *stroke* style because you use it for the line or stroke that defines shape outlines.

Help! I just want plain, solid paint!!!

Are you getting weird, patterned, or thin paint — perhaps not even in the color you chose — when you just want plain, unpatterned color? Are you getting no paint at all? The problem is that you have somehow chosen a fancier style than plain paint, chosen a texture, or turned off style altogether. Here's how to return to the ordinary, using controls in the Color palette:

Mouse down (click and keep your mouse button down) on the Foreground Style swatch. In the fly-out panel that appears, click the paint brush icon and release. The swatch displays foreground color. Repeat for the Background Style swatch.

Mouse down on the Foreground Texture panel. In the fly-out panel that appears, click the circle-with-a-slash icon and release. The panel displays that icon. Repeat for the Background Texture panel.

- ✓ **Background style:** This swatch works like the Foreground Style, but, like Background color, it determines the second style for two-style operations, or determines what style is used when you right-click or drag with many of the tools. Paint Shop Pro also refers to this style as the *fill* style because you use it to fill shape outlines.

- ✓ **Foreground Texture:** A kind of roughness, optional, that appears wherever you paint foreground color or style. The circle-with-a-slash icon says that texture is "off."

- ✓ **Background Texture:** A roughness that appears wherever your background color does.

- ✓ **Switchers:** Switchers switch foreground and background settings. Three switchers are available: one to swap colors; one to swap styles; and a third to swap textures. Click the switcher's two-headed arrow icon to switch.

- ✓ **Color Primary Values**: Three numbers *(primaries)* that define exactly what color your cursor is poised over in the Available colors area. These colors can be in either the RGB system or HSL system; see Chapter 10 to understand these numbers better.

- ✓ **Color Choice Preview:** A sample that shows a larger expanse of whatever color your cursor is poised over in the Available colors area.

Choosing Paint

How do you choose what color to paint with? To choose any color, from screaming chartreuse to insipid indigo, just click on Paint Shop Pro's palette of colors.

Or, in full and gory detail, it goes like this:

1. **Move your cursor over the Available Colors area, in the Color palette.**

   Figure 4-1 points out that area: the multi-hued box that (unless you've moved the Color palette) lives in the upper-right corner of the Paint Shop Pro window. (If you don't see the Color palette, display it by pressing the *C* key on your keyboard.) Your cursor is a dropper icon while it's over this area, to indicate that you'll pick up a color if you click.

   The Current Color area at the bottom of the palette gives you an enlarged sample of the color your cursor is over. The Primary Color Values give you the exact numerical color you are using.

2. **Left-click to choose your main painting color, called the *foreground* (or *stroke*) color.**

   That color appears in the Foreground Color sample, shown in Figure 4-1.

   This color is what I sometimes call your left-mouse-button color — it's the one that appears when you use the Paint Brush, Airbrush, or Fill tool by pressing the left mouse button. It really doesn't have much to do with foreground. It's just one of two colors.

3. **Right-click anywhere on the available colors area to choose a secondary color, the *background* (or *fill*) color.**

   See the sidebar, "Do you need a background color?" to figure out if you need or want a secondary color; if the answer is "no," you can skip this step. If you do choose a background color, it appears in the Background Color sample, shown in Figure 4-1. The term Background color, like Foreground color, is kind of a misnomer because it really doesn't have much to do with the background of your image. It just defines a second, or alternative, color you can work with.

Do you need a background color?

How do you know if you need or want a secondary color? It depends on the tool you're using and how you intend to use it:

✔ If you're using the Eraser tool, background color is the color the eraser leaves behind when you erase on the main, or background, layer, unless that layer is transparent. (On other layers, the Eraser tool leaves transparency.)

✔ If you're using a tool that involves two colors, say, the Color Replacer tool to replace one color with another, you need a second color — background color is that second color. Background color also provides the fill of filled shapes and text.

✔ If you want to be able to switch quickly between painting with one color and another, you can paint foreground color with the left mouse button on many tools and background color with the right mouse button.

Choosing paint for each tool separately or all tools together

Paint Shop Pro version 7, unlike earlier versions, mimics real life. In real life, if you paint with your brush dipped in red paint, then switch to spray-painting with a can of green paint, your brush remains red. Likewise, in Paint Shop Pro 7, you normally choose paint (including color, style, and texture) individually for each tool. If you change tools, your foreground and background paint changes with it.

If you prefer, however, you can choose colors, style, and texture and have those choices apply to *all* the tools. In that case, if you change tools, you continue to use the same colors in the new tool. (That mode of operation is also how all earlier versions of Paint Shop Pro worked.)

The secret between the two ways of working is the Lock check box in the Color palette. Checking Lock means that your current paint choice applies to all tools. Deselecting the Lock check box means that you choose paint individually for each tool.

Now you have *chosen* a color. To actually *paint* with your chosen color, make sure that you have chosen the style you want in the Foreground Style swatch (and Background Style swatch, if you're using a background color). Mouse down on the style swatch and click the paint brush icon for solid color style. See the section, "Working with Style — Beyond Plain Paint," later in this chapter for more help with styles.

Here are a couple of tips for choosing and using colors:

- **To swap the Background and Foreground colors, click the color Switcher, shown in Figure 4-1.** The background color becomes the foreground color and vice-versa.

- **To get pure black, white, or other colors, use the Recent Colors dialog box (I describe this in the following section).** You can also find pure black anywhere along the extreme left side of the Available colors area; pure white is anywhere along the extreme right. For pure black, the color values labeled R, G, and B (see Figure 4-1) should all be zero. For pure white, they should all be 255. (If you see H, S, and L instead of R, G, and B, then H and S should be zero for black or white. For black, L is also zero. For white, L is 255.)

Choosing a basic or recently used color

You may want to use that same fantastic shade of fluorescent orange you used before, but locating that same, exact, color in the Available Colors area is often next to impossible. Your eyes and fingers can't be that precise.

Fortunately, Paint Shop Pro gives you another way to choose a recently used color: the Recent Colors dialog box.

The Recent Colors dialog box also gives you basic black, totally-white white, and a variety of other basic colors that you can return to again and again.

Here's how to get this helpful box of recently used and basic colors:

1. **_Right_-click a color sample area — the foreground or background sample, whichever one you want to set.**

   The color samples are the small areas at the top of the Color palette. If you have chosen the style, solid color, you may instead right-click the style swatch. The Style swatches are the larger areas marked Styles.

   The Recent Colors dialog box appears, as Figure 4-2 shows. Ten standard colors appear in the top two rows of the dialog box (including black, white, and two shades of gray), and up to ten colors you have most recently used appear in two lower rows. If the colors have circles with slashes, you're using a palette image, and those colors aren't available. See Chapter 10 for a discussion of increasing the number of colors.

Figure 4-2:
Right-click the Foreground or Background Style swatch, and the Recent Colors dialog box gives you both basic and recently used colors.

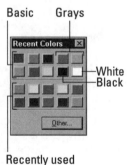

Basic   Grays

White
Black

Recently used

Colors in the top two basic-color rows are _pure_ colors — except for the grays — that is, they are the reddest red, bluest blue, magent-est magenta, and so forth.

Technically speaking, the top row contains the pure red, green, and blue primaries of radiant light. The second row contains the pure cyan, magenta, and yellow primaries of printed ink.

2. **Click any color to choose it (or press the Esc key if you see nothing you like).**

   The Recent Colors dialog box disappears immediately. The color you clicked on is now chosen and appears in the color sample in the Color palette.

   You might think that right-clicking in the Recent Colors dialog box would choose the background color, as it does in the Color palette. You would be wrong. Right-clicking does nothing here.

To get shades of color other than the ones you see in the Recent Colors dialog box, click the Other button. This button takes you to the Color dialog box. See the upcoming section, "Choosing a Color More Precisely," for details.

Choosing a color from your picture

Sometimes, the easiest way to choose a color is to pick up that color from your picture. You have two ways to pick up color. Choose the one that makes your life easier:

- ✔ When using any tool that applies paint (for instance, the Paint Brush tool), hold down the Ctrl button and your cursor turns into a dropper icon. Left-click to pick up foreground color, right-click for background color.

- ✔ In the Tool palette, click the Dropper tool icon shown in the margin. Your cursor turns into a dropper icon (or into crosshairs if you have chosen Use Precise Cursors in the Tool Options palette). Left-click to pick up foreground color, right-click for background color. As of this writing, you must have the Lock check box in the color palette selected if the colors that the Dropper tool picks up are to apply to other tools.

If your Style swatch is set to something fancier than plain paint, you can pick up a new foreground or background color, but you can't apply it until you switch to plain paint or a gradient that uses foreground or background color. Mouse down on the Style swatch and click the paintbrush icon in the little fly-out box that appears.

Choosing a Color More Precisely

Choosing a color from the Color palette's Available Colors area is all well and good, but if you're working with higher-quality color images, it's not a very precise way to go. The area is tiny and up to 16.7 million colors may be squished together in that area. (If your image has 256 or fewer colors, you can discern individual color boxes in the Available Colors area.)

To choose a color more precisely, *left*-click the color sample (foreground or background, whichever one you want to set) in the Color palette. (If the Style swatch is in solid color mode, you may alternatively left-click the Style swatch instead of the color sample.)

The amazingly colorful Color dialog box of Figure 4-3 appears. (Oh, the amazingly colorful Color dialog box of Figure 4-3 did *not* appear? The somewhat less colorful Select Color From Palette dialog box appears, instead? In that event, you're working with an image that has fewer than 32,000 colors. See the upcoming section, "Working With 256 Colors or Fewer.")

Drag this around the wheel

Figure 4-3:
It's time
to play
Wheel . . .
of . . . Colors!
Starring the
Color Wheel
and the
Saturation/
Lightness
box. Vanna
White, eat
your heart
out.

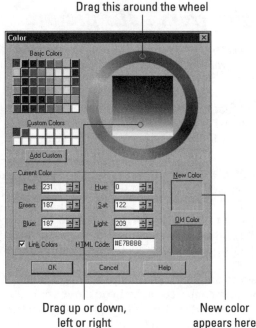

Drag up or down,
left or right

New color
appears here

Precise color using the color wheel

The callouts for Figure 4-3 give you the simplest way to be more precise. You only need to follow three steps:

1. Drag the little circle on the color wheel to the basic hue you want.

Hue has a technical meaning, but forget about that for now. Hue means basic color, apart from that color's exact shade.

The square in the middle of the circle turns to your chosen hue, showing you all kinds of variations in shade — or, more precisely, in color intensity (called *saturation*) and lightness. The square is called the Saturation/ Lightness box.

2. Drag the little circle on the square to the precise shade you want.

The New Color swatch at the bottom right of the dialog box shows exactly what color you're choosing. (The Old Color swatch shows what the foreground or background color is, currently.)

Drag this circle up to make your color darker or down to make it lighter. Drag the circle left to make your color grayer, or right to make it more intense (saturated).

3. Click OK.

Your foreground or background color has been changed.

Additional shades of basic colors

The Color dialog box (shown in Figure 4-3) is also home to 48 basic colors. These colors are shades of six primary colors — red, yellow, green, cyan, blue, and magenta — plus six shades of gray (including white and black).

Open the Color dialog box as usual by clicking either the Foreground Color or Background Style swatch in the Color palette. (Or, if you happen to be using the Recent Colors dialog box, click the Other button.)

Choose a basic color by clicking it in the Basic Colors area, in the upper-left corner of the Color dialog box. Click OK, and your foreground or background color is changed to your chosen color.

Creating shadows and highlights

For brushing highlights or shadows onto an object, you often want a color that's the same hue as an existing one, just a little lighter or darker. Pick up the existing color from your picture, making it the foreground color by clicking on it with the dropper tool.

Click the Foreground Style swatch to bring up the Color dialog box. In the Saturation/Lightness box, drag the tiny circle up to make a shadow color, or down to make a highlight color.

Very precise color adjustments —
by the numbers

Just as saying "1 foot, 3 inches" is a lot more precise than saying "a little bigger than my shoe," choosing a color by using numbers is a lot more precise than clicking it in a palette or color wheel. But . . . how can you do color by the numbers?

As it turns out, you can specify any color by using just three values. Adjusting these values independently gives you more control. For instance, you can change just the *lightness* of a color and be certain you haven't changed the *hue* at all.

Chapter 10 gives you more detail about how these values relate to colors. For now, knowing that you can set these three values in the Color dialog box can help you make more precise adjustments, if you need them.

Just as with specifying distance, where you can use either the English (feet, inches) or metric (meters) systems, you can use either of two alternative systems to specify colors: Hue/Saturation/Lightness (HSL to its friends) or Red/Green/Blue (known as RGB).

The Current Color area of the Color dialog box, shown in Figure 4-4, shows the three values that describe your currently chosen color, in both systems (RGB and HSL). The area displays values for Red, Green, and Blue (on the left), as well as Hue, Saturation, and Lightness (on the right). When you choose a new color using any control in this dialog box, those numbers change. In value, the numbers range from zero to 255.

Figure 4-4:
Being numerically precise. An optional visual control appears when you click and hold the down-arrow at the far right of a value box.

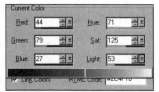

To adjust a color precisely, you can edit the numbers in either the RGB or HSL value boxes (your choice). For instance, do you want more red? Use the RGB controls and increase the value in the Red box. More yellow? Well, to use the RGB controls you'd have to know that red and green make yellow in the RGB system (perhaps having read Chapter 10) and then increase the values in Red and Green (perhaps decreasing the value in Blue).

Using the HSL values is sometimes a more intuitive alternative to using the RGB values. HSL values are connected to the controls in the Color wheel and Saturation/Lightness box. Here's how they work:

- **Hue:** The Hue value connects to your chosen position in the Color wheel, beginning at zero at the top (red) and increasing as you go around the circle counter-clockwise. As you increase the number, the hue passes through red, yellow, green, cyan, blue, violet, and magenta.

- **Saturation:** The Saturation value connects to horizontal motion in the Saturation/Lightness box: left (for a lower value) or right (for a higher value). Use a higher value for a more intense (saturated) color.

- **Lightness:** The Lightness value connects to vertical motion in the Saturation/Lightness box: up (for a lower value) or down (for a higher value). Use a higher value for a lighter color.

As with any value box in a Windows program, you can change the values either by typing in new numbers or by clicking the tiny up/down arrows to gradually increase or decrease the value.

 A more visual way to fiddle with the RGB or HSL values is to mouse down on the down-arrow at the far right of any of the RGB or HSL value boxes. As Figure 4-4 shows, a multicolored bar appears, showing the range of colors you can achieve by dragging left or right. Keeping the mouse button down, drag left or right to choose a color. Release the button when you're done.

Storing Custom Colors to Use Again

The Color dialog box also provides a place to store up to 16 colors that you want to use repeatedly. Choose a foreground color or background color that you want to keep. (For instance, click on the Available Colors area of the Color palette; the method you use to choose the color doesn't matter.) Then take these steps:

1. **Open the Color dialog box.**

    To store the current foreground color, open the Color dialog box by clicking the foreground color sample in the Color palette. (To store the current background color, click the background color sample.)

2. **Position your cursor over the New Color swatch and press the right mouse button.**

   Or, if you prefer, take this same action over the circle that appears in either the saturation/lightness box, or in the color wheel.

3. **Keeping the right mouse button pressed, drag to any of the 16 squares in the Custom Colors area, and release.**

   Your color is stored in your selected square. Click OK if you're done using the Color dialog box.

To create a batch of colors and store them in consecutive squares, begin by clicking the Custom Colors square in which you want to store the first color. Make a color choice in the Color dialog box and then click the Add Custom button. Each time you do so, Paint Shop Pro stores the color in the currently chosen square, and then selects the next square in preparation for your next choice.

To use one of your stored colors, open the Colors dialog box again (click either the Foreground or Background Style swatch) and then click on the color in its square. Click OK.

These colors remain stored with Paint Shop Pro. So, when you reopen Paint Shop Pro, they're still there. Unfortunately, however, Paint Shop Pro currently gives you no way to create different sets of those 16 custom colors and store them.

Working with 256 Colors or Fewer

Images that have 256 colors or fewer are called *palette* images. That means that they use only a specific set of colors — the image's palette of available colors. You can change any of those colors individually, but you can't have any more colors than the palette size (color depth) allows. (See Chapter 10 for ways to change color depth.)

When you work with a palette image, the Available Colors area of the Color palette shows you the palette. You can choose any of those colors by clicking on the color. The squares are tiny, however, and colors aren't always in a useful order.

To choose colors from larger squares or see them in more useful orders, click one of the color samples at the top of the Color palette (the foreground or background color sample, whichever color you wish to change). The Select

Color From Palette dialog box swings into action, displaying a somewhat larger view of the palette. To reorder the colors, click the Sort Order drop-down list box, choosing either Palette Order (an arbitrary, numbered order), By Luminance (ordered from light to dark), or By Hue (ordered by color). To choose a color, click on it; then click OK.

To change any color in the image's palette, choose Colors⇨Edit Palette. The Edit Palette dialog box that appears is identical to the Select Color From Palette dialog box, with one exception: if you double-click any color in the palette, you go to the Colors dialog box. See the section, "Choosing a Color More Precisely," earlier in this chapter, for instructions on choosing a color in this dialog box.

Working with Style — Beyond Plain Paint

In Paint Shop Pro 7, painting in a single, flat color is just the simplest of three modes of painting called *styles*. (Whether or not you can use the other two kinds of style depends upon what tool you're using.) Those styles, controlled by the Style swatches on the Color palette, are:

- ✔ **Solid color:** Delivers plain, old color.
- ✔ **Gradient:** Delivers a totally cool multihued shading.
- ✔ **Pattern:** Delivers a seamless photographic-quality surface like wood grain or gravel, or repeated images of your own design.

After you choose a style and it's displayed on the Style swatch, you can choose from a cool variety of shades and patterns by simply clicking on the swatch. The details are in the following sections.

Choosing a style

To choose a style, mouse down on the Style swatch (for either foreground or background). Figure 4-5 shows the result.

As you hold the mouse button down, a tiny panel flies out displaying icons for the three styles (paint, gradient, and pattern, in order), and one icon for "off." Any icons that are grayed-out are not available in your currently chosen tool. Release the mouse button. To choose an icon, click it and the following takes place:

✓ **Solid style (paint brush icon):** The Style swatch displays just a solid color, your currently chosen foreground or background color.

✓ **Gradient style (shaded icon):** The Style swatch displays the currently chosen gradient. To choose a gradient, click the Style swatch to access a gallery of gradients; see the following section, "Choosing gradients," for details.

✓ **Pattern style (waffle icon):** The Style swatch displays the currently chosen pattern. To choose a pattern, click the Style swatch to access a gallery of patterns; see "Choosing and making patterns," later in this chapter, for details.

Figure 4-5: Mousing down on a Style swatch gives you three choices: plain paint, gradient paint, or a pattern.

Choosing gradients

After your chosen Style swatch (foreground or background) shows a gradient style (see the preceding section), you may click the swatch to choose a different gradient. The Gradient dialog box appears, as shown in Figure 4-6.

Here's what to do:

1. **Choose a gradient style by clicking one of the buttons in the Style area that appears on the right side of the Gradient dialog box (see Figure 4-6).**

    Each button depicts a different kind of gradient: from side to side, from center to edges in a rectangular or circular fashion, or proceding radially around in a circle. The preview box on the left then displays a gradient in your currently chosen style.

2. **Click the down-arrow button to the right of the preview box and choose from the ultra-fabulous gallery of gradients that appears.**

   Figure 4-6 displays the gallery. The colors of all choices are pre-chosen, except for those that use the terms foreground and background. Those choices make use of whatever foreground or background colors are current at the time you paint with this gradient.

3. **Customize the angle or center of the gradient by dragging the control in the preview window.**

   Gradients in the linear style (linear is the top button in the Style column) have an angle setting. In the preview window, drag the gadget that looks like the hand on a clock to set the angle.

   Gradients in other styles have a center point. In the preview window, drag the crosshairs to set the center point.

4. **Make the gradient pattern repeat several times if you want.**

   Increase the number in the Repeats value box.

5. **Click OK.**

   Your chosen gradient appears in the Style swatch you selected.

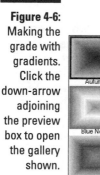

Figure 4-6: Making the grade with gradients. Click the down-arrow adjoining the preview box to open the gallery shown.

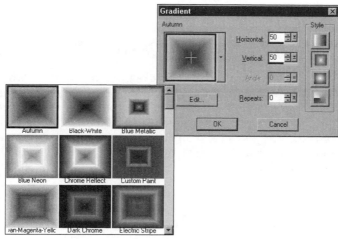

Creating gradients in your choice of colors is easy although not many patterns are available for that purpose. Choose a foreground and/or background color as the one or two colors for your gradient. In the gradient gallery, choose any gradient you like that uses the term foreground and/or background.

Creating your own gradient patterns is possible, as is altering the existing ones, but . . . wow! Definitely not a *For Dummies* kind of project. If you want to fool around with the controls, click the Edit button in the Gradient dialog box to access the Gradient Editor dialog box. Whoa! Have fun; try dragging the little pointers around, and good luck.

Painting with gradients

Gradients fill a painted area with a series of colors. When you paint with a gradient using the Text, Draw, or Preset Shapes tools, or fill with a selection using the Flood Fill tool, Paint Shop Pro scales the gradient to fit within the object you have created or area you have selected. For instance, to apply a sunset-like gradient from blue to orange to the sky in your photo, select the sky and use the Flood Fill tool. Paint Shop Pro ensures that the full range of colors (blue to orange) fills the sky area. Or, if you create text and use a gradient style, the text displays the full range of colors.

If you paint with the Paint Brush or Air Brush tool, however, the gradient is scaled to the *entire image*. If you paint with a sunset-like blue-to-orange gradient, anything painted near the top of the image is blue, and anything near the bottom is orange.

Choosing and making patterns

Patterns are interesting surface images, like brick or wood, or other more exotic or creative patterns not found in nature. Their colors are fixed, like those of a photograph, and are unaffected by your choice of foreground or background color. The patterns that come with Paint Shop Pro are seamless, which means that they can maintain an unbroken pattern, filling any area without appearing like tiles (with distinct edges). The process of choosing a pattern is very much like choosing a gradient.

With your chosen Style swatch (foreground or background) in pattern mode, click the swatch. The Pattern dialog box appears (somewhat resembling the Gradient dialog box of Figure 4-6, but not as complicated).

1. **Click the down-arrow button to the right of the preview box and choose from the boffo gallery of patterns that appears.**

   The preview window shows your choice.

2. **Customize the angle of the pattern by dragging the clock hand Angle control to point in any direction.**

3. Click OK.

Your chosen pattern appears in the Style swatch you selected.

To apply a pattern to an existing image, try the Sculpture effect described in Chapter 9, setting its Depth control to 1.

Creating your own patterns, or variants of existing ones, is easy. Create or open an image that you want to use as a pattern. Leave that image open in Paint Shop Pro. Then, when you open the pattern gallery in Step 1, you'll discover that at the very top of the gallery are patterns based on any image that is currently open in Paint Shop Pro — including the one you just created! You can use this feature to create differently colored or scaled versions of existing patterns. Create a new, blank image, fill it with an existing pattern, and then colorize or resize it. The image is now available as a new pattern in the pattern gallery.

To create your own *seamless* pattern, apply Paint Shop Pro's Pattern effect to the image you're using for a pattern (as in the preceding paragraph). Choose Effects⇨Reflection Effects⇨Pattern. Fiddle with the controls in the Pattern adjustment box until you get a seamless pattern, and click OK.

Applying a Texture

Textures give a result like rubbing chalk on concrete, or like rubbing a pencil on paper that is placed over a coin or another raised surface. Paint Shop Pro supplies a variety of textures, such as concrete, construction paper, and bricks. When you use one, anything you do with the Paint Brush, Erase, Airbrush, Fill, Text, Draw, or Preset Shapes tools displays that texture. Textures don't change your choice of color. Textures do work with solid color, gradients, or patterns — that is, with any choice you make in the Style swatches.

You can apply texture to either the foreground color, the background color, or both; each has its own control. Texture is normally turned off (disabled). To use a texture, do the following:

1. On the Color palette, mouse down on the Foreground Texture or Background Texture swatch.

Figure 4-7 shows the location of the texture swatches. When you click and hold down the mouse button (mouse down), a tiny enable/disable panel appears.

Foreground (or stroke) texture

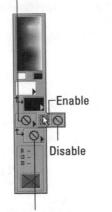

Enable

Disable

Figure 4-7:
Enable
texture by
mousing
down on a
texture
swatch and
dragging to
the textured
Enable
button
(where the
cursor
appears in
this figure).

Background (or fill) texture

2. Click the Enable button, which displays a rough texture, and release.

(In Figure 4-7, a mouse cursor appears over the Enable button.) When you release the mouse button, the texture swatch displays a rough texture.

3. Double-click your chosen (foreground or background) texture swatch.

A Texture dialog box appears, shown as part of Figure 4-8. It shows a texture sample.

4. Click the down-arrow button to the right of the texture sample.

A gallery of textures appears, as Figure 4-8 shows. Scroll down the gallery to find a texture you like.

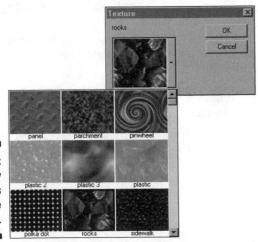

Figure 4-8:
A gallery
of textures
to choose
from.

5. **Click the texture you want in the gallery.**

   The gallery disappears and the sample area of the Texture dialog box shows your chosen texture.

6. **Click OK in the Texture dialog box.**

   The texture swatch displays your chosen texture. It's displayed in gray because the color you apply depends on your chosen foreground or background color.

Now, anything you create or erase appears textured. Here are a few more things you may want to do with texture:

✔ **To change texture:** Click the texture swatch to return to the Texture dialog box in Figure 4-8. Choose a new texture as Steps 4 through 6 describe.

✔ **To stop using texture:** Mouse down on the texture swatch (which now displays a sample of the texture). Click the Disable button shown in Figure 4-7. (The Disable button has a circle with a slash through it.)

✔ **To resume using your most-recently chosen texture:** Just mouse down on the texture swatch, and click the Enable button. You don't have to re-choose the texture from the Texture dialog box.

To apply a texture to an existing image, use the Texture effect that I describe in Chapter 9.

Texture thins your paint

When you use texture, paint goes on thin (with low opacity) with each click or stroke. Make repeated strokes or scribble with your paint tool to build up the thickness.

Likewise for the eraser: Only a thin layer of paint comes off with each pass. Disable Texture and, in the Tool Options window, set Opacity to 100 to erase fully in a single stroke.

When you use texture with the Fill tool, make repeated clicks if you need to increase the opacity.

Chapter 5

Fundamental Painting, Spraying, and Filling

- -

In This Chapter

▶ Choosing the tool

▶ Brushing

▶ Spraying

▶ Erasing

▶ Painting

▶ Using different brush sizes and shapes

▶ Controlling how paint goes on

▶ Replacing colors

▶ Filling

- -

*W*hether you paint like Rembrandt or like Phil (the guy who paints our house), Paint Shop Pro can help you do your thing. You can use a brush, a sprayer, an eraser, or simply pour the paint on. Use different sizes and shapes of brush. Use paint, chalk, markers, or even different kinds of paper. Paint Shop Pro can do nearly anything you can do with real artist's media. (Well, okay, body painting loses something in the translation.)

I'm talking about fundamentals of painting, spraying, and filling in this chapter, including basic tool options, such as brush size, that apply to many other tools. Paint Shop Pro has other features that I cover in other chapters of this book. For instance, Paint Shop Pro draws as well as paints. Its drawing features mimic tasks that you can do with a pen or pencil, using a straightedge or template of basic shapes. I discuss those tools in Chapter 16.

Paint Shop Pro also has fancy painting tools for a job that only a computer (or perhaps a character in a cartoon) can do, such as painting with pictures that flow right off your brush, or painting a copy of one part of the image onto another part. These special tools I discuss in Chapter 6.

As with most jobs you do in Paint Shop Pro, painting affects only the currently active layer and only the selected area. If it appears that a painting or retouching tool isn't working, make sure you're on the right layer and working within a selected area (or clear the selection by pressing Ctrl+D). If you don't use more than one layer or don't have any current selection, don't worry about those restrictions. Also, remember that by pressing Ctrl+Z, you can undo any painting or erasing.

Choosing the Tool for the Job

Figure 5-1 shows you Paint Shop Pro's fundamental painting tools in the Tool palette. (The palette is normally on the left side of your Paint Shop Pro window. You can drag it elsewhere; see Chapter 1.)

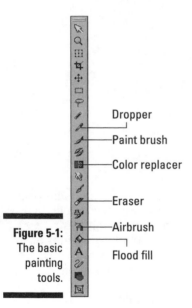

Dropper

Paint brush

Color replacer

Eraser

Airbrush

Flood fill

Figure 5-1:
The basic painting tools.

Choose your tool (say, the Paint Brush tool), by clicking its icon in the Tool palette. Your cursor then *becomes* that tool (it displays that tool's icon) whenever the cursor is over your image.

Throughout the rest of this chapter I give you the details, but here are the jobs you can do with each tool and the simplest description of how each works:

Don't forget textures, gradients, and patterns

In Paint Shop Pro, you can apply textures with any tool that applies paint by choosing one in the Texture swatches of the Color palette. Textures apply your chosen color as if you were rubbing on a surface of some kind, such as asphalt pavement. To apply plain, untextured color, you must disable textures. See Chapter 4 for help.

You can also apply gradients and patterns with any tool that applies paint. These special shadings and images are determined by the Style swatches in the Color palette. Again, see Chapter 4 for instructions.

- **Paint:** Click the Paint Brush tool, click a color in the Color palette, and then click or drag on your image to paint.
- **Erase:** Click the Eraser tool, and drag across the image to erase.
- **Spray-paint:** Click the Airbrush tool, click a color in the Color palette, and then click or drag on the image to mimic the effect of a spray can or airbrush.
- **Fill an area with a solid color or a fade:** Click the Flood Fill tool, click a color in the Color palette, and then click within a selection area or on an area of a particular color to fill that area.
- **Replace a color:** Click the Color Replacer tool, choose the color to replace and the replacement color, and then drag or double-click on the image.

Using Basic Artist's Tools: Paint Brush, Airbrush, and Eraser

Using the Paint Brush, Airbrush, and Eraser tools are much like using real paint, paper, and eraser. Okay, okay, you would never use an eraser on *paint* in real life, but you get the idea.

In Paint Shop Pro, however, you don't simply paint a color, you paint a style. A style *can* be simply a color, but it can also be a multihued thing or a patterned image. Chapter 4 tells you how to choose exactly what you want from the Color palette.

Painting a straight line

Can't draw a straight line? Paint Shop Pro comes to your rescue. The starting point of the line is the last place you clicked, or where your last brush stroke ended.

To create a straight line from that point, hold down the Shift key and click where you want the line to end. This trick works with all the brush tools (Paint Brush, Airbrush, and Clone Brush) and with the Eraser tool.

Like most of Paint Shop Pro's tools and commands, the Paint Brush, Airbrush, and Eraser tools do their thing on the currently active layer of your image. If they don't seem to be working correctly, or are grayed-out, you may be on the wrong layer. See Chapter 15 for more about layers. If you're too busy to do that, try pressing Ctrl+1, which makes the background, or main layer, active. That's most likely the one you want.

Painting with the Paint Brush or Airbrush tool

The Paint Brush tool, like a real paintbrush, paints a spot of paint when you click it on your image or a line when you drag it. The Airbrush works similarly, but, like a can of spray paint, it puts down a speckly spot or line that gets denser as you hold the button down.

The Airbrush tool paints speckly and the Paint Brush tool paints solid for a reason: Jasc initially gives the two tools different density settings in the Tool Options window. You could easily change their density settings and make the Paint Brush tool paint speckly or the Airbrush tool paint solid. The real difference between the tools is that you can manually increase the density of the paint using the Airbrush tool. If you pause the Airbrush tool or move it slowly while keeping the mouse button pressed, paint continues to fill in the speckles. As a result, you increase the paint density just as you can with real spray paint. Not so with the Paint Brush tool — you'd have to click repeatedly to get that effect.

Otherwise, the two tools work similarly. Here's how to paint with the Paint Brush or Airbrush (spray can) tools:

1. **Click the Paint Brush or Airbrush tool shown in the margin.**

2. **Inspect the Color palette's Foreground Style swatch and Foreground Texture swatch to make sure each displays the color and texture (if any) that you want to paint with.**

   See Chapter 4 for more about choosing colors, styles, and textures.

3. **Drag on your image (or click to make just a single spot).**

   As you drag or click with the left mouse button, you apply whatever is displayed in the Foreground Style swatch, modified by the Foreground Texture swatch. (To apply Background style and pattern, click or drag with the *right* mouse button.)

   If you're using the Airbrush tool, you may keep the cursor in one place and hold down the mouse button. The paint density gradually builds up.

If the spot or stroke doesn't look right, press Ctrl+Z (or click the Undo button on the Toolbar) to undo it. Then, you need to use the Tool Options window to change the brush features. See the upcoming section, "Controlling Strokes, Sizes, Shapes, and Spatters: Tool Options" for details on changing appearances.

In the Tool Options window on the second tab, select the Show Brush Outlines check box. Now you're less likely to accidentally paint with the wrong size, shape, or density. Your mouse cursor's outline shows the exact shape and size of your brush, and also the speckly pattern that results if density is less than 100.

Erasing with the Eraser tool

Erasing works a bit differently on different layers of your image.

✔ If you erase on the background layer, you actually *apply* background color! (If your image began its life with a transparent background, which is not usual, the erased area becomes transparent, instead.) The Background Style and Texture settings of the Color palette affect how that Background color is applied.

✔ If you erase on any other layer but the background layer, the erased area becomes transparent. If the background texture swatch shows a texture, you get textured transparency! Style settings don't matter.

Here's how to erase:

1. **Click the Eraser tool, shown here.**

2. **Check the Color palette's Background Style and Texture swatches to make sure that style, color, and texture (if any) are what you want to leave behind as you erase.**

   If the current selections in those swatches aren't what you want to leave behind, see Chapter 4. For unpatterned, untextured erasing, set Background style to solid color (paintbrush icon) and set Background texture to "off."

3. **Drag on your image to erase, or click to erase a single spot.**

   Drag with the *right* mouse button depressed if you want to leave behind *Foreground* style and texture.

If the size, shape, and density (speckliness) of your eraser aren't what you want, press Ctrl+Z (or click the Undo button on the Toolbar) to undo, then see the next section, "Controlling Strokes, Sizes, Shapes, and Spatters: Tool Options."

To unerase, drag across the erased area with the right mouse button pressed *(right-dragging)*. On layers other than the background layer, that action restores the original colors of those pixels. (On the background layer, that action simply paints with the background color, style, and texture.) Strangely, right-dragging across areas that were originally transparent (transparent for reasons other than being erased) may leave black or other marks behind! Paint Shop Pro is simply confused because you're trying to unerase something you didn't erase. Left-drag across those marks to erase the marks.

Controlling Strokes, Sizes, Shapes, and Spatters: Tool Options

The Painting and Eraser tools can do lots more than just create a plain, boring spot or line. The Tool Options window in Figure 5-2 is your key to variety, artistic success, and fame and fortune. The palette works the same, or nearly the same, for all painting and erasing tools.

One key role of your Tool Options window is to show you what your brush currently looks like. As Figure 5-2 shows, a preview area in the upper left corner shows you the size, fuzziness (hardness), and speckliness (density) of the spot you make if you clicked on your image. Consider leaving the Tool Options window open and unrolled on your screen so that you can check your brush before you paint.

Preview picture of brush shape and size

Figure 5-2:
The Tool Options window, key to making your paint tool work the way you want it to.

In Chapter 1, I tell you how to open, unroll, and hide palettes and windows. The Tool Options window (or its title bar, labeled Tool Options) is probably already floating around somewhere on your PC screen. If you can't find the Tool Options window, do this:

1. **Press the letter *O* key on your keyboard a few times, or click the Toggle Tool Options button on the Toolbar.**

   The palette appears and disappears. Leave it visible.

2. **If only the Tool Options title bar appears, pause your mouse button over that title bar to unroll the palette.**

   If you want to lock the palette window open, click the down-arrow button in its upper-right corner. After the window is open, proceed to Step 3.

3. **The Tool Options window has multiple tabs. To get the tab shown in Figure 5-2, click Tab 1, the leftmost tab. That tab is where you find most of the adjustments.**

The following sections show you how to achieve different effects, using adjustments you find in the Tool Options Window.

✔ You don't need to put away the Tool Options window before working on your image. Leave it up so that you can make adjustments as you go. Drag it out of the way, if necessary, by its title bar (where it says Tool Options).

✔ Not all tools offer all the adjustments that I discuss in the next few sections.

Using convenient controls in the Tool Options window

You can make adjustments in the Tool Options window by using the dialog-box gadgets you're familiar with from other programs. You can click the Size and other boxes and edit or type a new value, or click either of the *spin dial* buttons (the pair of up/down arrows) to increase or decrease a value.

Besides the usual ways of adjusting values, Paint Shop Pro has a unique and nifty adjustment feature, shown in Figure 5-3. Click on the tiny down-arrow at the far right edge of the box for any numerical value, such as the Size box (see Figure 5-3). Hold your mouse button down (called *mousing down*). A tiny ruler-like bar appears, with a pointer. Keeping your mouse button down, drag the pointer left or right to adjust the value down or up, respectively.

Most adjustments are on Tab 1 of the Tool Options window that Figure 5-3 shows. (Tabs, in Paint Shop Pro vernacular, are numbered from left to right; see Chapter 1.) Figure 5-3 shows the Paint Brush tool window, but all or most of these same controls exist for the other painting tools.

Mouse down here

Figure 5-3:
Mousing down on the far-right down-arrow for a given widget opens the adjustment slider.

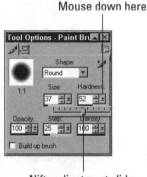

Nifty adjustment slider

Making lines wider or narrower: Size

You most frequently adjust *size*. One size of tool definitely does not fit all. Even Phil, our house painter, uses different sized brushes. (What an *artiste!*) In the Tool Options window, adjust the Size value in the Tool Options window to any value between 1 to 255 (meaning from 1 to 255 pixels).

You can see just how big your tool is at any time by moving your cursor over the image. (That is, unless you've disabled the Show Brush Outlines option, found on Tab 2 and which I describe when discussing the Tool Options window in Chapter 1.) Big brushes may need smaller step values (the number in the box labeled Step) to avoid painting dotted lines.

Shaping clicks, lines, and line ends: Shape

Shape changes the way the painted (or erased) line looks when it ends or bends. It also lets you stamp a shape by clicking on the image, as if you had a rubber stamp or were spraying paint through a template.

In the Tool Options window, click the Shape list box and choose from the list. Your choice appears in a preview area of the window, noted back in Figure 5-2. Using the square, round, left-slash, right-slash, horizontal, and vertical brushes, you can make your lines look as though you've drawn them with a calligraphic pen, as shown in Figure 5-4.

Figure 5-4:
Painting,
from left to
right, with
the square,
round,
left-slash,
right-slash,
horizontal,
and vertical
brush
shapes.

As you make strokes, you see repeated stampings of this shape. The Step control (which I discuss in the section, "Making lines more or less dotty: Step," later in this chapter) helps you change the separation between stampings.

For some really exotic shapes, like snowflakes and clouds that you can use for stamps, see "Brushing snowflakes and other custom shapes," later in this chapter.

Painting with a softer or harder edge: Hardness

Hardness determines how sharp the edges of your tool are. Maximum hardness (100) gives your tool a sharp edge; lower hardness applies a gradual fade to the edge. Zero hardness gradually fades the edge all the way to the center of the brush shape. At low hardness, you may need to decrease step to avoid creating a dotted line. Figure 5-5 shows the effect of changing hardness.

Reduce hardness to minimize jaggies (a staircase effect also called *aliasing*) where your line bends.

Figure 5-5:
A single spot
showing
hardness of
100, 80, 60,
40, and 20
(from left
to right).

Making paint thinner or thicker: Opacity

Opacity is how thick (opaque or solid) your paint is. A value of 100 means that your paint is completely opaque. Reduce opacity to make a more transparent paint. A value of 50, for instance, means an individual spot of paint (caused by clicking once with your mouse) is 50 percent transparent. Overlapping spots cause each stroke, or click of the mouse, to add paint and make the area more opaque. Figure 5-6 shows single spots with decreasing opacity.

Figure 5-6:
Spots with opacity of 100, 80, 60, 40, and 20 (from left to right).

A brush stroke (*dragging* with your mouse) is more opaque than a single spot (*clicking* with your mouse) because strokes are simply repeated, overlapping spots. If you increase the values of the step variable (which controls spacing of those spots), you make the stroke more transparent.

For the Eraser tool, opacity refers to how completely you erase. If you use maximum opacity (100), you erase the line entirely. Use repeated strokes or clicks with values under 100 to shave the paint thickness and reduce opacity.

Getting speckles of spray: Density

The word *density* doesn't accurately describe this adjustment. The words speckly-ness or speckle-osity are more accurate, but still confusing. Density works like this: When density is at its maximum (100), you get nice, solid paint coverage (or *eraserage*, if you're using the eraser). At lower settings of density, you get random speckles, as if you were spattering or spraying. Figure 5-7 shows the effect of different density settings.

For the Airbrush tool to do its job (which is spraying paint), you must set the density at less than 100. Yet, you can set density less than 100 for the Paint Brush or Eraser tools, too, and they also give a speckly result, very similar to the results you'd get with the Airbrush tool.

Figure 5-7:
A single spot, at densities of 100, 80, 60, 40, and 20 (from left to right).

Making lines more or less dotty: Step

It's time you knew the truth: Paint Shop Pro's paint tools don't actually apply paint continuously as you drag. (Gasp!) No, they actually apply repeated stampings of the brush's shape. (Imagine a jackhammer tipped with a rubber stamp.) The *Step control* determines the distance between those stampings.

If you set the Step value at its maximum (100, meaning 100 percent), the shapes don't overlap at all; the step is 100 percent of the tool size, and so you get a dotted line. At 50, the shapes overlap halfway, and at 25 they overlap three-quarters (25 is often a good choice). Figure 5-8 shows increasing step values:

Figure 5-8:
Step values of 20, 40, 60, and 100 (from top to bottom). The larger the step values, the more dotted the line.

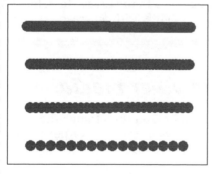

Scribbling to make paint thicker: Build Up Brush

In the real world, color often gets thicker as you scribble, as it does if you rub chalk on a sidewalk. In Paint Shop Pro, you have several ways that you can get that effect:

✔ **Enable the Build Up Brush option:**

  1. **Set opacity or density to less than 100 — preferably much less.**

     Otherwise (if both are at or near 100), you get the thickest paint possible within a stroke or two, and the paint can't build up much because it's already as thick as it can get.

  2. **Select the Build Up Brush check box.**

     It's available in the first tab of the Tool Options window for most paint tools. (It's not an option for the Airbrush, Color Replacer, Flood Fill, and Picture Tube tools.)

  3. **Scribble with your tool to get thicker paint.**

     By scribbling, I mean moving your mouse back and forth with the mouse button pressed.

✔ **Make repeated separate strokes or clicks.** If you don't use the Build Up Brush option, you can simply make repeated separate strokes or clicks, *releasing the mouse button* between strokes or clicks. (You must also set opacity or density to less than 100 in the Tool Options window.) Most people, however, find that kind of motion more awkward than scribbling.

✔ **Use a texture.** Another way that you can build up paint thickness is to use a texture (see Chapter 4). When you use a texture in Paint Shop Pro, scribbling with your tool gradually builds up paint thickness. (You don't have to set opacity or density lower to use paper texture in this way, either.)

You can use the Build Up Brush option with the Eraser tool, too. With the Eraser tool, the effect is like rubbing lightly with an eraser: each stroke or click removes a bit more paint.

Chalk, crayon, and other media

Like many artists, you may prefer to work in something other than paint. Paint Shop Pro doesn't seem to offer chalk, crayons, or pencils on its Tool palette, however, so what's the poor sidewalk chalk artist to do?

The answer lies in the Tool Options window. It has the power to turn your paintbrush into a piece of chalk, a crayon, a pencil, and more — or, at least, into Paint Shop Pro's idea of what those media look like.

With the Paint Brush, Air Brush, Eraser, or Clone Brush tool selected, do the following in the Tool Options window:

  1. **Click the tiny Brush Types button near the upper right-corner of the Tool Options window.**

     Figure 5-9 shows which button to click to access the drop-down list you're after. Aha! There's your chalk!

Click the Brush Types button

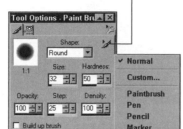

Figure 5-9:
Where your
chalk is
hiding.

2. **Choose your medium (say, Chalk) from the list that appears.**

3. **Adjust any other settings (size, shape, and so on) that you want to alter in the Tool Options window.**

You're ready to do your stuff. To return to normal, choose Normal in Step 2 (at the top of the media list).

Each medium is simply a particular set of values in the Tool Options window, values that are predetermined by Paint Shop Pro. In other words, each medium specifies particular settings for density, opacity, step, and hardness. Choosing chalk, for instance, simply sets Hardness to 90, Opacity to 80, Step to 25, and Density to 33 for whatever tool (say, the Paint Brush tool) you're currently using. Choosing the Marker produces different settings.

Brushing snowflakes and other custom shapes

Where I live, brushing snowflakes *off* things is a way of life for much of the year. But some of you may want to brush snowflakes (or stars, or clouds) *on* to your image. Figure 5-10 shows just such a flaky idea.

You can give any brush (Paint Brush, Airbrush, Clone Brush), the Eraser tool, or the Retouch tool a custom shape, turning the tool into a sort of maniacally fast automated rubber stamp. When you brush with a custom shape, you get repeated impressions, like the border of Figure 5-10. When you click, you get single impressions like the individual flakes in Figure 5-10. How very impressionistic all those impressions are.

Figure 5-10:
A few of my favorite things, created with a single snowflake brush shape that was then copied and distorted.

Paint Shop Pro offers a gallery of predesigned shapes, and you can also add your own artistry to that gallery. To use any shape in the gallery, do the following:

1. **Double-click the brush preview area near the upper-left corner of the Tool Options window (first tab).**

   Alternatively, click the tiny Brush Types button (which displays a brush icon) near the upper right-corner of the Tool Options window, and choose Custom from the drop-down list.

   The Custom Brush dialog box appears

2. **Click the down-arrow adjoining the sample shape that is displayed.**

   A gallery of available brush shapes appears.

3. **Click any brush shape.**

4. **Click OK.**

To return to a normal brush type, click the Brush Types button near the upper right-corner of the Tool Options window, shown in Figure 5-2, and choose Normal from the drop-down list.

When you make a stroke (drag your mouse), the overlap between repeated images is determined by something called *step*. (In "Making lines more or less dotty: Step," a few pages back, I describe what *step* is.) Step is pre-set for each shape, but you can adjust it in the Tool Options window each time you use the shape. You can also adjust size and opacity there.

To change the preset step value:

1. **Repeat Step 1 in the preceding list.**

   You return to the Custom Brush dialog box.

2. **Click the Edit button.**

   The Custom Brush Edit dialog box appears.

3. **Drag the Step slider left or right to set a new step value and click OK.**

4. **Click OK again to exit the Custom Brush dialog box.**

You can make your snowflakes or other shapes appear to turn or lie flat, as I did in Figure 5-10, by using the Deformation tool to shrink, add perspective, and rotate the shape. If you like, you can then use those shrunken, deformed images to make new, custom brushes! Speaking of which. . . .

To make your own custom brush shape, do the following:

1. **Draw (or otherwise create) the image that you want for a brush shape.**

   Using a white background color makes your life simpler in Step 2. The image can be a photo or anything you like, as long as it is 255 pixels across or smaller. If it has more than two colors, however, those additional hues are lost. You're creating a brush that applies whatever you choose for foreground color (or style). Any colors in this original image are reduced to various shades of a single hue when you use the brush.

2. **Select the image with one of the selection tools.**

   If the background color is white, you can use the Selection tool to drag a rectangle or other simple selection shape around your shape. Otherwise, you must make sure your selection closely follows the outline of the shape that you want for your brush. Use the Magic Wand tool, for instance, to select the hue that you used to create the shape.

3. **Choose the Paint Brush tool (or any brush, or the Eraser tool) in the Tool palette.**

   Which tool you choose doesn't matter, as long as the Tool Options window displays the brush preview area that you need in the next step.

4. **Double-click the brush preview area near the upper-left corner of the Tool Options window (first tab).**

   The Custom Brush dialog box appears.

5. **Click the Create button.**

   Your design is now in the gallery of brush shapes, where you can find it from now on.

6. **Click OK to choose that brush shape and exit the Custom Brush dialog box.**

If your brush isn't quite what you'd like it to be, you can delete it. Start with Step 3 in the preceding list. When you get to Step 5, click the Delete button instead of the Create button. Click OK in the Paint Shop Pro warning box that appears.

Coloring within the Lines by Using Selection

When you're using painting tools in Paint Shop Pro and have currently selected an area, those painting tools work only within that selection. This feature is great for keeping you "within the lines" as you paint.

First, select the area that you want to paint. (See Chapter 13 to make selections.) If you have chosen to use multiple layers in your image, make sure you're on the layer that contains the object you want to paint. (See Chapter 15 or the Cheat Sheet for help with layers.) Then, choose a painting tool and paint! Feel free to scribble or spray paint over the edges; the paint falls only within the selection.

Here's an example. In Figure 5-11, I'm trying to create the impression of an overcast, fall sky. I have selected the sky with the Magic Wand tool, so that I don't overpaint the tree line or mountains. (Squint and you may be able to see the selection marquee surrounding the sky.)

Figure 5-11:
Clouds may be moving in, but the selection marquee keeps them out of the trees and mountains.

On the right side of Figure 5-11, I've begun applying paint that's staying nicely within the selection. This selection technique works for any tool; I happened to choose a large airbrush and the Ocean texture for my job. (The fuzzy ball on the left is the Airbrush outline.) The Paint Brush tool or the Flood Fill tool would work, too, but with the Airbrush tool, paint builds up gradually, giving me a bit more control over its density.

Feathered selections work, too, for blending the edges of your painting efforts into the rest of the image. Paint Shop Pro applies less paint in the feathered zone. Feathering expands the marquee to include feathered pixels outside the selection, however. If the selection has Swiss-cheese-like holes in it (as the Magic Wand tool selections often do), those holes may now be invisible because the feathered expansion covers them. As you paint, because the holes are feathered areas, they reappear as fuzzy spots that resist being painted. If you don't want that effect, eliminate the holes in your selection before you apply feathering. See Chapter 13 for help.

Replacing Colors

Here's your chance to make that purple cow — the one that people always prefer to see, rather than be. The Color Replacer tool is your companion in creative cow coloring.

Color replacement, like most Paint Shop Pro actions, works only on the currently active layer and within any selection that you may have made. If you have chosen to use layers in your image, make sure that you're working on the correct layer during the following steps, or else replacement may not work.

Here's how to put new hue in your moo:

1. **Click the Color Replacer tool, shown in the margin, in the Tool palette.**

   Your cursor becomes a brush shape. As with the Paint Brush and other painting tools, the brush size, shape, and other properties are controlled by the Tool Options window. See "Controlling Strokes, Sizes, Shapes, and Spatters: Tool Options," earlier in this chapter.

2. **Holding down the Ctrl key, *right*-click in your image on the color that you want to *replace*.**

   The Background color sample in the Color palette takes on this color.

3. **Again holding down the Ctrl key, *left*-click on your new, replacement color, either in the image or in the Available Colors of the color palette.**

   The Foreground color sample takes on this color. Alternatively, you can use any technique I describe in Chapter 4 to set the new foreground color.

4. **To replace the color in specific areas, drag across those areas. Double-click anywhere to replace the color everywhere.**

   Like most tools, the Color Replacer tool's action is constrained by layers and selections. If you have used layers in your image, color is replaced only throughout the currently active layer. If you have a current selection, replacement only happens within that selection.

The Color Replacer tool replaces a range of colors that are close to the one you picked to be replaced. Adjust the Tolerance setting, on Tab 2 of the Tool Options window, to control closeness. (Press O if you don't see the Tool Options window; then click the second tab at the top of the palette.) The larger the Tolerance setting, the broader the range of colors the Color Replacer tool replaces. If you're replacing a single, uniform color, then set tolerance to zero. If you're purpling a cow in a photograph, you need to replace a range of browns (or blacks, or whites, depending on the cow). Set tolerance higher in that event; try 25 or so, to start. In short, do this:

- ✔ If the Color Replacer tool replaces more than you want, decrease tolerance. Press Ctrl+Z to undo the overenthusiastic replacement, and then drag or double-click again.

- ✔ If the Color Replacer tool doesn't replace enough, increase tolerance and then drag or double-click again.

Filling Areas

For flooding an area with nice, even color, nothing beats the Flood Fill tool, except possibly spilling a glass of red wine on a white sweater. (Fortunately, unlike the wine spill, you can undo the Flood Fill tool's actions by pressing Ctrl+Z.)

 Using the Flood Fill tool (known to its friends simply as Fill), shown in the margin, you can fill an area with uniform color — either solid (totally opaque) or partially transparent. Just as other tools can, based on your choolÿoolÿoolÿoolÿFF oFF oFF oFF ote, the Flood Fill tool can also apply a gradient fill, which is a smooth fade from one color to another. Alternatively, by choosing a pattern style in the Color palette, you can fill an area with bricks, bark, or any other repeated image you can find or devise. Moreover, by choosing a texture, you can give a virtual surface roughness to any area you fill. Chapter 4 describes how to choose a solid color, gradient, or pattern using the Style swatch of the Color palette.

Filling a selected area with solid color

The most basic kind of fill you can perform is filling a selected area with a uniform color (the sort of work that Phil, our house painter, does). For instance, the sky in your photograph may be gray — perhaps with clouds and power lines running through it — and you want to make it solid, cloudless blue with no power lines.

1. **Select the area you want to fill, using any of the selection tools.**

   For instance, click the sky in your picture with the Magic Wand tool. See Chapter 13 for help with getting exactly the selection you want. The selection marquee indicates your selected area.

If you have chosen to use layers in your image, you must also select the layer that contains the portion of the image that you want to fill. See Chapter 15 for more help with layers. If you don't use layers in your image, just make your selection and move on to Step 2.

2. **Click the Fill tool in the Tool palette.**

   Your cursor icon changes to the paint can, the Fill tool icon (unless you have chosen Use Precise Cursors on Tab 3 of the Tool Options window).

3. **Choose Foreground color and style to fill with.**

   For instance, left-click one of the available colors in the Color palette. Your chosen color appears in the Foreground color sample of the Color palette.

   Make sure the Foreground Style swatch is set to the style you want to fill with (solid color, gradient, or pattern). For instance, set it to solid color by mousing down on it and clicking the paint brush icon. You may also choose a Foreground texture. (See Chapter 4.)

4. **Open the Tool Options window.**

   If the Tool Options Window isn't visible on your screen, press the *O* key on your keyboard to display the palette. If only its title bar ("Tool Options") is visible, pause your cursor over that title bar to unroll the palette.

5. **Click Tab 1 of the Tool Options window (the tab with the paint can icon), and make the following choices from the drop-down lists there:**

   Blend Mode: Normal

   Match Mode: None

   Opacity: 100 percent for a fill that nothing shows through, or lower for a more transparent fill

6. **Click on your selection in the image.**

   The color completely fills the selected area (in your chosen layer, if you use layers). If you choose an opacity lower than 100, the color just tints the selected area and increases in thickness if you click again.

Figure 5-12 shows the effect of a solid fill in a selection of the sky, using deep blue to fill the sky uniformly. (The edge of the selection is feathered a bit, causing the white band to appear along the skyline.)

If you're modifying a drawing, a solid color may be exactly what you want. In my photo, however, a solid color doesn't look very natural as sky. Sky is never a uniform color in real life; it changes in color gradually as it approaches the horizon. For a more natural look, I need a gradient, or shaded, fill.

Figure 5-12:
A solid fill of the sky. In this image, a solid fill doesn't look natural.

Filling with a gradient, pattern, or texture

In real life, you rarely see a uniform color (even if you think you do). Changes in lighting or the angles at which light strikes an object cause a gradual change across the object from one color to another, lighter color. The surface of your desk, for instance, is probably a lighter color nearer your source of light.

If you need a realistic shading like that, or if for any other reason, you want colors in an area to make a smooth transition from one color to another, try a shaded, or *gradient* fill. Figure 5-13 shows the effect of a gradient fill on the sky area of my photograph.

Figure 5-13:
Gradient fills make filled areas (the sky, in this photo) more realistic.

What about tolerance?

Technical types may be wondering what the Tolerance control, in the Fill tool's Tool Options window, is good for. In this chapter, I bypass the need to use that control by instructing you to select the area you want to fill and then use a Match Mode of None. I think that's the easiest way to fill a specific area.

An alternative to selecting an area beforehand with a selection tool is to use the Fill tool itself to determine which pixels are to be filled, according to their color or other qualities. Choose a Match Mode other than None, and then set tolerance. The Fill tool determines what pixels to fill based on those settings, exactly as the Magic Wand tool does to determine what pixels to select.

For some fills, like filling a rectangle to look like a brick wall or a tree trunk, use a pattern instead of a solid color. To use gradients or patterns, you must first set your Foreground Style swatch to gradient or pattern mode. Mouse down on the Foreground Style swatch, release the mouse button when the fly-out panel appears, and click either the gradient icon or the pattern icon. See Chapter 4 for instructions on choosing the gradient or pattern you need.

Or, you may want to apply color with a textured appearance. Just like the other painting tools, the Fill tool can apply a texture such as canvas or asphalt as you paint a color. See Chapter 4 for details on using textures.

Blend modes

Sometimes, you don't really want to overpaint the underlying image; you want to just tint or infuse the image with a color, or increase or decrease color saturation, or apply some other quality. The Fill tool has some very fancy features, called *blend modes,* that combine attributes of your chosen fill such as hue and saturation with the underlying image in complex and subtle ways. In general, these blend modes are too obscure to be useful for any but the most dedicated graphics professional. For the rest of us, two of the modes, the Color and Hue modes can be occasionally useful, as they can infuse an area with color, although the Colorize command, which I describe in Chapter 11, does that job quite nicely.

To experiment with blend modes, click the Blend Mode drop-down list on Tab 1 of the Fill tool's Tool Options window, and choose a mode. Then try filling a selected area of your image.

Chapter 6

Painting with Pictures

· ·

· ·

*R*emember those cartoons where an image would flow, full-blown, off the tip of a brush? In just a few brush strokes, Daffy Duck would paint an image of a door on the wall, open the door, and run through.

Well, with Paint Shop Pro, you can have images flow off the tip of your brush, just like Daffy does. (You'll have to figure out how to run through walls on your own.) Paint Shop Pro offers two ways to paint with pictures that you'd be daffy *not* to use:

✔ **Clone Brush:** The Clone Brush tool simultaneously picks up an image from one area of an open image, while you brush a copy of that image somewhere else — either within the same image or within another open image. (It's a bit like a new-fangled version of the pantograph, for all you antique machinery mavens.)

✔ **Picture Tubes:** The Picture Tube tool lays down a series of images, fully-formed. As you stroke, the images are drawn from a collection of images that you choose, such as variously numbered billiard balls, different types of flowers, or an abstract shape in various orientations.

Why paint with pictures? The Clone Brush tool simplifies a lot of jobs. Using the Clone Brush tool, you can retouch a photo by copying a texture (like grass) or a background image (like sky) over some offending portion of the image. No need to worry about tedious color matching or finicky copying and pasting; the cloned image blends right in. Or, you can simply clone Aunt Kate from her photo at the beach on the lake and put her in the photo of the beach at Club Med. (Next time, though, invite her to Club Med.)

The Picture Tube tool does a fast job of creating backgrounds or swarm images — a great cloud of butterflies, a pile of candies, or a trail of footprints. A few individual images clicked off the Picture Tube can also quickly brighten up a poster, logo, or banner.

Cloning Around

The *Clone Brush tool* gives you results similar to copying and pasting, but allows you fingertip control over exactly what gets copied. In certain circumstances, clone brushing is also easier than copying and pasting. Here are the basic steps:

1. **Click the Clone Brush tool (shown in the margin) in the Tool palette.**

2. ***Right*-click on the source area (the area that you want to copy).**

   Clicking on an edge or corner of the desired object helps you with the next step.

3. **Brush (*left*-click or drag) on the destination area (the area that you want to paint).**

   As you brush, keep an eye on the source area, too. An X marks the spot on the source image where the Clone Brush tool is picking up (copying) pixels. As you move your brush, the X on the source image tracks your movement. Move so that the X sweeps across the object that you want to copy.

If, in Step 2, you right-clicked on the upper left corner of the area that you're copying, begin painting where you want the upper left corner of the clone to appear in Step 3. Stroke down and to the right so that the X traverses the original object.

Cloning between images or layers

The Clone Brush tool copies just as well from one image window to another window, as it does within one image. It also copies between layers, if you like.

To clone between images, open both images. They appear in separate windows in Paint Shop Pro. Just right-click on the source image where you want to copy, and then left-click or drag where you want to paint on the destination image.

To clone between layers, select your source layer in the Layer palette. Then, right-click on the image you want copied. Select the destination layer in the Layer palette, and then left-click or drag on the image.

Setting clone brush options for your specific needs

The size of the area copied in each stroke depends on your brush size, which you set in the Tool Options window. In fact, using the Tool Options window, you can set not only size, but *all* the usual variations available to Paint Shop Pro brushes: size, hardness, shape, opacity (transparency), step, and density (speckliness).

See Chapter 5 for the details of setting Tool Options for brushes in general. Here are some tips for setting those options for the Clone Brush tool:

- **Size:** Increase brush size for copying broad areas such as grass or sky. Decrease brush size for precision copying, such as cloning Aunt Kate without copying the barbecue pit behind her.

- **Hardness:** Reduce hardness to make your clone fade at the edges (which helps it blend into the background).

- **Opacity:** Lower opacity to make Aunt Kate a ghostly, transparent clone.

- **Step:** Decrease step value to get a continuous line as you make a stroke. If you increase step, your strokes look more like overlapping spots — and make Aunt Kate look a little dotty around the edges.

- **Shape:** Play with shapes to change the way a stroke ends and bends. If you simply click instead of dragging, you get a single impression in the shape of your brush. See Chapter 5 for more about interesting brush shapes, like stars and snowflakes. You can make Aunt Kate a star, if you like — literally!

Extending lawns or other textured areas

The Clone Brush tool is best suited for extending *textures* — randomly patterned areas, such as grass — into other areas of an image. In Figure 6-1, for instance, I begin filling my parents' woodshed — without sawing a single log. On the left is the original photo. On the right is an enlargement of the area marked by a rectangle on the original. The X (see the photo on the right) marks the log I'm copying. The brush is painting a copy of that log above, and to the left. (For clarity, the X is a bit brighter in Figure 6-1 than in real life.)

Don't paint too near what you're copying, if you can avoid it. If you left-click very near where you originally right-clicked, you may soon start cloning your clones. (Your X may traverse areas that you just painted.) You don't lose quality, but a pattern becomes apparent more quickly. If you look carefully at Figure 6-1, you can discern a pattern in the logs that I've cloned.

Figure 6-1:
Filling a
woodshed
by cloning
the existing
logs. X
marks the
original,
while the
brush paints
the clone.

Cloning Aunt Kate

When you copy individual people or objects, you can either use the Clone Brush tool or you can copy and paste. Which to choose? The Clone Brush tool is not really the best tool for copying objects because constraining the tool to just the object you're copying is difficult — but sometimes it's the fastest tool to use.

A couple of criteria for using the Clone Brush tool to copy objects are:

✔ When you're putting the copied object around an object or making it appear to be behind an object. For instance, you may want Aunt Kate to appear behind a palm tree at Club Med. With the Clone Brush tool, you can paint her image on either side of the palm tree. Paint Shop Pro has ways of doing this job (such as masking; see Chapter 17) that give cleaner results, but the Clone Brush tool is often simpler.

✔ When you want the object you're copying (say, Aunt Kate on a sandy beach) to have a similar background to the image where you're putting it (the sandy beach at Club Med). It's difficult to copy an object without picking up a few border pixels using the Clone Brush tool, so it works best when backgrounds match.

Otherwise, see Chapters 13 and 14 for instructions on selecting specific objects and copying them. Selecting enables you to precisely define the limits of the object you're copying and avoid copying background.

TIP

Cloning neatly within the lines

You can paint neatly within a precisely defined area by selecting that area in your destination image. (I describe selection in Chapter 13.) Paint Shop Pro paints only within the selection marquee.

To paint Aunt Kate behind a palm tree, for instance, you can select the palm tree's trunk and then invert the selection to select everything *but* the palm tree. Then your brush stroke can stop right over the tree withiout leaving paint on it.

Creating a selection around the *source* area doesn't help you copy *from* a precise area, however. A selection only works on the *destination* area.

Painting with Picture Tubes

Imagine a paint tube that, instead of containing paint, is crammed with images that pour out as you squeeze the tube. You now have a pretty good mental image of Paint Shop Pro's *Picture Tube tool.* Paint Shop Pro comes with a gallery of tubes, and you can even make your own.

Each tube contains a set of images on a particular theme. For instance, you can squeeze out a set of airplanes, butterflies, billiard balls, or coins. Each individual image in a tube is different. Figure 6-2 shows an illustration that uses two tubes: a tube of a child's ABC blocks, and a tube of letters in various styles.

Figure 6-2:
An illustration using two different picture tubes: blocks and letters.

Picture tubes have several purposes. They can serve as:

- A source of clip art on various themes.
- Brushes for interesting textures and shapes, such as grass, fire, or three-dimensional tubes.
- Creative painting tools that are sensitive to your brush strokes.

Basic tubing 101

Picture tubing is fundamentally easy. You choose what kind of pictures you want and then click or drag the picture tube across your image. Here are the details:

1. **Click the Picture Tube tool (shown in the margin) in the Tool palette.**

   You may have to wait a bit when you first choose this tool, as Paint Shop Pro loads its cache with pictures. A Cache Status box may briefly appear.

2. **Choose what picture set you want from the Tool Options window.**

   As I describe in Chapter 1, if the Tool Options window isn't visible, press the *O* key on your keyboard; if only the Tool Options title bar is visible, click the down-arrow near the right end of the title bar. If Tab 1 (the left-most tab at the top of the window) is not already selected, click it.

   A sample image from the currently selected picture tube appears on Tab 1. Click the down-arrow to the right of that sample to reveal a gallery of picture tubes of different types: airplanes, beetles, candy corn. . . . Scroll through those images to review them, and then click the one you want.

3. **Click in your image window to deposit one picture at a time or drag to paint a line of pictures.**

   As you click or drag, various pictures similar to the sample you chose appear at intervals on your image. (If your image isn't much bigger than an individual picture, very few pictures may appear. See "Adjusting basic tube behavior," just a bit later in this chapter, for instructions on reducing the picture size.)

The most basic way to use picture tubes is as a sort of randomly chosen clip art to ornament an illustration. Choose a tube and then click on your illustration in various places to drop in some art.

Basic tubing 102: Worms, grass, music, and fire

Some picture tube pictures aren't much to look at individually (for instance, when you see them in the Tool Options window), but they create cool effects when you drag your brush. For instance, choose one of the "3D . . ." shapes, such as 3D Rainbow, and you can make beautiful 3D worms.

Clouds, Fire, Grass Blades, Music, and Neon Spikes are among a few others you should try. Grass Blades, for instance, can create a field of grass. Music lets you paint a waving staff of musical notes. Fire creates an entire conflagration! Figure 6-3 illustrates the classic story of 3D worms fleeing a grass fire while music plays.

Figure 6-3: 3D worms flee a grass fire, whilst Nero (off-camera) fiddles a tune, courtesy of Paint Shop Pro's picture tubes.

Adjusting basic tube behavior

If the Picture Tube tool doesn't deliver images in quite the way you want, you can change its behavior. Behaviors you can modify include:

- ✔ **Picture size:** Reduce the number in the Scale value box (on Tab 1 of the Tool Options window) if the pictures are too large. Scale is initially set to 100 (meaning 100 percent), which is the largest setting you may have.

- ✔ **Spacing between pictures:** Pictures initially flow off your brush at a certain pre-set spacing. Increase step value (on Tab 1 of the Tool Options window) to separate pictures more. To jam them together, decrease step value.

✔ **Regular or random spacing:** The Picture Tube tool is initially set to randomly vary the spacing between pictures as you drag. To make it deliver an evenly-spaced stream of pictures:

   1. Click Tab 2 of the Tool Options window.

   2. Click the Placement Mode list box (which initially reads Random).

   3. Choose Continuous instead of Random.

✔ **Picture sequence:** The tool is initially set to choose pictures randomly from its set of images. To have it choose images in sequence:

   1. Click Tab 2 of the Tool Options window.

   2. Click the Selection Mode list box (which initially reads Random).

   3. Choose Incremental instead of Random.

The artist who created the tube determined the sequence. For each stroke you make, the sequence picks up where you last left off. The tube doesn't repeat the initial picture until it has delivered the last picture.

Advanced tubing: Stroke-sensitive behavior

For certain artistic effects, you may want the picture to change in response to your brush stroke. For instance, if you're painting a stream of butterflies emerging from the ear of your company's Chief Executive Officer, you want the butterflies to point in the direction of flight, not in random orientations. After all, you want your CEO to look good!

Certain Paint Shop Pro's picture tubes are designed to give some sort of logical response to the direction of your stroke. The Pointing Hands tube, for instance, works that way already: The hands point in the direction you stroke. Others, like Monarchs (butterflies), are normally random; you must specify a directional response. You can make all tubes change in some way in response to direction. For instance, you can make jelly beans change color — a creative, but not particularly intuitive, response.

To make a picture tube's choice of image sensitive to your brush direction, click Tab 2 of the Tool Options window. Choose Angular in the Selection Mode box. (Note that when Angular is selected, you must drag. A single click doesn't deposit a picture.)

Figure 6-4 shows Alex the dog pondering an orbiting circle of Monarch butterflies. I created the circle using the Monarch picture tube and an Angular Selection Mode.

Figure 6-4:
Alex and friends. Butterflies point in the direction of travel when you use an Angular Selection Mode.

If you're in a very creative mood, you can make a tube's pictures respond to the speed at which you stroke! Choose Velocity in the Selection Mode box. Likewise, if you have a pressure-sensitive tablet, you can make the response pressure-sensitive by choosing pressure in the Selection Mode box.

Making your own picture tubes

If the picture tube idea really excites you, you can make your own! Basically, you create a single image that contains all the pictures of your tube and then export it as a Paint Shop Pro Picture Tube. Here are the details:

1. **Decide how big you want the pictures in your tube.**

   For instance, you can make them 100 x 100 pixels.

2. **Decide how many different pictures you need in your tube.**

3. **Create a new image with a transparent background, just big enough to hold all your pictures.**

   For instance, if you wanted 12 pictures, each 100 pixels square, you can make a 300 x 400 picture, or a 200 x 600 picture. See Chapter 2 for instructions on creating a new, blank image.

4. **Set up Paint Shop Pro's grid with a horizontal spacing to match your picture width and a vertical spacing to match your picture height, and enable grid viewing.**

   For a 100 x 100 pixel picture, for instance, use spacings of 100 pixels. See Chapter 2 for help with the grid.

5. **Create a picture centered within each cell of the grid.**

   The inherent order of the pictures is reading each row from left to right, moving down the rows. They are delivered in that order if the user of the tube chooses Incremental as the Selection Mode.

   To make images correspond to the angle of the brush stroke (say, by pointing in the direction of the stroke), divide 360 degrees by the number of pictures you have. Create the pictures in the order given in the above paragraph, rotating each picture (perhaps using the Deformation tool) from its predecessor by that many degrees.

   For instance, if you have 12 pictures, rotate each one an additional 30 degrees from the last one you made. The first picture isn't rotated at all; the second picture, 30 degrees; the third picture, 60 degrees; and so on.

6. **Choose File⇨Export⇨Picture Tube.**

   The Export Picture Tube dialog box appears.

7. **Enter the number of cells in each row of your image in Cells Across.**

8. **Enter the number of rows in your image in Cells Down.**

9. **Choose the initial settings you want for placement mode, step size, and selection mode.**

   See the section, "Adjusting basic tube behavior," earlier in this chapter, for explanations of these settings. The tube user can change these settings at the time of use, in the Tool Options window.

10. **Enter a name for the tube in the Tube Name text box.**

11. **Click OK.**

    You can now close your tube image with File⇨Close. You're done.

To give you a better idea how tube images work, you can view Paint Shop Pro's own Picture Tube images. Choose File⇨Browse to open the browser and browse to the folder Program Files/Jasc Software Inc/Paint Shop Pro 7/Tubes. Double-click any tube image to open it.

Part III
Improving Appearances

The 5th Wave   By Rich Tennant

"You might want to adjust the value of your 'Nudge' function."

In this part . . .

This part is the place to turn when you have an image that needs work. If your image has individual defects, Chapter 7 is the place for you. There I show you which Paint Shop Pro hand tools can help. You can brush away freckles or paint speckles, repair scratches, or remove that evil red glow from the eyes of people or animals who were caught in a too-direct flash.

For overall appearance problems in photographs, check out Chapter 8. Over- or under-exposed photos? Green people? Blurry or speckly images? Dull colors? No problem. Paint Shop Pro version 7 offers several new effects specifically designed to fix common photo problems.

If your image needs to go beyond not bad and into the world of *wow,* Chapter 9 is the place to go. Paint Shop Pro provides all kinds of stunning and clever special effects. You can bend, twist, chisel, cut out, or translate your image into exotic media like neon or metal. In Chapter 9, I give you examples to work from. (See the color insert of this book, too, for samples of various effects.)

To get the most from your art, you need to understand your medium. With Paint Shop Pro, your medium is software. When you need to get precise about color, turn to Chapter 10, where I show you how to talk clearly to Paint Shop Pro about exactly what you need, whether it's more saturation or a color that's a bit more yellow.

When automatic solutions like Paint Shop Pro's effects don't quite solve overall image problems, your image may need fine tuning with Paint Shop Pro's color commands. I show you how to clean up subtle problems of contrast, brightness, and color in Chapter 11.

Chapter 7

Retouching Touchy Spots

- -

In This Chapter

▶ Softening

▶ Smudging

▶ Lightening

▶ Darkening

▶ Removing a scratch

▶ Removing red-eye

- -

C an Paint Shop Pro remove worrisome wrinkles, unwanted warts, or malevolent moles? Would Uncle Andrew look any less evil without red eyes? Can you do anything about the scratches and creases in that family heirloom photo?

Paint Shop Pro's answer to these questions is an emphatic "yes!" (For trickier tasks, like looking a bit skinnier or restoring lost hair, Paint Shop Pro's answer is an emphatic "Um . . . well, sort of." Believe me, I've tried.)

I focus on three Paint Shop Pro tools that you can direct towards problem areas in this chapter. They don't help you shed pounds or grow hair, but they do help you improve specific spots on your photograph or illustration:

✔ Retouch tool

✔ Scratch Remover tool

✔ Red-eye tool (or *effect*)

 None of these tools work on images with a color depth of less than 16.7 million colors. If you find that the tools or commands I describe here are grayed out or don't work on your image, try pressing Ctrl+Shift+0 to increase your color depth to 16.7 million colors.

Paint Shop Pro has other, automatic *effects* (features) that can enhance the entire image or selected areas of it. See Chapter 8 for more about those.

The Friendly Finger of the Retouch Tool

The retoucher's best friend in Paint Shop Pro is the friendly finger of the Retouch tool, shown in the margin. The Retouch tool, which lurks in the Tool palette, is a kind of virtual fingertip with which you can rub away many defects, like Mom rubbing a bit of soot off your nose.

The Retouch tool offers many possible effects to choose from. For many of these effects, using them well requires a pretty technical insight into computer graphics. In this chapter, I cover other effects that you're likely to use most.

Click the Retouch tool, and open the Tool Options window if it isn't already open (press the letter O on your keyboard). The Tool Options window lets you choose exactly what effect the Retouch tool will have. Read on to see how to apply this friendly finger to your photos.

Using layers? The Retouch tool, like most of Paint Shop Pro's tools, normally works only on the currently selected layer. (If you have selected an area, it works only within that area, too.) To have the retouch tool modify all layers at once, click Tab 2 of the Tool Options window (where you also set the Retouch Mode) and enable the Sample Merged check box. If the tool doesn't seem to be working, check to make sure you have the correct layer selected (see Chapter 15) and that you don't currently have a selection encompassing some other area (press Ctrl+D to remove any selection).

Adjusting your retouch stroke

You want to adjust size and other stroke attributes of the Retouch tool to match your task. After choosing the Retouch tool, click Tab 1, the leftmost tab in the Tool Options window for the Retouch tool, to control what size stroke the tool makes, as well as other stroke-related attributes.

Controls for size, shape, and other stroke-related qualities are like those for any basic Paint Shop Pro brush. See Chapter 5 for details, but here are the controls in a nutshell:

- **Shape:** Choose alternative shapes from the Shape selection box.
- **Size:** Set the brush's width in pixels. Reduce it for a smaller brush.
- **Hardness:** Decrease this value to give your tool softer edges (diminish its effect near its edges).
- **Opacity:** Decrease this value if you want to work more gradually (have the tool change the image less per stroke or click).
- **Step:** Leave this set at a fairly low value, like 25.

✔ **Density:** Leave this set at 100, unless you can think of a good reason to spray — that is, retouch in a speckly, spray-paint-like fashion.

✔ **Build Up Brush:** This check box has no effect in softening or smudging, but does affect lightening, darkening, and certain other modes. When enabled, it builds up the effect of your stroke as you scribble continuously over the same area. Without it, you need repeated strokes to accomplish the same result.

Having the size and shape of your Retouch tool depicted by your mouse cursor is useful. If your mouse cursor outline doesn't already exhibit your chosen shape and size, click Tab 3 of the Tool Options window and enable the Show Brush Outlines check box.

Softening

One of the Retouch tool's most useful effects is one that is great for retouching portraits: the Soften mode. We could all use a bit of softening.

In the Tool Options window, click Tab 2 (the middle tab) and choose Soften in the Retouch Mode selection box. In the Soften mode, the Retouch tool softens sharp edges — wrinkles, for instance. Just brush the tool across those edges or click on them.

Figure 7-1 shows a frighteningly close shot of the left eye of wrinkled, old Uncle Dave, namely me. On the left is an unretouched copy; on the right is the Retouch tool softening my wrinkles. O, kindly, friendly Retouch tool!

You could get the same result by selecting the wrinkled area and applying the Blur or Blur More Effect, but that's more work. (See Chapter 8 for help with Effects.)

To work more gradually and do less softening in each stroke, click Tab 1 of the Tool Options window. Set Opacity to a lower value.

Figure 7-1:
The Retouch tool in Soften mode removes a few years from the author's left eye.

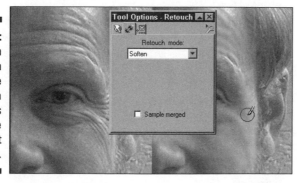

Smudging

Smudging is the closest thing to finger painting you'll find in a computer program. You can use smudging to soften edges, rub out pimples, or even blend in a dot of rouge (say, low-opacity red paint) you've added to the cheek of your CEO's portrait. It's also great for making artistic swirls and clouds or giving the effect of a pastel drawing (where real finger smudging is common).

In the Tool Options window, click Tab 2 (the middle tab) and then choose Smudge in the Retouch Mode selection box. In Smudge mode, the Retouch tool picks up paint from the place where you set it down and smears that paint as you drag to other areas. As it smears, it loses paint just as your finger would.

To minimize moles, pimples, and similar imperfections, don't start *on* the discolored area, but off to one side. Smudge across the discolored area and release the mouse button once you're through the area. Repeat in the opposite direction, again starting on clear skin.

Figure 7-2 shows the smudge effect as the Retouch tool is dragged from left to right, starting with white and passing through the center of three differently colored squares in a single stroke. Notice how the paint fades as the tool moves from left to right. The tops of the three squares have also been smudged, but with repeated, circular strokes.

Figure 7-2:
The Retouch tool in Smudge mode. A single stroke through the middle creates a "bullet through an apple" look, while circular motion smudges the tops.

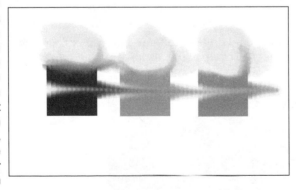

As in the center of Figure 7-2, a single stroke may reveal the inherent dotti-ness of computer stroking, which you can minimize by reducing the Step value on Tab 1 of the Tool Options window. Repeated strokes, as along the tops of the squares in Figure 7-2, tend to smear out those dots.

Lightening or darkening

You can do lightening or darkening in lots of different ways in Paint Shop Pro, but the most basic ways are called *Lighten RGB* and *Darken RGB* — two very useful modes of the Retouch tool. (Other modes — Dodge, Burn, Lightness Up, Lightness Down — can also be useful. See the following section, "Other modes.")

Click Tab 2 (the middle tab) of the Tool Options window and then choose Lighten RGB or Darken RGB in the Retouch Mode selection box. Each time you make a stroke (click or drag), the colors under your brush grow darker or lighter.

Enable the Build Up Brush check box on Tab 1 if you prefer to lighten or darken by continuous rubbing or scribbling over the same area (keeping the mouse button down), rather than by making repeated clicks or strokes (lift-ing the mouse button between repetitions).

The left side of Figure 7-3 shows an image of Alex, my Golden Retriever, that was taken a bit too close to the camera's flash. On the copy on the right side, I used the Retouch tool in Darken RGB mode to tone down the gleam on his nose and reduce the flash's reflection in his eyes.

To darken more gradually and gain more control over the results, click Tab 1 of the Tool Options window and then set Opacity to a lower value.

Figure 7-3:
The Retouch tool in Darken RGB mode takes the shine off Alex's nose and the glare off his eyeballs.

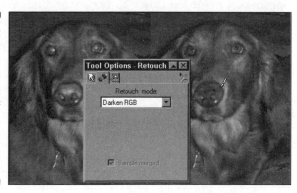

Other modes

The Retouch tool offers other modes, some of which are pretty obscure and some of which are more creative than restorative. Still, you may think a few of them worth a try. The following are brief synopses of what they do:

- **Sharpen:** Amplifies edges, wrinkles, and other sudden transitions (opposite of Soften).

- **Emboss:** Creates a grayscale image that appears to be embossed, like George Washington's face on a U.S. quarter.

- **Push:** Picks up the image area where you begin dragging and pushes it along, leaving a trail of finely overlapping copies of that area. (Overlap is controlled by the Step value on Tab 1 of the Tool Options window.)

- **Dodge:** Dodge is a term taken from photographic darkroom work, meaning to lighten areas that are already somewhat light. It lightens the image and enhances contrast at the same time.

- **Burn:** Burn is the opposite of Dodge — it darkens pixels that are already somewhat dark. It darkens the image while enhancing contrast.

- **Saturation Up/Saturation Down:** Provides more or less intense colors, respectively. Lowering saturation moves colors towards gray. Technically, this changes S (Saturation) in the HSL (Hue/Saturation/Lightness) primary system.

- **Lightness Up/Lightness Down:** Provides lighter or dimmer colors, respectively. (This changes L — Lightness — in the HSL system.)

- **Hue Up/Hue Down:** Gives you really weird colors, pushing colors counter-clockwise (red, yellow, green, cyan, blue, violet, magenta) or clockwise, respectively, in Paint Shop Pro's color wheel. (Technically, this changes H — Hue — in the HSL system.)

- **Saturation, Lightness, or Hue Up/Down to Target:** Enables you to choose a color of a desired saturation, lightness, or hue as your Foreground color (in the Color palette), and then, by brushing, to move image colors towards the saturation, lightness, or hue of that color.

The Scratch Remover Tool

Having photos come back from the developer with a scratch is heartbreaking. Usually, it means that a scratch is on the negative so making a new print can't help. Equally traumatic is having a valued print creased, torn, or scratched when you don't have a negative and can't replace the print. Paint Shop Pro has an answer for all your folds, creases, and scratches. After you scan the picture into Paint Shop Pro (see Chapter 2), here's what to do:

1. **Zoom in on your scratched area so that it fills the screen.**

   Click the magnifying-glass icon on the Tool palette; then left-click on the scratch to zoom.

2. **Click the Scratch Remover tool on the Tool palette.**

    This tool is the trowel-looking icon shown in the margin. (Actually, I suspect the icon is supposed to represent a *palette knife* — a painter's tool for scraping paint.)

3. **Position your mouse cursor at one end of the scratch and drag along the scratch.**

   As you drag, a frame area stretches to follow your mouse cursor and extends across the width of the scratch, as shown in Figure 7-4.

Figure 7-4:
Having a dog requires familiarity with scratching. Here, Alex looks pleased as I remove a scratch.

4. **Release your mouse button at the end of the scratch.**

   If you're following a curved or irregular scratch, release your mouse button at the point where the curve can no longer fit within the frame. (Later, you can go back and remove remaining segments of scratch.)

   When you release the mouse button, the Scratch Remover tool picks up paint from either side of the scratch and pushes it into the scratch. If you had to stop short of the end of the scratch, drag a second time to cover the remaining portion.

That's it! You now have a slightly fuzzy band where the scratch was, but it's probably a lot better than a scratch.

If your photo has lots of small scratches from improper handling, try the Automatic Small Scratch Removal effect I describe in Chapter 8.

If the scratch wasn't completely filled in, you may need to repeat your action for another segment of scratch or adjust some tool options and try again. For irregular scratches, remove the scratch in sections. To adjust options, first undo any failed attempt (press Ctrl+Z). Next, open the Tool Options window (press O to toggle the window on or off). Do one of the following:

✔ **If the scratch didn't fill in because the scratch was wider than the tool's frame:** A value box on Tab 1 gives the tool's width in pixels. Increase the value in that box and again try to remove your scratch. With tool settings larger than 20, the frame exhibits an inner and outer zone as you drag. As you drag, make sure that the scratch fits in the inner zone and that the outer zone is completely filled with the bordering colors you want to use for filling in.

✔ **If you end up with an unacceptably wide, fuzzy band where the scratch was:** The tool's width was set too high. Lower the width value on Tab 1 of the Tool Options window.

✔ **If the end points of the scratch didn't properly fill in:** An outline option on Tab 1 gives you an alternative shape to drag, one that has pointed ends instead of square ones. That shape is good for clicking in tight spaces or corners. Click that alternative shape button and then try scratch removal again.

If the scratch runs along an edge in the image, use the smallest width possible in order to avoid blurring that edge. For instance, in Figure 7-4, the scratch grazes my shoulder where my shirt ends and the trees begin. The scratch remover blurs that edge. Rather than removing the entire irregular scratch in one broad attempt, I may do better to remove that shoulder-grazing portion of the scratch separately, with the width value set very low.

The Red-eye Remover

In my youth, I longed for something to remove the telltale morning red-eye that bespoke a long, hard night out. Regrettably, Paint Shop Pro doesn't remove *that* kind of red-eye, where the blood vessels in the whites of your eyes throb reproachingly.

Paint Shop Pro's red-eye remover *does,* however, fix the evil red glow that sometimes appears in photographs, emanating from the pupils of the eye as the result of a camera's flash. In animals, that glow may not be red, but yellow or other colors.

The red-eye remover in Paint Shop Pro is actually a red-eye replacer. Rather than attempting to restore the original pupil of the eye, Paint Shop Pro says, "The heck with it" and paints a whole new pupil, complete with the glint of the flashbulb.

In fact, the red-eye remover can even construct a new iris (the colored portion of your eye) if you need one! Sometimes a camera's flash obliterates the iris, so the Red-eye remover comes complete with a set of spare irises of various colors. Ever wonder how you'd look with green eyes? Here's your chance!

Reconstructing the pupil

Usually, red-eye affects only the pupil. If it has affected the iris in your photo, see the section, "Replacing pupil and iris," later in this chapter. Here's how to get rid of red-eye if the flash hasn't affected the iris area:

1. **Choose Effects⇨Enhance Photo⇨Red-eye Removal.**

   The amazingly complex-looking Red-eye Removal dialog box appears. Figure 7-5 gives you the picture.

2. **Zoom in very close on one of the red eyes, in the preview windows.**

   To zoom in, click the button displaying a magnifying glass with a + sign, located between the two preview windows. Repeat until the eye practically fills the windows.

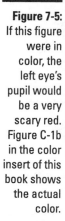

Figure 7-5: If this figure were in color, the left eye's pupil would be a very scary red. Figure C-1b in the color insert of this book shows the actual color.

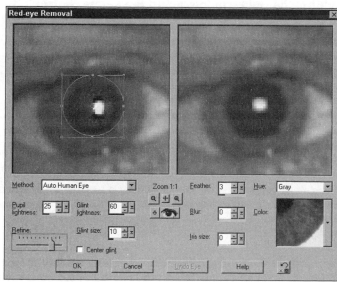

To move the photo around behind the window, drag in the *right* (not left) window. Your cursor displays a hand icon when it's over the right window.

If you mistakenly drag or click in the left window, click the Undo Eye button to remove the replacement iris you have accidentally created.

3. **Choose Auto Human Eye (if you're working on a human) from the Method selection box.**

   If you're working on an animal, choose Auto Animal Eye.

4. **Set Iris Size to zero.**

   Or, if you have changed your mind and decided that the red really does afflict the iris, see the section "Replacing pupil and iris," later in this chapter, at this point.

5. **Click once on the dead center of the (red) pupil of the eye in the left window.**

   A circle appears, with a dot in the center and a square frame surrounding the circle. The circle has handles on it (tiny squares that you can drag). Figure 7-5 shows this tool.

   You want the circle to just cover the red pupil and be centered over it.

6. **Adjust the circle's position or size if the circle doesn't cover the red pupil.**

   You can drag the circle by the dot in its center. To re-size the circle, drag one of the handles on the box surrounding the circle.

7. **Looking at the right window, adjust the Refine control left and right until the red is just covered by a dark spot (the new pupil).**

   The Refine control determines to what extent the new pupil covers the red. When you're done, very little or no red should be showing. For precise control of Refine, click the slider and press the left- and right-arrow keys on your keyboard to decrement or increment the slider. The new pupil should be no larger than the original and shouldn't cover the eyelid. If you can't achieve a result you like, return to Step 5 and resize the circle.

8. **Adjust the Pupil Lightness value box to set the lightness of your new pupil to your liking.**

   Decrease the value for a darker pupil. For a normal appearance, the pupil should be darker than the iris.

9. **Check the new, white glint in the right window against the original in the left window.**

   If the new glint isn't roughly the same size as the original, adjust the Glint Size control up or down until they match. Feel free, however, to make the new glint any size you like, including removing it altogether by setting Glint Size to zero. If you prefer the glint in the center of the eye, click to enable the Center Glint check box. Otherwise, the glint tracks the original one. Adjust the Glint Lightness control up or down to match the brightness of the original glint. If the new glint has a noticeably sharper edge than the old, adjust the Blur control upward.

10. **Increase the Feather control to get a softer edge or to mute any remaining red spots around the edge.**

   Alternatively, if the original photo is a bit blurry, try adjusting the Blur control upward instead. Fool around with these two controls until the edges look properly blended in to the rest of the eye.

11. **Click the Proof button (with the eye icon) to check your results in the main image window.**

   (Drag the Red-eye Removal dialog box out of the way, if necessary; don't close it yet.)

   Return to any earlier steps that seem necessary to adjust size, darkness, coverage, glint, and so forth.

   If you decide that you need to give up and start again, click the Undo Eye button. If you want to return all the settings to their original positions, click the Reset button in the bottom-right corner.

   If you can't get acceptable coverage of the pupil, click the Cancel button and see the next section, "Outlining problem pupils."

12. **Click OK.**

When you're done with one eye, repeat those steps for the other eye. When you proof your work in Step 10, make sure the eyes match!

Outlining problem pupils

As you undoubtedly remember from school, some pupils are troublemakers. They don't cooperate if you try to doctor their red-eye. In that case, change from using automatic red-eye removal to *manual outlining*.

Open the Red-eye Removal dialog box and zoom in as directed in Steps 1 and 2 of the preceding steps. Instead of choosing Auto Human (or Auto Animal) Eye in Step 3, which tells Paint Shop Pro to automatically outline the red area, choose one of the following two manual outlining options:

   ✔ **Freehand Pupil Outline:** Choose this option if you prefer to drag a continuous line around the red area to outline it. (Requires a steady hand but can give a more rounded outline.) When you release the mouse button, Paint Shop Pro connects the line's end with its beginning.

✔ **Point-to-Point Pupil Outline:** Choose this option if you prefer to click a series of points around the red area. Paint Shop Pro draws a straight line between the points. When you're ready to complete the circle, don't click again on the starting point. Instead, double-click somewhere short of that point. Paint Shop Pro completes the circle for you.

Drag or click an outline, according to your choice of options. After you outline the pupil, resume with Step 7 of the preceding steps to refine the red-eye correction.

Replacing pupil and iris

If the flash has affected the colored iris of the eye, first follow Steps 1–4 in the earlier list. (In those steps, you open the Red-eye Removal dialog box, zoom in on an eye, and click in its center.) Then, after Step 3, do the following:

a. **Enlarge the circle in the left-hand window to cover an area equal to the *iris* (not just the pupil) you need.**

   Drag any corner handle of the square frame surrounding the circle to enlarge the circle. Often the circle needs to overlap the top eyelid and possibly a bit of the bottom.

b. **Adjust the value in the Iris Size value box up or down, a little at a time, until the iris and pupil size either matches the other eye, or simply looks correct.**

   Click the tiny up-arrow or down-arrow adjoining the Iris Size value box to change the value by one.

c. **Click the Hue selection box and choose an iris color from the list.**

   Choose from Aqua, Blue, Brown, Gray, Green, or Violet.

d. **Click the down-arrow to the right of the Color sample box and choose a precise shade of color from the gallery that appears.**

   Pause your mouse cursor over any cell in the gallery to see a verbal description of the shade.

e. **Adjust the Refine control left or right to set the shape and extent of the iris.**

   The optimal setting of the Refine control is when the iris doesn't significantly overlap an eyelid and is reasonably round elsewhere. A black spot with a white glint should cover the pupil of the eye.

Now, resume with Step 8 in the preceding list of numbered steps. From here, you adjust the darkness of the pupil, set any feathering or blurring you need, and adjust the glint size, if necessary.

Chapter 8

Finessing Photos with Effects

. . . .

. . . .

*W*ith today's point-and-shoot cameras, you may wonder if anything could really go wrong. They autofocus, auto-expose, autoadvance, autoflash, and, therefore, autobedarnednearperfect. But, despite all this automation, we all still make seriously flawed photographs from time to time. Maybe we autogiveup?

Fear not, fellow photo flubbers. If your photos get an F for Faulty, you'll find a flock of effects for finessing your photos to a fare-thee-well. Even for people whose pictures are practically perfect, Paint Shop Pro is replete with photo polishing possibilities. Now, if only they had an answer for authors' unlicensed alliteration.

Effects in Paint Shop Pro encompass a wide range of image-processing doohickeys. You can use effects on photographs and images of all kinds. In this book, I have divided effects into two main categories, which I cover in two chapters:

✔ In this chapter, I describe effects that are most useful for improving photographs.

✔ In Chapter 9, I describe effects used mainly in a creative way, for doing artsy stuff.

Like most other features of Paint Shop Pro, effects work only on whatever layer of an image is currently active, and within a current selection. If your image has multiple layers, you need to choose the layer you want before applying an effect. See Chapter 15 for help with layers.

One limitation of effects is that they don't work on 256-color images. If your image has 256 or fewer colors, press Ctrl+Shift+0 to increase the image's color depth to the 24-bit level before trying effects.

Paint Shop Pro offers a special Photo Toolbar for all of the effects in the Effects➪Enhance Photo submenu. With that toolbar enabled, you can simply click a button for an effect rather than use the menu commands. To enable the toolbar, choose View➪Toolbars, select the Photo Toolbar check box in the Toolbars dialog box that appears, and click the Close button.

Using Effects' Adjustment Dialog Boxes

Many adjustment dialog boxes in Paint Shop Pro's Effects (and Colors) menu have similar adjustment, preview, and proofing features. The Automatic Color Balance dialog box provides an example in Figure 8-1.

Adjustments are made using three types of control:

- **Sliders:** You do many adjustments by dragging sliders. Dragging varies an associated value (number) that appears in a text box near each slider.

- **Slider values:** Instead of dragging the slider, you may click in its associated text box and type a value. Or, you can click on a slider, and then press the left- or right-arrow key on your keyboard to adjust the value by –1 or +1, respectively. These two methods give you more precise control than dragging the slider.

- **Value boxes:** Value boxes in Paint Shop Pro (like the Strength box in Figure 8-1) are just like value boxes anywhere, but with an additional feature. You can type in a value, or increment/decrement the value by clicking on the up/down arrows that appear in a pair to the right of the box. You can also adjust the value by mousing down (clicking without releasing) on the down-arrow to the right of the increment buttons, and then dragging the slider that appears left or right.

All the dialog boxes let you see the effect of your adjustments (preview them or proof them) before you commit to them. Here's how to preview or proof your changes:

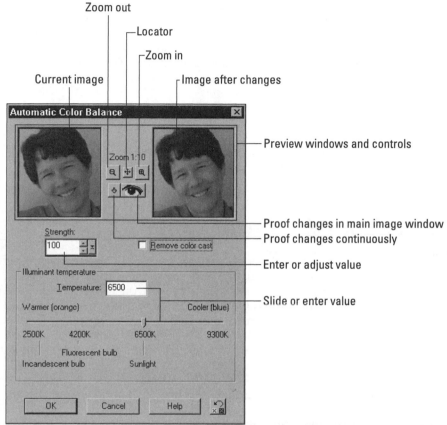

Zoom out

Locator

Zoom in

Current image

Image after changes

Preview windows and controls

Figure 8-1:
The
Automatic
Color
Balance
dialog box
illustrates
controls
common to
all the
adjustment
dialog boxes
in the
Effects
menu.

Proof changes in main image window
Proof changes continuously

Enter or adjust value

Slide or enter value

✔ **Zoom:** To zoom in or out in the preview windows, click the zoom in button (a magnifier with a +) or zoom out button (with a –) shown in Figure 8-1.

✔ **Drag:** To move an image behind the preview windows, drag the image within a preview window. In most dialog boxes, you can drag in either window, but some of them use the left window for defining areas of interest. It's better to get in the habit of dragging in the right window.

✔ **Locate:** To move quickly to a new area of the image, mouse down on the locator button shown in Figure 8-1 (keep the mouse button depressed). A small version of the entire image is displayed, with a rectangle representing your preview area. Drag the rectangle to the area you want to preview and then release the mouse button.

✔ **Proof:** To see the effect of your adjustments in the main image window, known as *proofing,* click the Proof button. (The changes you see aren't permanent until you click the OK button.) Click the Proof button again to remove the change.

✔ **Auto Proof:** If you would prefer to always proof your adjustments instead of just seeing them in the preview windows, click the Auto Proof button. Paint Shop Pro now shows the effect of your changes in the main image window every time you make a change. For large images, however, you may find this proofing method slow. Turn off auto proofing by clicking the button again.

After you make an adjustment, click OK to apply it to your image.

Changes are rarely final in Paint Shop Pro because you can undo them by clicking the Undo button on the Toolbar, by pressing Ctrl+Z, or by using the Edit⇨Command History command (see Chapter 1).

Correcting Lighting Color

Despite automatic flashes, lighting is still one of the prime photographic problems. Your flash fails to go off, the room is lit by incandescent or fluorescent light, the sunset casts an orange light, the forest reflects green, or the swimming pool reflects blue. Many of these problems go away almost magically with Paint Shop Pro's Automatic Color Balance effect.

Choose Effects⇨Enhance Photo⇨Automatic Color Balance. The Automatic Color Balance dialog box makes the scene, as shown in Figure 8-1.

Adjust the slider in the grandiosely named Illuminant Temperature area left or right, or edit the value in the Temperature text box. Dragging the slider left (lower Temperature value) makes the color of your photo visually warmer, or more orange. (Yes, lower Temperature makes color warmer.) Dragging right makes the color visually cooler, or bluer. Notice that the Temperature scale is labeled with various light sources, such as Sunlight; position the slider at a given label to simulate that light source.

Adjust the Strength value higher for greater effect, generally a brighter picture. Adjust it down for the opposite effect.

See the color section of this book for a color version of Figure 8-1, in which the Automatic Color Balance adjustment salvages a rather blue picture of my wife. That photo was accidentally taken indoors without a flash.

The Temperature thing is about an illumination term called *color temperature,* referring to the temperature of an incandescent light source. A lower-temperature light source generally gives a warmer (more orange) light. You can see the effect in a fireplace or barbecue; as the fire dies down, it gives off a more orange glow.

Correcting Contrast and Brightness

Paint Shop Pro offers several ways to adjust contrast (see Chapter 11 for additional ways), but for photos, the Automatic Contrast Enhancement effect is a great place to start. It simultaneously fiddles with brightness and contrast — two interlinked attributes — to optimize your photo's appearance. Whether your photo has too little contrast or too much, this tool can help.

Choose Effects➪Enhance Photo➪Automatic Contrast Enhancement and the Automatic Contrast Enhancement control of Figure 8-2 rushes to your aid. It has three control areas: *Bias* (or lightness), *Strength* (amount of effect), and *Appearance* (amount of contrast).

Choose overall lightness/darkness

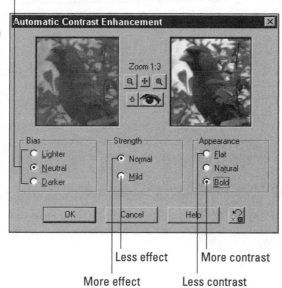

Figure 8-2:
The "cardinal" rule for contrast problems is to try the Automatic Contrast Enhancement dialog box first.

Less effect   More contrast

More effect   Less contrast

In Figure 8-2, a photo that I took of a cardinal (through a window) suffers from poor contrast — a dark fate for such a bright bird. The Automatic Contrast Enhancement effect restores his outstanding appearance. Use the controls of this effect in the following ways:

✔ If your photo needs contrast adjustment, use the Appearance controls. If your photo needs more contrast, click Bold; for less contrast, click Flat; and, if it's just right, click Natural.

✔ If your photo needs lightening or darkening, use the Bias controls. If it's overall too dark, click Lighter; if it's too light, click Darker; if it's just right, click Neutral.

✔ For a greater effect on contrast and/or brightness, click Normal in the Strength area. Otherwise, choose Mild.

Intensifying (or Dulling) Colors

The more common problem with photos is dull colors that need more intensity. However, if you're shooting, say, Ronald McDonald at a sunny tulip festival, I can imagine you may need duller colors, too. Either way, the Automatic Saturation Enhancement effect fills the bill.

Choose Effects➪Enhance Photo➪Automatic Saturation Enhancement to enter the land of more intense (or dimmer) colors. The Automatic Saturation Enhancement dialog box glimmers onto your screen.

Figure 8-3 shows you the dialog box in action. Showing you intensified colors in a black and white illustration is a bit too much of a challenge, however, so please turn to the color section of this book to see what kind of results you can achieve.

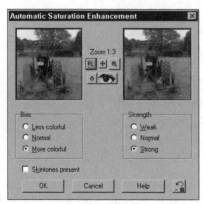

Figure 8-3: Brightening up a dull day at the farm with Automatic Saturation Enhancement.

Controls in the Bias area determine whether you intensify or dull your colors. Choose Less Colorful to dull your colors or More Colorful to intensify colors. Normal may intensify or dull your colors, depending upon how intense they are currently.

Controls in the Strength area determine to what degree you dull or intensify colors (according to your choice in the Bias area). Choose Weak to barely affect colors, Normal to moderately affect them, or Strong to have the most effect.

Removing JPEG, Moiré, and Other Patterns

Unwanted patterns, or other disturbances, are common in images created or stored in certain ways. Paint Shop Pro offers several effects to help you rid your images of these imperfections.

Unearthing JPEG artifacts

One kind of disturbance is typical of photos that you obtain from digital cameras or the Web. When these photos are stored in JPEG format, as they often are, the result is nice, small files. But they often exhibit strange patterns around text and other objects with sharp edges. JPEG can also make a checkerboard pattern. Figure 8-4 shows those patterns, also called *artifacts*. Problems are particularly noticeable when a JPEG file is stored with a low-quality, high-compression setting.

Speckles near sharp edges

Figure 8-4:
This farm grew a few artifacts when stored as a JPEG image. The JPEG Artifact Removal effect uproots them.

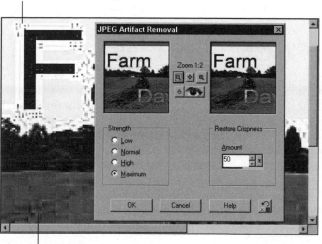

Checkerboard

To clean up JPEG images, choose Effects⇨Enhance Photo⇨JPEG artifact removal. The JPEG Artifact Removal expert appears on your doorstep in the form of the dialog box in Figure 8-4.

Checking your image either by looking in the right preview window or by proofing your choice, choose the strength (Low, Normal, High, or Maximum) needed to clean up your artifacts. Another casualty in JPEG files is a certain amount of detail, which you can restore by increasing the value in the Restore Crispness value box.

Don't want no moiré

Scanned-in photos from print media (books, magazines, newsletters, PC-printed images) often have moiré patterns. (See Chapter 3 for more about moiré and ways to avoid it in the first place.)

You can fix moiré patterns by choosing Effects➪Enhance Photo➪Moiré Pattern Removal. The rather simple Moire Pattern Removal dialog box arrives to do your bidding.

The Moire Pattern Removal dialog box offers two controls: Fine Details and Remove Bands. Adjusting Fine Details upward (sliding it to the right) blurs your image, removing fine, grainy moiré patterning. Adjusting Remove Bands upward counters the distracting bands that often are part of moiré patterning.

Unlacing your interlacing

Images captured from video cameras are often *interlaced.* The image is made up of horizontal lines created in two passes: The first pass fills in the odd-numbered lines, and the second fills in the even-numbered lines. Because the two passes occur at slightly different times, the result is often a motion-induced blur. Paint Shop Pro's answer to interlacing problems is the very straightforward Deinterlace effect.

Choose Effects➪Enhance Photo➪Deinterlace. The Deinterlace dialog box appears. It has one control called Scanlines To Retain. Choose which set of lines you like by clicking either Odd or Even. Paint Shop Pro fills in the eliminated lines by averaging between the lines you retain.

Rubbing Out Scratchiness

Some photos or their negatives can get pretty seriously abused, picking up tiny scratches, pits, or other imperfections while being handled, while living in suitcases or sandy beach bags, or while being badly processed. Hey, who wouldn't get a little abraded under those circumstances? To fix individual scratches, creases, or folds, see the Scratch Remover tool in Chapter 7. To get rid of lots of scratches at once, try the Automatic Small Scratch Removal effect.

Choose Effects⇨Enhance Photo⇨Automatic Small Scratch Removal. The Automatic Small Scratch Removal dialog box scratches its way onto your screen. Figure 8-5 shows this tool removing a rather serious sandblasting of my face — not that sandblasting wouldn't make a marked improvement.

Figure 8-5: I've been itching to remove these scratches and now the Automatic Small Scratch Removal effect does the job.

First, determine if your scratches are light or dark, or both. Next, select Remove Light Scratches, Remove Dark Scratches, or both. If the preview image on the right side isn't already adequately cleaned up, change the Strength setting from Normal to Aggressive. If the effect is removing things that aren't scratches, or making your photo too fuzzy, try changing Strength to Mild. (A necessary side effect of cleaning up scratches with this effect is a bit of added fuzziness, so you can't be too picky.) If the effect is removing too many tiny features, try adjusting the Local Contrast Limits. To restore low-contrast features, drag the pointer at the left end of the line to the right. To restore high-contrast features, drag the pointer at the right end of the line to the left.

If the result is still too fuzzy, check out "Removing Noise (Speckles)," later in this chapter, for alternative methods like the Salt-And-Pepper filter.

Clarifying the Details

You can't say that Jasc, the maker of Paint Shop Pro, isn't on the job. Often, people say that a photo "just isn't clear." What can a software vendor do about such a vaguely defined problem?

Come up with a solution with an equally vague name: the Clarifying effect. What this tool actually does is unclear, but it appears to increase the contrast of certain details by boosting contrast. It's like a smart contrast enhancement with an eye for detail.

Choose Effects⇨Enhance Photo⇨Clarify. The rather simple Clarify dialog box arrives with a clear intention to help you. It has only one control, the Strength of Effect value box. Increase that value to get more clarity (whatever it is). Clarify doesn't clarify everything, but it's worth a try.

Unfading the Faded

Photographs, especially those exposed to the sunlight, tend to yellow and fade with age. Paint Shop Pro can reverse the yellowing and other symptoms of age with its Fade Correction feature.

Choose Effects⇨Enhance Photo⇨Fade Correction to unleash this photo-graphic fountain of youth. The Fade Correction dialog box appears, sporting only a single control. Adjust the Amount of Correction value upward until the image in the right preview window looks young again.

Correcting for a Specific Color

Sometimes you don't know exactly what's wrong with the color of a photo. You may, however, know that the color of a specific object in the photo is wrong. For instance, skin color may be too blue in those underwater shots, or your cat is simply not that shade of brown. Would you recognize the correct color of that skin or cat if you saw it? If so, you have an easy way to correct the color of your photo: Paint Shop Pro's Manual Color Correction effect.

Note that Manual Color Correction adjusts the color of the *entire* image so that your selected object (say, skin or fur) is then the correct color. It pre-sumes that every object in your photograph was shot in the same, bad light. If it gets your selected portion of the image correct, the entire image is then correct. You *can* use it to correct just the object itself, but you must first select that object using Paint Shop Pro's selection tools.

Ready? Choose Effects➪Enhance Photo➪Manual Color Correction to give this targeted tool its instructions. The Manual Color Correction dialog box appears, as shown in Figure 8-6. (Refer to the color section of this book to see the difference in colors.)

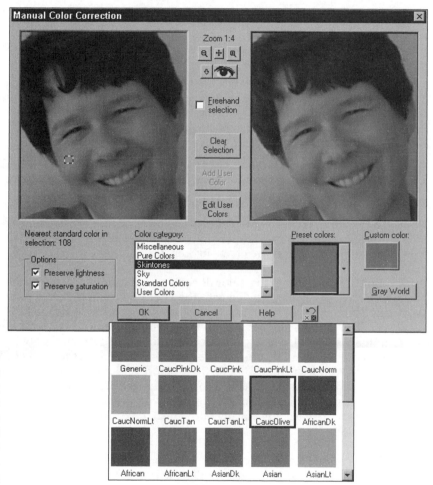

Figure 8-6: Correcting the entire photo so that Katy's skin tone is correct.

1. **Make the object which color you know fill the left preview window.**

   Use the zoom, drag, and locating features of the dialog box (see "Using Effects' Adjustment Dialog Boxes," earlier in this chapter).

2. **Click the Color Category selection box and choose a likely-sounding category for your object, like Skintones.**

3. **Click the down-arrow to the right of the Preset Colors box.**

   A gallery of color appears, as shown in Figure 8-6.

4. **Choose a color from the gallery.**

   If you can't find the color you want, click the Custom Color button to choose a color from Paint Shop Pro's Color dialog box. See Chapter 4 for the details of using this dialog box.

5. **Drag on the left image, creating an area in which you're certain what the color should be.**

   Drag diagonally to define a rectangular area. For instance, drag across the forehead of your subject, creating a rectangle that surrounds a fairly uniform skin color, if you intend to match his or her skin tone to a color. Choose an area that isn't strongly affected by highlights or shadows. Drag again if you want to change your selection.

   If the area you want to define is irregular in shape, enable the Freehand Selection check box. Then, drag (draw) the irregular shape you want to use on the left window.

The instant you have completed dragging an area, Paint Shop Pro alters the image in the right preview window, matching the hue of your selected area to the hue of the color you chose in Step 2.

"But," you may say, "the color doesn't match exactly." Don't panic. Unless you have previously fiddled with the check boxes in the Options section of the Manual Color Correction dialog box, the color *shouldn't* match exactly — yet. The Preserve Lightness and Preserve Saturation check boxes, which are initially selected, cause your photo's color to be corrected only to the *hue* (a kind of fundamental color) of the color you have selected, and not it's saturation or lightness. (See Chapter 10 for more about hue, saturation, and lightness.) If you want to make the color match your chosen sample exactly, you must clear both check boxes. However, you may find that you get good results more easily by leaving both check boxes selected and choosing different colors.

If you created a custom color in Step 4 (using the Color dialog box), you may save the color for future use, under the User Colors category. Click the Add User Color button, and in the Add User Color dialog box that appears, type a name (10 characters or fewer) in the Name field and a description (such as Katy's cheek color) in the Description field. Click the Add button.

You can now find your custom color by first choosing User Colors in the Color Category selection box. Then click the down-arrow for the Preset Colors box to choose from a gallery of user colors. Your description appears when you pause your cursor over the color swatch in the gallery.

Sharpening, Edge Enhancing, or Blurring

Many photos need sharpening — well, many of mine do, anyway. Not many *need* blurring. Blurring is more of an artistic effect (like those I cover in Chapter 9) than it is a photo enhancing effect but, as it's conceptually the opposite of sharpening, I discuss it here.

You can apply any of these effects repeatedly to increase their effect. Too much sharpening, however, can turn your image into a messy field of high-contrast dots. Too much blurring can turn it into a smeary mess.

Sharpening

Paint Shop Pro offers three sharpening effects. Choose Effects⇨Sharpen and then choose one of the following in the menu that appears:

✔ **Sharpen:** Does a little bit of metaphorical grinding and filing on the various edges of your photo, boosting the contrast at those edges. No dialog box appears, your image simply gets sharper.

✔ **Sharpen More:** The same as Sharpen, but more so.

✔ **Unsharp Mask:** Sharpens like its two siblings (Sharpen and Sharpen More), but operates incognito, like the Lone Ranger. No, just kidding. It wears, not a mask, but an adjustment dialog box. To use this box's controls, see Chapter 3 where I discuss unsharp mask when setting contrast and other adjustments in scanning software.

Technically, if your picture is taken out of focus, none of these effects can actually make it sharp. These effects can, however, give the illusion of doing so in some cases. The detail it restores is fake — but a good fake.

Edge Enhancing

Paint Shop Pro's Enhance edge effect is a close cousin to its sharpening effect. Both find adjoining pixels that contrast in lightness (an edge), and then make the contrast stronger by darkening or lightening those pixels. The pixels gradually move towards fully saturated primary colors, plus white and black.

Choose Effects⇨Edge⇨Enhance or its more powerful sibling, Enhance More. Neither uses an adjustment box, but just immediately does its thing.

How do sharpening and edge enhancing compare? The edge Enhance effect is more dramatic, focusing directly on even the tiniest edge. The sharpening effect makes a subtler change that influences a range of pixels around the edge.

Blurring

Blurring effects, although many and varied, are simple to use. Choose Effects➪Blur to access the following menu items:

- **Average:** Pops up an adjustment dialog box with a single control, Amount of Correction. Drag right for more blur.

- **Blur:** Applies a moderate amount of blurring. No adjustment dialog box appears.

- **Blur More:** Like Blur, only more so.

- **Gaussian Blur:** Pops up a single-control adjustment dialog box. Drag the Radius control to the right for more blurring. To the trained eye of the blur *aficionado,* this blur is a bit more refined than Average blur. To the rest of us, it's just a blur.

- **Motion Blur:** This is an artistic effect most people can understand, having tried to take a photo of a fast-moving child, car, or animal and ended up with a motion blur. This effect, using an adjustment dialog box, *produces* a motion blur! Drag the clock-hand-like Direction control in that box to point in the direction you want motion. Then set the Intensity slider, moving it to the right if you need more blur. See the following Tip.

- **Soften:** The distinction between blurring and softening is way too subtle to ponder. This effect uses no dialog box; it just, well, blurs in a particularly soft way. Try it, you'll like it.

- **Soften More:** Like Soften, only softer. Mr. Whipple, call your office.

Blur is often most effective when applied selectively, to a particular area of your image. Select an area with any of the selection tools that I discuss in Chapter 13 and then apply the blur effect. Blur applied selectively can help focus attention on the subject of your photo, and away from a confusing background. Photographically, that result is often achieved by using a narrow depth of field (due to a wide lens opening). You can simulate that effect by de-selecting all subject material that is within a certain distance from the camera, and applying blur to the remaining, selected area.

The Motion Blur effect is sometimes best applied to the background area *around* the object you want to appear speedy, so the object of interest is not blurred. It's a great way, for instance, to make Speedy, your lethargic Retriever, appear to live up to his name. Take a photo of Speedy in his fastest pose — say moseying towards his dinner bowl. In Paint Shop Pro, select the area around Speedy before choosing the Motion Blur effect. (Perhaps select Speedy first with the Magic Wand tool, as he is uniformly black and easily selected, and then invert the selection.) Apply the motion blur in the head-to-tail direction. Your photo looks like your camera tracked Speedy as he sped heroically to save his Gravy Train from a watery demise. Figure 8-7 shows this effect applied to Alex.

Figure 8-7:
Speedy
Alex. On the
right, by
motion-
blurring the
background,
I get a
camera-
tracking
effect. The
slight fringe
around Alex
comes from
feathering
the
selection.

Removing Noise (Speckles)

Removing noise from an image sounds a bit illogical, like subtracting apples from oranges, or removing odor from a TV program. Well, okay, you can perhaps imagine ways to do the latter, but apply that same imagination to how your TV looks when you run a vacuum cleaner: the screen is covered with speckles. That's *graphical noise:* pixels altered at random locations and in random colors.

The trick with removing speckles is to avoid removing freckles — and other speckly stuff that's supposed to be in the picture. (Unless, of course, you *want* to get rid of the freckles!) For that reason, Paint Shop Pro offers several choices, depending on what you need. Choose Effects➪Noise and then one of the following menu selections:

✔ **Despeckle:** Removes smaller, isolated speckles altogether. Good for removing a light coating of dust. Speckles that are closer to each other tend to form clumps, however.

✔ **Edge-Preserving Smooth:** Gives an effect like rubbing carefully within the shaded areas of a pastel drawing, using your finger. Speckles disappear into a uniform shade, and you keep the sharp edges of those larger areas. This effect is also good for removing the random discoloration of pixels that often results from shooting digital photos in low light. In the adjustment dialog box that appears, drag the Number of Steps slider to the right to make a smoother image.

Edge-Preserving Smooth, turned up high, creates a very nice oil-painting-like effect on photos! See Figure C-11 in the color insert of this book.

✔ **Median Cut:** Removes speckles by removing fine detail, a kind of blurring process in which each pixel is recalculated to be the average of its neighbors. Contrast is lost at the detail level.

✔ **Median Filter:** Removes detail as Median Cut does except that you can choose the fineness (size) of the detail you remove. You can also affect quite large details. An adjustment dialog box appears in which you drag the Amount of Correction slider to the right to remove increasingly large detail.

✔ **Salt-And-Pepper Filter:** Removes speckles of a particular size (or up to a particular size) that you choose. A Salt-And-Pepper Filter adjustment dialog box appears, with the following adjustments:

  • **Speck Size:** Adjust this value to match or slightly exceed the size of the speckles you're trying to get rid of. (You may have to zoom in close to figure out how big your speckles are.)

  • **Sensitivity to Specks:** If the right preview window shows clusters of specks remaining, increase this value. Too high a value blurs your photo.

  • **Include All Lower Speck Sizes:** Enable this check box to remove specks of Speck Size and smaller. Otherwise, you just remove specks close to Speck Size.

  • **Aggressive Action:** Enable this check box to remove specks more completely. Otherwise, you may simply reduce the specks' intensity.

✔ **Texture-Preserving Smooth:** This effect sounds like a sophisticated grade of peanut butter. Actually, it blurs and reduces the constrast of tiny specks while preserving the larger variations that give texture to grass, wood, water, and the like. The result is sort of like a crunchy peanut butter without small, gritty chunks. An adjustment dialog box appears in which you adjust the Amount of Correction value upward to minimize specks.

You can always select an area using Paint Shop Pro's selection tools, in order to apply noise-removal effects only to that specific area. See Chapter 13.

Chapter 9

Creating Artsy Effects

• •

In This Chapter

▶ Browsing through effects

▶ Simulating physical art media

▶ Creating 3D objects

▶ Performing geometric distortions

▶ Adding glints, lens flare, and spotlights

▶ Reflecting images into patterns

▶ Creating textures, weaves, and mosaics

• •

*P*aint Shop Pro has enough wild and crazy effects to satisfy the most *avante-garde artistes* (psycho art geeks). The Effects menu in Paint Shop Pro 7 hides over 70 different effects that you can consider creative. Jasc undoubtedly has even more coming down the pipeline. These gadgets are great fun and incredible time-savers when you need a striking effect in a hurry.

The color section of this book shows a gallery of 72 different, in-your-face effects and the various ways that they improve my eminently-improvable visage. I suppose, then, technically, they are in *my* face, but you get the idea. I call it the Gallery of Effected Ancestors.

Many of these effects use adjustment dialog boxes, which all have a set of common controls for zooming, previewing, proofing, and other functions. See Chapter 8 for help using these controls. I don't repeat those instructions here.

Paint Shop Pro categorizes its creative effects into the following six major categories:

- **3D:** For turning selected areas into raised buttons or cutouts, dropping shadows, or doing anything else that looks like it's raised above or dropped below the page.

- **Artistic:** For simulating physical art media, like pencil, colored chalk, and paint brushing, plus a few non-traditional media like chrome and neon.

✔ **Geometric:** For bending and distorting the image or a selected part of it, such as bending a corner up or wrapping around a cylinder.

✔ **Illumination:** For introducing a sunburst or lens flare effect, or placing one or more spotlights on parts of the image.

✔ **Reflection:** For creating mirrored images or patterns, including kaleido-scope and other patterns that arise from multiple reflections.

✔ **Texture:** For giving your image the effect of being laid upon different surfaces, like crinkled paper or leather, or seen through mosaic glass.

Effects, like most other features of Paint Shop Pro, work on whatever layer of a multi-layer image is currently active — and, if you have an area selected, only within that selection. This restriction is designed to let you modify just the portion of the image you want, but it can also be confusing if you forget that you have made a selection or changed layers: your effect may not appear to work. If your image has multiple layers, choose the layer you want before applying an effect. Effects don't work on Vector or Adjustment layers. If you use an Adjustment layer, you must merge it with your image if you want your effect to act upon that adjustment. See Chapter 15 for more about layers. If you haven't created any layers, or added text, lines, or shapes to your image, don't sweat the layer thing.

Effects don't work on 256-color images. If your image has 256 or fewer colors, press Ctrl+Shift+0 to increase the image's color depth to the 24-bit (16.7 million color) level.

If you use Paint Shop Pro's effects often, the Effects Toolbar speeds things up. With that toolbar enabled, you can simply click a button for an effect rather than use the menu commands. To enable the toolbar, choose View⇨Toolbars, select the Effects Toolbar check box in the Toolbars dialog box that appears, and then click the Close button. Only a few effects appear on the toolbar at first, but you can add more by following the instructions for customizing toolbars in Chapter 1.

Try 'em On: Browsing the Effects

An easy way to try an effect on your image is to use the *Effect browser.* Choose Effects⇨Effect Browser. The Effect Browser dialog box appears, as shown in Figure 9-1.

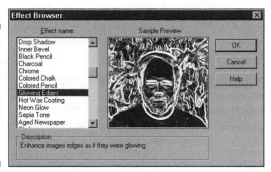

Figure 9-1:
Browsing
gives you
a rough
idea of an
effect's
influence on
your image.

Choose an effect on the left side. The preview window on the right side gives you a rough idea of what the effect does to your image. The preview can give you only a rough impression because many effects vary depending upon how you adjust them. Figure 9-1 shows the spooky, Glowing Edges effect.

If you have a selected area, or if the currently active layer contains only one filled-in area, that area fills the preview window. Remember that effects apply only to the currently active layer.

If you find an effect you think you may like, click the OK button. Some effects use adjustment dialog boxes, in which case that's the next thing you see. (See Chapter 8 for help with adjustment box controls.) Other effects just go right to work and do their thing. If it's the wrong thing, press Ctrl+Z or click the Undo button on the Toolbar.

3D: Holes, Buttons, and Chisels

Except for the Buttonize effect, you must select an area before you apply any of the 3D effects. The area you select is what is turned into a button, chiseled, cut out, or beveled inside or outside the selection marquee. Also, if you intend to use background color for the Buttonize or Chisel effect, choose it now.

Choose Effects⇨3D Effects. Then, choose one of the following from the menu that appears:

✔ **Buttonize:** Creates a raised appearance (inside your selection if you've made a selection). In the Buttonize dialog box, increase Height to make top and bottom edges wider. Increase Width to do likewise for left and right edges. Increase Opacity to darken the edges. Choose Transparent Edge to see through the edge, see margin button; otherwise, choose Solid Edge.

✔ **Chisel:** Creates a raised appearance by making an edge *outside* your selection. In the Chisel dialog box that appears, increase the edge width by increasing the Size value. Choose Transparent Edge to see through the edge, or Background Color otherwise.

✔ **Cutout:** Creates the illusion of a cutting out your selected area and extending a shadow in two directions. In the Cutout dialog box that appears, drag the Vertical and Horizontal sliders left or right to extend the shadow from different edges. Increase Opacity to darken the shadow, or increase Blur to blur the shadow's edge. You can change the color of the shadow or the underlying surface by clicking the Shadow Color swatch or the Fill Interior With Color swatch, respectively. Then choose a color from the Color dialog box that appears.

✔ **Drop Shadow:** Drops a shadow in any direction from your selected area, as if that area were floating over a surface. In the Drop Shadow dialog box that appears, drag Vertical and Horizontal sliders to change the shadow location. Increase Opacity for a darker shadow and increase Blur to blur the shadow's edge more. Click the Color swatch if you want to choose a shadow color from the Color dialog box.

✔ **Inner Bevel or Outer Bevel:** Creates an effect like raising a pyramid. The pyramid's sloping sides (the bevel) appear within your selection area for Inner Bevel or outside them for Outer Bevel. A rather complex-looking dialog box appears. Click the Bevel illustration to choose a bevel profile from a gallery. (Each profile is like the cross-sections you see of wood moldings in a hardware store.) To learn what other controls do, either fiddle with them or see the section "Common Adjustments," later in this chapter.

Artistic and Other Effects: Simulating Traditional Media

Paint Shop Pro offers way too many artistic effects for me to discuss them individually here. See the Gallery of Effected Ancestors in the color section of this book for an illustration of what each effect does, by name. I show you a couple of examples in this section.

Choose Effects➪Artistic Effects and Paint Shop Pro reveals a large menu of possibilities. Choose one from the list.

Nearly all these effects display an adjustment dialog box (see Chapter 8 for an explanation of the basic controls). See the section "Common Adjustments," later in this chapter, for help regarding more specialized controls. For the most part, your best approach is to fiddle with the controls for a while. A few effects take place immediately. If you don't like the result, press Ctrl+Z to undo it.

TIP

Not all the effects capable of making artistic results are neatly categorized in the Artistic Effects menu selection! For instance, I find that applying the Edge Preserving Smooth effect, found under Effects⇨Noise, creates a wonderful painted result. (Use a high value for Steps in that dialog box.)

A few more general tips for using artistic effects are as follows:

✔ If the result is too fuzzy, try decreasing various values, especially density if that adjustment exists. Most effects do some blurring, so if you turn it down a bit (decrease the effect), the image becomes clearer.

✔ If the result is too speckly or has too many lines, look for a detail adjustment and if you find one, turn it down.

✔ Some effects that do stuff with edges need a little help. Try running the Edge Enhance effect (choose Effects⇨Edge⇨Enhance) or boosting contrast before applying your artistic effect. Or, in the adjustment box for your edge-fiddling effect, look for an intensity control and increase it.

Example 1: Topography

Topography is, for no particularly good reason, one of my favorite artistic effects. Its result is an image that looks like stacked, cut sheets of cardboard or foamboard (like the ones that architects use in models to simulate sloping ground). Figure 9-2 shows the creation of Sir Topography in my Gallery of Effected Ancestors.

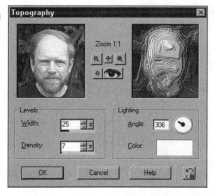

Figure 9-2: The Topography adjustments control the number of levels and the way the light strikes the stack.

The controls do the following:

✔ **Width:** At low Width settings, contours follow the details of the picture more closely. At high Width settings, contours are broad and without sharp turns; detail is lost.

✔ **Density:** Density controls the number of layers in the virtual stack of layers. A higher density results in a surface that conforms more to the original detail. A lower density gives a more abstract result.

✔ **Angle:** The Angle control in the Lighting section determines the direction that light is coming from to illuminate the side of the stack. Drag its clock-hand-like control to point in the direction you want this light to shine.

✔ **Color:** Color determines the color of light that strikes the stack from the side. Originally, the Color control is set to white. To change it, you may either left-click on the swatch (to choose from the Color Wheel), or right-click (to choose a basic or recently used color from the Recent Colors dialog box).

Example 2: Brush strokes

The Brush Strokes effect has lots of things to fiddle with, and you probably have to spend some time fiddling to get a result you like. It gives the appearance of applying thin or thick paint with a brush. In real life, the edges of paint strokes catch any incident light, and in this effect, you can simulate that appearance in varying degrees. Figure 9-3 shows a photograph of a cardinal in a bush, getting stroked.

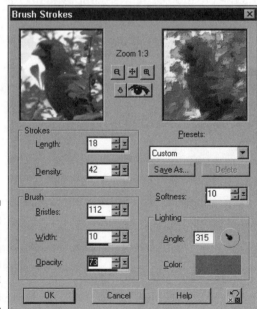

Figure 9-3:
Brush strokes, one of the more complex effects.

The Brush Strokes controls work as follows:

- **Length:** Short lengths (low values of Length) create a stippled effect, like someone poking the end of a brush into the canvas. Longer lengths produce visible stroke directions.

- **Density:** Density determines the number of strokes. The greatest sensitivity of this control is at the very low end. A very low density (1 or 2) gives the appearance of a few strokes made over a photograph. Higher density makes a more abstract effect of many overlaid strokes.

- **Bristles:** A higher value of Bristles gives the distinct patch of paint that a nice, new, neatly trimmed brush, packed densely with bristles, lays down. A lower value simulates the scratchy result of a brush where the bristles are few or frazzled.

- **Width:** The Width control determines the width of the brush stroke. A higher value makes a wider brush.

- **Opacity:** The Opacity control sets the density of the paint. A low value gives a blurred effect that is more like looking through frosted glass than anything else. A high value makes paint look like it was applied thickly, as if with a palette knife.

- **Softness:** The Softness control gives a smoother look to the paint surface, with less speckling.

- **Angle:** The Angle control determines the direction of the incident light that glints off the edges of thick paint strokes. Drag the clock-hand-like control to point *towards the source* of the light.

- **Color:** To change the color of incident light striking the paint edges, click the Color swatch and choose from the Color dialog box. (Or right-click to choose from the Recent Colors dialog box.) Black gives no incident light, a dark color (low lightness value) gives a little, and so on. High lightness values strongly emphasize the stroke edges.

Like many effects, if you return to this adjustment dialog box later, it normally resumes whatever settings you last used. This intelligent behavior saves you lots of time returning to settings that you like.

If you use this effect a lot, you may want to save any given combination of settings for later use. To do so, click the Save As button, enter a name for your settings in the Preset Save dialog box that appears, and click OK. Then, in the future, click the Presets selection box to choose your stored settings by name. Select Last Used in that box to tell the effect to resume your last used settings.

Geometric Effects: Curls, Squeezes, and Waves

The Geometric effects in Paint Shop Pro have enough curls, squeezes, and waves to outfit an entire army of cute toddlers. If you want anything bent, distorted, or wrapped, this is the place to go.

Choose Effects➪Geometric Effects, and then choose from the large list that appears. As with the Artistic effects, Paint Shop Pro has too many Geometric effects for me to try to cover completely. Fortunately, most of the controls are either self-evident or do something you can easily figure out by playing with them. I give you a couple of examples, though.

Here are a few tips for using Geometric effects:

- ✔ Some effects are centered on a particular location. To move the center, adjust the Horizontal and Vertical controls. A setting of zero centers the effect horizontally or vertically. Negative Horizontal values are to the left of center; negative Vertical values are *above* center.

- ✔ The Circle and Pentagon effects are immediate. No adjustment dialog box appears.

- ✔ Remember that you can apply any effect to a particular area by selecting that area first. Using a feathered edge on the selection feathers the modified image into the original image.

Need a thinner face? If you have a portrait on a plain background, Paint Shop Pro can help. First, carefully select the face. Then, equally carefully remove areas around the eyes, nose, and mouth from the selection. (See Chapter 13 for help on removing areas from a selection.) Apply the Pinch effect in the Geometric effects menu.

Example 1: Page curl

The Page Curl effect is, for some reason, one of the most enduringly popular geometric effects. It seems that we never tire of remarking, "Why, Martha, that photo looks like it's a-peelin' right off the page!" I guess the Page Curl effect is just plain a-peelin'. Figure 9-4 shows this remarkable effect.

Drag end points of line

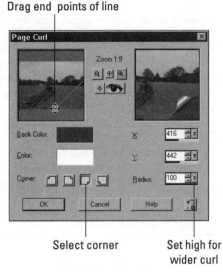

Figure 9-4:
Choose a
corner,
move the
curl line in
the left
window,
and set the
radius to get
a quick curl.

Select corner   Set high for
wider curl

Here's how to control your curl, with the most important stuff listed first:

✔ **Corner:** Which corner do you want to curl? Click the button depicting your chosen corner.

✔ **Curl line, or X and Y:** To set the position of the curl, drag either end of the white line that diagonally crosses the left preview window. As Figure 9-4 shows, your cursor becomes a four-headed arrow when it's over the line's end. Alternatively, you can adjust the X or Y values to move those points; watch the line as you do so, and see how the X and Y values affect it.

✔ **Radius:** How broad do you want curl to be? The smaller the Radius value, the tighter the corner is rolled up. The smaller the corner that you're curling (that is, the lower the X and Y values), the smaller the Radius value usually needs to be.

✔ **Back Color:** The color that appears on the flat page revealed by the lifted corner. Click to choose a different color from the Color dialog box, or right-click to choose from the Recent Colors dialog box.

✔ **Color:** The color that appears on the highlight of the curl (the underside of the curled picture). Paint Shop Pro makes the rest of the curl, the shaded part, the same hue, but darker.

Bear in mind that besides curling the edge of the entire image, you can select a rectangle — say, a stamp on an envelope — and curl that. (Other selection shapes don't usually work as well.)

Instant pond

Need a pond in your photo? Assuming your photo is on the main (background) layer, follow these steps blindly and exactly: Press Ctrl+1, Ctrl+D, Ctrl+C, Ctrl+L, then Ctrl+1, Ctrl+I (that's the letter i), and Ctrl+2. (You just copied your image to a second layer, inverted the original Background layer, and made the second layer active.)

Click the Eraser tool in the Tool palette and brush it across your image to create the pond. (You're creating a hole in the second layer.) Press Ctrl+1 (to switch to the Background layer), and then apply the Wave effect as I describe in the section "Example 2: Wave."

Example 2: Wave

The Wave effect is great for simulating reflections in bodies of water, although I'm sure you can think of other, more creative uses. It makes waves in your image (or a selected area of it).

Waves can go either horizontally (side-to-side — what you see looking out at the ocean) or vertically (up and down — what you see trailing behind a boat). Waves can also go both ways at once (what you may see as you row across ocean waves). Figure 9-5, in which I'm simulating the reflection of a tree in water, shows mainly horizontal waves.

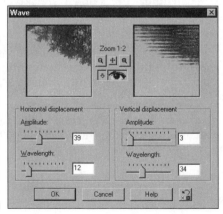

Figure 9-5: Making waves, in this case mostly horizontal ones, to create a realistic reflection.

The Wave adjustment box has two identical sets of controls: the Horizontal Displacement controls and the Vertical Displacement controls. Each has the following adjustments:

✔ **Amplitude:** Increase this value to get a stronger wave effect. In Figure 9-5, the horizontal amplitude is mid-range, at 39. The vertical amplitude is very low (3) because I don't want much vertical effect.

✔ **Wavelength:** Increase this value to spread the waves out more. In Figure 9-5, the horizontal wavelength is low to make tight ripples. The vertical wavelenth doesn't matter much because the vertical amplitude is set so low. A slow, low-amplitude vertical wiggle makes the horizontal ripples more realistic.

Illumination Effects: Sunbursts, Flare, and Spotlights

Paint Shop Pro sports two brilliant Illumination effects: Sunburst and Lighting. *Sunburst* gives the effect you see when a photo is taken into the sun, complete with lens flare — those light circles that often appear. *Lighting* lets you illuminate portions of your image with spotlights.

Choose Effects⇨Illumination Effects, and then choose one of the following effects (Sunburst or Lights). Paint Shop Pro has few illumination effects as of this writing, but they're neat.

Sunburst

If you need a sparkle of sunlight, unwrap Paint Shop Pro's Sunburst effect. It places a bright spot on your image, with rays of light and circles of lens flare. The adjustment dialog box appears, shown in Figure 9-6, on top of the image that it's modifying, to better show the effects.

The controls for the three different components each have their own area: Light Spot, Rays, and the Circle Brightness control. All share the same color setting. Here's how to use these adjustments:

✔ **Color:** Click the Color sample to choose some color other than white from the Color dialog box.

✔ Light Spot **Brightness:** Increase to brighten the light spot.

✔ Light Spot **Horizontal/Vertical:** Adjust to position the spot. Or, if you can see a tiny set of crosshairs on the left preview window, drag that instead. When your cursor is over the crosshairs, the cursor becomes a four-headed arrow.

✔ Rays **Brightness:** Set this higher to bring out the rays of light you can see in Figure 9-6.

✔ Rays **Density:** Adjust this lower to see fewer rays or higher to see more rays.

✔ Circle **Brightness:** Set this higher to make the lens flare circles brighter. On light photos, these circles are barely visible even at full brightness.

As with many effects, you can save these settings by clicking the Save As button and entering a name for the settings in the Preset Save dialog box that appears. To use them later, click that name in the Presets list box.

Figure 9-6:
A sunburst over the farm brings life-giving rays and artsy lens flare circles.

Lights

The Lights effect provides multiple spotlights for you to illuminate your image. It isn't quite the same as having a spotlight on your subject when you take a picture. It's more like shining a spotlight on a photograph. The spot doesn't conform to the shapes in the image, or cast shadows, but just lies flat. You can, however, select areas of your image to be struck by the spotlight, like the top of a cube, leaving other sides or other areas in shadow, or apply a mask that allows light to hit areas with varying strength (see Chapter 17).

The adjustment dialog box for this effect is a doozy. Here's how to bring it under control:

- **Changing overall brightness:** The Lights effect darkens your image, for contrast with the lighted areas. For an overall lighter picture, reduce the Darkness value.

- **Choosing a spotlight:** Click the button for the spotlight you want (1, 2, 3, and so on) to adjust. Spotlights shine down on the center of your image from four corners, starting at the top left corner with Spotlight #1, and proceeding clockwise. Spotlight #5 aims into the image, as if from over your shoulder. Each spotlight is also represented as a dot in the left preview image, which you can click to select. All the other controls now relate to your chosen spotlight.

- **Turning lights off:** All lights are initially on. To disable a light, choose it and then clear the On check box.

- **Adjusting the spot:** When you choose a spotlight, a shape (apparently an arrow) appears in the left preview window. Its *head* points toward the *origin* of a cone of light; its *tail* (a + in a circle) indicates the *direction* the light is shining — opposite to the direction you may expect a lighting arrow to point. This arrow is, however, actually a three-pronged control for your currently chosen spotlight.

  - **Elongation:** Drag the end of the tail away from or closer to the head to make the spot more or less elongated. If the tail's end is off-screen (and therefore inaccessible), change the Asymmetry value to adjust enlongation.

  - **Direction:** Drag the end of the tail around the arrow's head to point the spot a different way. If you can't reach the end of the tail, drag the clock-hand-like Direction control instead.

  - **Width:** Drag the tips of the arrowhead away from the arrow shaft to make the spot wider.

  - **Overall size:** Increase the Scale value for a larger spot.

  - **Position:** Drag the tip of the arrow to a new position. If you can't see the tip, adjust the Horizontal and Vertical values to alter position. The tip marks where the center of the light cone is if Asymmetry (elongation) is set to 1.

  - **Intensity:** Increase the Intensity value for a brighter spot.

  - **Color:** Click the Color swatch to choose a light color from the Color dialog box. Don't forget to click in the Saturation/Lightness box to set Saturation to something other than zero (the default).

  - **Sharpness:** Increase the Smoothness value for a more diffuse (fuzzier) spot.

To turn a spotlight off altogether, set its Intensity value to zero.

Reflection Effects: Mirrors and Patterns

The Reflection effects are a funhouse phenomenon. You can choose a single mirror, or multiple mirrors in various configurations, turning your image into a pattern. Choose Effects⇨Reflection Effects, and then one of the four menu items that appear:

✔ **Feedback:** The mirror-reflecting-into-mirror effect you get in barbershops with mirrors on opposite walls. See "Common Adjustments," later in this chapter, for help with this effect's controls.

✔ **Kaleidoscope:** A humdinger of an effect, like looking at your image through a kaleidoscope. See the following section.

✔ **Pattern**: Another way, besides Kaleidoscope, to turn your image into a pattern. See the upcoming two sections.

✔ **Rotating Mirror**: Like putting a mirror edge-down onto your image. You can rotate a reflection to any angle and position the mirror horizontally and vertically on the image.

You can limit any of these effects to a particular area by making a selection first.

Kaleidoscope

The Kaleidoscope pattern maker has an amazing number of settings for such an apparently simple concept. Actual kaleidoscope images, however, *do* depend on many variables. Here's how to control your variables:

✔ **Moving the center:** To point your virtual kaleidoscope at a particular portion of the image, adjust the Horizontal Offset and Vertical Offset controls. At zero, they point to the center of your image. Negative horizontal values move the center to the left; negative vertical values move the center up.

✔ **Rotation Angle:** Just as with a phyiscal kaleidoscope, rotating the mirror set changes the pattern. Drag the clock-hand-like Rotation Angle control to rotate the mirror.

✔ **Zooming in/out:** Adjusting the Scale Factor control is like zooming in (larger Scale Factors) or out (smaller ones) on your image.

- ✔ **Number of Petals:** How many mirrors would you like? Set this control accordingly.

- ✔ **Number of Orbits:** Kaleidoscopes can create concentric images if they're long enough. Set this value for the number of concentric images you want.

- ✔ **Radial Suction:** You gotta love a control named Radial Suction. It defies description. Fiddle with it.

Pattern

Patterns are particularly useful in Paint Shop Pro because you can use them to fill areas. See Chapter 4 where I discuss choosing a pattern to paint with. With the Pattern effect, you can make your own patterns to paint with.

The Pattern adjustment dialog box sets the position, angle, and number of times your image is reflected. Fiddle with the following:

- ✔ **Center of reflection:** Adjust the Horizontal Offset and Vertical Offset to position the center of your mirror that makes the pattern.

- ✔ **Rotation angle:** Oddly, this control gives ½ of the rotation it's set to. Set it to 90, for instance, to reflect something at 45 degrees.

- ✔ **Pattern size:** Set Scale Factor above zero to make the pattern larger than the original, or below zero to make it smaller.

- ✔ **Number of repetitions:** The pattern is built of repeated rows and columns. Set Columns/Rows values to the number of columns and rows you want.

- ✔ **Horizontal/Vertical Shift:** Adjust these values to move the pattern within your image boundaries. For instance, to get a horizontally seamless pattern, pixels along the left edge should match those along the right. The Horizontal Shift control helps you do that.

To get a truly seamless pattern requires constant fiddling with two or three controls, especially Scale Factor and the two Shift controls. (Paint Shop Pro comes with some seamless patterns that you can use as models. See Chapter 4.)

Texture Effects: Bumpy Surfaces from Asphalt to Weaves

Texture is the neglected third dimension of an image. *Texture,* the surface on which the image is constructed, is a quality most of us don't think about when we think about images, but it's very much a part of the visual experience. An image made up of mosaic tiles, for instance, feels very different from the same image painted on canvas.

To choose a Texture effect, choose Effects⇨Texture Effects and then choose from the extensive menu that appears. Paint Shop Pro has too many textures to cover in detail, but the next few sections should help you sort things out. All effects but one (the Emboss effect) open an adjustment dialog box, in which you should feel free to fiddle while watching the effect.

Relating texture effects to the Color palette's textures

You may be a bit confused because Paint Shop Pro gives you two ways to use texture in your images. If you're painting an image, you can apply texture by using the Color palette. If you already have an image, the Texture effects are the way to go.

Texture effects, however, offer more variety than the Color palette does. For instance, you can't paint fur texture but you can apply it as an effect. The Jasc Department of Redundancy Department has also put all those same Color palette textures, like asphalt and plastic, into a Texture effect cleverly called *Texture*. In that effect's dialog box, you can achieve all kinds of variations using the Color palette's textures that you can't achieve in the Color palette itself.

Just as the Texture effect gives you more leverage over the Color palette's textures, the Sculpture effect lets you leverage the Color palette's *patterns*. The effect's main job is to turn your image into a sort of etching or embossing, but it also applies patterns. Patterns are sort of like textures, but come with their own colors. The Sculpture effect applies a Paint Shop Pro pattern, allowing you to set a number of variables that are unavailable in the Color palette. In the Sculpture effect, for instance, you can give a pattern a (uniform) color or change its size (scale).

Using texture effect controls

Texture adjustments have, in general, two main types of controls:

- Those for the virtual substance that puts ridges and valleys in the image
- Those for the light that strikes at some oblique angle and reveals that unevenness

In addition, the virtual substances that make up some textures have optical qualities that you can adjust, like transparency and blurring.

If a texture or pattern is unclear at some settings, try zooming out in the adjustment dialog box. (Click the magnifier-with-minus-sign button.)

The best way to understand most of the texture controls is to fiddle with them while watching the right preview window in the adjustment dialog box. (Only the Emboss effect goes to work immediately, without displaying a dialog box.) Some of the more common controls you find in the adjustment dialog boxes are:

- **Length** (and occasionally **Width**), or **Size:** The dimensions of the ridges and valleys that make up the texture.
- **Blur:** The overall fuzziness imparted to the original image.
- **Detail:** How much detail the lines of texture inherit from the edges of the original image.
- **Density:** The degree to which ridges and valleys are packed closely together.
- **Transparency:** The ability to let the original image show clearly through the virtual substance that overlays the image.
- **Angle:** The direction from which incident light strikes the surface.
- **Elevation:** The height of the light source above the image. Low elevations show the ridges and valleys more strongly. High elevations make a brighter image. Some textures allow you to set the **Intensity** or **Luminance** and **Color** of the incident light as well.
- **Ambience:** The overall brightness (ambient light) of the image.

Example 1: The fur texture effect

A simple texture effect is Fur, disturbingly applied to a bird in Figure 9-7. The Fur effect causes fibers to radiate from clusters throughout your image, giving a result not unlike the fur of a cat engaged in discussion with a member of the canine profession.

You'll go fur with this effect if you interpret your controls in the following ways:

- **Blur:** A kind of fluffiness control. Increasing Blur minimizes the visibility of individual hairs and also makes the original image less clear.
- **Density:** Determines the number of hairs; very low settings give a cactus-like whiskered appearance.
- **Length:** Sets the length of individual hairs. High length values tend to give more of a frosted-glass appearance than a furry one.

✔ **Transparency:** Determines the extent to which the original image shows through the hair, undisturbed. High transparency values give an effect like hair sprinkled on a photograph.

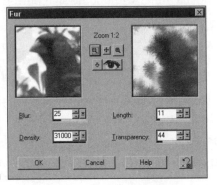

Figure 9-7:
A cardinal
with fur,
perhaps the
inspiration
for Big Bird.

Example 2: The texture texture effect

The Texture effect in the Effects⇨Texture menu gives you access to the same textures that you may use for painting with Paint Shop Pro's Color palette. Here, instead of painting with them, you apply them to an existing image. Figure 9-8 shows the same cardinal as Figure 9-7, this time more appropriately receiving a tree-bark texture.

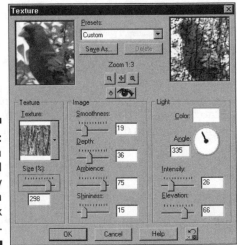

Figure 9-8:
Making a
cardinal
bark by
applying a
tree-bark
texture.

The controls of this dialog box provide enough fiddles to outfit a symphony orchestra. Here's how to make them play in tune:

- ✓ **Texture:** Click here and choose a texture from Paint Shop Pro's gallery of textures that appears.

- ✓ **Size (%):** Make the texture pattern larger by increasing this value above zero. Drag left (make the value negative) for a smaller pattern.

- ✓ **Smoothness:** To blunt the sharp edges of your texture, increase this value.

- ✓ **Depth:** To have deeper valleys and higher hills in your pattern, increase this value.

- ✓ **Ambience:** Adjust this control for a brighter or darker image.

- ✓ **Shininess:** A higher value of shininess puts a bright glint on the edges and corners of your texture pattern.

- ✓ **Color:** Click this swatch to choose a different color of incident light from the Colors dialog box.

- ✓ **Angle:** Drag the clock-hand-like control to point towards the imaginary light source that illuminates the texture.

- ✓ **Intensity:** Higher intensity increases the incident light that reveals the contrast.

- ✓ **Elevation:** Lower values emphasize the hills and valleys; higher values brighten the flat hilltops and valley bottoms. (Reduce ambience to avoid washout at high elevations.)

Common Adjustments

Effects use a wide range of adjustments to set their various variables. In most cases, the function of a control becomes apparent as soon as you fiddle with it, but in very complex dialog boxes you need to understand what does what. Following are descriptions to help you distinguish one variable from another.

- ✓ **Ambience:** General illumination. Determines the image brightness with the incident light source's intensity and elevation.

- ✓ **Amplitude:** Degree to which the effect is applied.

- ✓ **Angle:** Direction of incident light in the plane of the image. Drag the clock-hand-like control to point toward the source.

- ✓ **Blur:** A fuzziness that affects mostly the original image showing through the texture. Makes the texture fuzzier in some textures.

- ✓ **Color:** A swatch showing the color of light that glints off the texture's hills and valleys. Click the swatch to choose a new color from the Color dialog box. If you want something other than gray, increase Saturation in the square Saturation/Lightness area. Right-click the swatch to choose from the Recent Colors dialog box.

✔ **Density:** The closeness and number of hills and valleys in the texture.

✔ **Detail:** Degree to which the texture picks out the detail in the original image.

✔ **%Effect:** Degree to which the effect is applied.

✔ **Elevation:** Height of the incident light above the plane of the image. Low elevations show the ridges and valleys more strongly. High elevations make a brighter image.

✔ **Height:** Height of the hills in the texture.

✔ **Horizontal/Vertical Center:** Position of the center of the effect.

✔ **Horizontal/Vertical Offset:** Position of the overall resulting pattern.

✔ **Intensity:** Strength of the incident light that reveals the texture.

✔ **Length:** The length of the ridges and valleys that make up the texture.

✔ **Opacity:** The degree to which the blobs of virtual substance pick up color from the underlying image, as opposed to letting the image's original pixels show through.

✔ **Presets:** This drop-down list lets you choose among any named collection of settings you've saved or your Last Used settings. After you change any setting, the Presets selection says Custom.

✔ **Radius:** The broadness of any curve or curl; smaller radius values make curves or curls tighter.

✔ **Save As:** A button leading to the Preset Save dialog box, in which you enter a name to label your current collection of settings. Choose the name from the Presets list box to recall the setting.

✔ **Shininess:** The glare off the sloping sides of the hills and valleys of the texture.

✔ **Size:** The overall size of the elements of the texture.

✔ **Smoothness:** How rounded the bumps are that make up the texture.

✔ **Symmetric:** A check box that makes an effect work the same way in all directions.

✔ **Transparent/Background color:** Options that either make an edge reveal the underlying image color (Transparent) or color the edge with the current Paint Shop Pro background color.

Chapter 10

Adjusting Color by Bits

• •

• •

*F*or basic painting and image processing, you rarely need to give a hoot about how the computer handles colors. Sometimes, however, understanding a little bit about the bits behind computer color makes your life much easier and your results better. You likely need to know about the bits when:

✔ Someone gives you, or you have to create, an image file that is not *full color*.

✔ You want to adjust a color in a very precise way.

✔ You want to use a Paint Shop Pro tool that refers to Red, Green, Blue, or Hue, Saturation, and Lightness, or other technical color terms.

Fortunately, the challenge isn't so much understanding the computer as it's understanding the *illusion* of color that humans have been using for about a hundred years to print or display color images. The computer is just the latest step in creating that illusion.

Mastering the Color Illusion

When you look at color in the real world, you're seeing the real thing: the full spectrum of color from red sunsets to purple mountains, plus all the colors of fire engines, new Volkswagen Beetles, and the grassy and flowering plains in between. When you look at *mechanized* color images, however, from printed pictures to TV and computer screens, the colors that you see are almost always an illusion!

Understanding why the trick works

Although printed or displayed color images seem to be using a full range of colors, they really use a mix of just three (or, in print, four) colors. They can get away with this trick because your eyes have just three kinds of color sensors: one kind that is most sensitive to blue, another that is biased towards red, and a third that favors green. If truly yellow light from the real world strikes your eye, it has an energy partway between red and green, so it tickles both the red and the green sensors by certain amounts. Your brain says, "Aha! Red and green: must be yellow!"

PC and TV screens use this trick to create the illusion of colors like yellow: each pixel on the screen is made up of a red, blue, and green glowing dot, the brightness of which is adjustable. The PC turns the blue way down, cranks up the red and green, and you see yellow because your red and green sensors are tickled equally. To get gray, all three colors are made equal; to make white, they're all at full strength; and to make black, they're all zero. But it's all an illusion. Your PC screen cannot actually make yellow, orange, magenta, or anything but pure red, green, or blue.

Applying the trick: Combining two primaries

Your PC screen uses those three so-called primary colors (red, green, and blue, or *RGB* to their friends) alone or in various combinations to make all colors. If you learn how these primary colors combine, you easily achieve any overall change in tint or hue you want. First, here's how they combine in pairs, assuming equal amounts of each:

- Red and blue combined make violet.
- Blue and green make cyan (turquoise).
- Green and red make yellow.

Table 10-1 shows these same pairings (the intersection of each row and column gives the result of pairing the row color and column color). Of course, many shades of color exist, too, not just, say, violet. You get these finer shades by adjusting just how much of each primary you use. A little more red than green and you get orange.

Table 10-1 Combining Pairs of Red, Green, and Blue Primary Colors

Primaries	Blue	Green
Red	Violet or (if more red) magenta	Yellow or (if more red) orange
Blue	—	Cyan (blue-green)

Adding the third color for pastels or grays

What if you add a third color? The result is more pastel, or gray. Equal amounts of all three colors, set to maximum, make white. If equal amounts of all three colors are set to less than maximum, you get gray; and, if set to zero, you get black.

If you add enough of the third color, it can become one of the two dominant colors and change the hue. For instance, if you add enough blue to orange (which is red and some green), the blue exceeds the green component and you get magenta.

In computers, you control how much of each primary color you have by adjusting numeric values. In Paint Shop Pro, these values run from zero to a maximum of 255.

In short, every color in Paint Shop Pro has three numeric values, one each for red, green, and blue. Together, those three numbers completely describe the color.

Fiddling with the three values

To make use of this inside information, start with the Color palette. Whenever you're choosing a color in the Available Colors area, the primary color values (labeled R, G, and B for Red, Green, and Blue) appear at the bottom of the Color palette. (In fact, RGB values for colors appear all over Paint Shop Pro.)

Now that you have this color's number, so to speak, you can fine-tune it by the numbers using the Color dialog box that I describe in Chapter 4. For instance:

  ✔ Need a more pastel shade? You need less of the highest value and more of the lower values.

  ✔ Need a purer color? Decrease the lowest of the three values.

  ✔ Need a darker or lighter shade? Decrease or increase all three values, keeping the same proportions of each. White is when all values are 255. Black is when all are zero.

✔ Need to move a color towards a given primary (make a greener yellow, for instance)? Increase that primary value (in this instance, green); decrease the next largest value proportionately to keep the lightness the same.

Using Hue, Saturation, and Lightness

Fiddling with the primary color values that create the color illusion is okay, but not very easy. You may find it tricky to keep proportions adjusted, for instance, when you want a lighter shade of a color without changing the basic color of it.

For that reason, very clever people came up with a *different* set of three numbers you can use to specify colors: Hue, Saturation, and Lightness (or Luminance), called *HSL*. These values aren't perfectly intuitive, either, but they're a lot closer to how people think about colors than are red, green, and blue. These three values aren't really primary *colors*, but rather a primary color *system*: a few numbers that fully describe a color.

You may find yourself using either system in Paint Shop Pro, depending upon what controls appear in various places. Some effects, for instance, use saturation or lightness. The Color dialog box that I describe further in Chapter 4 lets you use either system.

The Color palette can display color values in either system. Initially, it shows R, G, and B. To make it show H, S, and L, choose File⇨Preferences⇨General Program Preferences. In the Preferences dialog box that appears, click the Dialogs and Palettes tab and then to enable the option, select Display Colors in HSL Format. Click OK.

Here's what H, S, and L are all about:

✔ **Hue:** You can think of hue as the basic color. If you and your spouse both want a room painted blue for instance, or even turquoise, you agree on hue. You still have lots of room for disagreement, however, in terms of how pure (saturated) or light that color should be. To a rough approximation, hue is the balance or proportion of primary colors.

✔ **Saturation:** Saturation is the least intuitive value. It is the purity, intensity, or richness of a color, independent of its hue or lightness. The most easily understood aspect of saturation is that at zero saturation, any color is a shade of gray (has equal amounts of red, green, and blue). Technically, to a rough approximation, it is the degree to which one or two primary colors are maximized. If any primary color is at or near maximum, saturation is at or near maximum.

> ✔ **Lightness:** Lightness — essentially brightness — is fairly intuitive. Technically, it's the combined (but not simply summed) values of the three primaries. It is independent of hue or saturation, so it doesn't significantly affect the balance of primaries except at extremes of H, S, and L. Paint Shop Pro sometimes calls Lightness *Luminance*.

To better understand how HSL works and how it relates to RGB, see the Hue color wheel and the Saturation/Lightness box in the Color dialog box in Chapter 4.

Primary Color Channels

Some of Paint Shop Pro's more advanced controls discuss channels, which relate to primary colors. To use those controls properly, you need to know what channels are.

Because every pixel in your image is made up of red, green, and blue elements, imagine separating out three separate images: one that just shows the red component of every pixel, one for the blue component, and one for green. So, for instance, where blue sky appears, the red image would be dark and the blue one would be light. Where gray appears, all three would be equally dark.

The computer embodiment of these images is *channels,* one each for Red, Green, and Blue. And, if channels can exist for RGB primaries, you can imagine that channels can also exist for the HSL primary system: one image for hue, one for saturation, and another for lightness. Finally, the primary colors used for *printing,* as opposed to light emanating from a screen, are different: cyan, magenta, yellow, and black, or *CMYK* for short. As you may expect, you can split out each component, or channel, of *any* primary system separately.

In addition to some controls using channels, some printing tasks can also require you to print out channels as separate images, called *color separations.* See Chapter 18 for more about this subject.

If you want to work on a channel image separately, follow these steps to *split it out:*

1. **Choose Colors➪Channel Splitting.**

2. **Choose your primary system: Split to RGB, Split to HSL, or Split to CMYK.**

   You end up with each channel as a separate monochrome image in a separate window, each with a telltale name like Red1, Green1, and Blue1.

Do your work on that channel (for instance, you can lighten the sky area of the blue channel's image to make the sky more blue). Then, to recombine the channels:

1. **Choose <u>C</u>olors➪Channel Com<u>b</u>ining.**

   The Channel Combining dialog box appears.

2. **Make sure that you enter the correct image names (such as Red1, Green1, and Blue1) into the three channel source selection boxes.**

3. **Click OK.**

You have created a new image in a new window from the three channels.

Color Depth/Number of Colors

Because computers use numbers to represent colors, computer images have a unique phenomenon called *color depth,* or a limited maximum number of colors. For some image types, known as *true color* or *24-bit* images, that limit is very high, like 16.7 million colors. 24-bit is known as the image's *pixel depth.*

In true color images, the limit of 16.7 million colors comes from the 256 different possible values of red, green, and blue. 256 x 256 x 256 = 16,777,216 — a number that requires 24 computer bits to store, hence the term 24-bit.

For other image types, called *palette images,* the limit is much less. Imagine making an image by using a box of colored markers holding only, say, 64 markers. That limit is your image's *palette size.* You can use fewer than 64, or you can change the colors in your box, but your image can have 64 different colors at most. In Paint Shop Pro, no matter how small the palette, any given marker in that palette can be one of 16.7 million colors.

In palette images, the palette size is given either in number of colors or in terms of pixel depth, meaning how many bits the computer needs to count up to the palette size. It needs 1 bit to count to 2 colors, 2 bits for 4 colors, 3 for 8 colors, 4 for 16 colors, 5 for 32 colors, 6 for 64 colors, 7 for 128, and 8 for 256. An 8-bit image, for instance, is a 256-color image.

Most cameras and scanners give you 24-bit, true color images by default. True color images are those that don't have palettes, but rather can contain up to 16.7 million colors. On the Internet, however, you may find 256-color palette images, typically of the GIF type. Those files are mostly used for drawings, but sometimes for color photographs. Most color photographs carried on the Internet these days are true color images (in JPEG file format).

See Chapter 2 where I discuss various types of files and of files having different numbers of colors.

Checking your image's color depth

To check your image's color depth, press Shift+I or choose Image⊃Image Information. On the Image Information tab of the dialog box that appears, look on the left, center for Pixel Depth/Colors.

For all you computer geeks, that value before the slash gives your depth in bits and the value after the slash gives a normal human count of colors. A true color image, for instance, reads 24/16 Million.

Increasing color depth to use more tools

For the greatest choice in color and for access to the greatest number of tools, work with a true color image. Many of Paint Shop Pro's advanced tools don't work with palette images. (Their menu commands are grayed out.)

To increase color depth to 24-bit, or true color, choose Colors⊃Increase Color Depth⊃16 Million Colors, or press Ctrl+Shift+0 on your keyboard. After you've performed whatever tasks you need to do at this color level, you can restore the original number of colors, if necessary. See the following section.

Reducing color depth for speed, size, or special effects

Many good reasons exist for working with images that have fewer — rather than more — colors. Some of those reasons are:

- Images with fewer colors make smaller files, use less memory, and don't slow down Paint Shop Pro as much.
- Some image file types, such as GIF (popular on the Web), don't allow more than 256 colors.
- Identifying and matching a color that you've already used is easier when you use fewer colors in the image.
- You may want fewer colors to create a poster-like look, although that job is better done by using the Posterizing color adjustment that I discuss in Chapter 11. The image can then remain a true color image in which you actually use only a few different colors. You can reduce the actual color depth of the image after posterizing if you want to save file size.

To decrease the number of colors in an image, choose Colors⇨Decrease Color Depth. From the menu that drops down, choose the color depth you want: 2, 16, 256, 32K (32 thousand), 64K, or X Colors, where X is any number you choose.

The Decrease Color Depth dialog box appears, offering all kinds of technical-sounding options. Paint Shop Pro now has to decide exactly what colors are going to be in the palette of the new image — because you're forcing it to eliminate colors — and also decide what colors to give the pixels whose colors are discontinued. Here's how to deal with that box:

- ✔ **The OK button:** Just click OK and don't fret about the other settings if you're not finicky about results.

- ✔ **Palette option buttons:** (These buttons don't appear for the 32K or 64K color depths.) For best accuracy of broad areas of color, at the expense of less commonly used colors, choose Optimized Median Cut. For best accuracy of all colors, choose Optimized Octree. For Web images where you want to make sure that even the most out-of-date PC users see accurate color, choose Standard/Web-safe Palette.

- ✔ **Reduction Method option buttons:** For minimal file size, at the risk of inducing blocks of dark and light colors, choose Nearest Color. For color accuracy at the expense of detail, choose Ordered Dither Method (not available unless you choose the Standard/Web-Safe palette option). For best color at the cost of graininess, use Error Diffusion.

- ✔ **Number of Colors value box:** If you choose the X Colors option for color depth, you must also enter the number of colors you want in the Number of Colors value box.

Don't sweat the other options as they aren't likely to be all that useful to you.

Saving and restoring a palette

You can save an image's palette of colors and re-use them for additional images later. (You must have a palette image: an image with 256 colors or fewer.) To save a palette, choose Colors⇨Save Palette to get a Save Palette dialog box. Enter a name for your palette in the File Name text box and then click OK.

To apply a saved palette to an open image, choose Colors⇨Load Palette From the Load Palette dialog box that appears and choose any of the palette files (ending in .pal). Paint Shop Pro does its best to translate the colors in your open image into the colors of the palette.

Chapter 11

Laundering Your Image for Brightness, Contrast, and Color

A common problem with images, especially with photographs, is that they need laundering: better brightness, contrast, or color quality. A wedding photo taken under a canopy, for instance, may make everyone look a bit dim. The groom's white shirt resembles his gray tux. Perhaps the problem isn't the whole crowd, but only Uncle Dave — who, as people have been saying for years, is comparatively dim. Or, maybe the poor light makes the colors of the bridesmaids' dresses, actually a charming sea green, look tattletale gray.

The secrets to brightening the family's dirty laundry lie within Paint Shop Pro's color adjustment features. Not all remedies are what you'd expect them to be. The remedy for what you may call a brightness problem, for instance, may turn out to be something called lightness or lightness and contrast both.

If you're tweaking photographs, check out Chapter 8. Paint Shop Pro has some effects that are very useful for solving specific photo flaws.

Paint Shop Pro's color features aren't just for fixing problems, however. They're creative tools that can change, say, a color photo into a sepia one (colorizing) or make your color image look like a silk-screened poster (posterizing).

Most of Paint Shop Pro's color features appear in two alternative forms; it's your choice which one you use:

- **Colors menu commands:** Use commands on the Colors menu if you're not comfortable working with layers. For example, you may use the Colors menu commands if you're working on a digital photograph, scanned-in picture, or a painted illustration.

- **Adjustment layers:** Use adjustment layers for more flexibility and control. The adjustment layer approach is Jasc's idea of a newer, better way. See Chapter 15 to understand layers before trying to use adjustment layers.

Whether you use the Colors menu commands or adjustment layers, the dialog boxes containing the color controls are practically identical, so the descriptions in this chapter work no matter which way you go. The Colors menu, however, also includes a few controls not available in adjustment layer form. These controls are older, simpler versions of the newer fancy-shmancy ones, so in some ways they're better *For Dummies* features!

Like most Paint Shop Pro effects, color adjustments can be limited to a particular area of an image, like the area occupied by dim, old Uncle Dave. Here are a few points to keep in mind about that phenomenon:

- If you've made a selection, only the selected area is affected by your adjustments.

- If you're using multiple layers in your image, commands in the Colors menu only affect the currently selected layer.

- If you're using multiple layers in your image, consider using an adjustment layer so you can affect color across multiple layers.

- If a feature doesn't appear to be working, check to see if you've selected an area or have made a particular layer active. If you have, then the tool is working only within that selection, or layer, and not necessarily in the area you're trying to change. Read all about selections and layers in Part III.

Using the Adjustment Dialog Boxes

All the dialog boxes for color adjustment have similar controls. I summarize those features in this section. The Brightness/Contrast dialog box that appears in Figure 11-1 provides an example. Note that the slider shown in Figure 11-1 only appears when you mouse down on the larger down-arrow at the far right of a value box.

Figure 11-1:
The
Brightness/
Contrast
dialog box
shows
controls
typical of
all color
adjustments.
Dialog
boxes for
adjustment
layers are
identical,
except that
they lack
previews.

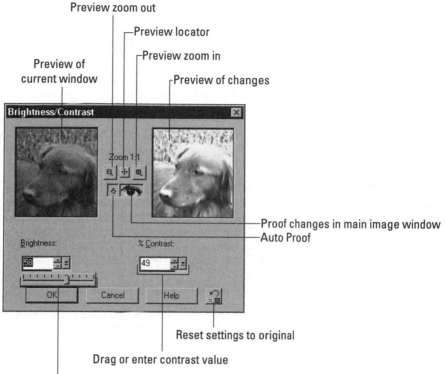

Preview zoom out

Preview locator

Preview of
current window

Preview zoom in

Preview of changes

Proof changes in main image window
Auto Proof

Reset settings to original

Drag or enter contrast value

Drag or enter brightness value

If you end up doing a lot of color adjustment work, you may want to add buttons for Brightness/Contrast, Hue/Saturation/Lightness, or other commands from the Colors⇨Adjust menu to the Toolbar. You can then click that button instead of making the menu selection. See Chapter 1 for the details of toolbar customization.

Making adjustments

You have several ways to adjust settings in the dialog boxes:

- ✔ In adjusting value boxes, you may type a value, click the associated up/down arrows, click in the value box and press the up/down keys on the keyboard, or mouse down on the larger down-arrow to the right of the box and drag the slider that appears.

- ✔ Some adjustments appear as sliders: Drag sliders to the left or right, up or down. Dragging varies an associated value (number) that appears in a text box to the right of each slider. Dragging left or down reduces that value and dragging right or up increases it. Alternatively, click a slider, and then press the up/down arrow keys on the keyboard to increase or decrease its value by one.

✔ To give precise values, double-click in the box where the value appears and type a new value.

✔ To reset adjustments to their original (default) levels, click the Reset button (shown in Figure 11-1).

After you make an adjustment, click OK to apply it to your image. Before you apply it, however, use the proofing or previewing tools that I describe in the following section, "Proofing or previewing your adjustments."

Changes are rarely final in Paint Shop Pro because you can undo them with Ctrl+Z or Edit➪Command History (see Chapter 1).

Proofing or previewing your adjustments

All the color adjustment dialog boxes let you see the effect of your adjustments in the main image window, a feature called *proofing*. The change isn't permanent until you click the OK button. If you cancel out of the dialog box, the change doesn't occur. You have two ways to proof:

✔ Click the Proof button — the one with the eye icon — after every adjustment.

✔ If you find yourself clicking the Proof button too often, try using Auto Proof. Click the Auto Proof down-arrow shown in Figure 11-1. Paint Shop Pro now shows the effect of your changes in the main image window every time you make a change. For large images, however, you may find this proofing method slow.

The dialog boxes for commands in the Colors menu also have preview windows that let you see the effect of your adjustments without the long wait that proofing sometimes entails. Here's how to preview your changes:

✔ To zoom in or out within the preview windows, click the zoom in button (marked with a +) or zoom out button (with a –) shown in Figure 11-1.

✔ To move the image in the preview window so you can see a new area, drag the image in either window.

✔ To quickly move to a new area of the image, click the locator button shown in Figure 11-1 and keep the mouse button depressed. A small version of the entire image is displayed, with a rectangle representing your preview area. Drag the rectangle to the area you want to preview and then release the mouse button.

Getting Brighter, Darker, or More Contrasty

I've been trying for years to be brighter, and now Paint Shop Pro has shown me the light. But just what is brightness? If you increase the brightness of an image, it basically looks whiter. You are, in effect, telling Paint Shop Pro, "More white, please." This whitening affects all shades uniformly, sort of like using bleach in mixed laundry: Lights get whiter, and so do the darks. (Decreasing brightness does the opposite — like washing a new pair of black jeans with your laundry.) This effect also changes your colors — noticeably, if they're very light or dark. Brightness alone rarely does the job you want.

Because brightness alone rarely does the job, Jasc puts Paint Shop Pro's adjustments for brightness and contrast together. Contrast is a bit like a laundry brightener that makes the lights lighter and the darks darker. (It isn't too picky about keeping your colors exactly right, though.)

Just how do brightness and contrast work?

Brightness changes all pixel values by the same amount. If, for instance, a pixel has a value of 100, 115, and 240 for its red, green, and blue primary colors, respectively, adjusting brightness by +50 pushes those values to 150, 175, and 255 (255 being the maximum possible value.) Any pixel value of 0 increases to 50, so blacks become grays. Light shades in any color may become pure white.

Increasing contrast pushes pixel values below 128 (mid-range) lower, and those above 128, higher. It does so not by a fixed value (by, say, subtracting and adding 50), but proportionately. Decreasing contrast pushes all values towards 128, so at –100% contrast, your image is a uniform medium-gray.

When should you use brightness and contrast adjustments? Brightness and contrast are often helpful for adjusting images that appear faded, images where you want the colors to be more vivid, or photographs taken under insufficient light. Where the accuracy of color in the highlights (bright areas) or shadows (dark areas) is important, however, you can try using the Hue/Lightness/Saturation controls instead (which I describe in the section, "Laundering for Lightness, Color Intensity, and Hue," elsewhere in this chapter).

If brightness and contrast adjustment sounds like the answer to your needs, you have two alternative solutions:

> ✔ **Choose Colors⇨Adjust⇨Brightness/Contrast.** The Brightness/Contrast adjustment dialog box of Figure 11-1 arrives, bringing enlightenment.
>
> ✔ **Choose Layers⇨New Adjustment Layer⇨Brightness/Contrast.** This adds a Brightness/Contrast layer. The Layer Properties dialog box appears, with the Adjustment tab displayed. See Chapter 15 for help with using layers.

Adjust the Brightness and % Contrast values up or down to see if you can achieve the results you want. Brightness ranges from –255 to +255; % Contrast ranges from –100 to +100. In Figure 11-1, I turned up both brightness and contrast.

Laundering Lights, Mediums, and Darks Separately

Sometimes, the best way to clean something up is to separately launder what I call three different *tonal ranges:* lights, darks, and mid-range colors. Paint Shop Pro gives you several ways to process these different tonal ranges separately:

> ✔ **The Highlight/Midtone/Shadow (HMS) control.** This guy is in the Colors⇨Adjust menu and is the most straightforward control. (It's not available as an adjustment layer, however.) Check out the upcoming section.
>
> ✔ **The Levels control and the Curves control.** Both are available in the Colors⇨Adjust menu and also as an adjustment layer. They are a bit more sophisticated and flexible than the previous control and avoid certain weirdnesses that can arise with the Highlight/Midtone/Shadow control. See the section, "Using More Sophisticated Color Adjustments," at the end of this chapter.

The Highlight/Midtone/Shadow controls enable you to adjust separately the darkest regions (shadows) of your image, the lightest regions (highlights), and the regions in between (midtones). To adjust these regions, do the following:

1. **Choose Colors⇨Adjust⇨Highlight/Midtone/Shadow.**

   The Highlight/Midtone/Shadow (HMS) dialog box appears, as in Figure 11-2.

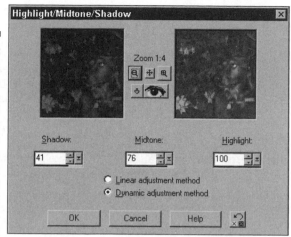

Figure 11-2:
Adjusting
highlights,
midtones,
and shadows
separately
lets me
brighten a
dark area
without
washing out
other areas.

2. **Click the Dynamic Adjustment Method option, if it's not already selected.**

   The other option, Linear Adjustment Method, is a throwback to an older (Paint Shop Pro 5) adjustment method. Jasc included it because some of the old-time users and experts prefer it. The older method is great for graphics geeks but pretty weird for the rest of us.

3. **Adjust any value downward to darken hues or upward to lighten them.**

   You can think of each value as a sort of brightness adjustment, one each for the shadow, midtone, and highlight areas. To darken shadows, for instance, adjust the Shadow value downward. To darken highlights, adjust the Highlight value downward. It's possible to even make dark areas lighter than the light areas, or vice-versa. A very weird effect.

   Refer to Figure 11-3 to see the effects of lightening dark areas using the HMS controls.

The more a pixel's value is within a given range, the more the control for that range affects it. The more shadowy a shadow, the more the Shadow control affects it. Likewise, brighter highlights are more affected by the Highlight control, and more mid-range midtones are more heavily adjusted by the Midtone control.

Just as with Paint Shop Pro's Brightness/Contrast control, adjusting brightness can affect the color of an area. If your shadows, for instance, have a slightly blue cast, they become noticeably blue if you lighten them. (Many shadows in outdoor photographs are slightly blue because of the incidental light cast by a blue sky.)

As I note, the strength of these adjustments varies with how far a pixel is into the highlight, midtone, or shadow zone. This effect is unlike Paint Shop Pro's brightness adjustment, which adjusts every pixel value by the same amount. The Shadow control, for instance, more strongly affects darker pixels within the shadow range than it does lighter pixels. (This variation in strength is true whether you adjust a control up or down.) Adjusting Shadow by +50, for instance, brings pixels with a value of zero up to 50, pixels with a value of 25 up to 63, and pixels with a value of 80 up to 85. As a result, if you lighten the shadows far enough, you can cause a sort of photographic negative effect in which the darkest portions are now lighter than formerly lighter pixels. The Highlight control, likewise, more strongly affects lighter pixels and the Midtone control more strongly affects pixel values near 128 (mid-range on a scale of 0 to 255).

Figure 11-3:
Left, brightening a dark sculpture using HMS controls. Right, equalizing gives better results in this instance. (See the sidebar, "Equalizing and stretching....")

Laundering for Lightness, Color Intensity, and Hue

Brightness and contrast are useful, but they're sort of like the laundry tools of yesterday. The way they work, which sometimes can alter colors, doesn't fully address the needs of a color world.

Paint Shop Pro's Hue/Saturation/Lightness control, on the other hand, lets you more safely launder a mixed color load. It gives you brighter colors (lightness) and richer colors (saturation) without risk to your delicate hand-washables, whatever they might be, metaphorically speaking.

Equalizing and stretching fix both highs and lows

If your images are either lacking in extremes of highlight or shadow, or have too much of both, Paint Shop Pro offers lots of alternatives: contrast, highlight/midtone/shadow (HMS) adjustment, saturation, gamma. A simple alternative worth trying is to give your image some gentle exercise: equalizing or stretching.

Equalizing gives a more even distribution of pixels from dark to light. Usually, it's the solution you want. Stretching tends to extend the highlights and brighten the overall picture. Either choose Colors⇨Histogram Functions⇨Equalize or Colors⇨Histogram Functions⇨Stretch. (Each command does its job immediately without providing a dialog box or any other means of adjustment.)

To access this modern wash-day miracle, as with most color controls, you have two choices:

- ✔ **Choose Colors->Adjust->Hue/Saturation/Lightness.** The Hue/Saturation/Lightness dialog box of Figure 11-4 springs colorfully into action.

- ✔ **Choose Layers⇨New Adjustment Layer⇨Hue/Saturation/Lightness** to add a Hue/Saturation/Lightness layer. The Layer Properties dialog box appears, with the Adjustment tab displayed. See Chapter 15 for help with using layers.

Whichever choice you make, I tell you how to adjust lightness, saturation, and hue in the next three sections of this chapter.

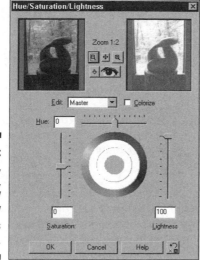

Figure 11-4: For brighter, richer colors, try the Hue/ Saturation/ Lightness adjustment.

Hue/Saturation/Lightness (or HSL to its friends) and Red/Green/Blue (RGB) are two totally different but equally valid systems for specifying colors on a computer. See Chapter 10 for more about these systems.

Lightness: Brightening without bleaching

Lightness is like a brightness adjustment, only without the bleaching effect on dark colors. Unlike the brightness adjustment, which makes everything brighter by the same amount, the lightness adjustment adjusts proportionately. Dark areas become slightly brighter and light areas become more bright. A second benefit of this proportional adjustment is that the colors remain more true to the original, except that some are pushed to near-white or near-black.

For a brighter image, increase the % Lightness value. (On an adjustment layer, the control is called % Luminance instead of % Lightness.) For a darker image, decrease the value. The range is from –100 to +100.

Lightness adjustment is something like brightness adjustment, but lightness gives a *percentage* change in pixel value for each primary color of a pixel, whereas brightness actually gives an *additive* change. At +50% lightness, for instance, the primary values of red, green, and blue for a pixel become 150 percent of their previous values (but no more than 255). Another way to think of the lightness control is that it stretches the range of pixel values (or compresses the range, if lightness is reduced). If the range in the original is from 0 to128 and you set the lightness value to +100%, the range then becomes 0 to 255 (255 being the maximum value).

Saturation: Getting more or less intense

Is your image a bit gray and lackluster? For more intense colors (increased saturation), increase the % Saturation value. Your reds get redder, your greens, greener, your chartreuses chartreusier, and so on. For less saturation, decrease the value. Values in the Saturation box range between –100 and +100.

The easiest way to understand what saturation does is to go the opposite direction from the way you're probably interested in: decrease saturation. Adjusting saturation downward makes a color image black and white (also called *grayscale*) by degrees.

Saturation adjustment is something like contrast adjustment in that increasing it pushes lower values of primary color even lower and higher values higher. Unlike contrast adjustment, however, saturation adjustment retains the overall lightness (a mathematical combination of red, green, and blue primary values) of each pixel. As a result, instead of washing out the image to a uniform gray (as low settings of *contrast* do), low settings of *saturation* turn the image into a grayscale image. In a grayscale image, the values for red, green, and blue for a given pixel are equal (say, 105), but that value varies *between* pixels. One pixel's red, green, and blue values may all be 105, another's all 84, and so on.

Following are a few tips for saturation adjustments:

- ✔ At low saturation settings (but not quite –100), your image may look like a black and white photo that someone has tinted with watercolors. This effect creates a kind of retro look that is effective for some artistic purposes.

- ✔ If only a *portion* of your image is too gray or too saturated, select that portion or activate its particular layer, and then change its saturation. You can use this method creatively to generate effects like those shown in the movie *Pleasantville,* where items and individuals become colored in a gray world.

- ✔ An easy way to make your image entirely gray is to reduce Saturation to the bottom of the scale (–100).

Hue-ing and crying

If your image is looking a bit blue, you can imagine cheering it up with a quick tint. You may turn to the % Hue slider of the Hue/Saturation/Lightness control. The slider's name, % Hue, makes it seem like a logical choice, after all. Wrong! This control is too weird for most common uses and probably doesn't change the hue in the way you would expect it to. If you want to change the overall hue of an image, use the Red/Green/Blue adjustment I describe in the next section, "Altering An Overall Tint."

If you feel compelled to fool with the % Hue control, here's what it does: It moves colors in color wheel order. Imagine a rainbow-hued circle in which red is at the top. Going counterclockwise around the circle, the colors are yellow, green, cyan, blue, violet, magenta, and then red again. So, if you adjust the % Hue control to +25%, any reds in your image become light green. However, *all* colors in your image are then rotated 25% around this wheel! Yellows become sea-green, greens become cyan, and blues become magenta. Lovely!

A funky, rotating display in the center of the dialog box attempts to show how the current colors are translated into new colors. It succeeds, sort of, but it's also way confusing! Proof your changes while you fiddle with the controls and look at the image, not the funky display — you see exactly what effect you're having.

What possible use is this control, other than a creative tool for merry mixups of color? If you get an off-colored image from someone, adjusting hue may solve the problem. (The originator's color wheel may not have started with the same shade of red, so the colors are offset some percentage from your wheel.) First, however, make sure you haven't been given a color negative. Choose Colors⇨Negative Image and see if that doesn't fix your problem.

Using a Hue/Saturation/Lightness layer doesn't give you *exactly* the same result as using the Hue/Saturation/Lightness command in the Colors⇨Adjust menu. The Color menu version gives you a gentler adjustment — it never washes out colors to pure black or white. For instance, using the Color menu command, a setting of +50 (meaning +50%) means "halfway between current and maximum (255)." A pixel with a Lightness value of 215 would therefore go to 235. Using the Hue/Saturation/Lightness layer, a setting of +50 means "50% higher than current." A pixel with a Luminance value of 215 would therefore max out at 255, or white, as would any value over 170.

A completely different control, which you get by choosing Colors⇨Adjust⇨ Hue Map, lets you rotate specific areas on the color wheel, rather than rotating all colors. You can rotate just the orange point, for instance, moving it closer to red or yellow. Colors in the vicinity of orange on the color wheel change, becoming more red or more yellow. (Try to imagine a stretchy, rubber color wheel, and dragging a point on it.) This control is also pretty weird for most users and usually not all that valuable, so I leave it for the curious to play with.

Altering an Overall Tint

Are your overalls the wrong tint? Paint Shop Pro can't fix that laundry problem — unless, of course, you have a picture of your overalls.

Images, whether the subject is overalls or not, sometime have — or need — an *overall tint.* Portraits taken in a forest setting, for instance, tend to make people look a bit green because of the light reflected off the leaves. Or, you may want to add a slight orange tint to a sunset picture.

Paint Shop Pro, as it does with most color controls, gives you several ways to alter tint:

✔ **Choose Colors⇨Adjust⇨Red/Green/Blue.** The Red/Green/Blue dialog box that appears is the simplest control for altering overall tint. (It isn't available, however, as an adjustment layer.)

✔ **Use the Color Balance, Curves, or Channel Mixer control.** All three controls are available either in the Colors⇨Adjust menu or as adjustment layers. Color Balance and Curves tint shadows, midtones, and highlights separately.

As I point out in Chapter 10, everything you see on your PC screen (or TV screen, for that matter) is made up of a mixture of red, green, and blue, so you can get any tint you like by adjusting the balance of those primary colors.

Choose Colors⇨Adjust⇨Red/Green/Blue and the Red/Green/Blue dialog box appears. Like all dialog boxes for commands in the Colors menu, it has preview windows and proofing controls, plus adjustable values — in this instance, one value for each primary color: % Red, % Green, and % Blue.

To make your image more red, green, or blue, the solution is straightforward: Increase the value for that color. (Decrease it for less of that color.) Values range from –100 to +100.

To gain or lose any *other* color, consult Chapter 10 for the discussion of mixing primary colors. For instance, to make your image more yellow, increase both red and green. Is your birthday photo a bit too orange because it was taken by the light of a few too many candles? Decrease the green and red sliders; note to decrease the red a bit more than the green because you're reducing orange, not yellow.

Going Gray with a Tint: Colorizing

We all go gray. Some of us try to add an attractive tint when that happens. The same scheme can be even more attractive when applied to images.

Paint Shop Pro calls this process *colorizing.* But, unlike the colorizing you may have seen used to make old black and white movies look as if they were shot in color, colorizing in Paint Shop Pro imparts only a single hue to the image. In effect, the result is a grayscale (monochrome) image done in your chosen hue instead of gray.

Paint Shop Pro gives you several tools that you can use to colorize:

✔ **Choose Colors⇨Colorize to get the Colorize dialog box.** This is the simplest control, offering a saturation and hue adjustment.

✔ **Choose Colors⇨Adjust⇨Hue/Saturation/Lightness to get the Hue/Saturation/Lightness dialog box.** This control gives you the additional ability to adjust the lightness of your new hue. The same control is also available as an adjustment layer by choosing Layers⇨New Adjustment Layer⇨Hue/Saturation/Lightness. See Chapter 15 for help with layers.

If you choose Colors⇨Colorize, the Colorize dialog box grabs its crayons and reports for duty. The Colorize dialog box sports two adjustments, as follows:

✔ **Saturation:** Increase this value to determine how much color is applied. If you set it to zero, the image is strictly grayscale (black and white). At 255, the image has no gray but is purely the hue you choose by adjusting the Hue control.

✔ **Hue:** Adjust this value from zero to 255 to proceed in color wheel order. At zero, the hue is red and, as you increase the Hue value, it proceeds through orange, yellow, green, cyan, blue, violet, magenta, and back to red.

If you choose Colors➪Adjust➪Hue/Saturation/Lightness, you get (not surprisingly) the Hue/Saturation/Lightness dialog box that I discuss earlier in this chapter. To colorize, however, you must check the Colorize check box. This control has the same Saturation and Hue adjustments that I just describe (except that they're sliders). It also has a Brightness control that gives you additional flexibility in choosing your hue.

Going Totally Gray or Negative in One Step

You're just one step away from going gray, or becoming completely negative. Paint Shop Pro's commands for Negative Image and Grey Scale, under the Colors menu choice, are simple enough to do their work in a single step: You get no dialog box and have no adjustments to make.

Choose Colors➪Negative Image and Paint Shop Pro gives you the negative of your image. Lights become darks, darks become lights, and the colors switch to their opposing colors on the color wheel. Reds become cyan, yellows become blue, and so on. Changing an image from positive (normal) to negative isn't often useful but, sometimes, you need to go the other way. That event occurs when you (or whoever is supplying your images) is using a film scanner and scans a film negative. The Negative Image command gives you the normal (positive) image you want.

To create a negative image by using an adjustment layer, choose Layers➪New Adjustment Layer➪Invert, and click OK in the Layer Properties dialog box that appears. See Chapter 15 for help with layers.

To turn your color image into shades of gray (like a black and white photo), choose Colors➪Grey Scale. This change can be useful for artistic effect, giving a more formal look to a photo, for instance. It can also reduce file size in certain file formats such as GIF if download times are a consideration. (Going from color to grayscale does not reduce file size if the image is in JPEG format, however.) Going grayscale affects the entire image, even if you have selected an area.

You can also turn an image grayscale by using a Hue/Saturation/Lightness control and reducing Saturation to the minimum. See the sections on Hue/Saturation/Lightness controls, earlier in this chapter. A Hue/Saturation/Lightness layer can turn an individual layer of an image gray, if you like. See Chapter 15.

Using More Sophisticated Color Adjustments

Paint Shop Pro is, after all, Paint Shop *Pro,* so it offers some sophisticated color adjustments for professional computer graphics mavens. Why, however, should those guys have all the fun?

Here are some rudimentary instructions for using a handful of these hifalutin controls. They are available in the same two forms that other color controls are:

- ✔ As commands in the Colors or Colors⇨Adjust menu. (Just poke around. You'll find 'em.)
- ✔ As adjustment layers, accessed through the Layers menu or layer palette (see Chapter 15).

Levels

The Levels control lets you adjust brightness and contrast within three different tonal ranges: shadows (darker pixels), highlights (lighter pixels), and mid-tones (pixels in the middle). As Figure 11-5 shows, the dialog box has two controls: Input Levels and Output Levels. Each control is a horizontal line, attractively studded with diamonds that you can drag.

You can think of the Input Levels control as a way to adjust contrast and the Output Levels control as a way to adjust brightness. (Neither description is perfectly accurate, but gets the idea across without getting *too* technical.) Here's how to use these controls:

- ✔ To heighten contrast by making shadows darker, drag the black diamond on the Input Level control (at or near the left end) to the right.
- ✔ To heighten contrast by making highlights lighter, drag the clear (unfilled) diamond on the Input Level control (at or near the right end) to the left.

✔ To adjust the mid-tones, drag the center (gray) diamond on the Input Level control. Drag it left to brighten or right to darken. The mid-tones diamond also moves a bit when the other two do, so you may need to readjust this diamond after moving the others.

✔ To lighten shadows, drag the black diamond on the Output Levels control towards the right. (Shadows and midtones get lighter.) To darken high-lights, drag the clear diamond towards the left. (Highlights and midtones get darker.)

Figure 11-5:
Making
shadowy
areas
visible by
redefining
mid-range
(dragging
the center
diamond of
the Input
Level
control
leftward).

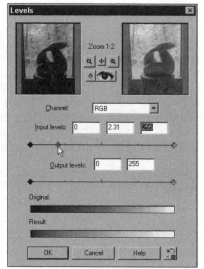

Other controls? To restore the original settings, click the Reset button. Leave the Auto Proof check box selected if you want to see how you're affecting your image.

What these controls actually do is to re-proportion and shift the range of tones. The three Input Levels diamonds specify which current pixel values are redefined as black, which ones are redefined as white, and where the mid-range falls between the extremes. The three Output Levels diamonds define how black that black is actually going to be and how white that white is going to be. If you have a good understanding of how images are made up of primary colors, you can alter the three primary colors separately: Click the Channel selection box and choose Red, Green, or Blue.

Curves

The *Curves* adjustment is a way to change brightness and contrast within a very specific range of tones that you specify. That range can be anywhere from shadows to highlights to anywhere in the middle. A Curves adjustment can, for example, help you pull out some of the detail that's lost in a specific range of a photograph by increasing the contrast in that range.

The main control (in the dialog box) looks like a chart and appears on the left side of Figure 11-6. (If the chart makes sense to you, great — otherwise, don't worry about understanding it.) The chart holds a curve — well, initially, it's just a straight, diagonal line between two points. The idea is to bend that line by adding and dragging points:

- ✔ In the chart, click on that diagonal line in the tone area that you want to change the most. Click more towards the left end of the line to adjust shadows and click more towards the right to adjust highlights.

- ✔ Clicking adds a point to the line. For instance, to change mid-tones, click near the middle and add one point. Click in two places to create two points slightly separated from each other. Adding more than one point gives you more control over exactly which tone range you adjust.

- ✔ Drag the point (or points) up to brighten or down to darken. Drag left to move your effect to darker pixels or right to move it to lighter pixels. You can also drag the end-points of the line: Drag the left end-point to affect shadows, and drag the right end-point to affect highlights.

- ✔ To get more contrast within a range of tones, drag points so that the curve is steeper (more vertical) in that range.

- ✔ To get less contrast, make the curve flatter. You may need to add points in order to focus your efforts on exactly the range you want.

- ✔ To remove a point that you've decided you don't need, drag it entirely out of the chart area.

- ✔ To adjust contrast and brightness only within a given primary color (red, green, or blue), click the selection box marked Channel and choose your color.

In Figure 11-6, the left column shows three curve settings. The right column shows an image that originally contains evenly distributed shades of gray from black to white. The first image shows those shades, unaltered. (The curve is straight.) The other two show the effect of the curve settings next to the images.

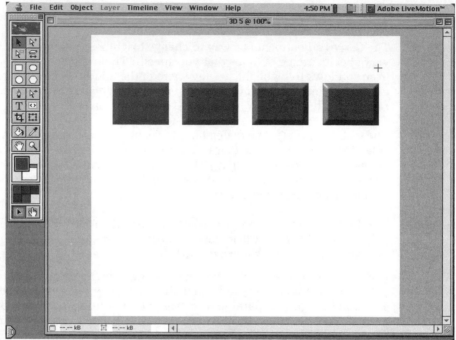

Figure 11-6:
Results of
various
Curve
settings.

Posterize

The Posterize control (under Colors⇨Histogram Functions) is well-named. In *posterizing,* an image takes on the appearance of a silk-screened poster, made up of areas of a few uniform colors. Posterizing reduces the number of colors that appear and results in blocks of color, like a paint-by-numbers painting.

Technically, posterizing only reduces the number of unique values of lightness that pixels may have in the image; pixels may have any value for hue or saturation. The effect, however, is to reduce the number of colors used.

The dialog box for posterizing has only one adjustment, called Levels. Reduce the value to reduce the number of colors or increase it to increase colors. The value in Levels determines the number of levels of brightness in the image.

Threshold

The threshold control (choose Colors⇨Adjust⇨Threshold) gives you images in pure black and pure white. With a threshold control, you're telling Paint Shop Pro, "Turn any pixel with a brightness below a given threshold black, and any pixel above that threshold, white."

The dialog box for this layer has a single adjustment. Reduce the Threshold value for a lower threshold (more white) and increase it for a higher threshold (more black). You can use a threshold value between 1 and 255.

Part IV
Changing and Adding Content

The 5th Wave   By Rich Tennant

©RICHTENNANT.COM

Jeez—that's impressive! Let's see that airbrush effect again.

In this part . . .

Part IV has solutions when you're concerned with your image's content, not its quality. Here's where you discover how to pluck out, put in, or move a person, product, or other object in your image. Here, too, is where to turn for cropping, resizing, rotating, or distorting an image (or just part of an image). To crop, resize, re-proportion, flip, mirror, re-orient, bend, spindle, or mutilate your image, turn to Chapter 12.

In Chapter 13, you see how to select parts of your image — the key trick for changing content. Want to abstract your better half from photo A into photo B? Paint Shop Pro can't tell your spouse from a sofa, so (assuming *you* can tell the difference), it's up to you to tell Paint Shop Pro, "Pat's the one in green," or to outline Pat by hand. You can even change the color, or other qualities such as contrast or sharpness, of the selected item. Selecting lets you apply nearly any of Paint Shop Pro's powers to particular items.

After you've selected your spouse, you may want to move, copy, or re-shape him or her. As inadvisable as such a project may be in real life, it's a simple matter in Paint Shop Pro. Chapter 14 is the place to turn for moving, copying, or other dimensional or reproductive changes.

Adding content is another trick that Paint Shop Pro can help you with. In Chapter 15, I show you how to combine multiple images or create layered images where you can manipulate different objects without affecting the underlying stuff. Layers make later editing much easier, produce cool image overlays, and can even make qualitative changes such as contrast or saturation easier to manage.

To add text and shapes to an image, a common requirement, turn to Chapter 16 where I show you how Paint Shop Pro's vector graphics and text tools can give you layers of easily-edited material.

Finally, in Chapter 17, I unveil a classic tool for combining images, — masking — that enables you to combine images by brushing them in or out of the picture.

Chapter 12

Getting Bigger, Smaller, and Turned Around

*I*t happened several times to Alice, of Wonderland fame: She needed to be bigger and smaller, or to change her orientation. Fortunately, you don't have to adopt her dubious pharmacological methods — eating and drinking mysteriously labeled substances — to change the size or orientation of your images.

No, to make your pictures bigger, smaller, rotated, or otherwise re-oriented, you only need to indulge in a few clicks upon well-labeled commands or icons. In this chapter, I illuminate your choices as you navigate the Paint Shop Pro rabbit-hole.

 If your image appears smaller than you think it should when you first open it, Paint Shop Pro has probably zoomed the image out to fit your window. To zoom in, click the Zoom (magnifier) tool on the Tool palette and then left-click on the image.

Getting Sized

Size may not be everything but it's certainly one of the things people are often concerned about — or ought to be. You don't need a 1024 x 768 pixel image, for instance (full-screen size on many PCs), for a snapshot of your new company CEO on your Web site. If you didn't get an appropriately sized CEO (okay, image of a CEO) in the first place, you can trim him or her down in Paint Shop Pro. Likewise, if you're rushing to prepare the opening screen for a company presentation and the only way you can get a logo is to scan in the tiny one on your letterhead, Paint Shop Pro can help you size it up to a more presentable image.

If you're preparing an image that someone else plans to place in a professionally prepared and printed document, don't scale it down yourself. Let your graphics designer or printer do the scaling to suit the printing process.

Start resizing by choosing Image⇨Resize from the menu bar. The Resize dialog box (see Figure 12-1) appears in order to help you size the situation up — or down.

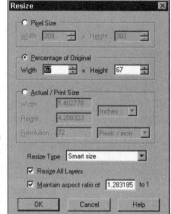

Figure 12-1: Sizing your image up — or down.

Proportioning

The Resize dialog box normally keeps the image's proportions (relationship of width to height) constant while you resize. That means that if you set width, Paint Shop Pro sets height for you (and vice-versa). Keeping image proportions constant avoids distortion.

If you prefer to change the proportions (which distorts your image), you can do it in one of two ways:

✔ Click to clear (deselect) the check box marked Maintain Aspect Ratio Of ___ To 1, shown in Figure 12-1, and Paint Shop Pro lets you set width and height independently.

✔ Or, if you have a particular aspect ratio in mind, leave the check mark in the Maintain Aspect Ratio Of __ To 1 check box. Then enter the ratio (width divided by height) in the Maintain Aspect Ratio Of __ To 1 text box and fiddle with either Width or Height to get the image size that you want.

Dimensioning

Using the Resize dialog box shown in Figure 12-1, you can adjust the size in one of three ways, all of which do the same thing: change the image's size in pixels. Use whichever way suits your mindset, as follows:

✔ **Specify size in pixels:** If you're using the image on the Web or in e-mail, you probably have a pixel size (probably a desired width) in mind. Click the Pixel Size button and enter a value for Width (or Height).

✔ **Make it X% of its current size:** Click the Percentage of Original button and enter a percentage value for Width or Height. In Figure 12-1, for instance, the setting of 67 makes the image ⅔ (67 percent) of its current size. To double image size, you would use 200.

✔ **Make it *print* bigger or smaller:** Click the Actual/Print Size button and enter Width or Height in inches (or centimeters; click the list box containing Inches to switch to centimeters). Paint Shop Pro multiplies this physical size (in, say, inches) by the resolution setting (pixels per inch) in this dialog box and comes up with a new image size in pixels. You can also change the value in the Resolution text box to adjust the image resolution (pixels per inch or centimeter). Don't confuse this setting with the printer's resolution (typically 300 to 600 dpi); see Chapter 18 if you *are* confused about printing and resolution!

If your image has several layers and you want them all resized the same, make sure to check the Resize All Layers check box. If you clear that check mark, you resize only the currently active layer. Click OK to make the resizing happen.

Avoiding degradation

Resizing sounds easy — just make the image bigger or smaller — what's to think about? Well, usually, you don't have to think about anything. Occasionally, however, your image's appearance degrades after resizing. It has jagged or fuzzy edges. These situations call for a little thought.

Behind the resizing issue is another difference between how computers and humans think. If you want your image to be 25 percent bigger, Paint Shop Pro has to figure out how to spread 100 pixels over 125 pixels. To get an idea of the problem, imagine dividing 100 cookies among 125 kids who don't accept broken cookies. Fortunately, Paint Shop Pro is pretty smart, so you don't have to smoosh up and re-bake these cookies yourself. Unless you instruct Paint Shop Pro otherwise, it uses *smart resize* to make these decisions — it chooses the right way to do it based on what your image looks like.

If your image doesn't look so hot after resizing, try second-guessing the smart resize that Paint Shop Pro uses by default. Press Ctrl+Z to undo the ugly resize you just did. Now, choose Image⇨Resize again. In the Image Resize dialog box that appears, click the Resize Type selection box to see the specific choices of ways to resize. Here's what to do with those choices:

- ✔ **Bicubic Resample:** Choose to enlarge a realistic-looking or complex image (like a photo) or to avoid jagged edges.

- ✔ **Bilinear Resample:** Choose to reduce a drawn image, one with well-defined edges, or one with text.

- ✔ **Pixel Resize:** Choose to enlarge a drawn image or one with well-defined edges. (Paint Shop Pro then simply removes or duplicates pixels in order to resize.)

Click the OK button to proceed with the resizing. If your image doesn't look better, press Ctrl+Z to undo your last resize. Choose a different resizing method and try resizing again.

Bilinear and Bicubic resampling only work for 24-bit color images (or grayscale images). You can use them on fewer-color images by increasing the color depth to 24-bit, resizing the image, and then reducing the number of colors to the original. See Chapter 10 for help with changing the number of colors.

Trimming (Cropping) Your Edges

Is your image a bit shabby around the edges, and in need of a trim? You can improve the composition of many pictures by trimming a bit off the top, bottom, or sides (a process called *cropping*). Often, for instance, snapshots are taken from too far away, so the subject is too small. You can enlarge the image in Paint Shop Pro, but you also need to trim it so that the overall picture isn't yards wide.

In a layered image, cropping effects all layers.

Dragging the Crop tool

Paint Shop Pro provides a special tool for your crops. Take the following steps to trim your image:

 1. **Click the Crop tool (shown in the margin) on the tool palette.**

   Your cursor icon displays a set of crosshairs. (Unless Use Precise Cursors is enabled on Tab 2 of the Tool Options window, a Crop icon also appears with the crosshairs.)

2. **Visualize a rectangular area that defines the new boundaries of your image.**

   For instance, if you're cropping a family photo taken in the backyard, next to the trash barrels, visualize a rectangle around the family, excluding the barrels.

3. **Move the crosshairs of your cursor to one corner of that visualized rectangle and then drag diagonally towards the opposite corner.**

   As you drag, a real rectangle forms. The status bar at the bottom of the Paint Shop Pro window gives you the exact pixel column and row where the cursor is positioned, if you should need that information. As you drag, the status bar also gives you the current cursor position, plus the resulting image's size and proportions, as Figure 12-2 shows.

   If the cropping rectangle isn't quite right, you can modify it in one of these three ways:

   - To remove the rectangle and try again, right-click anywhere on the image. The rectangle disappears.

   - To change any side or corner of the rectangle, drag that side or corner.

   - To position the rectangle, move your cursor within that rectangle; the cursor becomes a four-headed arrow and you may drag the rectangle to any new location.

4. **When the rectangle is correct, double-click on the image.**

   Paint Shop Pro crops the image. If you don't like the result, press Ctrl+Z to undo the crop and then try these steps again. Instead of double-clicking, if the Tool Options window is open (press the *O* key if it's not), you may click the Crop Image button on the first (left) tab.

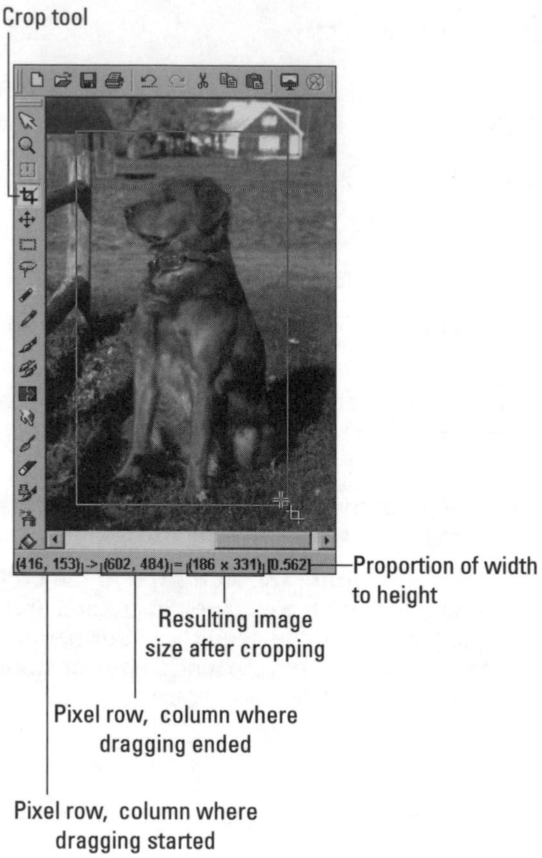

Crop tool

Figure 12-2:
Cropping a
furry dog.

(416, 153)) -> (602, 484)) = (186 x 331)) [0.562]

Proportion of width
to height

Resulting image
size after cropping

Pixel row, column where
dragging ended

Pixel row, column where
dragging started

Cropping by precise pixel positions

If you know exactly how many pixels from the left or top edge you want to crop your image, Paint Shop Pro offers an easier cropping method than dragging a rectangle. Do the following:

1. *Double-*click the Crop tool.

   The Crop Area dialog box appears.

2. **In the Crop Area dialog box, enter pixel position numbers in the boxes provided for the left, right, top, and bottom edges.**

   To crop an image's left edge at 10 pixels in from the current left edge, for instance, enter 10 in the Left box. To crop the image's top edge 15 pixels down, enter 15 in the Top box.

To crop the right edge, say, 10 pixels in, you need to do some quick arithmetic: Subtract 10 from the image width and enter that number in the Right box. Likewise, to trim the bottom edge by ten pixels, you would subtract 10 from the image height and enter that result in the Bottom box. You can find current image width and height at the very top of the Crop Area dialog box, labeled Image Size. The first number of the pair given (say, 600 x 350) is the width; the second is the height.

3. **Click OK in the Crop Area dialog box.**

   A rectangle appears on your image, showing the crop area you defined.

4. **Double-click anywhere on your image to perform the crop.**

   Alternatively, you can double-click the Crop tool again to revisit the Crop Area dialog box and change pixel positions.

Cropping to an existing selection

If you have selected an area (see Chapter 13), you can crop the image to the edges of that selection. The selection doesn't need to be rectangular; Paint Shop Pro crops to a rectangle that just surrounds your selection.

With an area selected, do the following:

1. ***Double*-click the Crop tool.**

   The Crop Area dialog box appears

2. **Click the Surround Current Selection button, and then click OK.**

   A rectangle defining the crop area appears, which you can move or modify as I describe in the section, "Dragging the Crop tool," earlier in this chapter.

3. **Double-click on the image to perform the crop.**

   Or, you may double-click the Crop tool again to revisit the Crop Area dialog box and change values in it.

 An even faster approach is to choose Image⇨Crop to Selection or press Shift+R. Your image is immediately cropped, but that means you have no opportunity to check or change the cropping rectangle.

Cropping out nothingness

Sometimes, you may have an image (or a layer in an image) that is surrounded by nothingness (no color, not even background). This nothingness is called *transparency* in Paint Shop Pro, and you may want to crop it away.

For instance, say you select an irregular portion of an image and paste it as a new layer in another image. Around that pasted image is nothing, or *no data,* usually represented by a checkerboard pattern if you view the layer separately.

To crop around that image, follow the directions in the preceding section for cropping to selection. In Step 2, instead of clicking the Surround Current Selection button, click the option buttons Select Opaque Area — Current Layer or Select Opaque Area — Merged. The first choice defines a rectangular cropping area surrounding all non-transparent pixels in the *currently selected layer.* The second choice does the same, but looks for non-transparent pixels in *all* layers. When you double-click to perform the crop, the entire image is cropped (all layers).

Getting Turned Around, Mirrored, or Flipped

I can't tell you how many people I've seen bending their necks to view a sideways image! Apart from providing work for chiropractors, this habit does nobody any good. Paint Shop Pro makes rotating the image very simple.

Mirroring or flipping an image is equally simple. Mirrored or flipped images are particularly useful for imaginative work, such as creating a reflection that isn't present in the original or making a symmetrical design, such as a floral border.

Does your image have layers, or have you selected an area? As with many Paint Shop Pro functions, the mirroring, flipping, and rotating commands apply only to the currently active layer. If you have a selected area, mirroring and flipping also restrict themselves to that area. See comments in the following two sections on layers and selections.

Rotating

To rotate an image, click Image⇨Rotate or press Ctrl+R. The Rotate dialog box appears, with a variety of option buttons, as follows:

- ✔ To rotate the image clockwise, click the Right button.
- ✔ To rotate counterclockwise, click the Left button.
- ✔ Choose 90 (a quarter-turn, good for righting sideways images), 180 (a half-turn), 270 degrees (three-quarters turn) of rotation, or Free (see next bullet).
- ✔ To rotate any desired amount, choose Free and enter any rotation (in degrees) in the highlighted text box.

Free rotation is particularly useful for correcting images that weren't scanned with perfect horizontal and vertical alignment. You may, however, have to make several attempts (perhaps undoing with Ctrl+Z between attempts) to get just the right amount of rotation. Such errors are usually very small, such as 0.5 degree.

If your image has multiple layers (or if you aren't sure if it does) and you want to rotate the entire image, click to place a check mark in the All Layers check box in the Rotate dialog box. Otherwise, Paint Shop Pro rotates only the currently active layer. Click OK to perform the rotation.

To rotate a portion of an image, select that portion first. Or, you can use the Deformation tool on the selection instead of the rotation command. See Chapter 13 for help with selection and Chapter 14 to rotate a selection.

Mirroring and flipping

To *mirror* an image is to change it as if it were reflected in a mirror held alongside the image. To *flip* an image is to exchange top-for-bottom as if the mirror were held underneath the image. Note that both transformations are unique: You can't achieve the same result by rotating the image!

If your image has layers, mirroring and flipping commands apply only to the currently active layer. If your image has an area currently selected, these commands float that selection and then work only on that floating selection. See Chapter 13 for more information about floating selections.

To mirror an image in Paint Shop Pro, choose Image⇨Mirror. Your image is transformed into its mirror image.

To flip an image, choose Image⇨Flip. Your image is turned head-over-heels.

Taking on Borders

Paint Shop Pro can add a border of any color and width to any image. (If your image uses layers, however, Paint Shop Pro has to merge them. For that reason, borders are often best left as the last thing you do to your image.) To create a border around an image, do the following:

1. **Choose a border color by setting the background color in the color palette.**

   For instance, for a white border, *right*-click the available colors panel in the palette at the extreme right edge (where the color is white).

2. **Choose Image⇨Add Borders.**

   The Add Borders dialog box appears — unless your image has multiple layers. In that event, Paint Shop Pro first displays a dialog box warning you that the layers must be merged to proceed. Click <u>Y</u>es to proceed or <u>N</u>o otherwise.

3. **Set your border widths, in pixels.**

   For a border that is the same width on all sides, leave the check mark in the Symmetric check box and enter your border width in the Top, Bottom, Left, or Right box. (It doesn't matter which you use; they all change together.) For different border widths on all sides, clear that Symmetric check mark and enter your border widths in all the boxes individually.

Click OK. Your image is now larger by the borders you have set.

Borders are no different than any other area of your image; they're just new and all of one color.

Achieving a Particular Canvas Size

Paint Shop Pro enables you to expand the *canvas size* of any image: to add a border area around the image to achieve a particular image width and height. The canvas size command has the same end effect as the add borders command.

"But," you say, wisely, "If 'add borders' has the same effect, why would I bother with the canvas size command?" You would bother if you were looking to end up with an image of a particular size — and didn't want to do the arithmetic necessary to calculate how much border to add to the existing dimensions.

You may use the canvas size command, for instance, if you were making a catalog using images of various heights and widths, but wanted all the images to be of uniform height and width. You couldn't resize the *images,* as that would distort them. If you used the add borders command, you would have to calculate border widths to fill out each image to the right dimensions. With canvas sizing, however, you can simply place each image on a uniformly sized background. Here's how:

1. **Choose a canvas (border) color by setting the background color in the color palette.**

   For example, for a white canvas, right-click the available colors panel in the palette where the color is white, at the panel's extreme right edge.

2. **Choose Image⇨Canvas Size.**

   The Canvas Size dialog box makes the scene.

3. **Enter a new width and new height for your image in the boxes of those names.**

   These numbers define how big your image is going to end up, with its expanded canvas (borders).

4. **Choose how you want your image placed (positioned) on the canvas.**

   To center the image horizontally, click to place a check mark in the Center Image Horizontally check box. To center vertically, click to place a check mark in the Center Image Vertically check box.

   To position the image off-center horizontally, clear the Center Image Horizontally check mark and enter border widths in the Left and Right boxes. Similarly, to position the image off-center vertically, clear the Center Image Vertically check box and adjust the Top and Bottom values. If you only adjust one value of a pair, say the Top value, click in the other box (Bottom, in this instance), and Paint Shop Pro automatically computes and enters the correct value to achieve the dimension you entered in Step 3.

Click OK and your image is mounted upon a fresh canvas of your chosen size and background color. If (as in the catalog example I use) you're trying to get many images centered on canvases of the same size, you find it convenient that your previous canvas size settings remain as you open each image. All you have to do is choose Image⇨Canvas Size for each subsequent image and click OK.

Fix Photo Lighting Flaws

Figure C-1a: My lovely wife, Katy overcomes bad photography when the Automatic Color Balance effect adjusts "color temperature."

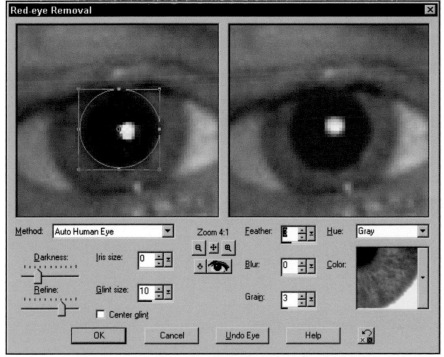

Figure C-1b: Paint Shop Pro's automatic Red-Eye Remover effect takes the evil glint from my eye.

Remedy Photo Flops

Figure C-2a: The original photo: a nice snapshot taken on a dim day needs some help.

Figure C-2b: First, some help from the Automatic Contrast Enhancement effect.

Figure C-3b: Second, a boost from the Automatic Saturation Enhancement effect.

Figure C-3d: Finally, a fake sky: the original was selected by Magic Wand, and a gradient blue-white fill was added with the Flood Fill tool.

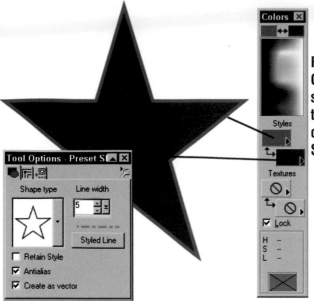

Figure C-3a: Plain painting. Color Palette Style swatches specify color and style; here, the outline and fill of a star, created with the Preset Shapes tool, are both plain.

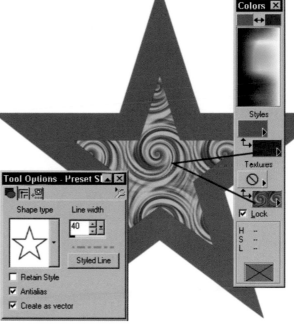

Figure C-3b: Fancier fill. Here, a Background (or Fill) texture is turned on. Combined with the Background or Fill color, a swirly blue fill occurs.

Figure C-3c: Fancier yet! Here, the foreground style is now a gradient, and a foreground texture is turned on, too. Textures tend to make paints transparent, so the fill can be seen through the inner half of the outline.

Layers Help Create Cool Text

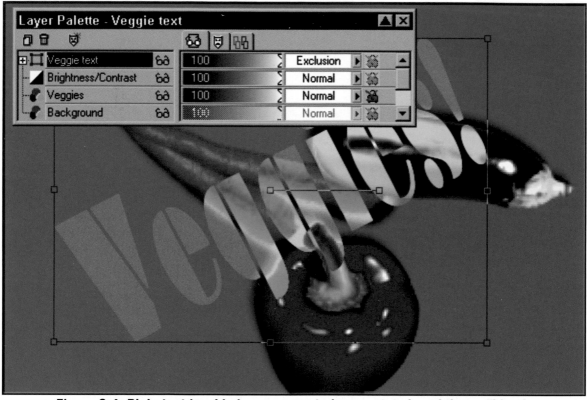

Figure C-4: Plain text is added as a separate layer, rotated, and then a "blend mode" of "exclusion" causes its color to interact with the background. The background uses veggies from Paint Shop Pro's Picture Tube tool.

Figure C-5: Text with multicolor gradients is bent to fit a hidden curved line. The skyline has a textured fill.

Gallery of Effected Ancestors

This "hall of ancestors" shows what many of Paint Shop Pro's various Effects do. The ancestors' progenitor is Sir Normal in the upper-left corner.

Sepia tone

Aged newspaper

Circle

Curly Qs

Horizontal cylinder

Vertical cylinder

Pentagon

Horizontal perspective

Vertical perspective

Pinch

Pixelate

Punch

Ripple

Skew

Spiky halo

Twirl

Warp

Wave

Wind

Feedback

Kaleidoscope

Pattern

Rotating mirror

Blinds

Tiles

Texture

Sculpture

Mosaic glass

Mosaic glass

Mosaic

Emboss

Soft plastic forms

Enamel

Sandstone

Topography

Brush strokes

Polished stone

Pencil

Colored edges

Lighting effects

Sunburst

Page curl

Contours

Fine leather

Rough leather

Colored foil

Straw wall

Fur

Select an Area by Color and Modify It

Figure C-9a: This cardinal's distinctive color makes selecting it easy. Clicking the Magic Wand tool on the red cardinal selects other red pixels. Sometimes additions to or subtractions from the selection have to be made using other tools.

Figure C-9b: Once an area is selected, you can do darned near anything to it. In this case, it was "colorized" a bright canary yellow!

Color Tricks for Instant Art

**Figure C-10a: The original photograph
(our Rusty, looking photogenic in Vermont)
in 16.7 million colors.**

**Figure C-10b: Reducing colors (here, to 16)
helps make a smaller file (useful for Web work),
but also creates an interesting artistic effect.**

Figure C-11: Other tricks for artistic effect: Using the Edge-Preserving Smooth Effect, set high, removes fine detail, then Posterizing reduces colors (here, to 17) and blends, for a watercolor effect.

Combining Images

Figure C-12a: The original, a low-resolution digital snapshot — but where's Mom?

Figure C-12b: Ah, here's Mom — at work, hugging a PC monitor. She'd much rather be hugging her family.

Figure C-12c: Mom is copied and pasted as a layer. The layer transparency is adjusted so she can be positioned properly and resized to fit.

Figure C-12d: The background on Mom's layer could simply be erased, but masking is more flexible; a mask was added and made visible, and in mask edit mode the background "painted out" with black "transparency paint."

Figure C-12e: Mom now with Dad and the kids. A little tweaking of Mom's layer was needed to compensate for different lighting; a little edge-feathering would make her fit more naturally.

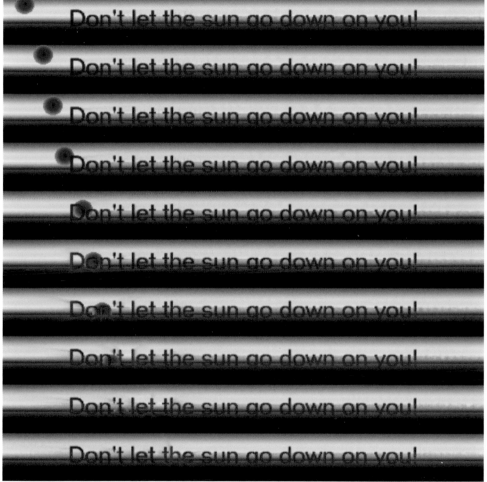

Figure C-13: Multiple frames of an animated banner. The sun is on a layer between sky and sea in Paint Shop Pro, and moved for each frame. An Animation Shop effect moves light rays through the text.

Logo Design

Figure C-14: Layering and fill tricks help make a logo. Text with an outline only is created in a vector layer, copied to a raster layer, selected, filled-around with white, and that layer is made transparent while the vector layer is hidden. Paint Shop Pro's Picture Tube tool made the background leaf pattern.

Printing Album Pages and Collections

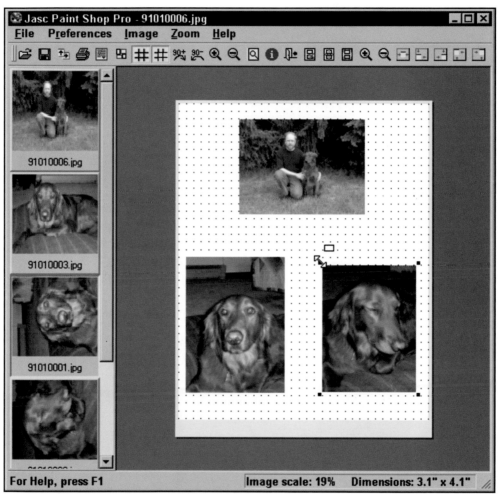

Figure C-15: Paint Shop Pro's Print Multiple Images feature lets you lay out, size, and rotate images to create pages for photo albums, simple collages, or other collections of images.

Smudging and Retouching

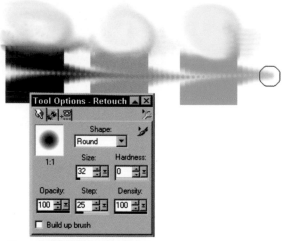

Figure C-16a: Paint Shop Pro's Retouch tool, in Smudge mode, substitutes for your finger in doing artistic smudging and blending. A straight line smudges through the center, and swirls smudge the tops of these colors.

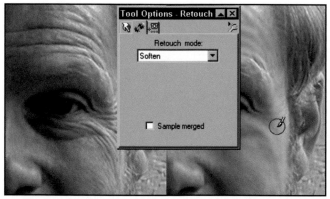

Figure C-16b: The Retouch tool in Soften mode makes quick work of the wrinkles this author acquired while doing this book. Balance reasserts itself in the universe.

Chapter 13

Selecting Parts of an Image

· ·

In This Chapter

▶ Selecting areas

▶ Feathering and antialising

▶ Disabling the selection marquee

▶ Selecting, deselecting, and inverting

▶ Saving and restoring selections

▶ Coping with layers in making and using selections

· ·

*I*f Uncle Dave is looking a bit dark and gloomy in your wedding picture, should the whole wedding party have to lighten up to make up for him? Heavens, no!

If the photographer for your brochure happened to photograph the vile, lime green version of your product, should you now be stuck with that color? Absolutely not.

You should be able to re-do your product in screaming magenta or lighten up Uncle Dave, maybe remove him entirely, while leaving the rest of the image alone. In short, you need to be able to select only that portion of the image that you need to work on.

The problem is that Paint Shop Pro hasn't the foggiest idea that your product or your Uncle Dave are in the picture. It's all just colored dots to Paint Shop Pro, so you need a way to tell Paint Shop Pro things like, "Select all those lime-green-colored dots," (no, not Uncle Dave) or "Select everything within this line that I'm drawing." After you accomplish that, you can restrict Paint Shop Pro's magic to the selected area and even move or remove selected portions of an image.

Paint Shop Pro has other features besides selection that restrict its actions to certain parts of an image: layers and masking. You can use those features to affect the way selection appears to work. See Chapters 15 and 17 for details of layers and masking, respectively.

Selecting is a key tool for altering the content of an image. Selecting in just the right way is key to altering exactly the content you want. Paint Shop Pro lets you be just as selective as you want.

I deal with selecting parts of your image that are bitmap *(raster)* images in this chapter. I don't, however, deal with the special case of selecting *vector* objects here. The text and shapes that the Text, Draw, and Preset Shapes tools make are almost always vector objects. To read about selecting vector objects, see the discussion of controlling your objects in Chapter 16.

Selecting an Area

Selecting is creating a restricted area in which you want Paint Shop Pro to do its thing — a sort of construction zone. "Its thing" is whatever operation you choose, whether it's moving, changing color, painting, filling, smudging, filtering, erasing, copying, pasting, mirroring — essentially any image change Paint Shop Pro can perform. For instance, you can select an elliptical area around Aunt Elizabeth in a group photo, copy that area to the Windows clipboard, and then paste it as a new image to create a classical cameo style oval image.

If you have layers in your image, selection can be slightly more complicated. See "Avoiding Selection Problems in Layered Images," later in this chapter.

The selected area has a moving dashed line around it, called a *marquee*. Figure 13-1 shows Rusty the Wonder Dog in his very own marquee.

Figure 13-1: A moving dashed line, called the *marquee,* shows your selection. I created this selection with the Freehand (lasso) tool.

Paint Shop Pro gives you a lot of flexibility in creating a selection, as I describe in the following bullets:

✓ **You can make a selection by:**

- Dragging a rectangular, circular, or other regular shape with the Selection tool

- Drawing an outline using the Freehand tool

- Clicking on an area that has a more-or-less uniform color or brightness using the Magic Wand tool

Figure 13-2 shows those three tools on the tool palette.

✓ **You can move, add pixels to, or remove pixels from your selection to modify it.**

✓ **You can *feather* or *antialias* the edges of a selection to keep natural-looking edges around your selected area.**

Your main tools for making a selection are on the tool palette, as shown in Figure 13-2. To make them work exactly the way you want, however, you need to use the Tool Options window. (See the following sidebar, "Keep your options open," for reminders about this window.)

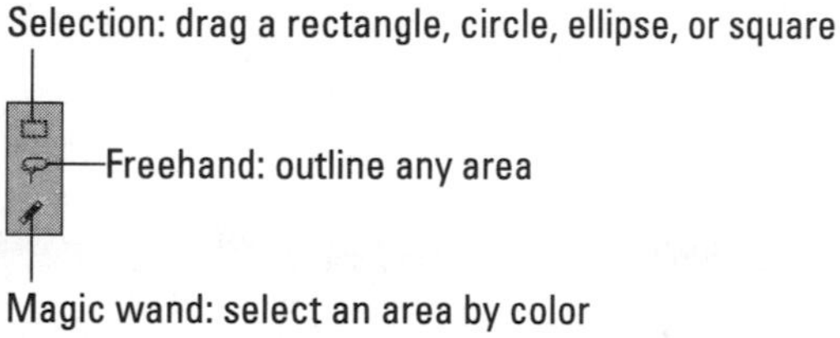

Figure 13-2: Three ways to make a selection.

Selection: drag a rectangle, circle, ellipse, or square

Freehand: outline any area

Magic wand: select an area by color

To make and modify selections, you can use the high-tech selection tools, shown in Figure 13-2, or give commands in the Selection menu. Because you can add to or subtract from a selection with any selection tool, you may also find yourself switching between tools to build or carve out a selection of a particularly tricky shape.

Selecting a rectangle or other regular shape

Selecting a rectangular area is particularly useful for copying portions of an image to paste elsewhere as a separate image. It's also useful for working on portions of your image that happen to *be* rectangular. Paint Shop Pro's Selection tool lets you select rectangles, circles, and other predetermined shapes.

Keep your options open

The Tool Options window is important for creating selections. When you use any tool on the tool palette, you can click the Toggle Tool Options Window button on the Toolbar or press the *O* key on your keyboard to view the Tool Options window (if it isn't already on-screen). If only the window's title bar appears, the window is rolled up; pause your cursor over its title bar to unroll it.

The Tool Options window has two or three tabs. If your Tool Options window doesn't match the illustrations in this chapter, you may be looking at the wrong tab. Click the leftmost tab (often called *Tab 1*). See Chapter 1 for more about roll-up windows, Toolbar buttons, and the Tool Options window.

Dragging a shape

To create the selection area, click the Selection tool, shown in Figure 13-2, and then drag diagonally on your image. You determine the shape that you drag in the Tool Option window of Figure 13-3.

Figure 13-3:
Choose your shape and any edge-smoothing options for the Selection tool.

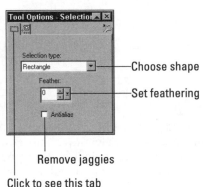

— Choose shape

— Set feathering

Remove jaggies

Click to see this tab

Click the Selection Type box to choose Rectangle, Circle, Ellipse, or Square. Drag diagonally to give your area both width and height. Following are a few tips for making and changing your selection:

✔ **Trying again:** After you define a selection, you can't resize it by dragging sides or corners, as you may expect. Right-click anywhere to clear the shape to try again. Or, you can simply drag a fresh shape if you begin your new drag anywhere outside the existing selection.

✔ **Dragging:** After you've selected an area, if you want to move that portion of the image, you may drag it. Unfortunately, this feature also makes accidental dragging very easy! Just press Ctrl+Z to undo an accidental drag.

✔ **Modifying:** To move, add to, or subtract from the selection, see "Modifying Your Selection," later in this chapter.

✔ **Smoothing edges:** The other features of the Tool Options window for the Selection tool are feathering and antialiasing, which both help smooth edges of a selection. The other selection tools use those features, too, so please see the sections, "Feathering for More Gradual Edges," and "Antialiasing for Smoother Edges," coming up soon, for help with them.

Selecting precise areas with the Select Area dialog box

If you want to select a rectangle very precisely and you know the pixel coordinates of the edges of that rectangle, double-click the Selection tool. The Select Area dialog box appears, in which you can enter Left, Right, Top, and Bottom coordinates for the rectangle, just as you do in the Crop dialog box. (See Chapter 12.) Click OK when you're done.

With that same Select Area dialog box, you can alternatively select a rectangle around an existing, non-rectangular selection. For instance, you may have selected Uncle Dave's head with the ellipse shape to brighten him up and now you want to select a rectangle around that ellipse in order to copy Uncle Dave to a separate wallet-sized portrait. Choose the Surround Current Selection option in the Select Area dialog box.

Finally, you can easily select images on transparent backgrounds. Perhaps you moved Uncle Dave's face to a separate layer, for instance, which is otherwise transparent. Using the Select Area dialog box, you can select just that filled-in *(opaque)* area. To base your selection on the opaque area of the current layer, choose the Select Opaque Area – Current Layer option in the Select Area dialog box. To base your selection on the opaque area of all layers combined, choose Select Opaque Area – Merged.

Selecting by outlining: The Freehand tool

I find the Freehand tool to be one of the most useful of the selection tools. It lets you define the area you want by outlining. It even helps you with that outlining, so you don't have to scrutinize every pixel you include or exclude.

On the tool palette, click the lasso icon (the Freehand tool) shown here in the margin. Your Tool Options window (Tab 1) then looks something like Figure 13-3. (Press the *O* key to flash the Tool Options window on or off, if you've misplaced that window.)

The Freehand tool gives you three ways to snare a selection. From the Selection Type drop-down list (opened, in Figure 13-4), choose whichever of the following methods best suits the area you're trying to select:

✓ **Freehand:** Drag an outline around the area you want to select. At whatever point you release the mouse button, Paint Shop Pro finishes the outline with a straight line to your starting point. This method is best for an area with a complex shape, especially if it doesn't have a clear edge. (If it does have a clear edge, try the Smart Edge method instead.)

✓ **Point to Point:** Click at points around the area you want to select. As you click, the outline appears as straight line segments connecting those points. To close the loop, double-click or right-click, and Paint Shop Pro draws the final line segment from that point back to the starting point. This method works well for areas with straight edges.

✓ **Smart Edge:** (This is my favorite.) If the area you want to select has a noticeable edge — a transition between light and dark, such as the edge of someone's head against a contrasting background — choose this type of selection. To begin, click at any point along the edge. A skinny rectangle appears, with one end attached to your cursor. Move your cursor to another point along the edge, so that a portion of the edge is contained entirely within the rectangle and click. Paint Shop Pro selects along the edge. Continue clicking along the edge in this way; Figure 13-5 shows the result. Double-click, or right-click, and Paint Shop Pro finishes the outline with a straight line back to your starting point.

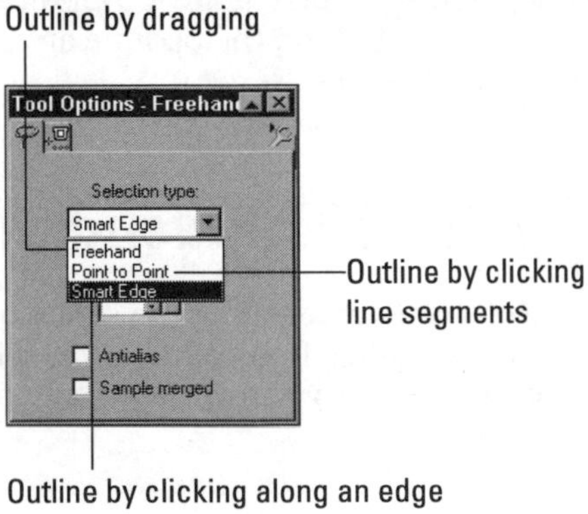

Outline by dragging

Figure 13-4: Three ways to outline your selection with the lasso (the Freehand tool).

Tool Options - Freehand

Selection type:
Smart Edge
Freehand
Point to Point — Outline by clicking
Smart Edge   line segments

☐ Antialias
☐ Sample merged

Outline by clicking along an edge

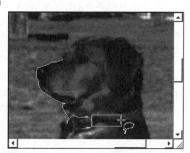

Figure 13-5:
Rusty's muzzle, then his bandana, form an edge that Smart Edge can detect.

Here are a few tips for selecting with the Freehand tool:

- ✔ **Aborting:** You can't abort the selection process once you begin. Instead, right-click (or release the mouse button if dragging) to finish the loop, and then press Ctrl+D or right-click again to remove the selection.

- ✔ **Undoing segments:** If you're in the middle of using Point to Point or Smart Edge and make a mistake, you can undo segments by pressing the Delete key on your keyboard.

- ✔ **Being precise:** When using Smart Edge, click directly on or near the edge as you go around the shape. (Or, said in other ways: Don't over-shoot any bends in the edge. Don't let the edge exit the rectangle from the side of the rectangle.)

- ✔ **Smoothing edges:** The Freehand tool provides antialiasing and feather-ing, which, if you're going to use them, you should set up before doing the selection. See the upcoming sections, "Feathering for More Gradual Edges" and "Antialiasing for Smoother Edges."

- ✔ **Using layers:** If your image uses layers, Smart Edge normally looks for the edge only within the currently active layer. If you want it to look at all layers combined, enable the Sample Merged check box.

Selecting by color or brightness: The Magic Wand tool

Sometimes you want to select an area that is so uniform in appearance that you would like to simply tell Paint Shop Pro, "Go select that red balloon," or whatever it is. To you, with your human perception, the area is an obvious thing of some sort. In software, anything that even slightly mimics human perception is often called *magic*. The Magic Wand selection tool is no excep-tion. It can identify and select areas of uniform color or brightness, somewhat as your eye does.

One benefit of this tool is that you can select areas with complex edges that would be a pain in the wrist to trace with the Freehand tool. For instance, a selection of blue sky that includes a complex skyline of buildings and trees would be relatively easy with the Magic Wand tool.

The Magic Wand tool doesn't, however, work as well as your eye. In particular, if the color or brightness of the area you're trying to select isn't uniform or doesn't contrast strongly with the surroundings, the selection is likely to be spotty, incomplete, or have rough edges.

Paint Shop Pro gives you lots of ways to improve an imperfect selection. See "Modifying Your Selection," later in this chapter, and, in particular, the subsection "Growing — fixing imperfect selections."

Making the selection

To make a selection, click the Magic Wand icon shown in the margin. Your cursor takes on the Magic Wand icon. Click the Magic Wand cursor on your image, and it selects all adjacent pixels that match (or nearly match) the pixel you clicked on. (Note that the selection does *not* include isolated pixels — pixels that, even though they match, are separated from the place you clicked by non-matching pixels.)

To get the selection you want when you use the Magic Wand tool, consult the Tool Options window. The Tool Options window for the Magic Wand tool looks like Figure 13-6. It lets you define (by using the Match mode list) exactly what you mean by match, and lets you adjust (by adjusting the Tolerance setting) how closely the selected pixels should match the one you clicked on.

Select by color, brightness, or content

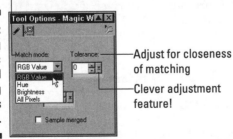

Figure 13-6: Fine-tuning your Magic Wand tool before using it ensures good magic.

—Adjust for closeness of matching

—Clever adjustment feature!

If your image uses layers, be sure the currently active layer is the one containing the area you want to select. Enable the Sample Merged check box in the Tool Options window so that the Magic Wand tool examines all layers combined. Otherwise, the Magic Wand tool selects a totally wrong area, and you'll wonder what's happening!

Choosing the Match Mode for better results

Click the Match Mode list box, as Figure 13-6 shows, and you can choose exactly how you want Paint Shop Pro to select the pixels around the place you clicked. The four choices are as follows:

- ✔ **RGB Value:** Basically, when you choose this, you tell Paint Shop Pro to "select pixels that match in both color *and* brightness." Clicking on a red apple using this choice may select only the highlighted side where you clicked, for instance. Technically, it selects all adjacent pixels with red (R), green (G), and blue (B) primary color values that match the one you clicked on.

- ✔ **Hue:** Like with RGB Value, you're telling Paint Shop Pro to "select pixels that match in color" when you choose Hue. Hue, however, is somewhat more independent of brightness than RGB Value. (See Chapter 10 for help understanding RGB and Hue.) Clicking on a red apple with this choice is more likely to select the entire apple than if you chose RGB Value. Technically, it selects all adjacent pixels with hues (in the Hue/Saturation/Lightness color system, or color wheel) that match the hue of the pixel you clicked on.

- ✔ **Brightness:** Brightness disregards color and selects all adjacent pixels whose brightness matches the one you clicked on. It's a useful choice for selecting things that are similarly illuminated, like shadows and highlights, or that are in a notably light or dark color compared with the background.

- ✔ **All Pixels:** This choice sounds odd, but it doesn't really mean *all* pixels. It's a special choice for when you're working on an image that has transparent areas — areas of no content whatever — usually displayed with a checkered background. It tells Paint Shop Pro to select the area that actually has content around the pixel where you clicked. For instance, you may have photos of various air freshener products on a transparent layer, artistically floating over a cow pasture in the background. With this choice, you can just click on one of the products to select it in its entirety.

If you really want to select all the pixels in your image, press Ctrl+A or choose Selections➪Select All.

Experiment to get the mode that works best for you! Press Ctrl+D to deselect each failed experiment, change match modes, and click again with the Magic Wand tool.

Setting tolerance to include more or fewer pixels

The Tolerance setting in the Tool Options window helps you determine how much of an area is selected by the Magic Wand tool. You may have to undo your selection with Ctrl+D, adjust Tolerance, and re-click with the Magic Wand tool several times to get the best selection possible. For an easier solution, see the discussion of growing a selection in the upcoming section, "Modifying a Selection."

Tolerance tells Paint Shop Pro how closely the pixels it selects should match the pixel you clicked on — in RGB value, hue, or brightness, depending upon which Match Mode you chose. (Tolerance doesn't matter for All Pixels match mode. A pixel either has content or it doesn't.) Here's how it works:

- Lower the tolerance value to make a less extensive selection the next time you click.
- Raise the tolerance value to make a more extensive selection the next time you click.

In Paint Shop Pro, low tolerance means that the Magic Wand tool tolerates little variation in color or brightness from the pixel you clicked on. The tolerance value itself has no particular meaning; it's just a number.

The Tolerance value box in the Magic Wand tool's Tool Options window has a clever adjustment feature that you find in similar boxes throughout Paint Shop Pro. As with such boxes in any Windows program, you can type a value into its text box (from 0 to 200) or click its up- or down-arrow to adjust the value. But, I find that the best way is to click the down-arrow, labeled *Clever adjustment feature!* in Figure 13-6, and hold your mouse button down. A tiny slider appears that you can drag left or right to set the tolerance value lower or higher.

Tolerance can be a very sensitive and picky adjustment. A small change can sometimes make a big difference in what gets selected. Unless you're trying to select an area that is well-differentiated by color, brightness, or content, you probably have to adjust your selected area afterward. I tell you how to do that in the next section.

Modifying Your Selection

If you didn't select exactly the area you wanted with one of Paint Shop Pro's selection tools, don't despair. You can fine-tune or completely rework your selection in any of the following ways:

- Drag the selection outline to another area of your image.
- Add to or subtract from your selection by using the selection tools.
- Expand or contract the selection's boundary by a given number of pixels.
- Grow the selection to include adjacent pixels of similar color or brightness.
- Select pixels of similar color or brightness anywhere in the image.

The following sections tell you how to do each one of those modifications. Read on!

Moving the selection outline

 To move the selection outline (marquee) to another area of your image, first click the Mover tool shown in the margin. Then mouse down with your *right* mouse button anywhere in the selection area and drag to move the outline elsewhere.

Adding to or subtracting from your selection

You can use the selection tools to add to or remove from your current selection. You can add any area at all, using any selection tool — not just the one you used to create the selection — to do any of the following:

- ✔ You can add or subtract areas around the edge of your selection. You can add cousin Alma's hat to a selection of her head, for instance, or remove it (the hat selection, not her head).

- ✔ You can select multiple, isolated areas throughout the image. You could select all the buttons on your product, for instance.

- ✔ You can remove isolated areas from the selection. For example, you could remove a policeman's buttons from a selection of his uniform.

- ✔ You can use the same tool you used for the initial selection, but you can also use any of the other selection tools. Although you may have used Smart Edge to select Rusty's head, you can add his red bandanna with the Magic Wand tool.

Performing the addition or subtraction is simple as, well, arithmetic. Simpler, even. Do either of the following:

- ✔ **To add areas to an existing selection:** Hold down the Shift key and, with any selection tool, make a new selection outside of (or overlapping) the original selection. A + sign appears next to the tool's cursor to remind you that you're adding.

- ✔ **To subtract areas from an existing selection:** Hold down the Ctrl key and make a selection within (or overlapping) the original selection. A – sign attaches itself to the selection tool's cursor.

Here's an example. In Figure 13-7, I originally clicked with the Magic Wand tool on my wife Katy's blue clothing, using Brightness for my Match Mode. (I chose Brightness over Hue because the contrast in brightness between dark blue clothing and white snow was stronger than the uniformity of the blue.) The selection extended over to sled dog Starr's darker markings, however, which I didn't want.

Figure 13-7:
Removing
Starr from
the
selection by
outlining her
with the
Freehand
tool while
pressing the
Ctrl key.

To remove Starr from this selection, I held down the Ctrl key and used the Freehand tool (set to the Freehand selection type) to draw a loop around Starr. Figure 13-7 shows this loop nearing completion. Note the – sign near the lasso cursor, indicating subtraction. When I released my mouse button, Paint Shop Pro completed the loop and subtracted Starr from the selection. I could just as easily have used the Selection tool and (with the Ctrl key pressed) dragged an elliptical selection around Starr. In real life, Starr was never this easy to lasso.

Expanding and contracting by pixels

Expanding or *contracting* a selection in Paint Shop Pro simply means adding or removing a set of pixels around the edge of the selection area. It's like packing snow onto a snowman or melting it away. You can expand or contract a selection by as many snowflakes . . . er, pixels as you like.

Choose Selections⇨Modify⇨Expand or Selections⇨Modify⇨Contract. The very simple-looking Expand Selection, or Contract Selection, dialog box appears. Set the Number of Pixels control to however many pixels you want to add or remove and click OK.

Growing — fixing imperfect selections

Growing a selection means to add pixels around the edge of an existing selection — pixels that are similar to the pixels within the selection. What it usually means from a practical standpoint is this:

If you try to select a colored area with the Magic Wand tool, but you don't succeed in selecting as much of that area as you wanted (the selection has holes or rough edges), you can often fix the problem by *growing* that selection. (Although growing works on any selection, no matter how you created it, growing is most useful for the often spotty selections you create with the Magic Wand tool.) Figure 13-8 shows a selection of a barn roof made before (top) and after (bottom) using the grow command.

Growing is a bit like clicking every pixel around all the edges of a selection with the Magic Wand tool in add mode (holding the Shift key down). It fills in holes in the selection as well as expanding the periphery.

Figure 13-8:
Fixing the barn roof by growing.

Choose Selections➪Modify➪Grow Selection from the menu bar. Paint Shop Pro expands the selection to include similar pixels.

How similar? First, adjacent pixels that exactly match *any* pixels in the current selection are added. Beyond that, similarity is determined by the Magic Wand tool's tolerance control. Click the Magic Wand tool and adjust the Tolerance setting in the Tool Options window to a value larger than zero; then apply the grow command. A higher tolerance enables the grow command to extend the selection to more pixels.

Often, the grow command only advances the selection a little, falling short of the area you want. In that event, try simply repeating the grow command a few times rather than fooling with the Tolerance control. That's how I did Figure 13-8. If the grow command overshoots your target, however, you have to knock tolerance down a bit. If grow still overshoots your target at zero tolerance, you need to use another technique to modify your selection.

Selecting all areas of similar color

Selecting all the areas of similar color throughout an image is a pain to do manually. You have to find each spot of similar color and click on it with the Magic Wand tool. Paint Shop Pro offers an automatic version of that same task.

First, use any selection tool to select one area of the desired color. Then, choose Selections➪Modify➪Select Similar. Paint Shop Pro selects all pixels similar to the colors within your selection.

How similar? As with the grow command, the select similar command looks to the Magic Wand tool's Tolerance control to determine how similar to the original color a selected pixel should be. Click the Magic Wand tool and adjust the Tolerance control in the Tool Options window. A high tolerance means a color can be significantly different and still be selected; a low tolerance selects only colors very close to those in your original selection.

If you're selecting areas of a particular color because you intend to change that color throughout the image, consider using the Color Replacer tool instead. See Chapter 5 for instructions.

Sometimes, you don't really want *all* the pixels of similar color, just those within a certain region of the image. Fussy, fussy. For instance, you may want all the sky, including that which peeks through the tree branches, but not the similarly colored pond, thank you. No problem. Just draw a freehand selection around the pond while pressing the Ctrl key to subtract that area.

Feathering for More Gradual Edges

When you copy or modify selected areas, you may notice that the edge between the selection and the background becomes artificially obvious. To keep a natural-looking edge on such objects, use *feathering* in your selection.

Feathering creates a blending zone of several pixels (however many you choose) extending both into and out of your selection. Whatever change you make to the selected area fades gradually within that zone, from 100 percent at the inner edge to zero percent at the outer edge of the zone. For instance, if you were to increase the brightness of the selected area, that increase fades gradually to zero at the outer edge of the feathered zone. If you delete, copy, cut, or move a feathered selection, you also leave a feathered edge behind.

You can apply feathering in either of two ways:

✓ **Before making the selection:** In the Tool Options dialog box for whatever selection tool you're using, set the Feather value to something greater than zero. When you next make a selection, the feathering is applied and the marquee's enclosed area expands to include the outer feathered pixels.

✓ **After making the selection:** Choose Selections➪Modify➪Feather, or press Ctrl+H, and the Feather Selection dialog box appears. Set the Feather value in that dialog box to something greater than zero and then click OK. The area within the selection marquee expands slightly.

When using the Magic Wand tool, I prefer to leave feathering set to zero in the Tool Options dialog box and do my feathering after making the selection. Selecting with a feather value of zero enables me to clearly see any holes in the selected area.

The value you set in the Feather control tells Paint Shop Pro how wide to make the feather zone — how many pixels to extend it into, and out of, the selection. (A setting of 4, for instance, creates a feathered zone 4 pixels into and 4 pixels out from the edge of the selection, for a total of 8 pixels wide.) A larger value makes a wider, more gradually feathered edge. When you feather, the marquee expands to include the pixels that are in the feathering zone.

Figure 13-9 shows the difference feathering makes. Normally, Alex is fairly fuzzy around the edges anyway. Feathering makes his edges even fuzzier. I copied the image on the left without feathering and the one on the right with feathering.

Figure 13-9:
Alex,
selected
and pasted
onto a white
background,
without
feathering
on the left
and with
feathering
on the right.

When you copy or move a feathered selection, you bring along a faint border — feathered copies of the original background pixels surrounding the selection. The image on the right in Figure 13-9 shows some grass background, for instance. One way to avoid copying background pixels is to (before you copy or move the selection) contract the selection by the same number of pixels that you set in the Feather control. See "Expanding and Contracting By Pixels," earlier in this chapter, for instructions on contractions. If the original background is fairly uniform in color — say, a green lawn — a better approach is to make that color transparent. Before copying or moving the selection, press Ctrl+T. In the Remove Transparent Color dialog box that appears, choose the background color of the original image in the Transparent Color list box. To the extent that the background wasn't entirely uniform in color, increase the Tolerance setting and click OK.

Because feathering a selection expands the marquee, it gives the appearance of filling in holes in a selection (adding them entirely to the selection). It doesn't really add those holes entirely to the selection, however; the pixels in them are simply feathered. As a result, if you feather a selection that has holes in it and then cut, delete, or move it, you leave behind faint images of those holes. (If you paste it, the pixels in those holes are faded.) If your selection has holes, try growing the selection before you feather it. (See "Growing — fixing imperfect selections," earlier in this chapter.)

Antialiasing for Smoother Edges

Computer images are made up of tiny squares (the pixels), so when a straight edge of a selection is anything but perfectly horizontal or vertical, those squares give the edge a microscopic staircase or sawtooth shape known as *aliasing*. Any changes you make to the selected area, or any cutting or pasting of the selection, may make that aliasing objectionably obvious.

To avoid aliasing when you next make a selection, click to enable the Antialias check box in the Tool Options window for your selection tool. Antialiasing is only available for the Selection and Freehand tools, not the Magic Wand tool. (With Magic Wand tool selection, you can use feathering to reduce most aliasing problems. Notice that Alex's edge isn't aliased in the feathered version you see in Figure 13-9.)

The antialiasing option, like other settings in the Tool Options window, only applies to selections you make *after* choosing that option, not to a *current* selection. You can't fix an existing aliased selection by clicking that option.

Hiding the Selection Marquee

The moving selection marquee sometimes gets in the way of viewing your image. For instance, complex selection outlines can hide your selected pixels under an apparent swarm of moving marquee bees.

You can choose Selections⇨Hide Marquee or press Ctrl+Shift+H to hide the marquee. (Repeat that command or key combination to restore the marquee.) Your selection still exists, but the marquee is gone.

The problem with hiding the marquee is that you tend to forget that an area is currently selected! As a result, all kinds of mysterious problems arise when tools apparently fail to work. (They work only in the selected area, which you have forgotten exists.) If a tool seems to be acting totally weird, make sure that your marquee isn't hidden.

Selecting All, None, or Everything But

Sometimes you want selection to be an all-or-nothing proposition! To select the entire image, press Ctrl+A or choose Selections⇨Select All.

To *select none* (also known as *clearing* the selection or *deselecting*), press Ctrl+D or choose Selections⇨Select None. You can also clear selections (except when the entire image is selected) by right-clicking anywhere on the image.

Sometimes you may want to select *everything but:* the part of the image that is *not* currently selected. For instance, now that you have painstakingly selected Uncle Dave and lightened him up, you may want to select everything *but* Uncle Dave and do some other image processing. This is known as *inverting* the selection. To perform it, choose Selections⇨Invert or press Ctrl+Shift+I.

Selecting complex shapes more easily

Selecting *everything but* and then inverting is a very useful trick when you may have a complex object on a comparatively uniform background. Rather than spend a lot of effort selecting the object, you can more easily select the uniform background with the Magic Wand tool and then, by pressing Ctrl+Shift+I, invert the selection (which selects the complex object).

Saving Selections

Getting a selection exactly the way you want it can be a lot of work, and you may want to use that selection again to do other kinds of image processing on the same area. Paint Shop Pro lets you save your selections in one of two ways:

- As a selection file
- As an alpha channel

You can then restore the selection at any time from the file or channel.

If your image has a selected area when you save it (as a Paint Shop Pro file), that selection is restored when you open the file again. You don't need to save that selection as a file or alpha channel.

Saving the selection as a selection file

For most purposes, the best way to save your selection is as a separate Paint Shop Pro selection (SEL) file on your hard drive. You can create a selection file for any file type, such as a GIF file from the Web, not just Paint Shop Pro (PSP) files. Here's how:

1. **With an area selected in your image, choose Selections➪Save to Disk.**

   The Save Selection Area dialog box appears.

2. **Enter a name and folder for your file.**

3. **Click Save.**

You can save as many different selections as you like by repeating those steps. The file name identifies the selection when you go to restore it.

You can use a selection file to re-create the same selection in *any* image file. You may find that feature useful if you use the same object, such as your corporate logo, in many images and need to select that object as you work on each image. An advantage of using selection files over using an alpha channel is that you can save many such files. Some image file types provide only one alpha channel, which may be needed for a mask, or no alpha channel at all. The disadvantage of a selection file is that it can get accidentally separated from the image file.

Saving a selection as an alpha channel

An *alpha channel* is a general-purpose auxiliary image-storage area that's part of an image file. You can use it to store selections or masks in Paint Shop Pro. (In fact, you can use stored selections as masks, and vice-versa, but that's another story. See Chapter 17.)

Use an alpha channel if you'd like to keep your selection with your image file. (That way, it doesn't get separated if you send your image to someone or reorganize your files.) Here's how to store your selection as an alpha channel:

1. **With an area selected in your image, choose Selections⇨ Save to Alpha Channel.**

   The Save to Alpha dialog box appears.

2. **Double-click New Channel in the Available Alpha selection box.**

   A New Channel dialog box appears.

3. **Enter a name for your selection in the text box provided (unless your image isn't stored as a PSP file) and click OK.**

   Both dialog boxes go away, and your selection is now stored as part of the image file. The name you entered helps you identify that selection when you go to re-create it from the alpha channel. (If you're storing your image as a TIFF, PSD, or TGA file, channel names aren't stored. When you go to re-create the selection, you see names like Alpha Channel 1.)

PSP (Paint Shop Pro) files, TIFF, and PSD (Photoshop) files can have multiple alpha channels, so you can store as many selections as you like by repeating these steps. TGA (Targa) files have only one alpha channel. Very few other standard file types offer alpha channels.

Restoring a saved selection

To restore a selection from a selection file, choose Selections⇨Load From Disk. In the Load Selection Area dialog box that appears, choose the selection file you want and click Open.

To restore a selection from an alpha channel, choose Selections⇨ Load From Alpha Channel. In the Load From Alpha dialog box that appears, double-click the alpha channel you want in the Available Alpha list box.

If you're restoring a selection into a different image than its original one, you probably need to move it. Remember that you can move any selection with the Move tool, dragging with the right mouse button.

Avoiding Selection Problems in Layered Images

Layered images can cause both the selection and the editing of those selections to go apparently screwy. The Magic Wand tool and Smart Edge features may appear neither magic nor smart, selecting areas not at all like you had in mind. Also, whatever changes you try to perform to the selected area (such as cutting, copying, or changing color) may apparently not take place. (If you're not sure if your image has layers, see Chapter 15.)

The basic trick is to work on the right layer. Here are some more detailed rules you can follow to keep the selection and editing process relatively sane.

- ✔ **Activate the right layer:** Before you make any changes to a selected area (no matter what selection tool you've used to create it), make sure to activate the layer that you want to change. You can't change all the layers within a selection at once, but only one layer at a time. You can merge all the layers (see Chapter 15) before making your change, but then you no longer have layers!

- ✔ **Use Sample Merged for combined layers:** Before you make a selection with the Magic Wand tool or Smart Edge feature, if the object you're trying to select is the result of various layers combined, enable the Sample Merged check box in the Tool Options window. That way, the Magic Wand tool or Smart Edge feature examines the combined effect, not just the currently active layer. For instance, if you added a party hat to Uncle Charley's head on a separate layer and now you want to select Charley-with-hat using the Smart Edge feature, you would use Sample Merged.

✔ **Consider the effect of higher layers:** If the changes you try to make to a selected area aren't visible at all, or seem only partially effective, a higher opaque or transparent layer may contain pixels that are obscuring your work. You may have to merge layers, do your changes to the higher, obscuring layer, or re-think your use of layers altogether.

Paint Shop Pro helps keep you sane. The preview window that certain adjustments provide (such as Brightness/Contrast) shows only the area that you're affecting: the selected part of the active layer. If the wrong layer is active, you don't see the area you're expecting!

When you make a selection, it extends to all layers — no matter which one is active at the time. *Changes* to selected image areas, however, affect only the currently active layer. So, for instance, you could activate one layer to make a selection with the Magic Wand tool and then switch to another layer to make changes within that selected area.

Chapter 14

Moving, Copying, and Reshaping Parts of Your Image

*I*n Chapter 13, I tell you how to identify a chunk of your image to Paint Shop Pro by creating a selection. In this chapter, you see how to move, copy, twist, and deform such selections — in short, how to do almost anything that changes the physical location or outline of a selection. (You may also rotate, flip or mirror a selection, but you have to go to Chapter 12 for those tricks.)

Before you get rolling, take the following notes to heart and staple them there:

✔ The instructions in this chapter assume that you know how to make selections. If you don't know how, see Chapter 13.

✔ A *selection* is a selected portion of the image, *not* the selection marquee (moving dashed line).

✔ If your image has multiple layers, make sure you're on the right layer to move, copy, float, or delete the image you want. See Chapter 15 for help with layers.

✔ You can press Ctrl+Z to undo any changes that you make. The changes that you can undo include selection, floating, moving, copying, pasting, or de-floating. See Chapter 1 for more about undoing.

✔ The instructions in this chapter deal only with image chunks that are made out of dots (called raster or bitmap images). Those are the kinds of selections that I describe in Chapter 13 and that you make with the Selection, Freehand, or Magic Wand tools. To deal with vector selections (typically text, lines, and geometric shapes), see Chapter 16.

Floating, Moving, and Deleting Selections

After you've made a selection, you can easily move it anywhere within your image, move a copy of it, or delete it altogether. Here's how to do it:

- **To move a selection:** Choose any selection tool (Selection, Freehand, or Magic Wand), if you haven't already, and then drag the selection. Selection tool cursors become four-headed move arrows when you position them over a selection, as Figure 14-1 shows. On the Background (main) image layer, dragging a selection in this way leaves behind background color. The image on the left in Figure 14-1 shows the effect.

Simply dragging leaves background color

Figure 14-1:
Dragging a
selection.
Float the
image first
with Ctrl+F
to drag a
copy.

Float, then drag to move a copy

- **To float a selection (make it moveable):** A *floating* selection simply means a moveable one. You can float a selection in one of two ways. When you click on an existing selection with a selection tool (as if to move the selection), that selection is floated automatically. Alternatively, you can choose Selections➪Float or press Ctrl+F. Floating a selection in that way (manually) leaves a copy of it behind. (Note that any floating selection also appears in the layer palette.)

- **To move a selection and leave a copy behind** (as the right side of Figure 14-1 shows): *Float the selection manually first* (choose Selections➪Float or press Ctrl+F) and then move it with the Mover tool (the four-headed arrow) or any selection tool.

- **To de-float the floating selection (or glue it back down):** To *de-float* a selection, press Ctrl+Shift+F or choose Selections➪Defloat. You can also *de-select* (press Ctrl+D) to de-float. The de-floating command leaves the area selected in case you want to do additional work on it. Whichever way you de-float the image, de-floating glues the image down. It's now part of the underlying image (or image layer) and its pixels replace whatever was there before. If you move the selection again, you find that the original underlying pixels are no longer there.

✔ **To delete the selection:** Press the Delete key on your keyboard. If the image has only one layer (or the Background layer is the currently active one in a multi-layer image), Paint Shop Pro's background color appears in the deleted area. If the selection is on a layer, the pixels within it simply go away. (Well, okay, technically, they're made transparent — same thing.)

✔ **To move a floating selection to another layer:** Drag the *Floating Selection* layer up or down in the layer palette. Leave the selection immediately above the layer that you ultimately want the selection to join. When you de-float the selection, it joins the closest underlying (raster) layer.

You can also flip or mirror a selection. See Chapter 12 for information on using the Flip and Mirror commands. Both commands leave a copy of the original image underlying the selection.

Cutting, Copying, and Pasting from the Windows Clipboard

To make lots of copies of a selection, use the conventional cut, copy, and paste features that employ the Windows clipboard. You can use these features for copying selections to or from other Windows applications, too, because nearly all Windows applications make use of the clipboard.

Looking snappy by aligning objects

Want your design to look a bit snappier? Line your objects up. To help align objects, you can make a selection *snap* to either a gridline or guide line, as you move the selection. (See Chapter 1 for more about gridlines and guide lines.) Snapping means that if one edge of your selection comes within a certain distance of a gridline or guide line, the edge moves instantly to that line.

To snap to gridlines, turn on gridlines and choose View⇨Snap to Grid. To snap to guide lines, create guide lines and choose View⇨Snap to Guides. To specify what edge or corner of your selection snaps to the line, choose View⇨Snap Alignment and choose an edge or corner among those listed.

To control how close the edge of your selection gets to a line before being snapped up, choose View⇨Snap Influence. In the simple Snap Pixel Influence dialog box that appears, enter a distance in pixels and then click OK.

If your image has multiple layers, first make sure that you have selected the right layer to cut, copy, or paste the image you want. Click the layer's name in the layer palette. (Press *L* if the palette isn't visible). See Chapter 15 for more help with layers.

Cut and copy

In Paint Shop Pro, *cut* and *copy* work very much as they do in any Windows program. First, select an area in your image. Then, do any of the following:

- ✓ **Cut a selection:** Press Ctrl+X, choose Edit⇨Cut, or click the familiar Windows Cut button (scissors icon) on Paint Shop Pro's Toolbar. Paint Shop Pro places a copy of the selected area on the Windows clipboard. If you're cutting on the main (Background) layer of the image, Paint Shop Pro fills the cut area with the current background color in the color palette. On other layers, it leaves behind transparency.

- ✓ **Copy a selection:** Press Ctrl+C, choose Edit⇨Copy, or click the Copy button (two-documents icon) on Paint Shop Pro's Toolbar. Paint Shop Pro puts a copy of the selected area (of the currently active layer) on the Windows clipboard. Nothing happens to your image.

- ✓ **Copy a selection on a multi-layer image:** The normal Edit⇨Copy command copies only from the currently active layer. If your image is made up of multiple layers, you may want to copy the combined effect of all layers. If so, choose Edit⇨Copy Merged (or press Ctrl+Shift+C).

- ✓ **Cut or copy from other applications:** Most Windows applications offer the same Edit⇨Copy and Edit⇨Cut commands so you can place text or graphics on the Windows clipboard. Paint Shop Pro enables you to paste a wide variety of clipboard content from other programs, such as text, vector graphics, or raster graphics.

Paste

After your selection is on the Windows clipboard, choose Edit⇨Paste to paste it into Paint Shop Pro (or nearly any other application). When you choose Edit⇨Paste in Paint Shop Pro, however, you get several different paste options, which I describe briefly below and in more detail in the following sections.

- ✓ **As a new image (Ctrl+V):** The clipboard contents become a whole new image, in its own window.

- ✓ **As a new layer (Ctrl+L):** The clipboard contents become a new layer for the current image. See Chapter 15 for a discussion of layers.

✔ **As a new selection (Ctrl+E):** Clipboard contents become a floating selection that you can place anywhere on the image (on the currently active layer.)

✔ **Into selection (Ctrl+Shift+L):** If you have a currently selected area in your image, this choice fits the clipboard contents exactly into the selection, scaling the contents up or down as needed.

If you're in the habit of using Ctrl+V for editing in other programs, you need to retrain yourself. In Paint Shop Pro, Ctrl+V creates a new image, rather than pasting your selection to the existing image, which is what you probably expect to happen.

Two paste selections that I cover elsewhere in this book are:

✔ **AS animation as multiple images:** To Paint Shop Pro, AS means *Animation Shop.* If you've copied multiple frames from one of these animations onto the clipboard, this command turns each frame into a separate Paint Shop Pro image. See Chapter 20.

✔ **As new vector selection:** This command is used for pasting text and shapes that you created using Paint Shop Pro's text and shapes tools. For more about vectors, see Chapter 16.

If you copy vector graphics from outside Paint Shop Pro (for instance, objects drawn using computer-aided design software, drawing programs, or Microsoft Word's draw feature), Paint Shop Pro converts them to raster graphics when you paste. Paint Shop Pro pops up a Meta Picture Import dialog box in which you can enter either height or width in pixels to determine the image's size. To enter height and width values independently, clear the Maintain Original Aspect Ratio check box.

Pasting to create a new picture: As New Image

The paste As New Image option creates a new image containing the clipboard contents. The image is just big enough to contain whatever is on the clipboard. The background of the image is transparent, which means that if your copied selection isn't rectangular, you see transparent areas; erasing also leaves transparency behind.

Choose Edit➪Paste➪As New Image or press Ctrl+V (the near-universal keyboard command for paste). Your new image appears in a new window.

If you prefer your new image to have a background color or to be slightly larger than the contents of the clipboard, create the new image first, separately (see Chapter 2). Then paste a selection or new layer rather than use the paste As New Image command.

Pasting onto an existing image: As New Selection

The paste As New Selection option pastes the clipboard contents as a floating selection on your image. This pasting option is the one most people want for editing an image, as it is the simplest and most intuitive.

If your image uses multiple layers, make sure to first activate the layer where you want to paste. See Chapter 15.

Choose Edit⇨Paste⇨As New Selection or press Ctrl+E. A floating selection appears on your image.

Because the selection is floating, you drag the selection to move it anywhere in the image. To de-float the selection (paste it down onto the underlying layer), press Ctrl+Shift+F. See the earlier section, "Floating, Moving, and Deleting Selections," for details about moving and de-floating a floating selection.

Pasting without background: As Transparent Selection

Often, you'd like to paste your clipboard contents onto an image, but without the background (or some other portion) of the contents. In that event, using the As Transparent Selection option to paste the clipboard contents may seem like a useful choice, because it can make the background transparent.

Frankly, however, I find this choice confusing to use. It assumes that you've *already* used the Selections⇨Modify⇨Transparent Color command to designate a background color as transparent in a selection.

Instead, I suggest you paste using the As New Selection option (see the preceding section). Then, remove the background color using the method I describe in the upcoming section, "Making Background or Other Colors Transparent."

Pasting to fit: Into Selection

Images that you copy onto the clipboard are often totally the wrong size to paste into another image. You could re-scale them after pasting, but Paint Shop Pro's paste Into Selection command saves you the trouble. Perhaps you're helping a client envision how a new drape will look in place of the old. You want to paste a page-sized drapery catalog photo that you've copied onto the clipboard into a photo of the room in which the existing drapes are much smaller. Take the following steps to paste to fit:

1. **Create the selection into which you'd like to paste, if you haven't already done so.**

   Use any selection tool and shape you like, although you can probably get the best results if you restrict yourself to the rectangular outlines that the Selection tool can make. In my example, you would select a drape in the photo of the room.

2. **Choose Edit⇨Paste⇨Into Selection (or press Ctrl+Shift+L).**

   Paint Shop Pro pastes the clipboard contents to best fit the selection outline. In my example, the new drape is compressed to fit the old drape's dimensions. If the clipboard image has a transparent background (as is the case for all non-rectangular selections copied onto the clipboard in Paint Shop Pro), the underlying image shows through that background.

If you need to paste just a portion of your copied image, say a drapery from a copy of an entire wall, first use the As New Image paste option instead of the Into Selection paste option to create a new, temporary image. Select just the area of interest to you (the drape) by using, say, the Magic Wand tool. Copy the selection onto the clipboard and then return to your original image and to Step 1.

What does *best fit* mean? If, as is likely, the outline of the image on the clipboard doesn't exactly match the outline of the selection, something has to go. Fitting a dog into a giraffe, for instance, would be awkward, not to mention a compromise to the strict vegetarian principles of the giraffe. To solve the problem, Paint Shop Pro squeezes and stretches first, and then trims where necessary. In the dog/giraffe example, Paint Shop Pro scales and distorts the dog to match the giraffe's vertical and horizontal dimensions and then trims it, cookie-cutter-like, to fit within the giraffe outline. For objects that are squeezable in real life, like drapes, squeezing doesn't matter much unless they also have a large pattern. As long as you don't mind the distortion of squeezing, using the Into Selection paste option is a good choice.

Pasting for maximum flexibility: As New Layer

Pasting directly onto another image is fine, as far as it goes. For maximum flexibility in making future changes, however, paste onto a new layer instead. When an image is on a layer, you can modify it to your heart's content without worrying about surrounding or underlying image areas. (In Chapter 15, I discuss the whys and hows of layers in detail.) Here's how:

1. **If your image already has more than one layer, activate (choose) the layer above which you want the new layer to appear.**

   For instance, click the layer in the layer palette to activate it. See Chapter 15 for more details on activating layers.

2. **Choose Edit⇨Paste⇨As New Layer (or press Ctrl+L).**

   Your pasted image appears on a layer of its own.

If the background of the image you pasted was transparent, the underlying image layer shows through those background areas. Otherwise, the pasted image and its background color fill an opaque rectangle. If you want to delete the background (make it transparent), use the Magic Wand tool, or another selection tool, to select it (see Chapter 13) and press the Delete key on your keyboard. Alternatively, see the following section, "Making Background or Other Colors Transparent."

Making Background or Other Colors Transparent

Sometimes you'd like to be rid of the background behind a selection you've moved or pasted. Often, for instance, a pasted object has a solid white or other colored background — perhaps because you copied and pasted it from the Web. Often, the background may not be perfectly uniform. A tree you moved may bring along some blue-ish sky around its edge, or a baby bring along a white blanket with gray folds. You, however, do not want the sky or blanket in the new location. Perhaps you're trying to copy the baby to a photo of a hay-filled manger with sheep looking on adoringly — or hungrily, which is easier, given the hay.

One solution is to make the background color transparent, if it's fairly uniform. (If that color appears elsewhere in the image, however, you may get unwanted transparent holes.)

With the area you're trying to affect selected in your image, do the following:

1. **Make sure the selection is floating: Press Ctrl+F.**

2. **Click the Dropper tool in the tool palette and right-click the background area you want to eliminate from the selection.**

   This step sets Paint Shop Pro's official background color (in the color palette) to match the soon-to-be-eliminated background in the selection.

   If the background color you want to eliminate is a standard color (white, black, red, blue, or green) or nearly so, you can skip this step.

3. **Choose Selections⇨Modify⇨Transparent Color.**

   The Remove Selected Color dialog box appears, sporting two controls: a Transparent Color list box and a Tolerance setting.

4. **Choose Background Color from the Transparent Color list box.**

   This tells Paint Shop Pro to make the official background color in the color palette transparent (but only in the selection).

   If the background color you're trying to eliminate is white, black, red, blue, or green, choose that color in the list box, instead of Background Color.

5. **Set the Tolerance value to something higher than zero.**

   I know this instruction is vague, but only experience or trial and error can really guide you in this setting. Try a value of 10 to 20 to begin with, if in doubt.

6. **Click OK.**

   Paint Shop Pro makes any pixel of the color you choose, or of a similar color, transparent. The higher the tolerance value in Step 5, the less similar the color needs to be, to become transparent.

If the process makes too many or too few pixels transparent, repeat these steps beginning with Step 3 and choose a new tolerance in Step 5. To make more pixels transparent, increase the tolerance value in Step 5; for fewer transparent pixels, decrease the tolerance.

Resizing, Rotating, Deforming, and Perspective-izing

Okay, so perspective-izing isn't a real word. Perspecting? In any event, you can resize, rotate, deform, or move your selection by using the Deformation tool, shown in the margin. (I tell you exactly how to use it in a minute.)

Removing fringe elements

After you paste (or promote to a layer) a selection that was taken from a black, white, or solid-colored background area, you often get a fringe or matte of that surrounding background color. The problem occurs particularly when the selection is feathered or antialiased because some of the background color remains in the edge pixels.

To remove that fringe from an object that's still selected, choose Selections⇨Matting. (To remove it from all the objects on a layer, choose

Layers⇨Matting.) Then, in the submenu that appears, choose Remove Black Matte (if the fringe is black), Remove White Matte (if the fringe is white), or Defringe (if the fringe is any other color).

If you choose Defringe, a Defringe dialog box wants to know how many pixels into the fringe area to extend the edge color(s) of the object. In the Width text box, enter the number of pixels wide the fringe is (use your Feather value, at minimum), and then click OK.

Making a shape look as if seen in perspective is one of the cool kinds of deformation you can do. You can make a rectangular area, for instance, look like a wall or road receding into the distance. You could paint a railroad track running vertically, flat, as if on a map and then make it lie down realistically by applying perspective.

Preparing for deformation

The Deformation tool is picky. A non-floating selection won't do. It needs either a floating selection or a separate layer (other than the background layer) to work with or else it remains grayed-out on the tool palette. Do one of the following if your selection isn't currently floating or on a separate layer:

✔ Float your selection, either by dragging it with a selection tool (which, on the background layer, fills background color into the original area) or by manually floating it with Ctrl+F (which leaves a copy of the selected area behind). Because you're about to change the size, shape, or position of the selection, you have to choose what background you want to appear within the original outline, if it gets revealed.

✔ Move your selection to its own layer. Choose Selections⇨Promote to Layer or press Ctrl+Shift+P. For more about layers, see Chapter 15.

If you have no selection at all, the Deformation tool works on the currently active layer. It encompasses all the non-transparent areas in that layer. In other words, if you have a blob of pixels on a layer, the tool encompasses (rather neatly, in my opinion) just that blob. If you have multiple blobs separated by transparency, it encompasses all blobs.

Doing the deformation

The easy and fairly intuitive way to do the deformation is by dragging various parts of the deformation grid with the Deformation tool. See "Deforming by dragging," coming up next.

The really geeky, but very precise, way to do the deformation is with the Deformation Settings dialog box. See "Deforming by dialog box," a bit later in this chapter.

Deforming by dragging

Click the Deformation tool icon on the tool palette (if it's grayed-out, see the earlier section, "Preparing for Deformation," for instructions), and your cursor turns into that icon. Click on your selection to get this cool-looking *deformation grid* with tiny squares (called *handles*) on it, as Figure 14-2 shows.

Drag anywhere inside grid to move selection

Re-sizing handles

Figure 14-2:
The Deformation tool's grid for stretching, rotating, and dragging the victim.

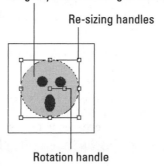

Rotation handle

Figure 14-2 shows you what to drag for resizing, rotating, or moving the image. Note that you can move the selection with this tool by dragging any-where *except* on one of the handles. (In areas where dragging is possible, the cursor changes to a four-way arrow.) Here's how to do various operations, using the handles of the deformation grid:

✔ **Resizing or repositioning sides:** Adjust width and height by dragging the handle in the center of any side. Drag corner handles to change both height and width at the same time. (The Deformation tool provides no way to automatically keep the proportions constant while you drag, but see "Precise Deformations," following, for help.)

✔ **Rotating:** Drag the handle, marked *Rotation handle* in Figure 14-2, in a circular motion around the center of the grid. (When your cursor is over the rotation handle, the cursor depicts the pair of curved arrows shown in Figure 14-3. The center of rotation is marked by a square that, in Figure 14-3, is at the face's nose.) Only the grid rotates until you release the mouse button; then the selection rotates.

Cursor

Figure 14-3:
Dragging
the rotation
handle.
Drag the
cursor away
from the
handle
before
rotating to
get more
precise
control.

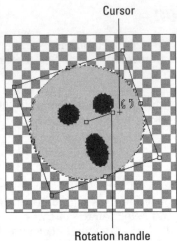

Rotation handle

✔ **Adding perspective:** In the real world, the farther away an object is, the smaller it appears to your eye. Here's how to create that illusion with your selection, so that one end looks farther away:

  • To shrink any side of the selection as if it were farther away, first hold down the Ctrl key. With that key down, drag one of the two corner handles that terminate the side; drag towards the center of that side. To expand the side, drag away from the center. The side shrinks or expands symmetrically about the center (both corners move). The perspective this distortion creates is as if your eyes were level with the middle of the selection, as the left side of Figure 14-4 shows.

  • To shink or expand any side asymmetrically (move one corner only), first hold down the Shift key. With that key down, drag a corner handle toward or away from the center handle of that side. When you apply this effect to the left or right side, as shown on the right in Figure 14-4, the result is as if your eyes were at a level above or below center. For instance, to get the illusion of a tall wall, drag the upper corner down.

  Tip: For a different way to apply simple perspective that doesn't involve as much head scratching, try Paint Shop Pro's Perspective effect. Choose Effects⇨Geometric Effects⇨Perspective Horizontal or Perspective Vertical. See Chapter 9 for help with effect dialog boxes.

✔ **Shear (or *skew*) distortion:** I got the shear effect of Figure 14-5 by dragging the right side of the selection down. To drag a side of your selection, hold down either the Ctrl or Shift key and drag the center handle on the side you want to move.

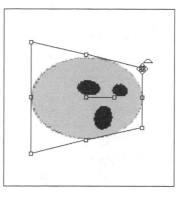 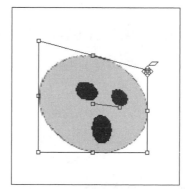

Figure 14-4: Getting perspective by dragging a corner while pressing Ctrl (left image) or Shift (right image).

Shear is useful for perspective when you want the virtual horizon (the vanishing point, in draftman's terms) to be higher or lower than dead center. Apply perspective distortion to shrink a left or right side first, and then use shear to drag one of those sides up or down. Dragging down, for instance, makes the image appear as it would if the viewer were looking up slightly (it lowers the horizon).

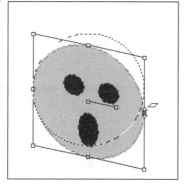

Figure 14-5: Shear brilliance! Dragging a center handle with Ctrl or Shift pressed applies shear distortion.

Deforming by dialog box

Dragging handles is convenient and intuitive, but not particularly precise. What if you know you need to rotate something 31.5 degrees, for instance? Or scale it down to 85 percent of its original dimensions?

Double-click the Deformation tool icon in the tool palette, and the Deformation Settings dialog box comes to your aid. (You may double-click the icon even if the tool is already in use and the deformation grid is visible.)

Deformation consternations

The Deformation tool can occasionally wrinkle your brow with certain weirdnesses. Here are a few typical problems and solutions:

✔ **The tool encompasses the wrong area:** You probably have the wrong layer currently active. Here's what happens: If you're on a layer that's transparent in the selected area, the Deformation tool chooses the non-transparent area instead. Press the *L* key to open the layer palette and click the layer that contains the image you want.

✔ **Can't find the deformation grid; you see only two squares and a connecting line:** The grid's there, all right, but you have applied the Deformation tool to a layer or selection that covers the entire image. Change layers or make a new selection.

✔ **Can't undo while using the tool:** It's true. You can't undo a mistake with the undo command while you're still using the tool. Try doing the opposite of whatever mistake you made (drag the other way, for instance). Your other option is to abandon the operation (see the final section of this chapter) and then try the deformation again.

✔ **An annoying background appears in the area the selection outline has vacated:** Well, Paint Shop Pro has to put *something* there and it can't invent a background image. (See "Preparing for Deformation," elsewhere in this chapter, for more about background.) If Paint Shop Pro could stretch the surrounding area to stay continous with your newly deformed selection, that would be nice, but it ain't so. Try dragging your selection elsewhere or filling in background with the Clone Brush tool. (See Chapter 6.)

Type the settings you want into this dialog box. It provides a column for X, or horizontal values, and Y, or vertical values, and rows for each of the various changes that the Deformation tool can make. Here's how to choose the values you need:

✔ **Position:** To move the selection, enter the X and Y coordinates where you want the upper-left corner of the deformation grid to go. (Remember that X and Y both equal 0 at the upper-right corner of the image.)

✔ **Scale:** Enter X and Y scale factors. Enter **80** in the X% scale box, for instance, to reduce the horizontal size of the selection to 80 percent of original. To keep the original proportions, put the same value in both the X and Y columns.

✔ **Shear:** To slide the top edge to the right, enter a positive value in the X column; enter a negative value to move the edge the other way. To slide the right edge down or up, enter a positive or negative value, respectively, in the Y column. The value tells Paint Shop Pro how far to slide. The value is expressed — not in pixels — but as a fraction of the length of the side. So, to move a side a distance equal to half its length, enter **.5**.

✔ **Perspective:** To make the right edge appear to recede into the distance by pulling the upper-right corner down and inward, enter a value between zero and 1 in the X column. A value of 1 drops the top edge to an angle of 45 degrees from horizontal. A value of .577 drops it to an angle of 30 degrees. (Yes, indeed, all you geometry geeks: That value is the tangent of the drop angle.) To make the top edge appear to recede, do likewise in the Y column. Use negative values to make those same edges appear to approach the viewer, instead.

✔ **Angle:** To rotate the selection clockwise, enter a positive number of degrees (say, 45) into the text box. Use a negative value for counterclockwise.

Click the OK button in the dialog box to deform the selection. You can change any setting at this point by again double-clicking the Deformation tool icon. Finally, apply (or abandon) the deformation as the next section describes.

Applying or abandoning the deformation

You have your object nicely deformed. Now what? The Deformation tool is still in your face. Or, perhaps you messed up so royally you want to abandon your effort and try again. Do any of these actions:

✔ In the Tool Options window (press the *O* key if the window's not visible), click the Apply button to carry out the the deformation or the Cancel button to abandon the deformation.

✔ Double-click anywhere in the image.

✔ Click any other tool in the tool palette. (The Arrow tool at the top of the palette is always a good choice.)

Either of the last two actions pops up a query dialog box asking `Apply Deformation?` Click Yes to keep your changes; otherwise, click No. You can always undo a deformation after you apply it by using the undo command (press Ctrl+Z).

Chapter 15

Layering Images

• •

• •

*T*he old masters of oil painting used layers of paint to give their paintings great depth and radiance. Today's artistic masters (who all work in Paint Shop Pro, of course) use layers for another reason: It makes changing stuff lots easier. It also lets you combine images more easily.

Layers are like transparent sheets of plastic that are laid over an opaque (non-transparent) background. You can put stuff on the background layer, or on the other, transparent layers.

As simple as this basic idea is, Paint Shop Pro uses it to give you a lot of flexibility and power in creating stunning images. To see what using layers can do for you, read on!

Putting Layers to Work for You

With layers, you can paint, erase, or move things around without worrying about ruining the underlying image. You can erase a line, for instance, without erasing the background. You can move an entire object or see how something looks without permanently committing yourself to it. You can also combine images in various clever ways.

Because Paint Shop Pro's layers are electronic, not physical, they can make your life easier in other ways, too. Here are just a few of the special tricks you can do, besides simply painting, moving, combining, or erasing images:

✔ Select an object painted on a layer without accidentally selecting other areas of the same color or that underlie that object.

✔ Make an image partly transparent, a sort of ghost on the background.

✔ Switch image objects into or out of the picture, as needed, or quickly change their stacking order.

✔ Combine layers into one layer, if you're certain no more changes are needed, or lock several layers together temporarily to form a movable group of objects.

✔ Make vector layers, which enable you to create basic shapes, text, and other objects in a special form that lets you easily change their shape.

✔ Make an adjustment layer (say, a brightening layer) that affects only the underlying layers and which effect you can vary.

✔ Create the frames of an animation by simply moving one or more layers.

✔ Make layers interact, for special effects. For instance, you can subtract one layer from another — a way to reveal changes between photographs.

Getting Layers

Your parents probably never explained where layers come from — unless, of course, you grew up on an egg ranch. Here's the real story.

You always have at least one layer: the background layer. That's the layer where nearly everything happens until you add more layers. If you download a digital photo from your camera, for instance, the image is on the background layer. If you happily paint away, ignorant of all knowledge of layers, all your painting is on the background layer.

You can get images with additional layers in a variety of ways:

✔ Make a new, blank layer by using the various New commands in the Layers menu (in the menu bar) or by using the layer palette.

✔ Turn a selection into a layer (*promote* it, in Paint Shop Pro terms).

✔ Incidentally make a new, vector layer by drawing lines or shapes, or by adding text.

✔ Paste an image from the Windows clipboard using Edit⇨Paste⇨ As New Layer.

✔ Open an image file that already has multiple layers, such as many Paint Shop Pro or Photoshop files have.

✔ Add a picture frame with the Image⇨Picture Frame command.

Calling a Pal for Help: The Layer Palette

The first thing you should do when you're working with layers is to call a friend for help. The Layer palette, shown in Figure 15-1, is your best pal. It's a small pal, hence the name *palette*. See how things make sense, after they're explained?

 If it's not on your screen already, call your little pal by pressing *L* on the keyboard or click the Toggle Layers button on the Toolbar (shown in the margin). Do the same to hide the palette again.

 Palettes can be shy and hard to find, sometimes. If only the title bar of the palette appears (which says Layer palette), pause your mouse button over that title bar to unroll the palette window. If you want to lock the palette window open, click the down-arrow button in the window's upper-right corner.

Create a layer

Delete a layer   Layers

Active layer   Blending control

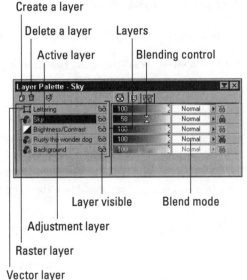

Figure 15-1:
Your pal, the Layer palette, is at your side to help you with layer stuff.

Layer visible   Blend mode

Adjustment layer

Raster layer

Vector layer

Here are a few basic factoids to help you get along with your new and complex-looking pal:

✔ **Each row of the palette represents a layer.** Your view of the image in the image window is down through the layers, from top to bottom (background). The layers' names are on the left side of the palette. You assign names when you create the layers, or else you allow Paint Shop Pro to create a boring but adequate name, like Layer3. Paint Shop Pro automatically calls the initial, background layer (the one that every image starts with) Background.

✔ **To work on a layer, click on its name.** Clicking its name makes that layer the currently active one. Nearly everything you can do to an image in Paint Shop Pro, such as painting, erasing, or fiddling with the colors, affects only the currently active layer. The palette helps you remember which one is currently active.

✔ **The icon at the left of each row tells you what kind of layer that row represents.** Three kinds of layer exist: raster, vector, or adjustment. You use raster layers most often. See the sidebar, "Choosing a layer that's just your type," elsewhere in this chapter, for details. In Figure 15-1, the row named Sky shows you a raster icon, the Lettering layer shows the vector icon, and the Brightness/Contrast layer displays the adjustment icon.

Don't bother trying to understand the palette all at once. I tell you how to use the rest of the palette's features as I go along.

Creating A New, Blank Layer

To create a new, blank layer, take the following steps using the Layer palette:

1. **Choose where, in your stack of layers, you want the new layer to appear.**

   (If this is the first layer you've added to an image, you can skip this step. The new layer appears just above the background layer.)

   Otherwise, in the layer palette, click on the layer above which the new layer should appear. In Figure 15-1, for instance, I've clicked on the layer labeled *Sky,* making that layer the currently active one.

2. **Click the New Layer button or choose Layers⇨New Raster Layer from the menu bar.**

   The New Layer button is in the upper-left corner of the layer palette, as shown in Figure 15-1.

   If you're savvy about the various types of layer and know you want a specific type, *right*-click on the New Layer button or choose Layer from Paint Shop Pro's menu bar. The menu that appears lets you choose New Raster Layer, New Vector Layer, or New Adjustment Layer. For more information about types of layer, see the nearby sidebar, "Choosing a layer that's just your type."

   The rather intimidating Layer Properties dialog box appears, trying to scare you. Forge ahead boldly.

3. **Type a name for the layer.**

The Name field of the Layer Properties dialog box is already highlighted, so you don't have to click there before typing. Whatever you type replaces the rather boring name (like Layer1) that Paint Shop Pro suggests. Enter a name in that field that describes what you're going to put on this layer. If you're not feeling creative, just skip this step and Paint Shop Pro uses the boring name.

You may set other attributes of your layer in this same dialog box, if you know what you're doing. See the section later in this chapter, "Setting Layer Properties," for more about those settings.

4. **Click OK.**

   Get the heck out of this boring, intimidating Layer Properties dialog box and get on with the fun!

Your image doesn't look any different, so maybe you're wondering, "Just what have I accomplished?" Fear not, you have indeed added a layer. The image doesn't look any different because your new layer is transparent and blank. It's just like a sheet of clear plastic placed over a painting.

Choosing a layer that's just your type

To make life a bit more complicated, Paint Shop Pro has three different types of layers for different kinds of stuff. All those types of layers appear in Figure 15-1, where you can see that they are distinguished by special icons. Here's more about those layers:

 Raster: This is the plain, vanilla type of layer that you use most of the time. Unless you specify otherwise, you get one of these when you create a new layer. A raster layer handles normal images — the kind made of dots, called raster or bitmap images. Raster layers are just like the background layer, which you're already familiar with. Raster layers are marked with the icon shown here.

 Vector: This special type of layer comes into play mostly when you use Paint Shop Pro's text, preset shapes, or line drawing tools. Vector images are made up of lines or curves connected together in a connect-the-dot

fashion. Paint Shop Pro normally creates text, preset shapes, and lines as vector images, although you can alternatively create them as raster images. Vector images can't appear on a raster layer, and raster images can't appear on a vector layer. Vector images are marked with the icon that appears here.

 Adjustment: This special type of layer doesn't contain any images at all! It's like a magical coating that imparts a particular image quality to the layers under it. It works almost exactly like color adjustments, so I discuss it in Chapter 11. The advantage of adjustment layers is that the enhancement is separated from the image, so changing your mind is easier. Adjustment layers are named according to the kind of adjustment they perform, and all of them wear the jazzy black/white icon shown here.

Look at the layer palette. You see your new layer, with the name that you gave it, highlighted. That means that it's the currently active layer, and any painting, erasing, selection, or color adjustment you perform now takes place on that layer.

To delete a layer in the layer palette, click that layer's name and then click the trash can icon. Or, drag the layer to the trash can. Everything that is on that layer goes away with the layer.

When you float a selection, it appears in the layer palette like a layer and is named *Floating Selection* (in italics). It's not really a full-fledged layer, but you can use Layer menu commands on it, like moving it down in the stack. See Chapter 13 for the details of floating.

Working On Layers

To work on a layer, click on its name in the Layer palette to select it (make it active). Then, working on the new layer is very much like working on the background layer. You can paint, erase, adjust color, cut, copy, paste, and do image transformations such as flipping, filtering, or deforming, and the results appear only on your selected layer. How tidy and organized!

As an artist who is using multiple layers, you're like a doctor who is seeing multiple patients. To avoid mistakes, you must know which one you're operating on. You can't tell what image is on which layer by simply looking at the image. The transparency of layers prevents you. So, instead, keep an eye on the layer palette to see which layer is active. The currently active layer is highlighted there. Pause your cursor over a layer's name to see a tiny thumbnail image of the layer's contents. If a tool doesn't seem to be working, you're probably trying to work on something that isn't *on* the currently active layer. Try turning various layers on and off to find the object you want.

Here are a few peculiarities of working with layers:

✔ **Moving:** You can use the Move tool (the four-headed arrow) to slide an entire layer around (but not the background layer). Click the Move tool in the Tool palette. Then, in the image window, drag the entire layer by dragging any object on that layer. To move an individual object independently of the others on that layer, select the object before you use the Move tool. (If the object still doesn't move independently, make sure that the object's layer is the currently active one, re-select the object, and try again.)

✔ **Selecting:** When you make a selection on a layer, the selection marquee penetrates to all layers. That means that you could select an object on one layer, switch to another layer, and then, say, fill that selected area (within the selection marquee) with paint on that other layer.

✔ **Copying:** When you copy, you copy only from the currently active layer — unless you choose Edit⇨Copy Merged. A merged copy includes all the layers.

✔ **Erasing:** When you erase or delete on a (non-background) layer, you restore the layer's transparency. (On the background layer, you leave behind background color when you erase, or transparency if the image was originally created with transparent background.)

✔ **Using the Text, Draw, and Preset Shapes tools:** The images created by these tools are, by default, vector-type images, not raster-type. (See the sidebar, "Choosing a layer that's just your type," elsewhere in this chapter, for more about these types.) That distinction means that, normally, these elements can't go on ordinary layers, which hold only raster type images. As a result, if you're not already using a vector layer when you choose one of these tools, Paint Shop Pro automatically creates a new vector layer for you. See the section, "Using Vector Layers," later in this chapter, for more about what happens in layers when you use these tools.

✔ **Grayed-out tools:** When you're working on a vector layer, the raster tools such as the Paint Brush tool are grayed out. You must switch to a raster (ordinary) layer to use them.

Seeing, Hiding, and Rearranging Layers

When you view a multi-layer image, you look down through all the layers just as you would look down through a stack of plastic sheets with stuff painted on them. To control which layers you see and also adjust the order in which they're stacked, use the following techniques:

✔ **To see just the currently active layer:** Choose Layers⇨View⇨ Current Only.

✔ **To see all layers:** Choose Layers⇨View⇨All.

✔ **To see specific layers:** In the layer palette, click a layer's Layer Visibility toggle, known to its friends as the eyeglasses icon. Each layer has this icon, to the right of the layer name. Click it once to turn the layer off (make it invisible) and click again to turn it on. When a layer is off, an X appears through the eyeglasses icon.

✔ **To move a layer up or down in the stack:** Drag it up or down in the left column of the layer palette. While you're dragging, the layer itself doesn't move; instead, a black line follows your cursor to tell you where the layer will go when you release the mouse button. An alternative to dragging is to click a layer, then choose Layers⇨Arrange⇨Bring to Top, Move Up, Move Down, or Send to Bottom.

Pinning Layers Together: Grouping

After you've carefully positioned objects on different layers, it's nice to pin those layers together so they can't reposition themselves. If you have painstakingly put Uncle Tobias' head on the neck of a giraffe, for instance, you want to keep them together while you get creative with other layers.

Paint Shop Pro does its grouping by the numbers. You assign a group number, 1–9, to any layer, using the following instructions. Layers that have the same number are part of that group. To assign group numbers to layers, open the layer palette (press *L* to reveal it, if necessary).

The first thing to do, as Figure 15-2 shows, is to click the Group tab near the upper right of the palette. The right side of the Layer palette then appears something like it does in Figure 15-2. You initially see the word None for every layer, indicating that the layer is not in a group.

Click to work with groups

Not in a group

Figure 15-2:
Grouping
eggplant
with pepper
(group 1)
and carrots
with squash
(group 2).

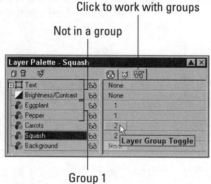

Group 1

Click where you see the word None for any layer you want to group. The number 1 then appears in place of None, making that layer part of group 1. (The button you click is called the Layer Group Toggle, which, incidentally, would be a great name for a new country-western line dance based on the Funky Chicken.) Do the same for any other layers that you want in group 1.

Need more than one group? If you click that Layer Group Toggle button again, the layer's group number increases by 1, putting the layer in another group. The numbers advance None, 1, 2, 3, 4, 5, 6, 7, 8, 9, and then back to None again. Right-click to make the numbers go down. To remove a layer from a group, just click until its Layer Group Toggle button reads None again.

Layers with the same group number behave as if they were pinned together: When you move one layer with the Move tool (the four-headed arrow thingy), you move the entire group. Members of a group keep their independence in other ways, though. If you change the appearance of a layer (say, make it brighter), its fellow group members don't change.

In Figure 15-2, you're looking at the Group tab of the Layer palette. You'll probably switch to the Appearance or Mask tab at some point, where you can no longer see which layers are parts of which group. To help you, Paint Shop Pro puts a tiny red dot on the Group tab when your currently active layer is part of a group. You can always see that tab and its dot, no matter which tab you're using at the time. So, at least you know that if you move the layer, you move something else, too.

Using Layers to Separate or Combine Images

The main reasons for using layers are either to break an image apart into several layers for more flexible editing or to combine multiple images into one. Here's how to do both.

Combining entire images

Do you have two entire images to combine? To combine an entire image file with the image you're currently working on, take the following steps:

1. **In the layer palette of the image you're working on, click the name of the layer above which you want to insert your new image.**

   If the current image doesn't have multiple layers, skip to Step 2.

2. **Choose File⇨Browse and open the image browser to the folder containing the image file.**

   Thumbnail pictures of the images in that folder appear. (See Chapter 2 for more about how to use the image browser.)

3. **Drag the thumbnail picture of the image file to the image you're working on.**

   Paint Shop Pro inserts the new image as a layer, above the layer that you selected in Step 1. (If the image you're dragging contains multiple layers, all its layers are grouped together.) The cursor turns into a four-headed arrow to indicate that Paint Shop Pro has selected the Move tool for you.

4. **Drag the new image to position it where you want it.**

After dragging, I often click the Arrow tool (at the top of the tool palette) or some other tool to avoid accidentally dragging the selection when I move the mouse again.

Separating image parts into layers

How do you get an object separated out and on its own layer? One answer is that you can select the object and turn it into a new layer, called *promoting a selection*. Take these steps:

1. **Select the desired chunk of any existing layer (the background layer, for example) using any of Paint Shop Pro's selection tools.**

   I cover selection tools for normal (raster) images in Chapter 13. To select an object on a vector layer, click the object with the Object Selector tool (at the bottom of the Tool palette).

   Is your selection tool not selecting on the object you want? Remember that selection only works within one layer at a time. Your object may be on a different layer than the currently active one. In the Layer palette, click on the layer where that object lives to make that layer active. Then try selecting again. If you're not sure where that object lives, pause your cursor over each layer's name, one at a time, and look for your object in the thumbnail image of the layer's contents.

2. **In the Layer palette, click the name of the layer above which you want to add the new one.**

3. **Choose Selections⇨Promote to Layer from Paint Shop Pro's menu bar.**

   A new layer, cleverly named Promoted Selection, appears in the Layer palette. Although nothing appears to change in your image, your selection is now on that Promoted Selection layer.

Your object is now on its own layer. A copy of that object remains on the original layer. You can now de-select the object if you like; press Ctrl+D or choose Selections⇨Select None.

If you would prefer that no copy be left behind when you promote a selection, drag the selection slightly after Step 1. On the background layer, this leaves behind an area filled with the current background color. On other layers, the area becomes transparent.

Another way to separate image chunks into layers is to select the chunks, then cut and paste the chunk as a new layer. See the next section.

Copying, cutting, and pasting with layers

A good way to get an image or chunk of an image onto a layer is to copy (or cut) it and then paste it as a new layer. This approach uses the same, familiar Windows clipboard system that other applications use, which is a great way to combine multiple images, even if the additional images come from a program other than Paint Shop Pro. In the following sections, I tell you how to copy, cut, and paste a selected image as a new layer.

Copying or cutting the image

You can copy or cut images from a variety of sources. Here's how to do it:

- ✔ **From a program other than Paint Shop Pro:** First, open that program and display the image you want. (You don't need to close Paint Shop Pro.) Exactly how to copy or cut an image from that program varies somewhat from program to program. Copying from a Web page in Internet Explorer, for instance, you could right-click the image and then choose Copy from the menu that appears. In many programs, click on the image to select it and choose Edit⇨Copy to put a copy onto the hidden clipboard of Windows.

- ✔ **From another layer within your Paint Shop Pro image:** In the Layer palette, click the layer containing the object you want. Select the image chunk you want with any of Paint Shop Pro's selection tools. (See Chapter 13 for help with selection tools. If the layer is a vector layer, use the Object Selector tool at the bottom of the Tool palette.) Then choose Edit⇨Copy (or Edit⇨Cut, if you want to remove the chunk from its current layer).

- ✔ **From another image file:** Open that file in Paint Shop Pro. (See Chapter 2.) A new window appears, displaying that image. Use any of Paint Shop Pro's selection tools to select your chosen chunk. Choose Selections⇨Select All if you want to select the whole image. Choose Edit⇨Copy to copy from the currently active layer. To copy combined images from all layers, choose Edit⇨Copy Merged.

Pasting the image as, or onto, a new layer

After you've copied (or cut) an image onto the Windows clipboard, you can paste it *as* a layer or *onto* an existing layer. Here's how to paste it as a layer:

1. **Click the title bar of the window in Paint Shop Pro where you want to paste.**

   This step makes sure that you paste in the right place.

2. **In the Layer palette, click the name of the layer above which you want the new layer to appear.**

   To put a layer above the background layer, for instance, click Background. If your image has only one layer, you can skip this step because Background is already selected.

3. **Choose Edit⇨Paste⇨As New Layer or press Ctrl+L.**

   Your image appears as a new layer, and Paint Shop Pro's cursor appears as a four-headed arrow. That cursor tells you that Paint Shop Pro has automatically selected the Move tool for you.

   (If you copy a vector object from outside Paint Shop Pro, such as a Microsoft Draw object from Microsoft Word, Paint Shop Pro converts it to a raster layer when you paste it. First, however, Paint Shop Pro displays a dialog box called Meta Picture Import. In that dialog box, set Width in Pixels and Height in Pixels to the sizes you want for the pasted image and click OK.)

4. **Drag your newly pasted image where you want it.**

When you're done dragging, consider clicking the arrow tool (at the top of the tool palette) or some other tool to avoid accidentally dragging the selection with subsequent mouse motions.

Paint Shop Pro assigns a clunky name, such as Layer3, to your new layer in the layer palette. To change that name, double-click the layer's current name. When the Layer Property box appears, type a new name in the Name field (already selected, for your convenience) and click OK.

You can also paste an image onto an *existing* layer, rather than pasting it as its own *new* layer. After you've copied or cut the image to the Windows clipboard, click the existing layer's name in the layer palette and choose Edit⇨ Paste As New Selection or press Ctrl+E. The image appears; drag it where you want it and then click to make it a floating selection. Press Ctrl+D to deselect the image.

Copying entire layers from one image to another

When you start using layered images, you may find that a layer that you created in one image is useful in another image. To copy a layer (or layers) from one image to another, you drag the layer from the Layer palette of the source image to the destination image. To do so, take these detailed steps:

1. **Open both images in Paint Shop Pro.**

   Each image gets its own window. Arrange the windows so you can see at least part of both images. (For instance, choose Window⇨Tile Vertically.)

2. **Click the title bar of the destination image.**

   By destination image, I mean the one where you want the layer to go.

3. **In the Layer palette, click the layer above which the new layer is to go.**

   Clicking makes that layer the currently active one.

4. **Click the title bar of the image containing the layer you want to copy.**

5. **In the Layer palette, click the name of the layer you want to copy and drag it to the destination image.**

   Drag the layer directly to the destination *image,* not the title bar of its window. When you release the mouse button, the copied layer appears.

Blending images by making layers transparent

Double your pleasure, double your fun. One very popular effect is a sort of double-exposure, which you do by making an overlaying layer on which the image is partially transparent. For instance, you may want to overlay a diagram on a photograph or add a faint image of a logo to a picture.

Figure 15-3 shows a few tasty vegetables overlaid with the word *Veggies,* perhaps to be used as a sign for a vegetarian buffet. (It looks a lot more appealing in color — see Figure C-2 in the color section of this book.)

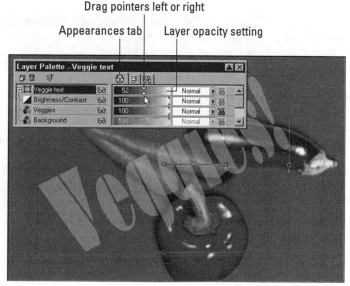

Figure 15-3: Making Veggies transparent makes them clearly a good menu choice.

To make a layer transparent, you merely adjust one little setting called *Layer Opacity*. Each layer has a Layer Opacity setting in the layer palette (the shaded bar noted in Figure 15-3). Until you change it, the setting for every layer is 100 to indicate that the layer is 100% opaque (you can't see through the image on the layer at all).

If the right side of your palette doesn't appear to have the controls shown in Figure 15-3, you're looking at the wrong tab. Click the Appearances tab indicated in Figure 15-3 to find the controls.

At the far, far, right end of each bar is a pair of pointers (triangles). Drag that pair to the left to make the layer more transparent. Drag it to the right to make the layer more opaque. The number on the bar changes as you drag, between 100 and 0. In Figure 15-3, the layer containing the text *Veggies!* is set to 52% (roughly half-transparent).

Blending images in creative ways

Sometimes, simply overlaying one image on the other doesn't give quite the effect you want. For instance, if you overlay colored text on an image that has like-colored areas, you can't read the text in those areas.

In that case, the result may be better if the layer could, say, lighten or darken the underlying image — or perhaps change the underlying color, no matter what color it is. With Paint Shop Pro, you can do those effects, and more, using something called *layer blending*. Layer blending is determined by two settings: the *layer blend mode* and the *layer blend levels*.

To use Blend Modes with forethought and skill requires pondering all kinds of technical stuff about computer graphics. So, do like I do — use blend modes with reckless abandon, instead of forethought and skill. Try one mode, and if you don't like the result, try another!

The right side of the layer palette contains Layer Blend Mode settings, shown in Figure 15-4, that you can change for each layer. Until you change a layer's blend mode, it's normal, which means that the paint on that layer simply overlays the paint on lower layers (like paint on transparent plastic).

Click the Blend Mode control for your chosen layer and choose a Blend Mode from the menu that appears. To restore the original appearance, choose Normal from the list of modes.

Blend mode control

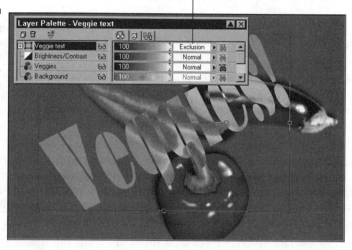

Figure 15-4:
To make
Veggies
tastier, try
another way
of blending.
Here, the
blend mode
is Exclusion,
which is
how some
kids prefer
their
veggies.

Here are a few tips:

✔ For maximum contrast between underlying and overlying images, try the Difference mode.

✔ Try making the color of the overlying layer lighter or darker, if you can't get the results you want otherwise.

✔ Make a layer more transparent if you want to reduce the effect of any blend mode, producing a more subtle result.

✔ For a speckly, spray-painted look, try the Dissolve mode and also make the layer partly transparent.

Creating and Using Adjustment Layers

An adjustment layer is sort of like a perfect facial makeup. It doesn't actually cover anything up, but magically changes the appearance of underlying layers. Changes include brightness or contrast, color, as well as other effects.

Many of these effects you can create in other ways, say with commands in the Colors menu. In fact, the dialog boxes for adjustment layers are so much like those for commands in the Colors menu that I cover them both with one set of instructions in Chapter 11.

So, why use an adjustment layer instead of a command in the Colors menu? Here are a few good reasons:

✔ Adjustment layers can affect the entire, combined, multilayer image (if placed on top of all other layers). Most commands in the Colors menu, on the other hand, affect only the currently active layer.

✔ Adjustment layers are useful when you're using different layers to combine two images. One image may have lower contrast than the other, for instance. You could put a contrast-adjustment layer above one image, and put the second image above that adjustment layer so it remains unaffected.

✔ An adjustment layer lets you make changes that are later easily reversible. You can simply delete the layer or change its settings if you later find the adjustment is wrong. Otherwise, you need to counter your earlier adjustment — a trickier job than undoing or changing it.

✔ You can paint the layer to apply the effect in different strengths in different places! This is admittedly a bit mind-boggling, but if you can imagine being able to paint, say, brightness (rather than a color), you've got the idea. Instead of painting, you can copy an image to the layer and the brightness of each pixel of the image determines the strength of the effect.

Adjustment layers only change the *appearance* of the underlying colors, not the actual colors of the layers. So, for instance, when you use an adjustment layer, the colors that the Dropper tool picks up and displays in the color palette are the real colors — the color of the paint in the layer, not the apparent color caused by the adjustment layer.

Creating an adjustment layer

To create an adjustment layer, take the following steps:

1. **Open the Layer palette (press the *L* key) if it isn't already on-screen.**

2. **In the Layer palette, right-click the name of the layer above which you want to add the adjustment layer.**

   Alternatively, you can left-click the layer above which you want to add the adjustment layer. Then, choose Layers in the Paint Shop Pro menu bar or right-click the Create Layer button.

3. **Choose New <u>A</u>djustment Layer from the menu that appears.**

4. **Choose the type of adjustment layer you want from the menu that appears.**

   (See the following section for choosing adjustment types.)

   The Layer Properties dialog box appears.

5. **Click the Adjustment tab near the top of that dialog box.**

   The tab shows various sliders and other adjustments appear, depending upon your choice of layer type.

6. **Make your adjustments and click OK.**

   I describe how these adjustments work in Chapter 11.

You can delete or move adjustment layers just as you do other layers. See "Working On Layers," earlier in this chapter, for instructions. To rename an adjustment layer, double-click its name in the layer palette; when the Layer Properties dialog box appears, click the General tab, enter a new name in the Name field there, and click OK.

To change these adjustments after you create a layer, double-click on the layer's name in the Layer palette. You find these adjustments on the Adjustments tab of the Layer Properties dialog box that appears. It's the same dialog box that appears when you create a new adjustment layer (see Step 5 in the preceding list).

Choosing the type of adjustment layer you need

Paint Shop Pro's adjustment layers give you lots of different ways to fiddle with the color, contrast, and brightness of the underlying layers of your image. Here are some suggestions for what to use to achieve various results:

- ✔ To adjust brightness or contrast, use the Brightness/Contrast layer.

- ✔ The Brightness/Contrast layer affects *all* three major tonal ranges — shadows, highlights, and midtones — at once. To independently adjust *any* of these three ranges — say, to just get darker shadows — try a Levels layer.

- ✔ If shadows, highlights and midtones aren't precise enough for your brightness and contrast adjustment — say, you need better contrast only within *specific* shadows — you can adjust brightness or contrast within *any* range of tone by using a Curves layer.

- ✔ For richer/grayer or lighter/darker colors, try a Hue/Saturation layer. The Hue/Saturation layer also lets you colorize underlying layers (give them a monochrome tint).

- ✔ To make a negative image, choose an Invert layer. (This layer has no adjustments, so I say no more about it. To use it, just choose it.)

- ✔ To reduce the number of colors, resulting in a kind of paint-by-numbers effect, try a Posterize layer.

- ✔ To get a truly black-and-white (two color, no shades of gray) effect, choose a Levels layer.

Applying adjustments only to certain areas

One cool feature of adjustment layers is that you can apply their effects selectively, to certain areas of your image. Paint Shop Pro uses paint on the adjustment layer to accomplish that result. Here are two ways to apply adjustments selectively:

 ✔ After you create the adjustment layer, you can paint out the areas on that adjustment layer where you *don't* want the effect, using black paint. Apply the paint to the adjustment layer with any painting tool, such as the Paint Brush tool. The paint doesn't show as black, but only as a masking out of the effect. Use gray paint to screen the effect out partially; the darker the paint, the less the effect.

 ✔ Before you create the adjustment layer, you can make a selection where you want the effect. When you create the layer, Paint Shop Pro paints out the remaining area so the layer's effect doesn't work there.

You can also paint in an area with white or gray, if that area is currently painted out. Notice that black, white, and shades of gray are the only colors that the color palette gives you to paint with when you're working on an adjustment layer. You can click any color you like in the Available Colors area, but it comes out in shades of gray in the Foreground Color and Background Color swatches.

Using Vector Layers

Most people discover vector layers accidentally. They use the Text, Draw, or Preset Shapes tools to create vector objects, and Paint Shop Pro automatically (and without telling them) creates a vector layer to contain the vector objects these tools produce. (I explain the difference between vector and raster images and layers in the sidebar, "Choosing a layer that's just your type," earlier in this chapter.) See Chapter 16 for more about using these tools.

You can also create vector layers intentionally, as I describe in the section, "Creating A New, Blank Layer," earlier in this chapter. After you create a vector layer, you can use the Text, Draw, or Preset Shapes tool to add objects to that layer. You can also use copy and paste to move these objects from one Paint Shop Pro vector layer or image to another. (See the section, "Separating and combining images by copying, cutting, and pasting," also earlier in this chapter.)

You can convert a vector layer to a raster layer, if you like. The command to use is Layers⇨Convert to Raster. Converting an image to raster form allows you to apply any of the raster paint tools to your vector shape, to get cool effects such as graduated fills or airbrush spraying. The drawback is that you can then no longer edit the shape by adjusting the lines and points that make up a vector object. You can't convert a raster layer to a vector layer.

As you add vector objects to a vector layer, each object gets its own entry in the Layer palette. The left side of Figure 15-5 shows the Layer palette with two layers: the background layer and a vector layer, Layer1. To see each individual object in the vector layer, click the white box with the + sign to the left of the vector layer's icon. That action reveals the individual vector objects, indented under the layer. (To hide the objects, click that same white box again, which now holds a – symbol.)

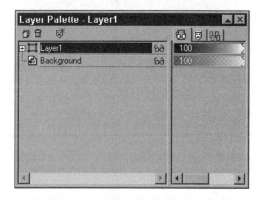

Group objects

Line object

Figure 15-5:
On the left, just layers. On the right, clicking the + symbol next to Layer1 has revealed individual objects on the layer.

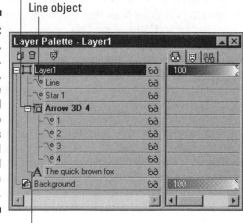

Text object

Paint Shop Pro has three kinds of vector objects: line objects, text objects, and groups of objects. Each kind of object has its own icon, as Figure 15-5 shows. Layer1 contains a line object called Line, a line object called Star 1, and a group called Arrow 3D 4. Star 1 is a single, multi-segment line that is part of the Preset Shapes object library (see Chapter 16). Arrow 3D 4, a group, is also one of the preset shapes. It's made up of line objects 1, 2, 3, and 4, which are listed and indented under Arrow 3D 4. You could collapse (hide) the list of component objects (1, 2, 3, and 4) by clicking the – symbol next to Arrow 3D 4.

Having objects listed in the layer palette lets you select, delete, hide, or reposition them in the stack, just as you would a layer. For instance, clicking an object in the palette selects it and displays its name in bold type. (Hold down the Shift key as you click to select multiple objects.) Pressing the Delete key deletes the selected object. Dragging it moves it up or down in the stack, enabling you to place it over or under other objects. Right-clicking it reveals a context menu with cut, copy, paste, and other commands you can experiment with. See Chapter 16 for more about managing objects.

Merging Layers

Using multiple layers usually makes working with images easier. Sometimes, however, you would rather have (or you need to have) everything on one layer. For instance, you may want to use one of the commands in the Colors menu on the entire image, but the command only works on a single layer. Or, if you try to save your image as something other than a Paint Shop Pro (.PSP) file, Paint Shop Pro may offer to merge all the layers for you. (Merging can sometimes be necessary because not many file types support multiple layers.)

If Paint Shop Pro merges layers when you're saving a file, it only merges layers in the file that you're creating on your disk drive. It doesn't merge the layers in the image you're working on in Paint Shop Pro.

Paint Shop Pro gives you two ways to merge layers into one layer. To merge all the layers (including those whose visibility is switched off), choose Layers⇨Merge⇨Merge All. To merge only the visible layers (leaving the hidden ones as layers), choose Layers⇨Merge⇨Merge Visible.

What happens when you merge? Nothing *visible* happens to your image when you merge. The merged layers, however, become one normal (raster) layer, named Merged, that you see listed in the Layer palette. Any vector layers (typically text, lines, or preset shapes) are converted into raster images, so you can't edit them any more with the text, drawing, or shape tools. When adjustment layers are merged, they no longer simply affect the image appearance, but actually modify the underlying colors.

Chapter 16

Adding Layers of Text or Shapes

• •

In This Chapter

▶ Vectorizing versus rasterizing

▶ Playing with text

▶ Fiddling with lines and shapes

▶ Changing colors, fills, and whatnot

▶ Positioning and arranging objects

• •

*G*iven a paintbrush, most of us would have trouble making nice, neat text, regular shapes like circles, or even straight lines. We'd clamor for a typewriter, a template, a ruler, or some other special tool that gives nice straight edges and shapes.

Well, clamor not. Paint Shop Pro offers three tools for creating such stuff and one to help you manage the stuff you create. Figure 16-1 shows those four tools as they appear at the bottom of the tool palette.

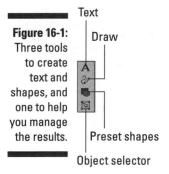

Text

Figure 16-1: Draw
Three tools
to create
text and
shapes, and
one to help
you manage
the results. Preset shapes

Object selector

Unless you tell Paint Shop Pro otherwise, these tools create text, lines, and shapes in a special vector form that makes them easier to change. Images in this form are known as *vector objects*. Unlike the other things you can paint or otherwise create in Paint Shop Pro, vector objects aren't a collection of pixels (colored dots). Instead, they're shapes that have color, line width, and other properties. These shapes can exist only on special *vector layers*.

So, you ask, "What's the upshot?" Here's the bottom line:

- **Creating stuff as vector objects:** If you use Paint Shop Pro's text, line, or shape tools in the normal, vector way, your creations are easier to modify — but you have to know how to deal with layers and the special features of vector objects. See Chapter 15 for help with layers, and I explain vector features in this chapter.

- **_Not_ creating stuff as vector objects:** If you don't want to bother with vector layers and special vector object features, you can create text, lines, and shapes as if they were painted with a brush. This form is called _raster_ form. If you're such a dedicated, um . . . rasterfarian, you must do this: If you use the Draw or Preset Shapes tool, on Tab 1 of its Tool Options window, click to clear the check mark in the Create As Vector check box. If you want text as a raster selection, click the Selection or Floating option boxes in the Text Entry dialog box that I talk about in the next section. Your choice of raster remains unless you change it. No problem, _mon._

If you need to work on vector objects with raster tools (like the Paint Brush or Eraser tools), you can convert a vector layer to a raster layer. Choose Layers⇨Convert To Raster Layer. You can't convert back, however.

Keeping Track of Objects and Layers

The most important thing to remember about adding text, lines, or shapes is this: If you try to add such vector objects to a normal, raster image (such as a digital photograph), Paint Shop Pro automatically, and quietly, creates a vector layer to hold the new object.

If you want to return to the rest of the image, you have to switch to the layer that the image lives on. So, for instance, if you add text to a photograph (which usually appears on the background layer), you need to press Ctrl+1 to return to the background layer.

To add text, lines, or shapes in a nice, controlled fashion where you know exactly what layer every object is on, create or select a vector layer before you create or paste a vector object. See Chapter 15 for help with creating and choosing layers. As you put vector objects on a vector layer, each object is listed separately, indented under the vector layer's name in the layer palette. Click the + sign to the left of the layer's name to display these objects individually. From within the layer palette, you can select, reorder, rename, or delete objects; see the discussion of using vector layers in Chapter 15.

Antialiasing for smoother edges

Shapes with nice, sharp edges tend to look a bit ragged when those edges run in any direction but perfectly horizontal or vertical. They develop an objectionable staircase look called *aliasing.* *Antialiasing* is a process of filling in those steps with a little bit of color, which gives the illusion of a straighter, if slightly fuzzier, edge. To antialias objects, do the following:

✔ When using the Preset Shapes or Draw tools, on Tab 1 of the Tool Options window, click to place a check mark in the Antialias check box.

✔ When using the Text tool, make sure the Antialiasing check box in the Text Entry dialog box is selected. (It is normally already selected for you.)

Adding and Editing Text

Text in Paint Shop Pro isn't just your grandfather's plain old letters and numbers. Oh, my gracious, no. Although you can certainly have plain text in a straight line, you can also have it filled or outlined with colors and patterns, bend it around curves, or rotate it into a jaunty angle. Truly, the cat's pajamas!

Creating, placing, and editing text

Text has two parts: an outline, set by the color palette's foreground controls, and a fill, set by the background controls. You can have both or either.

If you already have a vector layer (one that has text, lines, or shapes on it), you may put your text on that same layer; just choose the layer now in the layer palette. Or, you may create a new vector layer to put your text on. If your currently active layer is a raster layer (say, background), Paint Shop Pro creates a new vector layer for you in the following steps. If you're not familiar with layers, don't worry about all this layer stuff for now.

Here's how to create basic text:

1. **Click the Text tool (shown here) on the tool palette.**

2. **If you want outlined text, do the following:**

   a. Mouse down (that is, depress your mouse button and hold it down) on the Foreground Style swatch and drag to the paintbrush icon.

    b. Choose a foreground color. For instance, left-click on the Available Colors area of the color palette.

    c. In the Tool Options window (Tab 1), set the value in the Width dialog box to the width of the outline you want, in pixels. For instance, for an outline 4 pixels wide, set it to 4.

If you don't want an outline around your text, mouse down on the Foreground Style swatch and drag to the circle-with-slash icon.

3. **If you want solid (filled) text, do this:**

    a. Mouse down on the Background Style swatch and click the paint-brush icon.

    b. Choose a background color. For instance, right-click on the Available Colors area.

If you don't want your text filled (that is, you just want outlined text), mouse down on the Background Style swatch and click the circle-with-slash icon.

4. **Click on your image where you want the center of your text.**

The Text Entry dialog box appears, as shown in Figure 16-2. Note that it displays style and texture swatches that reflect your actions in Steps 2 and 3. You can change your choices here, if you like, by applying those same actions to these swatches. To turn off outlining and use fill only, click the Standard Text button.

Figure 16-2 shows how the Tool Options window controls the width (and style) of the text outline. It also shows, in the Layer palette, that the text object appears indented under the vector layer after you click the white square at the far left of the object layer (originally containing a + sign).

5. **Choose a font from the Name selection box.**

6. **Choose a font size from the Size selection box or manually enter any other size you want, in points.**

7. **Enter your text in the big box that is ingenuously labeled** Enter Text Here.

Your text appears in your chosen font and size. For long, multi-line text, you can press the Enter key to start a new line or just click on a second line and type. If you have multiple lines of text, decide how you want them aligned (left-justified, centered, or right-justified) by clicking the appropriate button at the upper right of the Enter Text Here box.

8. **To selectively apply any font style (Bold, Italic, Underlined, or Strikethrough), drag across the text you want styled to highlight it. Then click the B, _I_, U, or A (strikethrough) buttons as you would in most word processors.**

You can also selectively change the font or size of any text by highlighting the text and then choosing a new font or size.

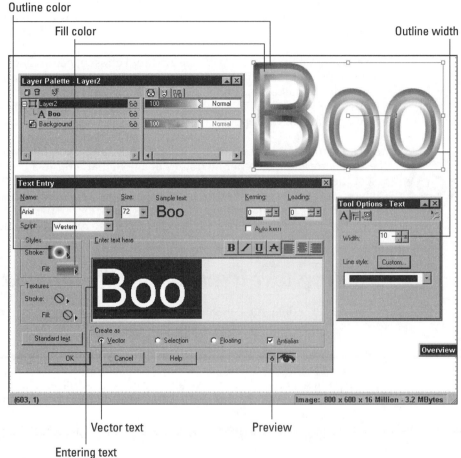

Outline color

Fill color

Outline width

Figure 16-2:
Have it your
way: text,
antialiased,
with
gradient
outline and
fill. Hold the
pickles.

Vector text

Entering text

Preview

9. **For vector text, remember to select the Vector option box.**

   If you prefer raster text, choose Selection to create a non-floating selection (or Floating to create a floating selection). See Chapter 14 to understand the very minor difference between those selection types.

10. **Click the OK button when you're done.**

    You can see the result of your work in the image window. While you're
    using the Text Entry dialog box, it normally displays a continuously
    updated preview of your work in the image window. (The preview
    button shown in Figure 16-2 is normally pressed. Click it to toggle pre-
    viewing on or off.)

Your text appears attractively displayed in a rectangular frame that has
squares *(handles)* around it. This *selection frame* means your text object is

selected. You can do several things to the text object now, including move, resize, rotate, or delete it. See the section, "Controlling Your Objects," later in this chapter.

You can also edit your text. With the Text tool chosen, carefully click directly on the body (outline or fill) of the text. The A icon that follows your cursor gets a pair of brackets around it, like this: [A], when your cursor is properly positioned to click. The Text Entry dialog box then reappears, where you can change the text or its appearance.

You can turn text into shapes, if you like. For instance, you may want to alter the shape, rotation, or other attributes of a text character in a creative way. Select the text that you want to convert and then choose Objects⇨ Convert Text to Curves. Then, to make each character an individually selectable, movable, rotatable object, choose As Character Shapes. If you want the characters to remain part of a single object, choose As Single Shape.

Creating text with fancy fills and outlines

For fancier lettering, you can choose Paint Shop Pro's gradients, patterns, or textures instead of solid color. Basically, it works like this:

- To choose a snazzy outline before creating your text, choose a *foreground* texture, gradient, or pattern in the color palette (Step 2 of the preceding steps). Or, if you've already clicked with the text tool, you can make these same choices in the Styles or Textures swatches of the Text Entry dialog box (Step 4).
- For a zippy fill, choose a *background* texture, gradient, or pattern in Step 3 or 4.

To make existing text fancier, edit it by clicking the text with the Text tool as the preceding section describes. Make your changes using the Styles and Textures swatches in the Text Entry dialog box that appears.

How do you make those choices? When you mouse down on the Foreground or Background Style swatches, click the gradient fill icon or the pattern icon instead of the paintbrush icon. To use a texture, mouse down on the Foreground or Background Texture swatches and click the texture icon instead of the circle-with-slash icon. Chapter 4 gives full details of choosing fancy stuff from the color palette.

Figures 16-2 and 16-3 show you the sort of text you can achieve with fancy fills and outlines. Figure 16-3 also bends text to fit a line (which I discuss in the following section). See the final version of this illustration in fabulous color, in the fabulous color section of this book (Figure C-3).

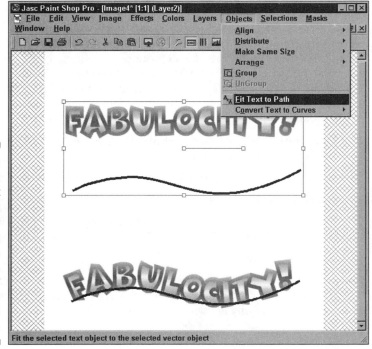

Figure 16-3:
Text with a
gradient
outline and
fill is bent to
follow a
curved line.
In real life,
you may
want the
line to be
invisible.

Bending text to follow a line or shape

Is your theatre company performing the *Wizard of Oz?* Well, before you can click your heels together three times and say, "There's no place like home," you can make the text on your advertising posters follow the yellow brick road — or any other (vector) shape or line in Paint Shop Pro. Figure 16-3 shows a before (top) and after (bottom) picture of fitting text to a line. Here's how to do your own:

1. **Create your (vector) text.**

   See the preceding two sections for help with text. While entering your text, choose an alignment in the Text Entry dialog box: three buttons at the top right of the Enter Text Here area depict left, center, and right alignment. Click one to choose how Paint Shop Pro aligns your text on your shape or line: squooshed to the left, centered across, or squooshed to the right.

2. **Create your shape or line.**

   See the rest of this chapter for help with lines or shapes. Bear in mind that if a line is created left-to-right, text ends up on top of that line. If a closed shape is created clockwise, text ends up on the inside. In both instances, the opposite direction gives opposite results.

3. **Click the Object Selector tool at the bottom of the tool palette.**

   If you just want to shape the text — you don't really want the line (or shape) itself to appear — take one additional step before proceeding to Step 4. The selection frame is still around your shape or line from its creation, and you have chosen the Object Selector tool. Now, click the Properties button in the Tool Options window. In the Properties dialog box that now appears, click to clear the Visible check box and click OK. Your chosen shape becomes invisible, but the selection frame remains.

4. **Hold down the Shift key and click the text, so both line and text are now within the selection frame.**

   The top illustration of Figure 16-3 shows this stage of the game.

5. **Choose Objects⇨Fit Text to Path.**

   Zap! Wanda the Good Witch puts your text safely on the yellow brick road to Oz. The bottom of Figure 16-3 shows the result of fitting text to the path.

Don't use solid-color-filled shapes if you intend your text to be on the inside of the shape — your text is hidden by the fill! A gradient, textured, or patterned fill, however, usually allows your text to be seen.

Straight, single lines

To draw a straight (vector) line, click the Draw tool on the tool palette and then do this:

1. **Choose a foreground color, style, and/or texture.**

   For instance, left-click on the Available Colors in the color palette. See Chapter 4 for more help.

2. **On Tab 1 of the Tool Options window, choose Single Line in the Type selection box.**

3. **Also on Tab 1, set the Width value to the width (in pixels) of the line you want.**

   All of Paint Shop Pro's value boxes offer you a nifty way to adjust them: Mouse down on the big down-arrow on the right side of the value box and drag left or right in the slider that appears.

4. **Drag.**

   Not only does your line appear, but it appears within a selection frame, a rectangle with square dots (handles) around the perimeter.

Drag any of the handles around the perimeter of the rectangle to re-size or re-orient your line. Drag the handle that sticks out to the right of the center to rotate the line.

Setting line and fill color for lines and shapes

To determine how lines and outlines look, choose a foreground color, style, and/or texture in the color palette before creating the line or shape. To determine how fills look (unless you're making a single straight line segment, where fill doesn't apply), choose a *background* color, style, and/or texture in the color palette before creating the line or shape. See Chapter 4 for help in making these choices. Note that, for open shapes (say, a curvy line), if you use fill, it fills the area between the starting and ending point of the shape. In many such cases, you may want to turn off background (fill) style altogether: mouse down on the background style swatch and drag to the circle-with-slash symbol.

If you've already created a line or shape and want to change its appearance, see the later section in this chapter, "Changing Colors and Other Properties."

Freehand lines or shapes

Freehand lines are basically any old scribble you want to make (or almost so). Here's how to scribble in high-technology land. Click the Draw tool on the tool palette, choose colors (together with any styles or textures) in the color palette, and then do the following:

1. **On Tab 1 of the Tool Options window (if the window isn't on-screen, press *O*), choose Freehand in the Type selection box.**

2. **Also on Tab 1, set the Width value to the width (in pixels) of the line you want.**

3. **If you want a shape (closed line), click to enable the Close Path check box on Tab 1 of the Tool Options window.**

   Otherwise, if you want an open line, clear the Close Path check box. Also, turn off fill if you just want a line. Mouse down on the background style swatch and click on the circle-with-slash icon in the panel that flies out.

4. **Drag on your image.**

When you release your mouse button, your line appears within a selection frame — a rectangle with square dots (handles) around the perimeter. Drag any handle around the outside of the rectangle to re-size or re-orient your line. To rotate the line, drag the handle at the end of the arm sticking out to the right of the center dot.

Your line is actually a very clever, automatically constructed connect-the-dots line. If you want to drag a line that follows your tight turns more smoothly, you need dots that are closer together. For a line that is more obviously made up of line segments that connect dots, the dots need to be farther apart. On Tab 2 of the Tool Options window, you can set that closeness by adjusting the Curve Tracking value: smaller for closer dots and larger for more widely spaced dots.

Connecting dots

A game that many of us loved as children endures in Paint Shop Pro: connect the dots. In this case, however, because you're a grown-up now, *you* place the dots and Paint Shop Pro draws the lines.

The Draw tool's connect-the-dots system can be as simple as child's play, but it can also go way beyond crayons. The Draw tool can give you straight lines between dots or a snaky line passing through the dots in a smooth fashion that you control. It can also remove dots, break the line into multiple lines, and more.

To play connect the dots with Paint Shop Pro, choose the Draw tool on the Tool palette, choose your foreground (stroke) and background (fill) color/style/texture, and then do the following:

1. **On Tab 1 of the Tool Options window, choose Point To Point Line in the Type selection box.**

2. **Set the Width value, also on Tab 1, to the desired width of your line (in pixels).**

3. **Turn off fill if you just want a line or outline; leave fill on to create a filled shape.**

   To turn off fill, mouse down on the background style swatch and click on the circle-with-slash icon in the panel that flies out.

4. **Make a sequence of clicks on your image, leaving dots *(nodes)*.**

   As you do, Paint Shop Pro connects the nodes with straight lines. If you prefer nicely curved lines, see "Connecting dots with curved lines," a bit later in this chapter. For now, the line is just one pixel wide in black, not your chosen width or chosen foreground color/style/texture. Width, color, and other style options are applied when you're done.

   As you create this line, if you discover you have placed an earlier node in the wrong position, you're free to return to the node at any time and drag it to another position.

   Technically, you're in *node editing* mode during this process. See "Picking at Your Nodes," later in this chapter, for more about this node mode.

5. **To end line drawing, right-click on your image and choose <u>Q</u>uit Node Editing from the context menu that appears.**

   Your line now appears in all its colorful, patterned, or textured glory.

As always occurs when you use the Draw tool, your completed line appears within a selection frame. If necessary, drag any handle that appears along the edge of the rectangle to resize or re-orient your line. To rotate your line, find the line that sticks from the center handle of the frame and drag the handle on the end of it.

Connecting dots with curved lines

To connect your dots with curved lines, don't just click when you place your dots — click where you want the dot, but then keep your mouse button down and drag a little. As you drag, you pull out an arrow by its tip. Your line no longer bends sharply at the dot. Here's how that arrow works for you:

✔ As you drag the arrow longer, the curve gets broader at the dot. If you make the arrow shorter again, the curve gets sharper at the dot.

✔ When the arrow appears, you can release the mouse button and make your adjustments by dragging either end of the arrow.

✔ If you drag either end of the arrow around the dot, your line rotates to stay parallel to the arrow where the line and arrow pass through the dot.

Figure 16-4 shows the effect of dragging the tip of the arrow. On the left, a curved line is created and the arrow appears for the latest dot. On the right, the arrow's tip is being extended and dragged upward a bit. You can see how the curve broadens and changes angle to follow the arrow's direction.

Figure 16-4:
Making a curved line. On the right, dragging the arrow's tip to adjust the curve.

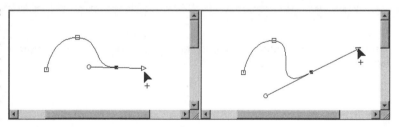

When you click to create another point in your curvy line, don't forget to drag that new point a little if you want to continue the line, avoiding kinks. If you mistakenly create a kinky node, see the next section to correct the problem.

Picking at Your Nodes

Paint Shop Pro users have an old saying, "You can pick your friends and you can pick your nodes, but you can't pick your friend's nodes." It's not true, of course, but that doesn't keep users from saying it. You can freely pick, or pick at, all your nodes — including your friend's nodes, if he or she gives you a Paint Shop Pro file with vector lines or shapes in it.

You can move nodes, remove them, or change how the line passes through them. The secret to picking at your nodes in this way is to enter the Node Edit mode. Yes, indeed: nodes have modes.

Nodes are the dots that Paint Shop Pro plays connect-the-dots with to create lines and shapes.

If you're in the middle of creating a line, you're already in Node Edit mode. You can tell you're already in Node Edit mode if your line or shape is thin, black, has no fill, and you can see nodes (tiny squares) along the line. Also, your cursor is solid black and has a + sign next to it.

 To enter Node Edit mode, do this:

1. **Click the Object Selector tool at the bottom of the tool palette (shown in the margin).**

2. **If the object (line or shape) you want to change doesn't already have a rectangular frame around it, click that object.**

3. **Either right-click the object and choose Node Edit from the context menu that appears or click the Node Edit button on the Tool Options window.**

Once in Node Edit mode, you can manipulate your nodes all you want. Here are some changes you can do:

- ✔ To move a node, drag it.

- ✔ To delete a node, click it and then press the Delete key on your keyboard. The line now connects the neighboring nodes of the deleted node.

- ✔ To select a node for any action (like deleting, dragging, or changing its type), click it.

- ✔ To select several nodes, hold down the Shift key while clicking on them.

- ✔ To break a line at a node, either right-click the node and choose Edit⇨Break from the context menu that appears, or select the node and press Ctrl+K. Now you have two unconnected nodes and two lines, where previously you had just one line. Both lines are still part of a single vector object, however.

✔ To join two line segments that are part of the same object (for instance, if they were created by breaking a line), select the two ends you want to join, then either right-click on your image and choose Edit⇨Join Select or press Ctrl+J.

✔ To convert a sharp kink at a node into a smooth curve, right-click the node and choose Node Type from the context menu that appears. Then choose one of the following:

- Symmetric: This choice makes the line curve symmetrically out from the node in both directions. You get this kind of node if you drag a little when you initially create a point-to-point line (the same arrow control appears).

- Asymmetric: This choice enables you to make the line curve more on one side of the node than on the other. An arrow appears through the node. To broaden the curve that emerges from the node, lengthen the arrow by dragging its head. To broaden the curve where it enters the node, lengthen the arrow by dragging its tail.

- Tangent: This choice allows a straight line segment to join smoothly to a curved segment.

✔ To convert a smooth curve at a node to a sharp kink, right-click the node and choose Node Type⇨Cusp. When you now rotate either the tip or the tail of the arrow that appears through the node, a sharp kink appears.

✔ A node can join either two straight lines, a straight line to a curve, or a curve to a straight line. To determine what kind of line segments enter and leave a node, right-click the node, choose Node Type from the context menu that appears, and then choose one of the following:

- Line Before/Line After: Line Before makes the line that is entering the node into a straight line. Line After makes the line that is leaving the node into a straight line.

- Curve Before/Curve After: Curve Before makes the line segment that is entering the node into a curve. Curve After does the same for the line leaving the node.

To get the inside story on your nodes, pause your mouse cursor over a node and examine the status bar (at the bottom of the Paint Shop Pro window). Figure 16-5 shows several different types of nodes.

Note that a line has *direction,* based on the order in which you create the line. The control arrow that appears on a node in Node Edit mode points in the line's direction. The word Start or End that appears when you pause your mouse cursor over end nodes of a line also tells you the direction. A few things that you do may be dependent on direction, such as aligning text to the line or shape. If you need to reverse the line direction, select the entire object with the Object Selector tool and press Ctrl+Shift+R.

Smooth, asymmetric,
curve after, line before

Smooth, asymmetric,
curve after, curve before

Figure 16-5:
Knowing
your nodes.
Notice the
asymmetric
arrow on
the
asymmetric
node.

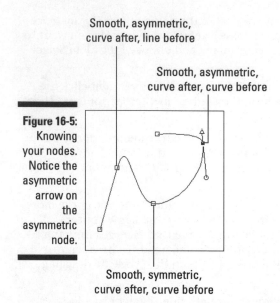

Smooth, symmetric,
curve after, curve before

Using Dashedly Stylish Lines

To add a dash of style to your lines or to the outlines of your shapes, try
styled lines — in simpler words, *dashed lines*. Whether you choose an existing
style or make your own, Paint Shop Pro has more dashed capability than
you're likely to want.

Choosing an existing style

Paint Shop Pro comes with a set of predesigned line styles that you can
choose either before you create a line or shape, or afterward.

- To choose a style to use *while* creating a line or shape, open the Tool
  Options window (press the *O* key if the window's not open). On the
  bottom of Tab 1 of that window, click the Line Style drop-down list and
  choose one of the offered styles.

- To apply a style *after* you've created a line or shape, first select that
  object with the Object Selector tool (at the bottom of the tool palette).
  Then right-click the object and choose Properties from the context
  menu that appears. In the Vector Properties dialog box that appears,
  click the Line Style drop-down list and choose one of the offered styles.
  Click the OK button.

You can add your own design to this list of styles. See the next section.

Making your own style

To create your own line style, you use Paint Shop Pro's Styled Lines. You get into the editor in one of two ways:

- ✔ To specify a dashed line *before* creating a line or shape, click the Custom button on Tab 1 of the Tool Options window. (If you're using the Preset Shapes tool, you must first clear the Retain Style check box on Tab 1, or else the Custom button is grayed out.)

- ✔ To give an *existing* object (line or shape) a custom dashed line, first select that object with the Object Selector tool (at the bottom of the tool palette). Then right-click the selected object and choose Properties from the context menu that appears. Click the Custom button in the Vector Properties dialog box.

The Styled Lines dialog box takes up residence on-screen and attempts to impress you with its wide range of doohickeys. Figure 16-6 shows the box in all its splendor. Stride forth boldly.

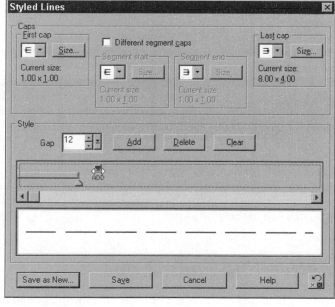

Figure 16-6: Click once in the gray box to define a dash. Click there again to define a gap and create the pattern displayed in the white box.

To create a dashed line, do this:

1. **Find the wide gray area that extends across the width of the dialog box, in the Style area.**

   Your cursor becomes a two-headed arrow marked Add when your cursor is within the correct area, as Figure 16-6 shows.

2. **Click within that area, near the left end, to create a dash.**

   A dash extends itself from the left end of that bar, ending in a green marker below where you clicked.

3. **Drag the green dash marker left or right to make the dash shorter or longer.**

   The Dash value box displays the length of your dash in pixels.

4. **Click to the right of the end of your dash to add a gap.**

   A red marker appears above where you clicked. The white box at the bottom of the dialog box shows the dashed pattern you've created. The pattern simply repeats the dash and gap you've chosen.

5. **Drag the red gap marker left or right to make your gap shorter or longer.**

   The Gap value box (formerly labeled Dash) indicates the length of your gap. The white box shows the changing pattern. Figure 16-6 shows the gap marker as it's dragged, and the result in the white area of the Styled Lines dialog box.

Continue to adjust those two markers (the lower, dash marker and the upper, gap marker) until you get the effect you want. If you want a more complex pattern, such as long-short-long, add dashes and gaps by clicking to the right of your pattern in the gray bar. Each time you click, you alternate between placing a dash and placing a gap, just as in the preceding steps. Drag the red or green markers to adjust the length of these dashes and gaps.

To return to a simpler pattern, or to a solid line, you must remove dashes and gaps. Drag each dash marker off the gray bar until your cursor is tagged with DEL and then release your mouse button. Any gap marker that follows the dash marker also disappears. When no markers remain, your line is solid again, as you can see in the white area.

Alternative line ends: Caps

The starting and finishing ends *(caps)* of lines in your object can be jauntier than just flat, which is how they come out normally. In the Styled Lines dialog box, the First Cap and Last Cap controls, respectively, are the means for determining those ends. (The caps do nothing for a closed shape, like a rectangle, as a closed shape ends where it begins. It has no ends to cap!)

Click the down arrow for either the First Cap or Last Cap control and choose a shape from the gallery that appears. The normal, flat-ended cap is the one that looks like a pitchfork, or the letter E.

To adjust the proportions of either the First or Last cap, click the cap's Size button. In the Cap Size dialog box that appears, increase the Height value to make the cap wider; increase the Width value to make the cap longer. Click OK when you're done.

Saving your style

Click the Save button when you're done adjusting your line. To save your line's style as a named style, click the Save as New button, type a name in the Style Line Name dialog box that appears, and click OK. If the Vector Properties dialog box remains on your screen (because that's how you got into the Styled Lines dialog box), click OK there, too.

Adding Preset Shapes

Need a square? Need a star? Need an outline of the Statue of Liberty? Paint Shop Pro's Preset Shapes tool lets you choose from a wide range of predetermined shapes, including circles, rectangles, stars, triangles, and cool icons. It can also deliver the Statue of Liberty but there's a catch: You have to draw the Statue (or whatever shape you want) and store it in the Preset Shape tool's library of shapes.

 To use a preset shape, click the Preset Shapes tool, shown in the margin. It lives near the bottom of the tool palette.

 Preset shapes are normally vector objects (as are text, lines, and arbitrary shapes). If you prefer them as raster (normal, bitmap) objects, make sure that the Vector option box is cleared on Tab 1 of the Tool Options window. If you create any vector object, it must be on a vector layer. If your currently active layer isn't a vector layer, Paint Shop Pro adds a vector layer for you and places the shape there.

If you like, you can edit the shapes of preset shapes after you've placed them in your image. Follow the instructions in the section, "Picking at Your Nodes," earlier in this chapter.

When you're done adding preset shapes and you want to work on other parts of the image, you probably need to change to another layer. If you're not layer-literate, press Ctrl+1 to return to the Background layer and see if that gets you where you need to go. Otherwise, refer to Chapter 15.

Dragging a shape

The Preset Shapes tool can deliver a shape from its library of shapes in any size, proportions, colors, gradients, patterns, or textures you like! Like text and drawn shapes in Paint Shop Pro, preset shapes have two parts: the outline and the fill. (It can even have dashed lines for its outline. See "Using Dashedly Stylish Lines," earlier in this chapter.) Do the following:

1. **Click the Preset Shapes tool on the tool palette.**

2. **If you want your shape to have an outline, do the following:**

   • Mouse down (that is, depress your mouse button and hold it down) on the Foreground *(Stroke)* Style swatch and, for a plain, colored outline, click the paintbrush icon. For a gradient or patterned outline, click those icons. See Chapter 4 for help with gradients, patterns, or textures.

   • Choose a foreground *(Stroke)* color. For instance, left-click on the Available Colors area of the color palette.

   • In the Tool Options window (Tab 1), set the value in the Width dialog box to the width of the outline you want, in pixels. For instance, for an outline 4 pixels wide, set it to 4.

   If you don't want an outlined shape, mouse down on the Foreground Style swatch, and click the circle-with-slash icon.

3. **If you want a solid (filled) shape, do this:**

   • Mouse down on the Background *(Fill)* Style swatch and, for plain color, click the paintbrush icon. For gradient fill or patterned fill, click those icons. For texture, choose a Background texture as I describe in Chapter 4.

   • Choose a background *(Fill)* color. For instance, right-click on the Available Colors area.

   If you don't want your shape filled (that is, you want just the outline of a shape), mouse down on the Background Style swatch (more properly called the Fill Style swatch for this tool) and click the circle-with-slash icon.

4. **In Tab 1 of the Tool Options window, click the down arrow next to the Shapes preview box and choose a shape in the gallery of preset shapes that appears.**

   The Tool Options window and its gallery of shapes appear in Figure 16-7.

5. **If you want to use the colors, styles, and textures you chose in Steps 1 and 2, make sure that the Retain Style check box is cleared on Tab 1 of the Tool Options window.**

Otherwise, if that box is checked, Paint Shop Pro uses the colors, line width, and other properties of the original shape that is stored in the shape library.

6. Drag diagonally on your image.

As you drag, your chosen shape appears and expands. (The colors and other style attributes don't appear until you release the mouse button.) If you drag more horizontally than vertically, the shape is flattened. Likewise, dragging more vertically gives you a skinny shape. Drag at a 45-degree angle to create a shape with the original proportions. To keep proportions more exact, see a description of the grid and snap-to-grid features in Chapter 14.

When you release the mouse button, your shape appears fully colored and filled according to your choices. The shape appears within Paint Shop Pro's usual object selection frame, which means you can re-dimension the shape by dragging any of the handles (squares) around the edge of that frame. To rotate your shape, drag the handle at the end of the arm that sticks out from the center of the frame. A star is born: Figure 16-7 shows the various elements that I discuss in the preceding steps.

Figure 16-7: A star is born, using the Preset Shapes tool. Because the Retain Style check box is cleared in the Tool Options window, the outline and fill chosen in the color palette apply.

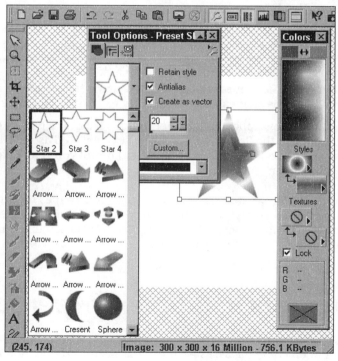

Creating custom shapes

If you can draw a shape, you can store it in Paint Shop Pro's preset shapes library and re-use it with the Preset Shapes tool.

Begin by drawing your (vector) shape or shapes in an image and then do this:

1. **If you've made your shape from various vector objects (say, text inside some shape), group the objects together.**

2. **Use the Object Selector tool to drag a rectangle to surround all the objects and choose O̲bjects⇨G̲roup.**

3. **Give each shape you want to export a name: select it, right-click it, and choose Properties from the context menu that appears.**

   In the Vector Properties dialog box, type a name for the object in the Name field and click OK.

4. **To export only one object, or only certain objects, select them with the Object Selector tool.**

5. **To select all shapes in the image, press Ctrl+D (select none). Then, choose F̲ile⇨Export Shape.**

   If you have selected any objects, a Warning dialog box appears, telling you that you're going to export only selected shapes. Fine! Click OK.

   The Export Shape Library dialog box appears.

6. **In the Enter File Name text box, enter a name for the shape file that contains all the shapes you're currently exporting and click OK.**

   The shapes now appear in the Tool Options window's gallery of shapes when you use the Preset Shapes tool. They're stored as a JSL file type, with your given filename, in the Shapes folder of your Paint Shop Pro program folder.

 When you go to use the stored shape with the Preset Shapes tool and want to use the original colors, styles, and textures, you must enable the Retain Style check box in the Tool Options window. See Step 5 in the list under the section, "Dragging a shape," earlier in this chapter.

Changing Colors and Other Properties

Don't like the color or some other look of your vector text, shape, or line? No problem. Put on colored glasses — or use the Vector Properties dialog box. Sound like fun? No? Well, it *is* fun. Do this:

1. **Click the Object Selector tool at the bottom of the tool palette.**

2. **Select the object or objects you want to modify.**

   The selection frame appears around your chosen object or group of objects. See the following section for different ways to select objects.

3. **Right-click the object and then choose Properties in the context menu that drops down.**

The Vector Properties dialog box of Figure 16-8 makes the scene. With this puppy on-screen, you can change all kinds of features.

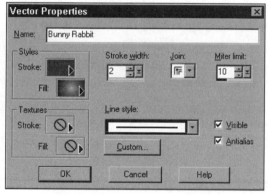

Figure 16-8: Change color or darned near anything else in the Vector Properties dialog box.

Here's a list of what you can change:

- **Object name:** If you have lots of different objects in your image, you may find naming them useful. Enter a name in the Name text box, if you like.

- **(In)visibility:** Clear the Visible check box to make your object invisible. What good is an invisible object? It's mainly useful as a hidden curve for text to follow. See "Bending text to follow a line or shape," earlier in this chapter, on making text follow a curve.

- **Aliasing (staircasing):** Place a check mark in the Antialias check box to avoid the jaggies (jagged edges) that afflict edges of computer-generated shapes.

- **Color/gradient/pattern/texture:** The Styles and Textures swatches work just like the ones in the color palette. For instance, to turn off outlines, mouse down on the top Styles swatch and click the circle-with-slash icon. See Chapter 4's discussion of styles and textures for help.

- **Thickness of line or outline:** For a thicker line, adjust the Stroke Width value upward.

- **Dashed line or outline:** Click the Line Style drop-down list and see the earlier section, "Using Dashedly Stylish Lines."

The rest of the controls have to do with joins. The term *join* refers to the point that forms where line segments meet. Paint Shop Pro offers three basic types of join, which you select by clicking the Join drop-down list box, and then choosing one of these:

- **Miter:** A miter join (what Paint Shop Pro normally creates) is one that ends in a point. Well, it tries to end in a point, anyway. If the lines meet at a really acute angle, Paint Shop Pro gives up in disgust and creates a flat (beveled) end. The point at which it gives up is controlled by the value in the Miter Limit value box. Fiddle with it this way:

    - If you want a point, increase the Miter Limit value.

    - If you want a flat end, decrease the Miter Limit value.

- **Round:** A round join is one that is, well . . . round at the point. 'Nuff said.

- **Bevel:** A bevel join is one that is flat at the point, like a miter join that has reached its Miter Limit. Or a computer user who has reached his or her limit and has been banging his or her head against the wall.

These join settings are available when you first create a line or shape, on Tab 2 of the Tool Options window.

Controlling Your Objects

Creating objects is one thing; getting them to do what you want is another — sort of like having kids. If the time has come to discipline your vector objects, Paint Shop Pro can make them straighten up and fly right.

Lots of illustrations need objects that are precisely centered, balanced, or distributed evenly. You can certainly arrange objects by dragging them and rotating them. For drill-team precision, however, you should also check out Paint Shop Pro's vector object positioning talents.

Snapping objects to a grid is one simple way of aligning them. See Chapter 14 for help with grids and snapping.

Selecting and grouping vector objects

In order to do anything to an existing object, you need to select it first. Vector objects (Paint Shop Pro's usual form of text, lines, and shapes) have their own selection tool — the Object Selector tool. Paint Shop Pro's other selection tools (the Magic Wand, Freehand, and Selection tools) don't work on vector objects.

Click the Object Selector tool that appears in the margin and then do one of the following:

✓ **Click on your vector object to select it.** If the object has gaps in it (spaces between letters, for instance), don't click on the gaps. Even if the object isn't on your currently active layer, the tool selects the object. Your layer selection doesn't change.

✓ **Drag around one or more objects.** Whatever vector objects you drag around become selected. Selecting multiple objects lets you treat them as a group for many purposes: You can change their color, change other properties, or use Paint Shop Pro's automatic arrangement features.

✓ **Hold down the Shift key and click multiple objects to select a group.** To remove objects from that selection, hold down the Ctrl key and click them.

You don't need to use the Object Selector tool. With the Layer palette open, you may click the object's name in the list of layers. See the discussion of using vector layers in Chapter 15.

A selection frame appears around your object or group of objects, with squares (handles) that you can drag to move, re-size, or rotate the object or group.

To create a single object out of multiple objects, select them all and choose Objects⇨Group. To ungroup them again, select the group and choose Objects⇨UnGroup.

To de-select, press Ctrl+D or choose Selections⇨Select None from the menu bar. To select all objects, press Ctrl+A or choose Selections⇨Select All.

 Paint Shop Pro selects an object automatically after you create it, so you can move, resize, or rotate the object. You can tell the object is selected by the rectangular frame that appears around it. Even though the object is selected, however, you can't access the same context menu (the thing that pops up when you right-click) that you could access if you had selected the object with the Object Selector tool! For instance, you can't change the object's color unless you first select the object with the Object Selector tool.

Deleting, copying, pasting, and editing

As with nearly any Windows program, you can delete, cut, copy, or paste selected objects in Paint Shop Pro using the Windows clipboard. First, select the object with the Object Selector tool. Next, do any of the following:

✓ **Copy, cut, or delete:** Use the conventional Windows keystrokes (Ctrl+X to cut, Ctrl+C to copy, and the Delete key to delete) or the familiar Toolbar buttons, Cut (scissors icon) or Copy (two documents icon).

✔ **Paste:** You can use the conventional Paste command (Ctrl+V) and Paste button (clipboard with document icon). These conventional methods, however, create an entire, new image from the clipboard contents. More likely, you want to paste the object as a new object on the current layer. For that, choose Edit⇨Paste⇨As New Vector Selection or press Ctrl+G on your keyboard. Your copied object appears and is selected you can position it; click to anchor it. Another alternative is to paste your object as a new layer: Choose Edit⇨Paste⇨As New Layer or press Ctrl+L.

✔ **Edit a selected vector object:** Right-click it and choose the kind of editing you want to do from the context menu that appears. For instance, to change text, choose Edit Text. To edit the nodes of a shape, choose Node Edit. See the sections of this chapter that deal with shapes and text for more detail.

Paint Shop Pro doesn't provide a Toolbar button for pasting vector objects as new selections or layers, but you can add such a button by customizing the Toolbar — see Chapter 1 for help.

Positioning, arranging, and sizing by hand

To move an object (or group of objects), select it with the Object Selector tool. You can then position it in the following ways:

✔ **Move it:** Mouse down anywhere on an object (on the outline or fill, but not in gaps like the spaces between letters), and then you can drag it anywhere. Or, you can drag the object by the square handle in the center of the selection frame. You can tell when your cursor is properly positioned over the square handle because the cursor displays a four-headed arrow.

✔ **Re-size or re-proportion it:** Drag any corner of the frame, or any side of the frame, by one of the square handles to resize the object or group. If you drag more horizontally than vertically (or the other way around), the object expands or contracts more in the direction you drag. To keep the object's original proportions, drag a corner at a 45-degree angle. Turning on the grid and snap-to-grid features can help you do that better. (See Chapter 14.)

✔ **Place it on top of or underneath another object:** Vector objects can overlay one another, so sometimes you need to control which object is on top of which. Envision them in a stack and the following menu choices in the Objects⇨Arrange menu make sense:

- Bring To Top (puts your selected object on top of all)

- Move Up (raises your object in the stack)

- Move Down (lowers your object in the stack)

- Send to Bottom (puts your object on the bottom of the stack)

Alternatively, you can actually see the stack of objects in the Layer palette and adjust an object's positioning by dragging it up or down. See Chapter 15 where I discuss using vector layers.

✔ **Deform it:** For creating perspective and other distortions, the object selection frame works like the Deformation tool that I describe in Chapter 14. Holding down the Ctrl or Shift button while dragging a handle creates different kinds of distortion.

✔ **Rotate it:** Sticking out from the center square is an arm that ends in a square handle. Pause your mouse cursor over that handle so that the mouse cursor displays a pair of circling arrows. Drag the handle around the center square to rotate your object.

✔ **Delete it:** Press the Delete key on your keyboard.

Positioning and sizing objects automatically

Paint Shop Pro can help you arrange or size objects automatically in lots of different ways. First, select the group of objects you want to arrange with the Object Selector tool (or press Ctrl+A to select all).

Open the Tool Options window for the Object Selector tool (press O on your keyboard if the window isn't already open), and click Tab 2 of that window. Tab 2 displays a whole raft of buttons for alignment, distribution, and sizing. Pause your mouse cursor over any button to see its name. Figure 16-9 shows the tab.

Figure 16-9: Select a few objects with the Object Selector tool and use Tab 2 of the Tool Options window to arrange or size them.

Features in the <u>O</u>bjects menu on the menu bar are the same as those on the context menu that appears if you right-click the group. I just prefer the Tool Options window because seeing all the options at once is nice. Plus, the icons show you graphically what to expect.

The useful changes you can make with those buttons (or menu choices) are as follows, with key distinctions in italics:

- **Alignments:** Align Object buttons move your selected objects so that they line up *with each other.* Those objects' edges or centers are used as alignment points. The Align Top, Align Bottom, Align Left, and Align Right choices shuffle the objects so that they align along a particular edge (the top edge, for instance). The Horizontal Center and Vertical center align the objects' centers.

- **Distributions:** The Distribute Object buttons move your selected objects so that they're distributed as evenly as possible, but *still fit within the area of the current selection frame.* They use particular edges or objects' centers as alignment points. The Vertical Distribute Top, Center, and Bottom buttons distribute the objects vertically, using the objects' top, center, and bottom edges respectively. The Horizontal Distribute buttons work similarly, but on the horizontal axis. When objects are different sizes, perfectly even spacing isn't always possible within the selection frame area.

- **Can. (on canvas) centerings and distributions:** The five buttons labeled Can. center or distribute your objects *across the entire image.* The Horizontal and Vertical buttons for Center on Canvas, for instance, move your objects to an imaginary line running through the center of the image. The Horizontal and Vertical buttons for Space Distribute your objects evenly in either the horizontal or vertical direction.

- **Sizing:** The Make Same Size buttons automatically make the width, height, or overall size of your selected objects uniform. Those three choices are Make Same Width, Make Same Height, or Make Same Size, respectively. All objects are made as large *as the largest object selected.*

Clicking multiple buttons in succession can have interesting and useful effects. For instance, clicking the alignment buttons Horizontal Center and Vertical Center makes objects concentric. But — because the selection frame often shrinks when you align objects (it's always just large enough to contain your selection objects) — the order in which you click buttons can make a difference in the outcome. If you're both distributing and aligning objects, for instance, distribute them before you align them.

Chapter 17

Masking Layers

• •

In This Chapter

▶ Knowing why and when to mask

▶ Working with a mask

▶ Saving the mask

▶ Deleting and merging a mask

• •

*Y*ou've probably used masking tape, or at least admire those people who do. (They are so tidy!) Masking tape hides certain areas and lets others remain visible.

In Paint Shop Pro, *masking* is likewise used to hide certain areas of an overlaying layer's image while letting other areas remain visible. The similarities between masking and masking tape end there.

First of all, masking is more like a paint than a tape because you can brush it on or off. And, rather than actually covering parts of an image like masking tape does, masking makes areas transparent — just as erasing on a layer does in Paint Shop Pro. That allows the underlying image to show through.

In fact, you can think of masking as applying a special transparency paint to a layer. In this chapter, I use that metaphor a lot: transparency paint — although if you read the Paint Shop Pro documentation, they don't refer to it that way. At first glance, applying transparency paint doesn't seem like it should be a big deal, but . . . read on!

The technical truth about masks is that they're simply monochrome images that you apply in a special way to a layer. Where the image is darker, the layer's pixels are more transparent. Where the image is lighter, the pixels are more opaque.

Putting Masking to Work for You

Any layer of an image can have this special transparency paint known as *masking* which makes portions of that image layer transparent. But what, exactly, can masking do for you that erasing, selecting, cutting, and pasting can't do? Here are a few instances where masking may work better for you than some alternatives:

✔ **Brushing instead of cutting and pasting intricate shapes:** Rather than meticulously selecting the area of an image you want to combine with another and then cutting it and pasting it as a layer, do this: Paste the entire image or a roughly-selected portion of it as a layer and mask out the portions you don't want. This approach lets you brush an area in or out, which is often easier than trying to carefully select the area.

✔ **To gradually feather or fade an image into another image:** If you fill a selected area in an opaque layer with a gradient fill of transparency paint, you fade the overlaid image into the underlying image smoothly.

✔ **To cut shapes or letters out of an opaque layer:** If you create letters or shapes on the mask of an opaque layer, the transparency paint that the letters and shapes are printed in cuts holes in the opaque layer, letting your background image show through those objects.

✔ **To *etch* an image out of an opaque layer:** You can apply an image as a mask, which makes the layer's pixels most transparent where the imge is darkest.

✔ **To brush or spray transparency in a creative way:** You can use any of the painting, drawing, or shape tools on a mask. For instance, you can spray (using the Airbrush tool) creative transparent (or opaque) images. You can even brush picture tube pictures that etch transparent tube images into an opaque layer.

✔ **To create transparency on the background layer:** A mask's transparency paint can create transparency on the Background layer. Normally, you wouldn't care because — after all — nothing is behind the background layer to show through! But if you move the background layer up in the stack of layers (yes, you can), you may want transparency. (Erasing creates transparency, too, after you move the background layer up.)

Figure 17-1 shows the basic idea of masking. On the left is a diagram showing the general idea of layering and masking and on the right is the resulting image.

Figure 17-1:
Applying the trans-parency paint to a layer (left) lets the underlying background image show through (right).

In the left image in Figure 17-1, a background layer full of flowers is on the bottom and over that is a layered image of Alex, the dog, running. To that layer, I applied the transparency paint, appearing as a pink (okay, gray, here) coating, brushed around Alex. On the right is the ultimate result, a layer that is transparent wherever I applied the paint, allowing the flowered background to appear.

Creating a Basic Show All Mask

Masks are applied to layers, so opening the layer palette is a good starting point. (Press the *L* key on your keyboard if the layer palette isn't visible.) I refer you to the layer palette regularly throughout this chapter.

To create a blank mask on which to apply transparency paint, do this:

1. **Choose the layer to which this mask will apply — the one you want to make partly transparent.**

   Click that layer's name in the layer palette.

2. **Choose Masks⇨New⇨Show All from the menu bar.**

   Nothing visible happens to your layer's image because you haven't applied any transparency paint yet to make it transparent. All its pixels are opaque and therefore cover up any underlying images. However, a tiny mask icon appears after your layer's name in the layer palette.

A Show All mask has no transparency paint on it. If you prefer, you can start with a mask that is completely covered in transparency paint and then either erase that paint or brush *non-transparency* onto the mask. In Step 2, choose Masks➪New➪Hide All or press Ctrl+Y. Now your layer is entirely transparent until you paint something on its mask. See "Choosing your paint," later in this chapter, to understand how to brush non-transparency.

Painting, Editing, and Viewing the Mask

In order to paint on the mask, or do anything else to it, you must first put the layer in mask edit mode. Otherwise, you end up just applying regular old paint to the layer, not transparency paint to the mask.

Choose Masks➪Edit from the menu bar or press Ctrl+K. This puts the layer in mask edit mode. The title bars of the image and of the layer palette display *MASK* to tell you so. When you're done editing the mask, repeat the command to toggle the mode off again and return to plain old layer painting.

You can slip out of mask edit mode very easily — and accidentally. When you change layers, for instance, Paint Shop Pro takes you out of mask edit mode. Always check the title bar of the image (or layer palette) for the word *MASK* before you try to edit the mask.

You're ready to paint. But one problem with applying transparency paint is that . . . it has no color! To see what you're doing as you apply the paint, you can do one of three things:

- ✔ Simply watch the underlying image appear as you paint areas transparent.

- ✔ Pause your mouse cursor over the mask icon that appears next to the layer's name in the layer palette to see a thumbnail image.

- ✔ Turn on a special mask-viewing feature that makes the transparency paint look pink and checkerboard-patterned, as in Figure 17-1. To turn on the mask-viewing feature, choose Masks➪View Mask or press Ctrl+Alt+V. (Repeat the command to turn the feature off again.)

Choosing your paint

When you're working in mask edit mode, notice that the Available Colors area in the color palette is no longer in color! It's in black, white, and shades of gray. That's because, in this mode:

- ✔ Black makes the layer's pixels fully transparent (invisible).

- ✔ Gray makes the layer's pixels partly transparent.

- ✔ White makes the layer's pixels fully opaque.

So, for instance, to make your chosen layer transparent in some area, apply black (or some shade of gray). To restore opacity in some area, paint them white. White is your non-transparency paint.

If your mask is the wrong way round — black where it ought to be white — choose Masks⇨Invert.

You can try to use other colors on the mask. For instance, you can right-click on the Foreground Style swatch and choose a color from the Recent Color dialog box. But when you paint color on the mask, only the darkness or lightness of the color applies. (This phenomenon enables you to use color images as masks.)

Painting and filling

You can use any of Paint Shop Pro's tools on the mask, including selection tools. The Paint Brush, Airbrush, and Flood Fill tools are very straightforward to use, as long as you keep in mind that you're brushing transparency (or opacity, if you're brushing white). Tools like the Eraser, Retouch, and Clone Brush tools work normally, too, but sometimes are a bit mind-boggling to think about: "Let's see, I'm erasing transparency paint, so the layer will become, um . . . more opaque! Right!"

The Flood Fill tool is fun for masks because it lets you apply gradient fills, patterns, or textures of transparency! Do you want your layer to become increasingly transparent in the center? If you use the Flood Fill tool and choose a gradient fill for your foreground style (see Chapter 4), you can fill the layer with a black-white sunburst style gradient. Likewise, you can choose a pattern for foreground style or choose a foreground texture.

Painting not working?

Getting confused with masks is easy. One important thing to remember is that with a mask you are *modifying* a layer, not *painting* a layer. For instance, if you create a new layer with nothing on it (completely transparent), you can create a mask and fill it with all the white (non-transparency) paint you like, but you don't see any change: The layer has no pixels to modify! You have to fill the *layer* with paint first, making it opaque, then apply black transparency paint selectively to the *mask*.

Also remember that you can't work on a mask unless you're in mask edit mode. The title bars of the image and of the layer palette read *MASK* in that mode. If *MASK* doesn't appear, you're working on a layer, not a mask. If that happens, press Ctrl+K to restore mask edit mode.

Finally, if you find painting directly on the mask too confusing, see the section, "Making a mask from an image," later in this chapter.

Drawing, shapes, and text

Paint Shop Pro's Draw, Text, and Preset Shapes tools also work on masks, so you can make transparent lines, holes, and text. These tools don't, however, do a few things that they do normally:

- ✔ They don't offer vector shapes, only raster shapes.
- ✔ As of this writing, gradients, patterns, and textures are possible, but not reliable. Sometimes they work, and sometimes they don't. Final releases of Paint Shop Pro 7 may correct this problem.

If your objective is simply to make cutouts of shapes or text through which an underlying layer appears, you don't need a mask. Apply your line, text, or other shape to the layer, select it with the Magic Wand tool and press the Delete key to cut a transparent hole. A mask is the way to go when you want a gradient fill of transparency, or other pattern. When you want total transparency (a hole) in a layer, deleting or erasing a selected area works fine.

Making a mask from an image

A mask is just a black and white (grayscale) image, applied to a layer, that makes the layer more transparent where the image is darker. So, rather than trying to paint in transparency paint (sometimes confusing), why not paint the grayscale image in the first place, then apply it as a mask?

Why not, indeed? In the first place, painting in shades of gray is a lot less mind-boggling than painting transparency. In the second place, you may already have some images that would make cool masks. You can even use a photograph as a mask, giving the appearance that it has been etched into your overlaying layer.

Figure 17-2 shows, on the top, an image that was used for a mask. The image on the bottom began as a background layer of vegetables (which I created with the Picture Tube tool). I overlaid it with a layer that I painted solid green. Then I applied the image on the top as a mask to the green overlaying layer. Notice how the black and dark gray of the mask make the layer more transparent.

Can you create the picture in Figure 17-2 in other ways? Sure — you can create a blank (transparent) overlaying layer and paint it with a set of concentric rectangles, using paint of increasing opacity. Then, you can place the text on that layer *as a selection* (rather than as a vector object). Pressing the Delete key makes the text selection transparent — et voila! Same result. But, I happened to have the concentric squares in the left image of Figure 17-2 lying around, so I added the text and used the image as a mask!

Figure 17-2:
An image
(top)
becomes a
mask for a
solid-
painted
layer that
overlays a
background
of fresh
produce.

To apply an image as a mask, do the following:

1. **Create an image or open an image file to use as the mask.**

   Your masking image can be either a monochrome (grayscale) image or a color one. Make it the same size, or at least the same proportions, as the image you're masking. Instead of creating an entirely new image and fussing about its dimensions, you can create a new layer in the image you want to mask and use that layer for your mask image. If you take that approach, make your new layer the topmost one.

2. **Click the title bar of the window containing the image to be masked, and then click the layer that you want to mask in the layer palette.**

   Make sure that you are *not* in mask edit mode or the command in Step 3 is grayed out. If the title bar of the layer palette reads *MASK*, press Ctrl+K to exit the mask edit mode.

3. **Choose Masks⇨New⇨From Image.**

   In the Add Mask From Image dialog box that appears, click the Source Window selection box and choose your mask image's name from the list that appears. It lists the images currently open in Paint Shop Pro, by name. (Look in the image title bars to check the image name if you're not sure which is the right one.) If you're using a new layer in your image as your mask image source, choose This Window.

4. **Choose an option in the Create Mask From area of the dialog box.**

   - Choose Source Luminance to make a mask from the varying brightness of the image — this basically treats the masking image like a black and white photograph.

   - Choose Any Non-Zero Value to pick up just the black areas.

   - Choose Source Opacity if your mask image is paint on a transparent background. For instance, if you're using a layer of your about-to-be-masked image, you may simply have painted on that layer's transparent background.

   - Enable the Invert Mask Data check box to switch black for white (make a negative) in the masking image.

5. **Click OK.**

   Your masking image is now a mask on your chosen layer. (If you created your masking image as a layer of the masked image, you can now delete that layer.)

Controlling the Mask

As the Phantom of the Opera knew, controlling your mask is important. Sometimes you want it on, sometimes you don't. You may even want to get rid of it, save it for a rainy day, or make it a permanent part of your face . . . er, image.

Disabling, enabling, or de-linking the mask

The layer palette has a special section for masks: On the right side of the palette, click the tab with the mask icon. On the row for any layer that has a mask, two icons appear: a mask icon and a link icon.

- ✔ To turn the layer's mask off or on, click its mask icon. An X through the icon indicates the mask is off.

- ✔ The mask is normally linked to its layer. If you move, flip, or mirror the layer, the mask goes with it. If, for some reason of your own, you want to unlink the mask so that you can manipulate the layer without its mask, click the link icon. An X goes through the icon. Click again when or if you want to re-link.

Saving, deleting, and merging a mask

When you save your image as a Paint Shop Pro type of file, your mask is automatically saved along with your image. You may, however, want to save it separately. You can be doing a series of images, for instance, all of which have the same look and need the same mask. Or, you may be saving your image as something other than a Paint Shop Pro file.

Choose Masks and at the bottom of the menu, you discover that Paint Shop Pro lets you save your mask for reloading in one of two ways:

- ✔ **Save To or Load From Disk:** These choices let you save your mask as a special Paint Shop Pro mask file on disk, and then later reload it into any layer of a new image.

  - To save your mask, first click the layer with the mask in the layer palette. Choose Masks➪Save To Disk; the Save Mask Channel dialog box appears. Enter a name for your mask in the File Name text box, choose a folder, and click OK.

  - To load a mask stored in this way and attach it to a particular layer, first click the layer in the layer palette that you want to mask. Then choose Masks➪Load From Disk. In the Load Mask Channel dialog box that appears, choose your named mask file. (All mask files end in the extension .MSK.)

- ✔ **Save To or Load From Alpha Channel :** Use these menu choices when you're saving your image as a TIF, PNG, or TGA type of file, and want that file to retain the mask information. (Note that these file types don't store layer information, however, so you aren't able to re-apply your mask to its original layer, unless that layer is the background layer.) These menu choices preserve your grayscale mask image in a special, second image storage area of the file called the alpha channel. (You can also use the alpha channel to store a selection.) You can use the alpha channel of Paint Shop Pro files to store a mask, but you don't really need to, as the mask is automatically saved with the Paint Shop Pro file.

- To save your mask in an alpha channel, first click the layer with the mask in the layer palette. Choose Masks➪Save To Disk and the Save Mask Channel dialog box appears. Double-click New Channel in the Available Alpha list box. In the New Channel dialog box that appears, enter a name for your mask and click OK.

- To restore your mask from an alpha channel, first click the layer in the layer palette that you want to mask. Then choose Masks➪ Load From Alpha Channel. In the Load From Alpha dialog box that appears, you see your mask's name highlighted. Click OK.

To delete a mask, select the mask's layer in the layer palette and choose Masks➪Delete. Paint Shop Pro asks Would you like this mask merged into the current layer? If you click Yes, the mask's transparency is imparted to the layer's image. If you simply don't want the mask any longer, click No.

Part V
Taking It to the Street

The 5th Wave   By Rich Tennant

©RICHTENNANT

"HONEY! OUR WEB ANIMATION GOT OUT LAST NIGHT AND DUMPED THE TRASH ALL OVER MR. BELCHER'S HOME PAGE."

In this part . . .

In the end, you probably want your image to appear somewhere else besides Paint Shop Pro: on a piece of paper, on the Web, or as part of an animation. Check out this part for help with taking your image that last mile.

For printing on paper, I show you how to get the size and proportions right in Chapter 18. It also tells you how to print multi-image pages for photo albums, collages, or portfolios.

Web work often involves getting the right kind of file and making some trade-offs. In Chapter 19, I tell you how to choose and create the best image file type, including special Web effects such as transparency or different kinds of fade-in as the image downloads.

Whether for Web banners or other applications, Paint Shop Pro's Animation Shop can quickly give you results you never dreamed you could produce on your own. In Chapter 20, I explain how Animation Shop's wizards and effects automatically generate animated text or images and describe how to use your own frames, created or modified, in Paint Shop Pro.

Chapter 18

Printing

· ·

In This Chapter

▶ Sizing and positioning the print on the paper

▶ Printing a single image

▶ Printing thumbnail images from the browser

▶ Creating multi-image pages

▶ Adjusting print speed and quality

▶ Printing color separations

· ·

*A*ll this electronic image stuff is just fine but in the end, many of us want our images printed on dead and flattened, bleached trees — paper. As a good friend once said, "The paperless office of the future is just down the hall from the paperless bathroom of the future." Paper is going to be around for a little while yet.

Paint Shop Pro has some great features for making the printing job easier: automatically fitting the image to the page, printing a collection or album page of images, printing browser thumbnails, and more. Read on for ways to make paper printing work better and faster for you.

Save a tree, and save time, too. Always preview your printout before committing it to paper. Choose File⇨Print Preview, and the Print Preview window comes to your aid. Click the Zoom In or Zoom Out buttons if you need to examine your print more closely or distantly. Clicking the Setup button takes you to the Page Setup dialog box where margins and scaling happen. Click the Close button when you're done previewing.

Fitting Your Print to the Paper

"Let the punishment fit the crime," said Gilbert and Sullivan's Mikado, who prescribed the death penalty for flirting. With the help of the few hints in this section, your image should fit your page with far less pain.

If you have multiple images open in Paint Shop Pro, click the title bar on the window of the image you want to print. That makes it the active window.

All the controls for sizing and positioning your print on paper are in the Page Setup dialog box. Choose File➪Page Setup to access that dialog box, shown in Figure 18-1, and then consult the following bullets for help.

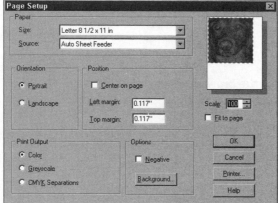

Figure 18-1: The Page Setup dialog box fits your print to the paper. A preview window shows the current setup.

Keep in mind that when Paint Shop Pro changes the size of your *print,* it's not changing your *image.* It's resizing the printed output only; the image itself is not changed in any way. If your image is 500 pixels across, it remains 500 pixels across.

Here's how to use the Page Setup dialog box to fit your print to your paper:

✔ **Centering:** Often, you want your print centered on the page. Click the Center on Page check box to do that.

✔ **Filling the page:** To fill the page with your image (to the maximum extent possible), click the Fit To Page check box under the preview window. Your print is enlarged until it fills either the width or height of the paper, within the allowable margins of your printer. The margin value boxes are grayed out, so you can't change margins.

✔ **Making the image larger or smaller:** You can print your image at scales from 100 percent down, or up to 1000 percent (ten times larger). Adjust the Scale value under the preview window to whatever percentage you want. 100 percent means that the image's resolution, assigned at its creation, is observed. An image 144 pixels wide, for instance, at a typical resolution of 72 pixels per inch, is printed 2 inches wide.

✔ **Setting margins:** Paint Shop Pro initially sets the initial left and top margins to the minimum that your printer can handle. You can move your print around on the page by adjusting the Left Margin or Top Margin values.

✔ **Printing sideways (orientation):** Paint Shop Pro initially sets you up to print in the *portrait* orientation on the paper, meaning the paper's long dimension runs vertically. For prints that are wider than they are high, however, you may want to print sideways, or in *landscape* orientation. Click either Portrait or Landscape to choose orientation.

Another option that happens to live in the Page Setup dialog box is printing your image in grayscale (black and white). If you would like that result, click to enable the Greyscale option box, in the lower left corner.

Click OK when you're done setting up.

When you print an image at a scale much greater than 100 percent, your pixels may begin to show. Scandalous! Instead of scaling your print, try exiting the Page Setup dialog box (click Cancel) and scaling your *image* by that same percentage, using a Resize Type of Smart Size. See Chapter 12 for help with resizing. Your image may be a bit blurred, but it doesn't look as pixelated. Figure 18-2 shows the difference.

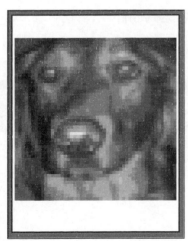 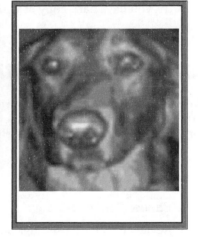

Figure 18-2: Rather than printing small images at large scales (left), try resizing the image larger first (right).

Printing an Image

After you've visited the Page Setup dialog box (see the preceding section), you're ready to print your image.

1. **Choose File➪Print, press Ctrl+P, or click the Print button on the Toolbar.**

   The Print dialog box appears.

2. **Choose your printing options.**

   You have the usual controls that come with any Windows program: the printer you're using, the number of copies you want, and a Properties button that takes you to the printer's driver software. (That's where you can set the print quality, speed, paper type, and other variables. See the section, "Printing at Different Speeds or Qualities," later in this chapter.)

3. **Choose more options.**

   - If you're going to print a lot of images, you may want the filename of the image on the print. If so, enable the Title check box. (If you've entered a title in the Creator Information tab in the Current Image Information dialog box, that title appears in place of the filename.)

   - In some instances, you may want to trim the margins off the print when you're done. If your image has a white background, however, finding those margins may be hard. To solve that problem, enable the Print Corner Crop Marks and Print Center Crop Marks check boxes.

4. **Click OK after you've set all the options you want.**

Shortly, you have hard copy of your hard work.

Printing Browser Thumbnails

When you have a lot of images, printing out a collection of thumbnail images from the image browser creates a very useful reference to keep on file. Each image is printed along with its filename.

With the browser window open and active, go first to Page Setup to specify your layout.

1. **Choose File➪Page Setup.**

   Review the margin settings and page size there to make sure that's what you want.

2. **Choose a Portrait or Landscape orientation.**

3. **Click OK.**

If you want to print only certain images, select them first by holding down the Ctrl key and clicking on them.

Choose File➪Print, press Ctrl+P, or click the Print button on the Toolbar. The Print dialog box that appears gives the usual controls (number of copies, choice of printer) plus some controls for Print Range. The All choice prints all pictures displayed by the browser. The Pages choice lets you specify one or a range of pages. The Selection choice prints only your selected images.

Printing Collections or Album Pages

One of Paint Shop Pro's newest and most popular features is the ability to print multiple images. It's a great way to create album pages or make collages of photos to celebrate an event.

First, open all the images you want to print. See Chapter 2 for help with file opening. The method I prefer is to open multiple images in the image browser as I describe in Chapter 2.

Then, make any alterations you need to the images: cropping, fixing exposure problems and red-eye, retouching, and the like. If you don't want to be bothered, you don't need to rotate pictures or to adjust their sizes.

If your images need no cropping or retouching, you can save a step: select them all at once in the image browser (hold down Ctrl and click them), right click any one of them, and then choose Print Multiple Images from the context menu that appears. That opens your chosen images and takes you directly to the multi-image printing tool.

After you have your images open in Paint Shop Pro, choose File➪Print Multiple Images. Your entire Paint Shop Pro window changes to the multi-image printing tool that appears in Figure 18-3.

The multi-image printing tool occupies your entire Paint Shop Pro window. To exit from it and return to the normal window, choose File➪Close. Unless you've saved your layout (see the section, "Saving and re-using your layout," later in this chapter), exiting the tool discards your layout.

With the multi-image printing tool on-screen, the basic procedure is as follows:

1. **Choose your page orientation.**

   Paint Shop Pro initially gives you a portrait-oriented page (long dimension vertically). If you want a landscape- (sideways-) oriented page, choose File➪Page Setup, and then click Landscape in the Page Setup dialog box that appears. Click OK.

Drag handles to resize

Drag images from here

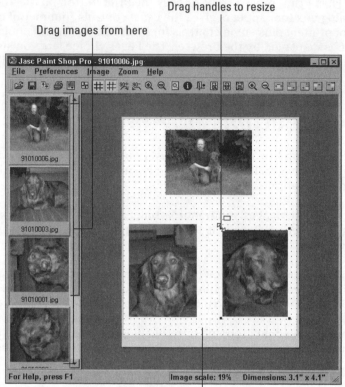

Figure 18-3: Composing a multi-image page.

Align images on optional grid

2. **Drag images, one at a time, from the left column onto the page.**

   If the images are too large for the page, Paint Shop Pro asks if you want to scale it. If you click <u>Y</u>es, your image appears with handles (square dots) at the corners that you can drag to resize the image. Choose <u>N</u>o if you want to use Paint Shop Pro's autoarrange feature (Step 4) to place and size the image for you.

   If an image is rotated 90 degrees the wrong way, drag it onto the page and click the *90+* (clockwise) or *90–* (counter-clockwise) button on the toolbar to rotate the image.

3. **If you want to position the images yourself, drag them into position.**

   Otherwise, just drop them anywhere on the page — even slopping over the side. The next step takes care of them.

4. **If you want Paint Shop Pro to position and size the images automatically, choose P<u>r</u>eferences⇨<u>A</u>uto Arrange.**

5. **To print your page, click the Print icon on the Toolbar or choose <u>F</u>ile⇨<u>P</u>rint.**

Neither choice gives you a Print dialog box, but immediately sends the page to your printer. If you need to change any printer settings, do so before sending the page to the printer. Choose File⇨Page Setup and click the Printer button in the Page Setup dialog box that appears.

If you're done, return to the normal Paint Shop Pro window by choosing File⇨Close or click the Close button on the toolbar (door-with-arrow icon).

Fooling with the pictures and layout

You can fiddle with the pictures and their arrangement all you want, after they're on the page. Most controls for fiddling are duplicated in the menu bar, the toolbar across the top of the window, or, if you right-click an image, in the context menu that appears. Nearly everything can be done fastest by the right-clicking approach, so that's mainly what's listed below. Here are some basic fiddlings you may want to do:

- ✔ To select a picture so you can do something with it, click it. (Handles appear at its corners.)

- ✔ To move a picture, drag it.

- ✔ To position a picture in the center or at any of the four corners of the page, click any of the five positioning buttons at the far right of the toolbar. The icon indicates the position the button delivers. Pause your cursor over the button for a text indication of its positioning.

- ✔ To resize a picture, drag any of its handles.

- ✔ To remove a picture from the layout, either click it and press the Delete button on your keyboard or right-click it and choose Remove from the context menu.

- ✔ To rotate a picture, right-click it and choose Rotate 90+ or Rotate 90– from the context menu that appears. (+ is clockwise.)

- ✔ To see an alignment grid, right-click on the white page background and choose Show Grid from the context menu. (Repeat to turn the grid off.)

- ✔ To make photos snap to the grid when you move them, right-click on the white page background and choose Snap To Grid from the context menu. (The grid must be on, first, or this command is grayed out.)

Saving and re-using your layout

The thing that you're creating in this tool is a *layout,* not an image. (A layout doesn't actually contain your pictures; it's a description of how to lay out your pictures.)

To save your work, choose File⇔Save Layout. In the Save As dialog box that appears, enter a name for your layout in the filename text box. Choose a folder to save your layout file in, if you like, and then click the Save button.

To re-use this layout, choose File⇔Open Layout and choose your layout by name in the Open dialog box that appears. (You must be in the multiple-image print tool; this command doesn't appear on the File menu of the regular Paint Shop Pro window.)

Because a layout file *uses* but doesn't contain your images, you can save your layout, exit the multi-image print tool, and do work on any of the images, at any time. For instance, you may decide to do some retouching on an image. When you re-use the layout, it brings up the image in its current condition, whatever that may be. For that reason, be sure not to move any images to other folders or rename them, because then the multi-image print tool can't find them.

Printing at Different Speeds or Qualities

Paint Shop Pro itself doesn't have much to do with choosing the quality or speed of printing that your printer delivers. That falls in the province of the software that runs your printer, known as its *driver*. To access that piece of software, either click the Properties button in the Print dialog box or click the Printer button in the Page Setup dialog box. Then, click the Properties button in the dialog box that appears. Because what happens next depends on your printer, I can't tell you exactly what you'll see from then on.

One quality that Paint Shop Pro does control is whether or not your image prints in color or grayscale. To print in grayscale (black and white), click the Greyscale option in the lower left corner of the Page Setup dialog box.

Speed, size, and ink

Quality comes at the cost of speed and of ink. Most printers have a *draft* and a *quality* setting. If you just want a general idea of how your image is going to look, and want to save time and ink, choose draft. Your image is printed lighter and fuzzier than if you choose the quality (or non-draft) setting, but is printed more quickly.

The size of your printed image also costs you time and ink. Doubling the size increases the amount of ink you need by four.

Many ink-jet printers do a much better job on special photograph-quality paper. In that case, the printer driver generally has a setting where you can tell it that you're going to use special paper.

Printer and image resolution

One aspect of print quality is *resolution*, or dots per inch. A higher resolution generally gives a better quality image. That resolution number is often confusing because your image has resolution, too, in pixels per inch. The two don't match, either. The printer resolution is always a higher number than image resolution.

What's going on? Your printer creates its range of colors by putting out tiny dots in four colors: cyan, magenta, yellow, and black. It needs many tiny dots to make a pixel of a particular color, so your printer needs many more dots per inch (dpi) than your image has pixels per inch. My printer, for instance, can print 1440 dpi. So, each pixel of a 72 pixel per inch image covers an area 20 x 20 dots of ink. For an image twice that resolution, I get an area only 10 x 10 dots, giving me ¼ the number of possible colors.

The bottom line? Although using a higher image resolution when you create your image gives you more detail in your prints, don't push it too high and don't try to match your printer's resolution. If you use a higher image resolution (pixels per inch), each pixel uses fewer printer dots, so color accuracy may suffer. Your printer driver does a few tricks to keep things accurate, but the laws of physics eventually win.

Printing Color Separations

If you're dealing with a professional printer who is reproducing your image in quantity, you may need to produce what are known as *color separations*. Color separations consist of a separate image for each primary color. Printers use four primary colors, cyan, magenta, yellow, and black (CMYK), so you would print four separate images for your one image. The printer also needs to align these four images, so the images need *registration marks* — crosshairs — to line them up.

First, choose File⇨Page Setup. Then, in the Page Setup dialog box, click the CMYK Separations option. Click OK.

Next, press Ctrl+P to print. In the Print dialog box, click to enable the Print Registration Marks check box. Click OK when you're ready to print. Remember: you're creating four separate prints!

Chapter 19

Creating Web Images

● ●

In This Chapter

▶ Improving download times

▶ Choosing the best file type

▶ Creating GIF and JPEG images

▶ Creating hot spots and rollovers

● ●

*T*he Web makes special demands on graphics. Images have to be stored as particular file types, and they can't take too long to download or people get bored.

What's more, popular tricks and techniques have been developed for Web graphics. On some pages, you can click on different spots of an image to go to different Web pages. Other pages provide rollover graphics that respond to the viewer's mouse position and actions. These techniques aren't part of the images themselves, but part of the Web page. Paint Shop Pro's new Webtools feature lets you create these Web page features.

In this chapter, I show you how to make your Web images look their best while downloading as fast as possible. I also show you how to use Paint Shop Pro's automated Webtools to more quickly generate special effects like hot spots and rollovers.

 Paint Shop Pro offers a special Web toolbar for the Web features that I discuss here. With the Web toolbar enabled, you simply click a button for an effect rather than use the menu commands. To enable the toolbar, choose View➪Toolbars, select the Web Toolbar check box in the Toolbars dialog box that appears, and click the Close button.

Making Images Download Faster

The key trick with images on the Web is to make sure that they don't take any longer to download than they have to. Web users are fickle and if you make them wait, they won't stay around. Images download faster when their files are smaller. Following are a few general tips for making sure your images download as fast as possible — some you do when you're creating the Web page and others you do in Paint Shop Pro:

- **Reduce image size:** The main mistake made by beginners is to use excessively large images on their Web pages. Web page authoring tools sometimes give the illusion of having made an image smaller, but in fact they may just squeeze a large image into a small space. Size or resize your image in Paint Shop Pro to exactly the size you need on the Web page.

- **Repeat images:** In your Web page authoring software, if your page uses the same image over and over again (say, for a bullet icon), insert the exact same image file each time. Don't use multiple files that are identical copies of the same image.

- **Reduce colors:** If you're painting or drawing an image in Paint Shop Pro for Web use, don't use any more colors than you have to.

- **Use solid colors:** Gradient fills, dithered, or airbrushed areas (hues made up of multicolored pixels), and scanned printed images (made up of visible dots) require larger files. Paint with solid colors wherever possible if you want to keep file size down. Noise effects such as Edge Preserving Smooth in Paint Shop Pro's Effects menu can help reduce dots to uniform colors.

Exporting Images for the Web

The images that appear on Web pages are almost always stored as one of two main types of file: GIF or JPEG. Sometimes, they're stored as PNG files, a new and improved type of file, but that type is still rarely used. To make your image viewable on a Web browser, all you have to do is make sure to save a copy of the image as one of these file types.

To create a Web file from your image, you can go either of two ways:

- You can save the image *as* a particular type of file (choosing File⇨Save As or File⇨Save Copy As, as I describe in Chapter 2).

- You can *export* it to a particular type of file.

Exporting takes you immediately into an optimizer dialog box for that type of file, where you choose features and tradeoffs. Using a Save As command, you can access that same optimizer by clicking the Options button in the Save As or Save Copy As dialog box, and then clicking the Run Optimizer button in the Options dialog box that appears.

Always store your image as a Paint Shop Pro file before you create Web image files from it. Paint Shop Pro files retain lots of features that are lost when you store an image as a Web image.

Choosing features and file types

Each file type has its own advantages and features. Table 19-1 lists attributes you may want, and the file type or types that are generally best to use. *Best* considers both image quality and speed of downloading (file size).

Table 19-1 Images, Image Features, and What File Types to Use

Image Attributes	File Type to Use	Notes
Is (or is like) a photograph	JPEG	Color photographs are much smaller in JPEG than in GIF.
Uses patterns/textures	JPEG or GIF	More complex patterns or textures are better as JPEG.
Uses mainly solid colors	GIF or PNG	Solid color images often have thin or sharp edges, all pixels of which are entirely preserved in GIF or PNG.
Has transparent areas	GIF or PNG	Transparency lets page background show through. See Figure 19-1.
Fades in during loading	GIF, JPEG, or PNG	Fade-in *(progression)* is an optional feature.

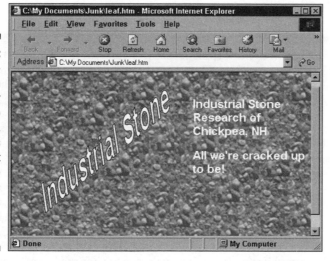

Figure 19-1: Transparency, a popular Web feature, allows this slanted-text image to float over a Web page's background image.

Creating GIF files

GIF files are the most widely used graphics files on the Web. They offer certain popular features, such as transparency, but are also limited to 256 colors, as I note in Chapter 2. To export a GIF file from your image, do the following:

1. **Choose File⇨Export⇨GIF Optimizer.**

   The Transparent GIF Saver dialog box (the *optimizer*) appears, containing five tabs of settings that I cover throughout the next few sections. The optimizer has before-and-after preview windows (left and right, respectively) that show what effect your choices have. To zoom in or out, click the magnifier icons. Click the magnifier with the + to zoom in, or with the – to zoom out. To view different parts of your image, drag in a window.

   If you aren't doing a transparent image, or have no desire to fool around with trading off quality for faster download speed, you can skip all these tabs and move on to Step 2.

2. **Click the OK button.**

   The familiar Save As dialog box appears.

3. **Choose a filename and folder for the file and click OK.**

You can make image files smaller so they download faster, but you trade off image quality. Click the Colors tab if you want to adjust this tradeoff. Keep an eye on the resulting image quality in the right preview window as you fiddle with the controls. Also, pay attention to the file size, given under that window as Compressed: # bytes.

Creating transparent areas

To prepare an image to have transparent portions on the Web, first save your image as a Paint Shop Pro file. Then choose *any one* of the following alternative approaches to mark a transparent area — whichever approach seems easiest to you:

✔ **Color:** If all the pixels in the area you want to become transparent are roughly the same color (say, a white background), you don't need to do much more in preparation. Just make sure that your chosen color does *not* appear in any pixels where you *don't* want transparency, such as the whites of people's eyes. If the color *does* appear elsewhere, try one of the two following approaches instead.

✔ **Selection:** Select either the object that you want to be visible (opaque), or the background that you want to be transparent.

✔ **Transparency:** If the object (say, your logo) that you want to be visible (opaque) is not already on its own layer or layers, select it and promote it to a layer. In the layer palette, turn off the visibility of the background layer and any other unwanted layers, and the transparent portions of the logo layer are apparent (display a checkerboard pattern).

Opening and using transparent GIF files

If you open a transparent GIF file in Paint Shop Pro, you may be surprised at what you see: Areas that appear transparent in a Web browser are filled in with a color. That result occurs because GIF transparency is a special trick used mainly in Web browsers. Paint Shop Pro shows the reality behind the trick.

GIF files achieve transparency by designating a particular color in the palette transparent. Web browsers pay attention to that designation and, where that exact color occurs, show the underlying Web page background in pixels, instead of the color. Paint Shop Pro, however, shows the color itself — unless you tell it otherwise.

To tell Paint Shop Pro to show the transparency, choose Colors⇨View Palette Transparency. Repeat the command to return to viewing the color.

If you want another color in the file's palette to be displayed as transparent, choose Colors⇨Set Palette Transparency. In the Set Palette Transparency dialog box that appears, click the option, Set the Transparency Value to Pallete Entry __, and then click on your chosen color in the image window. To turn off transparency altogether, choose the No Transparency option. Click OK when you're done. Be careful when choosing a color that the color is not used in places where you're not expecting it. White, for instance, may appear in someone's eyes, giving a very spooky result when the whites of their eyes become transparent!

Remember that GIF files are palette-type files, and so many Paint Shop Pro features don't work unless you convert the file to 16.7 million colors first. (Press Ctrl+Shift+0.)

To have edges of a selected area blend gradually into the Web page's background, contract the selection by a certain number of pixels (say, 4). Then feather the selection by that same number of pixels. (See Chapter 13 for help with contracting and feathering a selection.)

A tab in the GIF Optimizer dialog box lets you translate your chosen area into a transparency. Choose File⇨Export⇨GIF Optimizer. In the GIF Optimizer dialog box that appears, click the first tab, Transparency. This tab asks, "What portion of your image would you like to be transparent?" Your choices are:

- ✔ **None:** Choose this option if you want no transparent areas whatsoever.

- ✔ **Existing image or layer transparency:** Choose this option if your image already has transparent areas (appearing as a gray checkerboard pattern) that you want to remain transparent on the Web page. This is the Transparency approach in the preceding bulleted list.

- ✔ **Inside The Current Selection:** Use this option if, using Paint Shop Pro's selection tools, you have selected the area (say, the background) that you want to become transparent (the Selection approach in the preceding bulleted list). If, instead, you have selected the area that is to remain opaque, choose Outside the Current Selection.

✔ **Areas that Match This Color:** Choose this option (the Color approach in the preceding bulleted list) if the areas that you want transparent are all the same color. If the color that is already displayed in the adjoining color swatch is *not* the one you want to make transparent, move your cursor outside the dialog box, over the image, and click on any area of your chosen color. The result appears in the right preview window. Increase the Tolerance value to make a wider range of similar colors transparent or decrease it to narrow the range of colors made transparent.

Coping with partially transparent areas

Partial transparency of an image, possible in Paint Shop Pro (revealed by a faint checkerboard pattern shining through the image) isn't really possible in Web images. A pixel is either 100 percent transparent or 100 percent opaque. Paint Shop Pro can fake intermediate values, however, by dithering an area — alternating pixels between opaque and transparent. Click the second tab in the GIF Optimizer, Partial Transparency, if you want the appearance of partially transparent areas in your image. For instance, perhaps you selected an area with a feathered edge to become transparent.

The Partial Transparency tab asks two questions. First, How would you like to represent partially transparent pixels in this image? Your possible choices are:

✔ **Use Full Transparency For Pixels Below __% Opacity:** This option simply draws a dividing line at a certain opacity: Pixels with a lower opacity value than the percent value you enter become totally transparent. Pixels with higher opacity values become totally opaque.

✔ **Use 50% Dither Pattern:** This option makes one out of every two pixels in the semitransparent area transparent. The entire semitransparent area appears to be 50 percent transparent.

✔ **Use Error Diffusion Dither:** This option (my favorite) makes randomly chosen pixels transparent in the semitransparent area. The density of transparent pixels varies, giving a result that more closely matches original transparency, such as the varying transparency that occurs within a feathered selection.

The second question, Would you like to blend the partially transparent pixels?, you should normally answer by choosing No, Use the Existing Image Color at 100% Opacity. Choose Yes, Blend With the Background Color *only* if you must accommodate the relatively few people using browsers that don't display transparency. Instead of transparency, those browsers display the background color, shown in the sample swatch that follows the Yes . . . option. You can change the background color by clicking the swatch and choosing from the Color dialog box that appears.

Choosing image fade-in

As GIF images download, they build gradually on-screen. You can choose whether they build from top to bottom, or fade in from fuzzy to increasingly detailed. For small images that download quickly, the choice doesn't matter much. To choose a method, click the Format tab.

On the Format tab, choose Non-Interlaced if you want the image to build from top to bottom. Choose Interlaced if you want the image to fade in. Leave the "What version do you want your file to be?" option set to Version 89a unless someone specifically requests a file of Version 87a.

Creating JPEG files

JPEG files tend to be smaller than GIF files for many kinds of image, so they download faster. The main tradeoff is that JPEG files are *lossy.* They lose some of the detail in your original image. You can choose how much detail to trade off for a reduction in file size, however. The second tradeoff is that JPEG files can introduce *artifacts:* blurs, spots, and rectangular blocks that weren't present in the original image. Again, however, you can choose how many artifacts you're willing to live with to get a smaller file.

To export to JPEG, do the following:

1. **Choose File⇨Export⇨JPEG Optimizer.**

   The JPEG Saver dialog box (the optimizer) appears. It has three tabs. It also has before-and-after preview windows (left and right, respectively) that show the effect of your choices. To zoom in or out, click the magnifier icons. Click the magnifier with the + to zoom in or with the – to zoom out. To view different parts of your image, drag in a window.

2. **Click the Quality tab to trade off file size for quality.**

   Adjust the Set Compression Value To __ value box to a value from 1 to 99. Higher values make the file smaller, but gives it lower quality. You can see changes in the file size under the right preview window, in the line Compressed: XX bytes. You can see changes to image quality in the right window.

   To see estimates of how fast your file downloads, depending upon the viewer's Internet connection speed, click the Download Times tab. A table there gives estimated download times for various connection speeds. 56K is probably the most commonly used.

3. **Click the Format tab to control how the image fades in.**

   JPEG files normally assemble themselves from top to bottom as they download to a Web browser. If you would rather have your image fade in from blurry to detailed, choose Progressive on this tab. Otherwise, leave the choice set to Standard.

4. **Click the OK button.**

   The familiar Save As dialog box appears.

5. **Choose a filename and folder for the file and click OK.**

Doing Common Webbish Tricks

Web pages often employ special tricks. Here are two that Paint Shop Pro can help you with.

Creating buttons

Paint Shop Pro offers an effect that is great for creating graphical buttons for Web pages. The *buttonize* effect makes any image (or selected part of an image) look like a raised button by shading around the edges.

Choose Effects⇨3D Effects⇨Buttonize. The Buttonize adjustment dialog box that appears offers two styles of button. Click the Solid Edge option box for a button that has flat sides or Transparent Edge for a button with rounded sides. The Buttonize dialog box also offers three adjustments:

- **Height/Width:** These controls adjust the vertical and horizontal dimensions, respectively, of the top surface of the button.
- **Opacity:** Increasing Opacity makes the edges of the button darker, obscuring the underlying image more.

The right preview window in the Buttonize dialog box shows the result of your choices.

Matching image colors to HTML colors

You may want to match colors used in your image to colors used in the text of your Web page — or vice-versa. Text colors are often given in cryptic, geekish codes called *hexadecimal* in the HTML code used to write Web pages. They're written like this: #FFC0FA. Such codes always begin with a # symbol, followed by 6 characters — digits or the letters A–F. (To see examples, open any Web page in your browser and then choose View⇨Source, View⇨Page Source, or a similar command, depending upon your browser.)

If you're creating a Web page and want to match the text color to a color in your image, the Color dialog box can help. Click the Dropper tool in Paint Shop Pro's tool palette and then click on your chosen color. Click the foreground color sample in the color palette and the Color dialog box appears (or, for GIF images, the Select Color from Palette dialog box). Use the HTML code (near the bottom of the dialog box) in your Web page authoring software to set the color of your text.

If you're creating an image and want to match a color in your image to a text color, the solution is similar: Open the Color dialog box. (In a 64-million color image, click the foreground or background color sample to open the Color dialog box. In a palette image such as a GIF file, press Shift+P to edit the palette and then double-click any color swatch in the Edit Palette dialog box that appears.) In the HTML code value box of the Color dialog box, enter the HTML code you obtain from your Web page authoring tool. Click OK and your chosen color swatch now matches the HTML document's text color.

Creating Interactive Web Pages from Graphics

Paint Shop Pro not only creates static Web images (images that just sit there), but it can create the interactive graphical portion of the Web page itself. For instance, Paint Shop Pro can help you do the following:

- Create a Web page in which the image has *hot links* — areas you click on to jump to other pages.
- Slice a single image into a multi-image grid, and create the Web page that assembles the pieces into a grid and makes each image a hot link.
- Create graphical *rollovers* — images that change as you pass your mouse cursor over them, and write the Web page code to make the rollover happen.

To accomplish its Webbish wonders, Paint Shop Pro actually writes HTML files (Web pages), not just image files. You can then use these HTML files on their own, or copy their HTML code (including JavaScript code) into other Web pages.

You probably need to understand how Web pages, hot links, and rollovers work before trying to use Paint Shop Pro to make these features. Check out the IDG Books Worldwide Web site at www.idgbooks.com to find various books on Web pages and design.

Creating an image map

An image map is an image that appears in a Web page and that has certain *hot spots* on it. Hot spots are regions of the image where, if you click, you activate a hyperlink to another Web page (make the browser display that new page). For instance, if your image showed a bouquet of flowers, each different flower in your image may be within a hot spot leading to a page describing that flower. Hot spots can have different shapes, depending upon the underlying image. For instance, the flower hot spot would be an irregular polygon of some sort. Text may be in a rectangular hot spot. A round button image can have a circular hot spot.

Curiously, when you create an image map, you add nothing to the image! The Web image remains a simple GIF, JPEG, or PNG image. All the fancy mapping — the relating of a particular image region to a hyperlink — is done in the HTML code that makes up the Web page that displays the image. So, image mapping is a feature of Paint Shop Pro that does two things: it spits out a GIF, JPEG, or PNG version of your image, and it writes the necessary HTML code (a Web page file).

Here's how to make it work:

1. **Choose File⇨Export⇨Image Mapper.**

   The Image Mapper dialog box appears, as shown in Figure 19-2.

Figure 19-2:
Paint Shop Pro's mapping tool. Here, a rectangular area is mapped to the Web document tips.html.

2. **Zoom and position your image in the Image Mapper so you can easily see the place where you intend to create your hot spot.**

   To zoom, click either of the magnifier icons below the image: + to zoom in or – to zoom out. To position *(pan)* your image, mouse down on the four-headed arrow icon (under the image, just under the Zoom label). In the window that appears, drag the rectangle displayed there so that it outlines the area you're interested in.

3. **In the Tools area, choose the tool that best matches the shape of the hot spot you need to define.**

   Each tool displays its name when you pause your mouse cursor over it. To define a rectangular hot spot, click the Rectangle tool. Choose the Circle tool for a circular hot spot and the Polygon tool for an irregular shape.

4. **Draw and position your hot spot on the image.**

   - If you use the Rectangle or Circle tool, drag across the image area to create a hot spot; start at the center point of the object you're outlining.

   - If you use the Polygon tool, left-click around the image area; close the shape by right-clicking anywhere.

   - If you make a mistake, finish the hot spot and then delete it. Click the Delete tool and then click the hot spot.

   - To adjust the position of your hot spot, click the Mover tool in the Tools area and drag the hot spot.

4. **Repeat Steps 2 through 4 until you've defined a hot spot for each area that needs one.**

The next step is to specify what page appears when someone clicks on a hot spot. See the section, "Entering the links," later in this chapter.

Creating image slices

An alternative to image mapping is to *slice* an image into multiple images (known as *cells*) and assign a link to each cell. Paint Shop Pro creates the HTML code (a table) that's necessary to hold the images in a grid and also creates a series of new images from your original, single image.

Slicing has advantages over image mapping:

- ✔ With Slicing, the viewer doesn't have to wait for a large image to download before he or she can see any clickable items. Each slice forms individually, one at a time.

- ✔ Slicing lends itself, better than mapping, to using *rollovers* — images that change in response to various mouse actions.

To slice an image, follow these steps:

1. **Choose File➪Export➪Image Slicer.**

   The Image Slicer dialog box appears.

2. **Zoom and position your image in the Image Slicer so you can see the whole area that you intend to slice.**

   To zoom, click either of the magnifier icons below the image: + to zoom in or – to zoom out. To position *(pan)* your image, mouse down on the four-headed arrow icon (under the image, just under the Zoom label). In the window that appears, drag the rectangle displayed there so that it outlines the area you're interested in.

3. **Click either the Slice tool or the Grid tool in the Tools area.**

   The Grid divides your image using a grid of evenly spaced lines. You're able to adjust the lines and their positions afterward. The Slice tool, although tricky to control, enables you to slice wherever you like.

4. **Slice your image.**

   If you use the Grid tool, click anywhere on the image. In the Grid Size dialog box that appears, enter values for the number of rows and columns in your grid.

   If you use the Slice tool, mouse down anywhere on the image and drag either horizontally or vertically. You don't need to drag entirely across the image. The tool automatically extends the line to the image edge or to the next line it encounters.

5. **With the Delete tool, remove any extra lines.**

   Click the Delete tool in the Tools area and click on lines you don't want.

6. **With the Arrow tool, drag any lines that need moving.**

If your image has any solid white cells, you can improve the Web page's downloading speed by not placing an image in that cell at all. With the Arrow tool, click the cell and then clear the Include Cell In Table box. This trick also works for other solid-color areas, but you have to edit the resulting HTML file to set the background color to match the image color.

At this point, you're ready to enter the hyperlink (Web address) information that describes what Web page appears when the person viewing your page clicks on a cell. See the next section.

Entering the links

After you've created your hot spot areas or cells, the next step is to enter the Web address that you want each hot spot or cell to link to when someone clicks it on the Web. Take these steps:

1. **Choose the Arrow tool (in the Tools area) and click a hot spot or cell.**

2. **Enter the URL (address of the Web page) you want to link to in the URL text box.**

If you intend the page to appear in a named frame of the current page, enter the frame name in the Target area.

3. **Enter a text description of that new page in the Alt Text text box.**

4. **Repeat Steps 1 through 3 for all hot spots or cells that you've created.**

After you enter your links, you're ready to create your Web page and images; see "Outputting the result," later in this chapter. You may also want to save the work you've done so far, which I describe how to do in the next section.

Saving and reloading your work

You may want to go back and change your hot spots, cells, or links later, or perhaps use similar settings on a slightly different image. For those reasons, save your work as a file. (Note that this file isn't the Web page file or an image file; to create those, see "Outputting the result," later in this chapter.)

Click the Save Settings button. The Save Map (or Slice) Settings dialog box that appears works just like any other file saving dialog box. Enter a name and choose a folder for your file, then click Save.

If you want to use or edit your settings later, open the Image Mapper or Image Slicer tool as before and click the Load Settings button. Open your file in the Load Map (or Slice) Settings dialog box that appears. The hot spots or cells you defined earlier are now set up for the current image. (In some early releases of Paint Shop Pro 7, you may need to select each cell and enable the Include Cell in Table check box for that cell, after loading settings.)

Outputting the result

For all this slicing and dicing or hot spotting to be of any use, you need to output Web files. Paint Shop Pro's Webtools output the two kinds of file that you need for your Web page: one or more image files (in GIF, JPEG, or PNG format), and a single HTML file. If you're image mapping, you output one image file. If you're image slicing, you output as many image files as you have cells. The Web page (HTML) file that you output incorporates those image file(s) and provides the links, hot spots, and other programming that makes it all work.

First, decide how you want your image files: what format, and what (if any) optimizations. To choose format, click the Format drop-down list and choose GIF, JPEG, or PNG. To optimize image files for the Web, click the Optimize button and, for GIF or JPEG files, see the sections "Creating GIF files," and "Creating JPEG files," earlier in this chapter. (PNG's optimizer is similar, but PNG isn't yet sufficiently popular to warrant its own section in this chapter.)

Before you output the final files, you can test your Web page by viewing it in your Web browser. In the Image Mapper or Image Slicer, click the button with the eye icon below the image window. Your Web browser launches and displays the result. You can test all the hot spots or other features you've created.

To output your Web files, click the Save button in the Image Mapper or Image Slicer dialog box. If you haven't created any Web files since you launched the Image Mapper or Image Slicer, the Save As dialog box appears. As with the Save As dialog box in any program, you enter a filename and choose a folder. The name and folder you choose is the name and location of the HTML, or Web page file, you're creating. (The Save As dialog box doesn't appear if your Web page file already has a name and folder.)

If you're image mapping, and if you haven't yet created Web files since the launching of this dialog box, Paint Shop Pro now displays an Image Map Save As dialog box. Here, you choose a name and a folder for the GIF, JPEG, or PNG image Paint Shop Pro is creating. If you're image slicing, Paint Shop Pro creates a series of cell images in the same folder as the HTML file; each cell file's name begins with the name of the original image file, but Paint Shop Pro appends additional characters to distinguish the cell. (At least, that's how early releases of Paint Shop Pro 7 work; later releases may change.)

Making rollovers

Rollovers are images (typically buttons) that change appearance when you position your mouse over them, or when you do various other mouse or keyboard actions. For instance, a button may get darker. Rollovers are popular Web page features because they provide immediate feedback to the user's cursor motion.

The basic *mouseover* rollover, which I describe here, simply changes as the mouse passes over it. It requires two images: the original image (say, a button) and the one that substitutes for the original when a mouse cursor passes over it (a darkened version of the button, for instance).

To create a rollover, do this:

1. **Prepare the pair of images for each rollover.**

   For each rollover, you need the image that first appears on the Web page and the image that takes the first image's place. If you like using sliced images, first use the Image Slicer to slice a large image into separate cell images and save your settings. Exit the slicer, load all the cell images created by the slicer into Paint Shop Pro, and modify them in some way; for instance, you can make them darker. Save each one with a modified file name so that the original cell images remain unchanged. If you prefer working with mapped images, create several different versions of the entire original image. You can create one image, say, for each button in which that button is darkened.

2. **Open the original image in Paint Shop Pro, if it isn't already open.**

   For instance, open the large image you originally sliced in Step 1 or the image you mapped with hot spots.

3. **Launch the Image Slicer and load your earlier settings.**

   If you're using image mapping, launch the Image Mapper instead. Load the settings you saved in Step 1 to restore the slicing or mapping.

4. **With the Arrow tool, click the cell in the Image Slicer that you want to program with a rollover.**

   If you're working with the Image Mapper, click the hot spot that triggers the rollover.

5. **Click the Rollover Creator button.**

   The Rollover Creator dialog box appears.

6. **Click the Mouse Over check box.**

7. **Click the file folder icon on the same line as the Mouse Over check box.**

   The Select Rollover dialog box appears.

8. **Choose the image file you want to appear when the mouse passes over and click Open.**

   For instance, this file is the darkened version of the original file.

9. **Click OK in the Select Rollover dialog box.**

10. **Repeat Steps 4 through 10 for each cell or hot spot.**

Proceed to save your settings and output your Web files as I describe in the earlier sections of this chapter.

Chapter 20

Animating in Animation Shop

. . . .

In This Chapter

▶ Using Animation Shop windows and controls

▶ Saving and opening animation files

▶ Creating animated text banners

▶ Creating animations from your own images

▶ Applying animation effects to frames

▶ Working on individual frames

▶ Creating animations for the Web

. . . .

*A*nimation Shop, a separate program that comes with Paint Shop Pro, creates animated images ranging from simple text Web banners to, say, your own knockoff of the *South Park* TV series. You're limited mainly by your own illustration skill — or, in the case of the *South Park* knockoff, your own taste.

Never made an animation before? You'll be amazed at how easy it is. For those of us with limited time and limited drawing skills, Animation Shop is great. It offers wizards and special effects that can crank out nearly instant and highly gratifying results. For those with more time and talent, Animation Shop works hand-in-hand with Paint Shop Pro, where you can do professional-grade work.

Keep your animations as small (a small fraction of your PC screen) and as short as possible. Otherwise, you may spend a lot of time waiting for Animation Shop, and the resulting files may also be too big to be useful — especially on the Web.

Getting to Know Animation Shop

Animation Shop is all about creating and manipulating *frames,* the individual images that make up an animation. You can launch Animation Shop from the Windows Start➪Programs menu or, in Paint Shop Pro, by choosing File➪ Jasc Software Products➪Launch Animation Shop. Figure 20-1 shows a short animation in progress in Animation Shop.

Style bar

Toolbar   VCR controls   Tool palette

Play view toggle

Figure 20-1:
A frame
window
shows you
the
individual
frames, and
an
animation
window
shows you
the frames
in action.

Play view window

Frames view window

Using Animation Shop windows and controls

Animation Shop has two main windows and a series of controls that you'll find useful.

- **Toolbars** contain buttons that do the same things as many of the menu commands that I give you in this book. Pause your mouse cursor over any button to see what it does.

- **VCR controls** let you control the animation that appears in the play view window as you would a videotape. They only work when the Play View window is active.

✔ **The tool palette** contains several of the same tools that the Paint Shop Pro tool palette offers: a paint brush, an eraser, a flood fill tool, and so on.

✔ **The Style bar** provides controls for various options for whatever tool is currently selected in the tool palette. In Figure 20-1, for instance, the Zoom tool is chosen, so the Style bar gives you a zoom factor selection box.

✔ **The Frames View window** lets you examine, select, or modify individual frames. It appears once you have started or opened an animation. You can zoom in or out with the Zoom tool, just as you do in Paint Shop Pro, and scroll left or right. Frame numbers appear after the letter F: and display times for each frame appear after the letter D:.

✔ **The Play View window** shows you the animation in action. Click the play view toggle button on the Toolbar to switch this window on or off.

Saving and opening animations

To save your animation, choose File➪Save. The conventional Save As dialog box that appears is initially set to save your file as a GIF animation, which is the correct file type for Web animations. To save as a different type of animation file, click the down-arrow in the Save As Type list box (in the Save As dialog box) and select a type. Enter a name and then click the Save button. Note that animated GIF files rarely run as fast as you intended because of limitations of the GIF file format. If speed is an issue, you may want to try AVI format.

Depending upon the type of file you're creating (such as GIF), an Animation Quality Versus Output Size dialog box may appear. It offers a Quality vs. Size slider with which you can adjust this tradeoff. Choose a setting and then click the Next button. As additional screens appear, just keep clicking Next until the final screen and then click the Finish button. If you don't like the result, press Ctrl+Z to undo it. Then, save again and choose a different Quality vs. Size setting.

Animation Shop can also read many existing animation file types. Just choose File➪Open and select the file.

Making Instant Text Banners

One of the easiest of the cool animations you can make in Animation Shop is a text banner, like the banners you see across the top of many Web pages. The Banner wizard is the place to start. Take these steps, clicking Next after each step:

1. **Choose File⇨Banner wizard.**

2. **Select a background on the Background screen that appears. Select one of the following:**

   Transparent Background for Web applications where you want the Web page's background to appear behind the text.

   Opaque Background to create the animation on a solid, colored background. Click the color swatch shown to choose a background color from the Color dialog box.

   Use A Background Image if you have an image file you want to use behind the text animation. Click the Browse button to select the file. Use small images (a tiny fraction of your PC screen) for Web work.

3. **Size: Choose a banner size from the Size screen. Choose one of the following:**

   Use A Standard Banner Size to select any of several suggested sizes from the selection box.

   Same As The Background Image to make the banner the same size as a background image you selected in Step 2.

   As Defined Here to enter any height and width dimensions in the associated Width and Height value boxes. Keep Web animations small to avoid excessive download times.

4. **Timing: Give timing values in the Timing screen.**

   Enter a value in the first value box for the duration of the animation. Enter a value that is ten times your desired duration in seconds; 30 for 3 seconds, for instance. Keep Web animations as short as possible, or else download times become excessive.

   Enter a value in the second value box if you'd like more frames per second (fps) than the default of 10 that's given. (10 fps is a reasonable value for Web animations. Professional animations use 15 fps or more.)

   If you'd like the animation to run over and over again endlessly, select the Yes option. Otherwise, click the Play It __ Times option box and enter a number for how many times you want the animation to loop.

5. **Text: Enter the text you want on your banner.**

   Click the Set Font button to choose typeface, size, style, and alignment from a Font dialog box similar to many Font dialog boxes you've seen in other applications.

6. **Text Color: Select text colors.**

   Choose Opaque Text for a solid color, which you then choose by clicking the color swatch and selecting a color from the Color dialog box that appears.

To fill the text with an image instead, choose Image Text, and then choose an image by clicking the Browse button. The result is as if the text were cut out of a mask overlying the image. If your animation moves the text, different parts of the image are revealed.

7. **Transition: Choose an animation style.**

Choose from the Transition Name drop-down list box. To change the way the animation works, click the Customize button. I can't possibly describe all the different transitions and customizations, so just fool with stuff until you like how it appears in the preview window on this screen. Pause your mouse cursor over your chosen transition's name in the list box to see a written description of the effect.

8. **If you have a result you like, click the Finish button.**

Otherwise, click the Back button to return to any earlier screen and make changes. Click Next buttons to proceed from that screen.

All the frames of your animation appear in the Frames View window. To see the animation in action, click the View Animation toggle button in the Toolbar (see Figure 20-1). The animation appears in the Play View window.

Making Quick Animations from Your Images

Just as the Banner wizard can conjure a text animation out of thin air, the Animation wizard can create an animation from a single image, or two, or as many as you'd like. After you have the frames of an animation, the wizard helps you assemble them into an animation file. That process is like making the flip-pad animations that kids make, but in this case all the pieces of paper (frames) haven't yet been assembled into a pad and may even be different sizes.

The images can come from anywhere. You can create the images in Paint Shop Pro, or you can take a series of images from your digital camera. For instance, you can create a vector shape in Paint Shop Pro and fiddle with its shape or position, saving each change as a new file using File⇨Save As. With your digital camera and some Play-Doh, you can create Claymation animations like the movie *Chicken Run!* To make assembling the animation easier, end the name files with successive numbers, such as `chick001.jpg`, `chick002.jpg`. You can save your images as nearly any type of file, but any layers in Paint Shop Pro (PSP) or Photoshop (PSD) files must be flattened: choose Layers⇨Merge⇨Merge All. Otherwise, Animation Shop turns each layer into a separate frame.

Although you certainly *may* make every single image for every frame of an animation, you don't *have* to. If you have only one image, Animation Shop can create frames to gradually fade an image to or from a blank screen; or it can wiggle, rotate, or distort your image in various ways. If you have two or more images, Animation Shop can give you clever *dissolves* (where one image slowly disappears to reveal another) or other transitions between images. You can also add frames in which text dances around on top of your image.

If you want a transparent Web animation, your frame images must have transparent areas. They can either be transparent GIF files or Paint Shop Pro files where transparent areas are visible (appearing as checkerboard areas).

Building your animation with the Animation wizard

After you obtain or create the images that you want to make part of your animation, take these steps, clicking the Next button after each step:

1. **Choose File⇨Animation wizard and then type your animation's dimensions in the first screen that appears.**

   Choose Same Size as Image Frame if you want to make all frames of the animation the same size as an image you're going to use to start the animation. If you don't want to start with one of your images (say, you want to start with a blank frame of some solid color), or if you want your animation to be a different size than the first image, choose As Defined Here and enter the Height and Width you want.

2. **Default canvas color: Select a background color or transparency.**

   Choose Transparent if the frame images you created for this animation are transparent. Otherwise, choose Opaque, then click the color swatch to choose a color from the Color dialog box. If your frame images are different sizes but have the same canvas, or background, color (say, white), choose that color.

3. **Aspect ratio: Tell the wizard how to resolve any differences in size or proportions between your frame images.**

   If your frame images are all the same size, skip this step.

   If you want all images to be aligned on their centers, choose Centered in the Frame; alternatively, you may choose Upper Left Corner of the Frame.

   If you want the area around smaller frames to be filled with the color you chose in Step 2, choose With the Canvas Color; otherwise, choose With the Preceding Frame's Contents.

   If you want all frames to be scaled to fit within the dimensions you chose in Step 1, click to enable the Scale Frames to Fit check box. (Image proportions are retained, so no distortion results.)

4. Looping and timing:

If you want the animation to run over and over again endlessly, select the Yes option. Otherwise, select the Play It __ Times option box and type a number for how many times you want the animation to play.

For the How Long Do You Want Each Frame to Be Displayed value box, enter a value that is 100 times longer than the period of time you want each frame to be displayed. A reasonable time is 0.1 seconds (producing a frame rate of 10 frames per second), for which you enter a value of 10.

5. Choose images: Select and order the image files for your animation.

Click the Add Image button to add one or more frame image files to the list (initially blank) that is displayed on this page. In the Open dialog box that appears, choose a file. To choose multiple files, hold down the Ctrl key on your keyboard and click files. If your files happen to be listed in order, click the first one, hold down the Shift key, and then click the last one.

To remove an image from the list or change its position in the animation, click the image's file name in the list, and then click the Remove Image, Move Up, or Move Down buttons. To add more images from files, click the file after which you want to add the images, and then click the Add Image button.

6. Finish: Click the Finish button on the last wizard screen.

The wizard goes off and does its thing. The frames of your animation appear in the Frame View window.

If your animation is complete — that is, you don't want Animation Shop to create any additional frames — you're done. To run your animation, click the Play View toggle button near the right end of the toolbar. The Play View window appears and the VCR controls on the Style bar control playback.

If you used only one or a few frame images in Step 5, you can now "insert transitions" (fade from one image to the next) or "insert effects" (make text or a given image do wacky things in subsequent frames). See the next three sections.

Creating frames by inserting transitions

One way that Animation Shop can automatically create frames for you is to insert a transition. *Inserting a transition* creates frames that gradually replace one image with another image (or a solid color) in a creative way. For instance, if your animation currently consists of photos of your product line, you can fade from a photo of one product to another. Here's how:

1. **Click the Arrow tool in the tool palette (the leftmost icon).**

2. **In the Frames View window (where your frames appear individually), click the frame that you want to place new frames after.**

If you can't see the frame you want, drag the scroll bar along the bottom of the window. To see multiple frames at once, click the Zoom tool in the tool palette (the magnifier), and *right*-click the Frames View window to zoom out.

3. **Choose Effects⇨Insert Image Transition.**

The Insert Image Transition dialog box of Figure 20-2 appears. Your selected image appears in the left, Start With window, and the next image in the animation (if any) appears in the right, End With window. Animation Shop immediately begins to create the currently selected effect and show it in the Transition window.

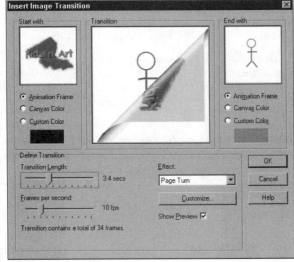

Figure 20-2:
Creating a real page-turner of an animation between two frames.

4. **Select the image to end the transition with.**

If you have an image following your selected frame, as I do in Figure 20-2 (the stick figure), you may end the transition with that image by clicking the Animation Frame option in the End With area. To end with a blank frame in the animation's background (canvas) color, choose the Canvas Color option. To end with a blank frame in any color, choose the Custom Color option and then click the color swatch to choose from the Color dialog box. (If, instead, you would like a transition *from* a blank frame to your End With image, you can also choose canvas color or custom color in the Start With area.)

5. **Select a transition from the Effect selection box.**

In Figure 20-2, I have chosen the Page Turn transition. Try different choices until you find a transition you like. To see a written description of an effect, choose the effect and then pause your mouse cursor over the transition's name in the Effects selection box.

6. **Adjust the Transition Length slider left or right for a longer or shorter animation.**

7. **Adjust the Frames Per Second slider right for a smoother animation (more frames) or left for a jerkier animation (fewer frames).**

   Bear in mind that the longer and smoother the transition, the larger the animation file size. Large animation files aren't generally appreciated on Web pages (due to long download time), if that's your intended use.

Click OK after you finish, and Animation Shop adds the transition frames after the frame you selected in Step 2.

Creating frames by inserting image effects

A second way to create frames within your animation is to have Animation Shop play with one of your images for a while, adding frames after that image. For instance, you can rotate the image, twist it into a spiral, or cycle it through all the colors in the color wheel. Here's how.

1. **Click the Arrow tool in the tool palette.**

2. **In the Frames View window, click the frame image you want Animation Shop to play with.**

   If you can't see the frame you want, drag the scroll bar along the bottom of the window. To see multiple frames at once, click the Zoom tool in the tool palette (the magnifier), and right-click the Frames View window to zoom out.

3. **Choose Effects➪Insert Image Effect.**

   The Insert Image Effect dialog box of Figure 20-3 appears. Your selected image appears in the left, Start With window. Animation Shop immediately begins to create the currently chosen effect and show the result in the right, Effect window.

4. **Select an effect from the Effects selection box.**

   Try different effects until you find one you like. For a written description of a chosen effect, pause your mouse cursor over the Effect selection box. To run the effect the opposite way, click the Run Effect in Reverse Direction check box.

5. **For variations on the effect, click the Customize button and make changes in the effect dialog box that appears.**

   They're all different, so I can't give you details.

6. **Adjust the Effect Length slider right for longer or left for a shorter transition.**

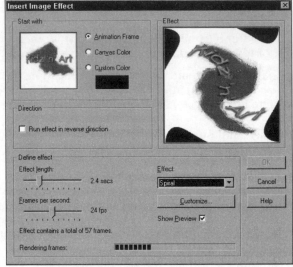

Figure 20-3:
Manipulating
an image to
create
animation
frames.

7. **Adjust the Frames Per Second slider to the right (for a smoother animation) or to the left (for a jerkier animation).**

A longer effect length or a higher frames-per-second rate makes for a larger animation file. Larger files may be unacceptably slow on the Web.

Click OK after you finish. Animation Shop adds the new frames after the frame you selected in Step 2.

Creating frames by inserting text effects

A third way to automatically create an animation is to insert animated text frames. These frames duplicate the initial image that you select, adding text animation on top of those copies. The procedure that you follow is like the procedure used for inserting transitions or image effects that I describe in the preceding sections. Choose Effects⇨Insert Text Effects. A dialog box appears that includes controls like those in the Insert Transition Effects box of Figure 20-2.

The Insert Text Effect dialog box also includes a Define Text text box; enter your text to be animated there. Click the Font button to open a conventional Font dialog box, where you can choose typeface, style, size, and other font attributes. To choose the way in which the text is animated, make a choice in the Effects selection box.

For text color, you have three choices in the Text Appearance area on the right side of the dialog box. Click Canvas Color to use background color. Click Custom Color to choose your color by clicking the Custom Color color swatch, which opens the Color dialog box. Click Animation Frame to use the coloring of the next image frame in the animation. In that case, the text looks like it was cut out of a mask covering the image, wherever the text happens to fall.

Applying Effects to Existing Frames

In the preceding two sections I describe how you can create frames by inserting image or text effects. If you already have a series of frames, you can simply apply those same image or text effects to the existing frames.

The process is nearly identical to the processes that I describe in the preceding sections. You begin, however, by selecting, not one frame, but the group of frames to which you want to add the effect. Click the initial frame of the group, and then, holding down the Shift key, click the last frame of the group.

Then, choose either Effects⇨Apply Image Effect or Effects⇨Apply Text Effect. The essential controls of the dialog boxes that appear work just like their cousins in the Insert Image Effect and Insert Text Effect dialog boxes.

Working Frame-by-Frame

Although Animation Shop offers lots of tricks for animating lots of frames at once, you can work on one frame at a time, if you like. Here are the basics of creating and editing on a frame-by-frame basis.

Starting from scratch

To start an animation from scratch, choose File⇨New. In the Create New Animation dialog box that appears, enter the dimensions of your animation in the Width and Height boxes and choose either Transparent or Opaque for your canvas color. If you choose Opaque, click the color swatch to choose a color from the Color dialog box. Click OK when you're done. A single frame appears in the Frame View window.

To paint an animation frame from scratch or to modify a frame by hand, use the painting tools in the tool palette. These tools work very much like the ones in Paint Shop Pro, but offer fewer options. Instead of a Tool Options window, the controls for each tool (like brush width) appear in the Style bar (just above the tool palette) when you choose the tool. Animation Shop's color palette also works like the one in Paint Shop Pro but doesn't have the fancy style or texture options for foreground or background.

Managing and adding frames

Managing your individual frames or adding new ones is also straightforward. Here's how:

- To select a frame, choose the Arrow tool from the tool palette and then click the frame.

- To select multiple frames at once, hold down the Ctrl key and click the frames. To select a sequence of frames, click the frame at one end, hold down the Shift key, and then click the frame at the other end.

- To delete a frame, select it, and then press the Delete key on your keyboard.

- To move a frame, drag it with the Arrow tool to the border between two other frames, where your cursor suddenly depicts three-pages-with-turned-corners. Release the mouse button.

- To cut or copy a frame as you would nearly anything in any Windows program, select it, and then either click the Cut or Copy icons on the Toolbar. You can also press Ctrl+C to copy or Ctrl+X to cut.

- To paste a frame that you have cut or copied, you have several choices. First, select whatever frame you want to paste on, before, or after. Choose Edit⇨Paste⇨ and then one of the following:

    - **Into Selected Frame** replaces whatever frame image is currently selected.

    - **Before Current Frame** and **After Current Frame** paste exactly where they say.

    - **As New Animation** starts a whole new animation.

- To insert a new frame (or frames) from files, first select the frame that you're going to insert frames before. Then choose Animation⇨Insert Frames⇨From File to insert an image from an image file. An Insert Frames from Files dialog box appears with various controls, as follows; click the OK button when done:

    - To add a frame before the currently selected frame, click the Add File button. In the Open dialog box that appears, click a file. To add multiple files, hold down the Ctrl key and click the files. Click the Open button when you're done.

    - To add a frame before any other frame than the selected one, enter the existing frame's number in the Insert Before value box. To add a frame after the currently selected one, increase the current number in that box by 1.

    - Frame Delay Time, a value in $\frac{1}{100}$ths of a second, controls how long the frame appears on-screen.

- If the frame or frames you add aren't the same size or proportion as the rest of the animation, visit the options in the bottom of the Insert Frames from Files dialog box. If you want all images to be aligned on their centers, choose Centered; alternatively, you may choose Upper Left Corner. If you want the area around smaller frames to be filled with the animation's canvas color, choose Canvas Color; otherwise, choose Preceding Frame's Contents. Finally, if you want all frames to be scaled to fit the animation's dimensions, then select the Scale Frames to Fit check box. (The images' proportions are maintained, so no distortion occurs.)

- To remove an image from the list or change its position in the animation, click the image's file name in the list and then click the Remove Image, Move Up, or Move Down buttons. To add more images from files, click the file after which you want to add the images and then click the Add Image button.

✔ To insert one or more blank frames, or copies of the preceding frame, choose Animation⇨Insert Frames⇨Empty. The Insert Empty Frames dialog box appears; click OK after you finish.

- Enter the number of frames you want in the Number of Frames value box.

- The Insert Before Frame value box gives the frame number you have currently selected. Change that number to insert before a different frame.

- Frame Delay Time is in $\frac{1}{100}$ths of a second.

- For a blank frame in canvas color, choose the Blank To Canvas Color option. To copy the frame before the currently selected frame, choose Carry Forward Contents of Preceding Frame.

Working on frames in Paint Shop Pro

To work on an individual frame in Paint Shop Pro, select it and then choose File⇨Export Frames⇨To Paint Shop Pro (or simply press Shift+X). The image appears in a window in Paint Shop Pro.

Make your changes to the image in Paint Shop Pro. When you're done, click the X in the image window's upper-right corner. (Make sure you don't click the X in *Paint Shop Pro*'s upper-right corner, as that closes Paint Shop Pro). A dialog box appears, asking if you want to save changes; strangely, you must click No! The window closes, and you return to Animation Shop with your edited frame.

You can work on multiple frames in Paint Shop Pro, but not quite as conveniently as the single-frame editing that I just described. Select multiple frames, and copy them by pressing Ctrl+C. Open Paint Shop Pro and choose

Edit⇔Paste⇔AS Animation as Multiple Images. Each frame becomes a separate image. After editing a frame in Paint Shop Pro, copy it with Ctrl+C. Return to Animation Shop, select the original frame and choose Edit⇔Paste⇔Before Selected Frame (or press Ctrl+L). Delete the original frame, which now follows the one you pasted.

Creating Animated GIF Files for the Web

The Web uses the GIF file format for most animations. See the first section of this chapter for instructions on saving animations in various formats, including GIF.

A useful command in Animation Shop, especially when you're creating transparent animations, is View⇔Preview in Web Browser. In the Preview in Web Browser dialog box that appears, click one of the browsers in the Web Browser list box and then click the Preview button. (If you're previewing a transparent animation, you may first click the Background Color swatch to choose a background color that better shows your transparency.) Animation Shop launches the Animation Quality Versus Output Size optimizer that I describe in the section "Saving and opening animations," earlier in this chapter. (Click Next buttons in each screen to proceed.) When that optimizer is done, the Web browser launches and displays your animation. It also displays the animation's file size, estimated download times, and palette size.

Part VI
The Part of Tens

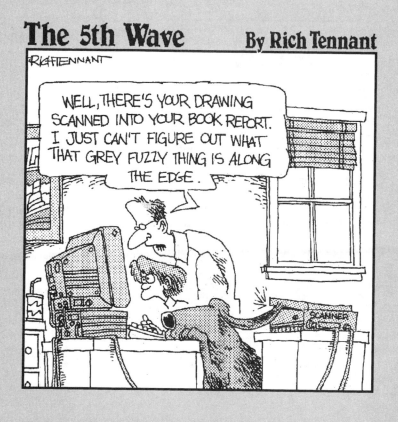

The 5th Wave   By Rich Tennant

WELL, THERE'S YOUR DRAWING SCANNED INTO YOUR BOOK REPORT. I JUST CAN'T FIGURE OUT WHAT THAT GREY FUZZY THING IS ALONG THE EDGE.

In this part . . .

*I*f you find yourself throwing your hands up in the air in despair, your ten fingers are telling you something: "Turn to the Part of Tens!" You can find quick solutions for common problems and issues in this part. I give you remedies for the ten most common headaches that afflict new users of Paint Shop Pro in Chapter 21. In Chapter 22, I give you ten quick fixes for the most common photographic failures. If the solution isn't here, turn off your PC, take a walk, and join millions of others in reciting the comforting (and true) mantra, "I am smart; software is stupid."

Chapter 21

Ten Perplexing Problems

*I*n real life, your paintbrush doesn't suddenly start painting in plaid, your canvas doesn't double in size, and (unless you have kids) your tools don't suddenly become unavailable. In software, however, all the laws of nature are repealed and then reformulated by people whose idea of a good time is to *make* your brush paint in plaid: software engineers.

When the bright colors you see before you are the result of a migraine, and not paint, this chapter is a good place to start. Take a deep breath, get a chocolate chip cookie, and repeat, "I am smart, software is stupid . . . I am smart, software is stupid. . . ." Then read on.

Grayed-out Tools

Tool gray-outs happen in three main circumstances:

▸ You've added text, drawings, or shapes to your image, and tools near the center of the tool palette are grayed out.

✔ You're trying to use the Deformation tool, but it's grayed out.

✔ You're trying to use the Object Selector tool (at the bottom of the tool palette).

If your problem is the first one in that list, here are some things to try:

✔ If you're now trying to work on something *other* than the text, drawings, or shapes, press Ctrl+1. Text, drawings, and shapes often live on their own special layers (overlying images). The stuff you're trying to work on lives on another layer, probably the Background layer, which you can get to by pressing Ctrl+1. If pressing Ctrl+1 doesn't work, then you need to understand layers better: See Chapter 13.

✔ If you're trying to work *on* the text, drawings, or shapes with the grayed-out tools, choose Layers⇨Convert to Raster Layer. This turns the objects on the current layer into the more conventional form where the tools in the middle portion of the tool palette work. The objects still reside on a separate (conventional) layer from the rest of your image, so you need to refer to Chapter 13 to understand how to navigate layers.

✔ Make the text, drawings, or shapes part of the main image by choosing Layers⇨Merge⇨Merge Visible. Now those objects are no different than if you had painted them on (very neatly) with the Paint Brush tool.

If you're trying to use the Deformation tool and it's grayed out, one of the following may be your problem:

✔ You haven't selected anything and you're using the Background layer. You have to select some area before you can use the Deformation tool. Or, you have to switch to a higher layer that has the object on it that you want to deform.

✔ You have selected something, but it's not floating. Press Ctrl+F.

If you're trying to use the Object Selector tool and it's grayed out, your problem is that you're not currently working on a vector layer (an overlying image where text, drawings, and shapes often hang out). Try pressing Ctrl+2, or Ctrl+3, or Ctrl+4, and so on until the Object Selector tool is no longer grayed out, and you're able to select the object you want.

Grayed-out Menu Commands

If menu commands are grayed out, chances are that your image has only 256, or fewer, colors. The solution is to increase (at least temporarily) the number of colors to 16.7 million. Press Ctrl+Shift+0 (that character is *zero,* not the letter O).

If one of your requirements is to end up with an image that is exactly the same type as you started with, you can later reduce the number of colors again. For instance, if you started with a GIF type of file (a type used on the Web that has only 256 colors), you may want to end up with a GIF file. In that particular case, however, when you go to save your image, Paint Shop Pro automatically offers to reduce the number of colors back to 256, so you don't have to worry about it. To manually reduce the number of colors, see Chapter 10.

Image is Wrong Size Inside or Outside Paint Shop Pro

Paint Shop Pro displays your image in different sizes to fit the Paint Shop Pro window. It doesn't actually change the size of the image — it just displays it with a different zoom factor. As a result, your image may look a lot smaller in Paint Shop Pro than it does in some other program. To see your image in its actual size in Paint Shop Pro, press Ctrl+Alt+N.

If you need to change the actual size of your image — which is the size it usually appears in other programs (like in Web browsers) — see Chapter 12. If you need to change its size as it's printed on paper, see Chapter 18.

Tool or Command Doesn't Do Anything

If a tool or command doesn't seem to do anything at all as you apply it to your image, the cause is probably related to selections or layers. Specifically, your problem may be one of the following:

✔ **You currently have a selected area (called a *selection*) in your image that you're unaware of.** Tools and commands are almost always constrained to working within a selection, if one exists. Probably you're either not working on, or not looking at, that selection. If you don't really want to be working within a selection at the moment, simply press Ctrl+D to remove the selection.

   • One reason you may be unaware of this selection is that you have somehow hidden the selection *marquee,* the moving dashed line that indicates a selection's presence. Choose <u>S</u>elections and examine the button next to <u>H</u>ide Marquee in the menu that appears. If the button is depressed, your marquee is hidden. Click Hide Marquee to un-hide it.

- Another reason that you may be unaware of the selection is that your image is larger than your window and the selected area isn't visible. Zoom out (right-click with the Zoom tool — the magnifying glass icon on the tool palette) until you can see your whole image, including the selection marquee.

✔ **You're mistakenly working on an image layer that's empty (transparent) in the area you're trying to work in.** If you're unfamiliar with layers and the layer palette, press Ctrl+1 (a shortcut that switches you to the main, or *background* layer) and try your tool again. If that doesn't work, press Ctrl+2 to go to the next layer, and so on, until your tool works.

If you're familiar with the layer palette, pause your mouse cursor over the names of the various layers to see tiny, thumbnail images of the contents of each layer. Click the layer that contains the content you're trying to modify. See Chapter 15 for more help with layers.

✔ **You're painting in exactly the same color as the background you're painting on!** Change your foreground color or background color. (See Chapter 4).

If you've been trying a menu command with no apparent effect, you may actually have been having an effect within your selection, without knowing it! When you find the area, check it. If it has been altered unintentionally, press Ctrl+Z repeatedly until the change goes away.

Paint Doesn't Come Out Right

Paint Shop Pro 7 adds a lot of new features to the color palette that can make life pretty complicated if you're not sure what's going on. The usual result is that you end up applying paint that isn't what you had in mind. The best solution is to get a good grip on the Color palette's features, so turn to Chapter 4. In addition, settings in the Tool Options window can make paint come out in unwanted ways. Check Chapter 5 for help with that. Here are a few specific things to check:

✔ **As Paint Shop Pro is configured out of the box, each individual tool has its own Color palette settings.** When you switch to a new tool, the paint (colors, patterns, textures) changes, a behavior that you may find confusing. This arrangement is very different from earlier versions of Paint Shop Pro, where, once you set a Foreground or Background color, it remained set no matter what tool you chose. To change back to the older, "one setting for all" system, click to enable the Lock check box in the color palette.

✔ **If the paint is too light and kind of dappled, you may be applying a texture unintentionally.** Examine the two swatches marked Texture on the Color palette. To paint without a texture, mouse down (depress your mouse button and hold it) on a Texture swatch and then click the circle-with-slash icon in the fly-out panel that appears. (Release your mouse button.) Do this for both Texture swatches.

✔ **If the color you're applying doesn't match either of the small foreground or background color swatches at the top of the color palette, you're applying a *gradient* or *pattern,* not plain paint.** Mouse down on the foreground or background Style swatch, and drag right to the paint brush icon to resume using plain paint.

✔ **If paint comes off your brush too quickly, building up to a heavy application within a short distance after starting the stroke, check the Tool Options window to make sure the Build Up Brush check box isn't enabled.** Or, try increasing the Step value so that the spots laid down by the brush don't overlap as much.

✔ **If paint doesn't get thicker as you brush your tool (and you would like it to), either release the mouse button between strokes, or click to enable the Build Up Brush check box in the Tool Options window.** Opacity must be less than 100 percent to build up paint.

✔ **If paint is too thin or too thick, adjust Opacity in the Tool Options window; higher Opacity makes a thicker paint.**

Brush Stroke is Wrong Size or Too Fuzzy

Anything to do with the way paint is applied, like the size of the spot or the fuzziness of the edges, is controlled by each tool's Tool Options window. Press *O* on your keyboard to toggle that puppy on or off. If only a title bar labeled Tool Options is visible, pause your mouse cursor over that bar to unroll the window.

To set size or edge-fuzziness, click the leftmost tab (Tab 1) of the Tool Options window. Size is set by (surprise!) the Size value; a larger value makes a larger spot. Edge-fuzziness is set by the Hardness value. A higher value makes a sharper edge. If the entire spot (not just the edge) is kind of fuzzy or speckly, then you can reduce the Density value to make it less so.

New Text Appears When You Try to Change Text

The Text tool, in its normal *vector* mode of operation, lets you click on existing text to change it. When you click, the Text dialog box is supposed to appear, displaying the current text so you can edit it. But . . . you have to click right on the text character, not the space between characters. Not even within a character's outline, if that character has no fill! Otherwise, you start creating new text. The cursor displays an A in brackets, like this: [A] when it's positioned correctly for editing text.

Text or Shape Comes Out the Wrong Color, Texture, or Pattern

Although you may logically expect your text, drawings, and shapes to appear in foreground color, sometimes they appear in background color! Sometimes, too, the colors can be weak, or mottled, or otherwise weird. Here's what's going on.

Shapes, drawings, and text are made up of outlines in one color and are filled with another color. The Color palette controls those colors. The outlines are done in foreground color (or gradient or pattern) and in foreground texture — but outlines can be very thin or even turned off altogether. In that case, nearly all you can see is the fill color. The fill color is the background color (or gradient or pattern), and in background texture (if any). If the Background Style is off altogether (circle with a slash), you may see very little at all — just the outline.

If patterns or gradients are unintentionally turned on in the Foreground or Background Style swatches, the result can be strangely mottled, or even nearly invisible. Likewise, if a texture is turned on for either foreground or background.

To get plain text, choose a background color, and in the Text Entry dialog box, click the Standard Text button. Your text appears in your chosen background color.

Magic Wand Tool Doesn't Select Well

The Magic Wand tool, which selects an area based on color (or other pixel qualities) is sometimes not so magic. What looks like a perfectly uniform color to you — one that the wand should be able to select cleanly without gaps or overlaps into unwanted areas — is apparently not so uniform. You may find that when you increase Tolerance, you close the gaps, but get more unwanted areas. Here are a couple of things to try besides fiddling with the Tolerance:

✔ Try different Match modes in the Tool Options window. Click the Match modes selection box on Tab 1 of that window and try RGB Value, Hue, or Brightness.

✔ Don't fuss any more with the Magic Wand tool. Use the Magic Wand tool to do the basic selection job, then use other selection tools to add or subtract from the selected area. For instance, switch to the Freehand tool, set it to Freehand (in the Selection Type box on Tab 1 of the Tool Options window), and with the Shift key depressed, drag a circle around any gaps in the selection. Likewise, hold down the Ctrl key and drag a circle around any unwanted areas.

Tool Works, But Not Like You Want

The key to a tool's behavior is its Tool Options window. For painting tools, it controls brush size, shape, how fuzzy the edges are, how speckly the paint comes off, how thick or thin the paint is, and how close together the individual dots are that make up a stroke. For other tools, it may also control how the tool chooses what pixels to operate on (by color, hue, or other attribute) and exactly what effect the tool has.

See Chapter 1 for details about the Tool Options window. The window floats on your screen and you can enable or disable it either by pressing *O* on the keyboard or clicking the Toggle Tool Options Window button on the Toolbar. Like nearly all of Paint Shop Pro's windows, it's initially set up to roll and unroll itself automatically. To unroll it, position your mouse cursor over the Tool Options title bar.

Chapter 22

Ten Fast Fixes for Photo Failures

Despite all attempts by camera makers to make photography foolproof, we still all make less than perfect pictures sometimes. Sometimes, we're the problem — we're too close, too far away, or can't figure out how to use the camera's foolproofing features. Sometimes, the problem is that reality stubbornly refuses to comply with our expectations: the sky is overcast, Great-Grandma can't be present for the family photo, or management has decided to cancel a product that appears in our product-line photograph.

Fortunately, Paint Shop Pro has a wide range of solutions, ranging from quick-and-dirty fixes to professional-level retouching. In this chapter, I give you some of the fastest solutions to the most common problems. See Chapter 8 for more details and more ways to fix up photos.

Rotating Right-Side Up

Photos that lie on their side are a pain in the neck. Don't put up with it! Take these simple steps:

1. **Press Ctrl+R — a fast way to pop up the Rotate dialog box.**

2. **In the Direction area of the dialog box, click either the Right (for clockwise rotation) or Left (for counterclockwise rotation) option boxes.**

   If you've added layers to your photo, click the All Layers check box. You probably haven't done so, however, or your neck would already be pretty stiff from turning your head sideways!

3. **Click OK or press the Enter key on your keyboard.**

Chances are, all of your sideways photos need rotating in the same direction. Fortunately, the Rotate dialog box remembers which rotation you chose in Step 2, so for future corrections, all you may need to do is press Ctrl+R and the Enter key!

Getting the Red Out

Suffering from a little too much red-eye? Photo flashes tend to make the normally black pupil of the eye glow red. Here's the fast fix for getting the red out. It works in nine out of ten cases — where only the pupil is red and the iris is unaffected; for tougher cases or more finicky retouching, see Chapter 8. Do this:

1. **Choose Effects⇨Enhance Photo⇨Red-eye Removal.**

   The Red-eye Removal dialog box appears.

2. **In the right preview window, drag the image to center the eye.**

3. **Click the Zoom In icon (the magnifier with the + sign) repeatedly until the eye fills the preview windows.**

   Repeat Step 2 as needed to keep the eye centered.

4. **Set Iris Size to zero.**

   This setting should be zero unless the red covers any of the iris (the colored part of the eye). If the red does affect the iris, see Chapter 8 for help.

5. **In the left window, click on the red.**

   A circle appears in a square frame in the left window. The circle should be centered on the pupil and cover it to some degree. (If not, see Chapter 8.) In the right window, the red area is partly or entirely obliterated. (If that isn't true at first, drag the Refine slider a bit to the left.)

6. **Drag the Refine slider left until a bit of red re-appears, then to the right just until that red is gone.**

7. **Click OK.**

Now repeat these steps for the other eye.

Photos without Enough Flash

If things are looking a bit dim in your photograph, Paint Shop Pro can often brighten your outlook. Follow these steps for a too-dim photo:

1. **Choose Effects⇨Enhance Photo⇨Automatic Contrast Enhancement.**

   The Automatic Contrast Enhancement dialog box springs into action. Your photo may already show sufficient improvement in the sample in the right window. If so, click OK and skip the rest of these steps.

   The preview window on the right shows the result of any changes in this and the following steps.

2. **To make the picture brighter, click Lighter (on the left).**

3. **To improve contrast, click Bold (on the right).**

4. **To get more brightness or contrast, click Normal (in the center).**

   The Mild option gives you less brightness or contrast.

5. **Click OK.**

One problem the preceding steps may not solve is feeble colors (*inadequate saturation,* in geek-speak). If your colors appear a bit too gray, see the section "Making Color Zippier," at the end of this chapter.

If this effect doesn't do the job, check out Chapter 11 for more help with brightness, contrast, and saturation. Nothing can restore image data that just isn't there, however. Things that are way dim are never going to look natural — unless you do some touchup brushing.

If you can't see your image very well in the right preview window of this dialog box, click the button with the eye icon to see the effect in your main image window. Click it again whenever you want to see the result of your changes. See Chapter 8 for more help with effect dialog boxes.

Photos with Too Much Flash

If you got a little too close in your flash photo, Paint Shop Pro may be able to help you back off a bit. Try this fast fix:

1. **Choose Effects⇨Enhance Photo⇨Automatic Contrast Enhancement.**

   The Automatic Contrast Enhancement dialog box comes to your aid. Your photo may already look better in the sample in the right window. If so, click OK and skip the rest of these steps.

The preview window on the right shows the result as you make any changes in this dialog box. If you can't really see enough of your picture there, click the button with the magnifier and – icon to zoom out.

2. **To make the picture darker, click Darker (on the left).**

3. **To reduce contrast, click Natural (on the right).**

   You can try Flat, too, but it's often too flat.

4. **For the maximum darkening, constrast-reducing effect, click Normal (in the center).**

   For a lesser effect, click Mild.

5. **Click OK.**

Photos with way too much flash are washed out, which may be harder to fix. If, for instance, portions of someone's face are practically white, you're going to need to restore skin tone without affecting the rest of the picture. A little work with the Retouch tool in Smudge mode (see Chapter 7) can help you push skin color into small white areas. Alternatively, try carefully selecting the entire face area with a feathered edge and then using the Manual Color Correction effect, which I describe in Chapter 8, to change the white area to skin tone. (You may have to disable the Preserve Lightness check box in that effect.)

Revealing Dark Corners

If you need to cast light into the dark corners of your life, Paint Shop Pro can help. Of course, nothing can reveal totally dark details and — as in life, itself — details that are *very* dark are generally not too attractive anyway, when brought to light. But, given those limitations, here is something you can do to reveal dark corners or other dark areas of your photo.

This approach is the computer equivalent of an old darkroom trick, known as *dodging*. Dodging requires a little eye-hand coordination because you, in effect, brush lightness and contrast onto just the dark portions of your photo. Do this:

1. **Choose the Retouch tool (pointing finger icon) in the Tool palette.**

2. **Locate or open the Tool Options window.**

   Press *O* on your keyboard to toggle the window on or off. If only the title bar of the Tool Options window appears, pause your cursor on that bar to unroll the window.

3. **Click Tab 1 of the Tool Options window (with the pointing finger icon) and make the following choices:**

    Size: To lighten broad areas, the best setting for this value is about 25 percent of the width or height of your image, whichever is larger. (Image dimensions appear in the Status bar, at the bottom right of the Paint Shop Pro window.)

    Hardness: Set this very low, or at zero, unless your dark area has very well-defined edges and you have a very steady hand.

    Opacity: A good typical setting is about 10. A higher number gives you a stronger effect per stroke. A lower number gives you a weaker effect.

    Step: A good typical setting is about 25. If you set it too high, you may see a dotty effect.

    Density: 100.

4. **Click Tab 2 of the Tool Options window (with the meshed gear icon) and choose Dodge in the Retouch Mode selection box.**

5. **Drag over the dark areas of your image to lighten those areas.**

    Keep the mouse button down and do a first pass over the area. Then release the mouse button and drag again over areas that need further lightening. Return to Step 3 and adjust any settings you think may be necessary, especially Opacity (strength of effect) or Size. Press Ctrl+Z to undo your most recent pass at the image, if necessary.

As you brush the image, objects in the dark become brighter and contrast against any black or very dark background is increased. The improvement can be pretty dramatic!

Removing Unwanted Relatives

Removing unwanted relatives is much easier in Paint Shop Pro than in real life. You're not limited to relatives, though. You can use the same Paint Shop Pro tricks to remove other unwanted features, like power lines or passing automobiles.

Like removing unwanted relatives, the task requires some skill. It also requires some sort of continuous or repeated background, like the clap-boarded side of a building, a grassy field, a rail fence, water, or shrubbery. If the unwanted relative is blocking more than half of some unique feature, like a fireplace, chair, or china cabinet, the job is going to be nearly impossible.

The main tool for the job is the Clone Brush tool, which you use to extend the background over the unwanted feature. For instance, you can brush out junk on a lawn by brushing lawn, taken from just below or alongside the junk. See Chapter 6 for help with the tool, but here's the general idea:

1. **Click the Clone Brush tool (two-brush icon) in the Tool palette.**

2. **Right-click on the background you want to brush over your object, in an area that has no unique features.**

   For instance, if you're removing lawn junk, right-click in grass, not near other junk. Don't click too near the object you want to remove, either. Because backgrounds tend to have horizontal strips of stuff, like grass at the bottom, trees in the middle, and sky at the top, clicking to the left or right of the object you want to remove usually works best.

3. **Drag carefully across the object you want removed.**

   If, in Step 2, you right-clicked to the left or right of that object, move your cursor only horizontally before you drag. That precaution ensures that you extend the correct strip of background and don't paint grass, for instance, where you want trees. As you brush, the Clone Brush tool picks up pixels from under an X that starts where you right-clicked and follows your motion. Keep an eye on the X to make sure that doesn't pick up pixels you don't want. You may need to re-set the X in a new location periodically; return to Step 2 to do so.

You probably need some trial and error to get a feel for the process. Press Ctrl+Z to undo any errors.

One problem with removing relatives and other objects is that if they were initially blocking a unique object, that object now has a hole in it. For instance, the relative may well be blocking one arm of a person or half of a piano (if that relative is fairly wide). Fortunately, many objects are symmetrical; if Aunt Katy's left arm is now missing, you may be able copy her right arm and paste it in place of the left one. (You can even mirror half a face to make a whole one in some instances. Results may be unsatisfactory.)

Use any selection tool — say, the Freehand tool — to select the object you need to copy. (See Chapter 13.) Press Ctrl+F to float the selection, press Ctrl+M to mirror it, drag it to the correct position, and then press Ctrl+Shift+F to defloat it. Press Ctrl+D to remove the selection marquee. You may need to do a little painting and retouching, because any light striking the object is now coming from the wrong direction.

Adding Absent Relatives

If Great-Grandma just couldn't make the wedding, boost her spirits (or seriously confuse other missing relatives) by creating a picture that includes her with the happy couple. The same trick works for adding anyone or anything. Have a new product to add to your product line? Just add it in to the product family photo. Following are the basic steps, with references to other parts of the book that provide more detail:

1. **Open your original photo (the one *without* Great-Grandma) in a window.**

2. **Press Ctrl+B or choose File⇨Browse to open the image browser.**

   The browser window opens. Arrange the browser and image windows so you can see both. (For instance, choose Window⇨Tile Vertically.)

3. **Drag the thumbnail of the new image (Great-Grandma) from the browser to the main image window.**

   The new image becomes a new layer of the original photo. You can close the browser window now, if you like. (Click the X in its upper-right corner.)

4. **With the Eraser tool (see Chapter 5), erase everything but the part of the new image that you want (leaving Great-Grandma).**

   A somewhat more complicated, but more forgiving approach is to use a mask. See Chapter 17 for help with that.

5. **Click the Deformation tool on the Tool palette (third from the top) and drag your new image (Great-Grandma) to the place you want it.**

   See Chapter 14 for help with the Deformation tool.

6. **If the image isn't the correct size or rotation, drag the handles (squares) that appear around your new image to make adjustments.**

   The image may need some repositioning; if so, drag it from any place *but* on one of the handles.

7. **Double-click on the image, when you're done sizing and positioning, to apply the deformation.**

Repeat Step 4 to make any additional erasures that you discover are necessary at this point. For instance, if Great-Grandma's head and shoulders are to appear behind the wedding couple, erase her from shoulders on down. You're done! Note that you now have an image with layers, so if you save it, Paint Shop Pro asks you if you want to merge layers. Reply Yes.

Zapping Zits

One noticeable difference between professionally done portraits and the ones you and I take is that the pros retouch their photos to get rid of unsightly blemishes. Throughout this book, I describe lots of tools useful for retouching and even devote one whole chapter to retouching tools, Chapter 7. To get rid of a simple blemish, however, is a matter of a few steps. Zoom in on the blemish and then try this:

1. **Choose the Retouch tool (hand with pointing finger icon) in the Tool palette.**

   (See Chapter 7 for more about this tool.)

2. **Open its Tool Options window, if it's not already open.**

   Press *O* to toggle the window on or off. See Chapters 1 and 5 for more about this window.

3. **On Tab 1 of that window (with the pointing-finger icon), set the brush size to roughly zit-size.**

   See the discussions of setting tool options in Chapter 5 for help with other options.

4. **On Tab 2 of that window (with the meshed-gears icon), choose Smudge in the Retouch Mode selection box.**

5. **Mouse down just to one side of the blemish, on clear skin of similar (but unblemished) color.**

6. **Drag across the blemish.**

   Dragging *along*, rather than *across*, any natural folds or wrinkles is usually a good idea. Also, don't drag from one area of unblemished skin color into a differently-colored area.

7. **Repeat Steps 5 and 6 from the opposite direction.**

Making Gray Skies Blue

Don't let an overcast day rain on your parade. You can make the skies blue in your photo, and, even though your snapshot may never look completely natural, it will probably be more attractive. You can't make a gray day look too natural because if it were really taken on a sunny day, the sun would appear to shine on all the subjects in your photo, casting highlights and shadows. Paint Shop Pro has several tools you could use. The following steps, however, outline the simplest approach:

1. **Click the Magic Wand tool on the Tool palette.**

2. **In the Tool Options window, set Tolerance to about 20 or 30 for a typical gray sky.**

   Press *O* on your keyboard to toggle the Tool Options window on or off. See Chapters 1 and 5 for more about this window and its options, like brush size.

3. **Click on the overcast area of your image, to select it.**

   If the whole sky is not selected, press Ctrl+D to clear the selection, and then try again with a higher Tolerance value in the Tool Options window. If more than sky is selected, try again with a lower value. Chapter 13 has more ways to help you select just sky.

4. **Press Shift+U to open the Red/Green/Blue dialog box.**

5. **Increase the number in the Blue value box.**

   As you adjust, keep an eye on the right preview window in the Red/Green/Blue dialog box, which is showing you the new sky color. Stop adjusting when you like the color, and click the OK button.

Making Colors Zippier

As I take a photo, I find that my mind's eye makes the colors livelier than they turn out to be in reality, and the photo looks a bit dull. Perhaps it's just that my antidepressant dose needs adjusting, but if you have the same problem, try adjusting saturation (of your image, that is). Take these steps and don't call me in the morning:

1. **Choose Effects⇨Enhance Photo⇨Automatic Saturation Adjustment.**

   The Automatic Saturation Adjustment dialog box springs into action.

2. **Choose the More Colorful option on the left side of the box.**

3. **If the photo contains a significant amount of skin, click the Skintones Present check box.**

4. **Choose the Weak, Normal, or Strong option on the right side of the box, depending upon which choice gives better results in the right preview window.**

   Click the button with the eye icon any time you want to see the effect of your chosen options in your actual image window.

5. **Click OK.**

If that doesn't brighten up your day, check out Chapter 11 or see your friendly primary care physician.

Index

IDG BOOKS WORLDWIDE BOOK REGISTRATION

We want to hear from you!

Visit **http://my2cents.dummies.com** to register this book and tell us how you liked it!

- Get entered in our monthly prize giveaway.

- Give us feedback about this book — tell us what you like best, what you like least, or maybe what you'd like to ask the author and us to change!

- Let us know any other *For Dummies* topics that interest you.

Your feedback helps us determine what books to publish, tells us what coverage to add as we revise our books, and lets us know whether we're meeting your needs as a *For Dummies* reader. You're our most valuable resource, and what you have to say is important to us!

Not on the Web yet? It's easy to get started with *Dummies 101: The Internet For Windows 98* or *The Internet For Dummies* at local retailers everywhere.

Or let us know what you think by sending us a letter at the following address:

For Dummies Book Registration
Dummies Press
10475 Crosspoint Blvd.
Indianapolis, IN 46256